Genteel Revolutionaries

Anna and Thomas Haslam
and the Irish Women's Movement

Genteel Revolutionaries

Anna and Thomas Haslam
and the Irish Women's Movement

Carmel Quinlan

CORK UNIVERSITY PRESS

For Paul, Hugh and Sarah Farrelly
and in memory of Pat Connolly

First published in 2002 by
Cork University Press
Youngline Industrial Estate
Pouladuff Road, Togher
Cork
Ireland

Library of Congress Cataloging-in-Publication Data

Quinlan, Carmel, 1944–
    Genteel revolutionaries : Anna and Thomas Haslamand the Irish Women's Movement / Carmel Quinlan.
       p. cm.
Includes bibliographical references and index.
ISBN 1–85918–328–X
    1. Haslam, Anna Maria, 1829–1922. 2. Haslam, Thomas Joseph, 1825–1917.
3. Feminists–Ireland–Biography. 4. Social reformers–Ireland–Biography.
5. Quakers–Ireland–Biography. 6. Feminism–Ireland–History. 7. Women's rights–Ireland–History. I. Title.

HQ1600.3.Z75 H376 2002
305.42'092'2415–dc21   2002074107

ISBN 1 85918 328 X (HB)
       1 85918 394 8 (PB)

Typeset by Mark Heslington, Scarborough, North Yorkshire
Printed by Colourbooks Ltd., Baldoyle, Co. Dublin

Contents

Acknowledgements

I owe a huge debt of gratitude to Tom Dunne for his enthusiasm for this project, and for his incisive criticism and constant encouragement. I am very grateful to all my friends in the Boole Library who helped and encouraged me. I have received practical assistance and support from many of my UCC colleagues, especially Trudy Ahern, Linda Connolly, Patricia Connolly, Larry Geary, Rachel Hutchinson, Breda Long, Jill Lucey, Seán Ó Coileáin, Clare O'Halloran, Phil O'Sullivan, Elizabeth Pettit, Sheila Spalding, Elizabeth Steiner-Scott and Éibhear Walshe, all of whom I would like to thank.

I am especially grateful to Mary Cullen for allowing me access to the archive of the Irish Housewives' Association, which was vital to my research, and for generously encouraging me in this endeavour. Maria Luddy very kindly gave of her time and expertise and sent me a copy of Thomas Haslam's rare pamphlet on prostitution. Cliona Murphy was most generous with her help, encouragement and friendship.

Richard Harrison was enormously helpful in sharing his knowledge of the Irish Society of Friends with me and in alerting me to obscure sources. Michael Ahern helped me in many ways particularly by sharing the result of his extensive research with me, and his wife Deirdre was generous in her hospitality, tea and sympathy. Thanks to Margaret Quinlan and Loughlin Kealy, Prue and Jo Horwood, Anthony Quinlan and Maura O'Sullivan, and Freda Smith all of whom provided me with lavish hospitality (sometimes too much so) while I was researching in Dublin and London.

I owe a debt of gratitude to the staff of libraries that I consulted in Ireland and England. A special thank you to Verity Murdoch and all Friends in Dublin Friends' Historical Library and to Justin Furlong of the National Library of Ireland. David Doughan of Fawcett Library, a living encyclopaedia of the women's movement, generously and entertainingly shared his knowledge with me. The staff of Girton College Library, Cambridge was especially helpful and hospitable. Lesley Hall of the Wellcome Library for the History and Understanding of Medicine, herself a witty and erudite chronicler of nineteenth-century sexuality, was of great assistance to me. Thank you also to the staff of Hull University Library for their help.

I am indebted to the International Federation of University Women who awarded me the Winifred Cullis Fellowship which facilitated my research in London. My gratitude especially to Deirdre O'Shea and Mary Horkan of the Irish Federation.

I would also like to acknowledge the grant awarded by the National University of Ireland towards the publication of this book

Finally, to my family to whom I dedicate this book, my love and thanks.

Abbreviations

AH	Anna Haslam
AOSA	Ackworth Old Scholars' Association
BL	British Library
CAISM	Central Association of Irish Schoolmistresses and Other Ladies Interested in Education
CDA	Contagious Diseases Act
CMAC	Contemporary Medical Archive Centre
DFHL	Dublin Friends' Historical Library
DWSA	Dublin Women's Suffrage Association
HSS	Hanna Sheehy Skeffington
IAWG	Irish Association of Women Graduates
ICW	International Council of Women
IHA	Irish Housewives' Association
ILP	Independent Labour Party
IWCLGA	Irish women Citizens' and Local Government Association
IWFL	Irish Women's Franchise League
IWSA	Irish Women's Suffrage Alliance
IWSF	Irish Women's Suffrage Federation
IWSLGA	Irish Women's Suffrage and Local Government Association
LNA	Ladies' National Association
MWFL	Munster Women's Franchise League
NARCDA	National Association for the Repeal of the Contagious Diseases Act
NAI	National Archives of Ireland
NLI	National Library of Ireland
NSWS	National Society for Women's Suffrage
NUWSS	National Union of Women's Suffrage Societies
NUWW	National Union of Women Workers of Great Britain and Ireland
TJH	Thomas Joseph Haslam
WFL	Women's Franchise League
WSPU	Women's Social and Political Union

Introduction

The image of Anna Haslam going to the polls in 1918, surrounded by flowers and flags, flanked by a disparate crew of unionist, constitutional nationalist and Sinn Féin women united in her honour to celebrate the victory of votes for women, has a powerful resonance. That the election represented a resounding victory for Sinn Féin and the corresponding death rattle of unionism adds the dimension of paradox to the occasion; Anna was a unionist who was almost ninety when she first cast her vote. Born in the year of Catholic emancipation, active in relief work during the Great Famine, lifelong campaigner for social reform, the scene of her triumph was marked by the trappings of modernity. She was driven by motorcar to vote for the unionist candidate and her arrival at the polling station was filmed by a news camera crew. The scene is allegorical, an image of the birth of a new Ireland in which women, despite their representational victory for women, were destined to play a reduced, rather than an increased role. The small indomitable figure at the centre of the stage, acknowledging the homage paid to her for her part in the battle for votes for women, was about to cast her vote in an election which signalled the breaking of the link with Westminster which she did not want; she represented not only victory for women, but the dying fall of an older Ireland, an Ireland in which people of different, and sometimes opposing political loyalties, and of a variety of religious persuasions, worked together for a common cause. Yet, here too, is paradox. This old woman, pacifist and law-abiding, was modern and forward-looking, more socially radical than the Young Turks who were overthrowing the Ireland to which she gave allegiance.

Anna Haslam and her husband Thomas devoted most of their lives to furthering the cause of rights for women. Thomas Haslam was a loving husband who admired and supported his wife in all her endeavours. Forced by ill-health to retire from paid work in his forties, the resulting leisure allowed him time to write on many topics, including birth control, sexual morality and suffrage for women. Thomas's writings, and correspondence pertaining to them, reveal his thoughts on love, sex and marriage and they illuminate, and are illuminated by, his own life and marriage; they are a useful indicator of his influences, his interest in contemporary social theory and the evolution of his feminism. The Haslams devoted their lives to reform. Their campaign against the Contagious Diseases Acts, which is discussed here at some length, was a practical application of their beliefs and ideals and also forged a link between the theory developed by Thomas in his writings, and the ongoing and evolving work for suffrage that was the main focus of their lives for many years. Thomas Haslam was a feminist theorist; his wife was an activist who put his theories into practice, and in her person epitomized his assertion that women, intellectually and morally, were deserving of equitable treatment in politics and before the law.

The story of Anna and Thomas Haslam is part of the social, political and cultural history of Ireland. Thomas was born in 1825 and, despite his ill health, lived until 1917, while Anna who was born in 1829, survived until 1922. Her early life is a useful illustration of the philanthropy practised by a typically prosperous Quaker merchant family. Her feminism was rooted in Enlightenment ideas of individual natural rights. She was educated and, from an early age, involved in reform and in philanthropy, a classic case of the evolution of a feminist. The experience of her Quaker upbringing, her education and work for reform, had empowered her to demand equality for women in the political sphere. Thomas, also born and brought up a Quaker, trained as a teacher. He was interested in social theory and informed on contemporary thinking on evolution and heredity. He was an avid reader of intellectual theorists such as Herbert Spencer and John Stuart Mill. His marriage to Anna meant that she had a partner who shared her beliefs and actively supported her work for reform. Early campaigners for women's rights were male as well as female. The Haslam marriage provides an example of the extent to which enlightened and altruistic men and women worked together to further the cause of women and of society generally.

The place of Anna and Thomas Haslam in recorded Irish history has been minor to the point of invisibility. They are commemorated in St Stephen's Green, Dublin by a Kilkenny limestone seat sculpted by Albert C. Power, bearing an inscription honouring them for their 'long years of public service chiefly devoted to the enfranchisement of women'. They are mentioned in works on suffrage and on Quakers in Ireland, and Anna is the subject of a scholarly essay.[1] The reasons why they are relatively unknown are obvious. The public lives of the Haslams were contemporaneous with the major political and social movements of late nineteenth- and early twentieth-century Ireland. They were not part of these movements however. The associations with which they were involved never became mass movements, and were non-party and non-sectarian. The history of Irish women in this era has, understandably perhaps, been dominated by the nationalist agenda and by the women of Inghinidhe na hÉireann and Cumann na mBan. Anna Haslam cannot hope to compete with Maud Gonne MacBride or Countess Markievicz as a national icon. She was unionist, uninvolved in the 'terrible beauty' of 1916, alienated from the independent Ireland that she lived to see, as much by extreme old age and physical discomfort as by ideology. In the resurgent Ireland of the turn of the twentieth century everything was run by the young; 'youth, eagerness, brains, imaginations' were the characteristics that marked the renaissance.[2] Anna Haslam was seventy years old at the start of the century and Thomas was seventy-five. Because the historiography of the Irish suffrage movement has concentrated on the twentieth century, she emerges as an 'old dear' – an assessment influenced, perhaps, by the suffragette Margaret Cousins's 1908 description of her as the 'dear old leader'.[3] From 1908 to 1918, however, she continued to lead an active public life, travelling to and from London to meetings and to lobby at the House of Commons and undertaking fresh fields of endeavour after the outbreak of war. Thomas penned his last work in 1916 at the age of ninety-one.

The history of the women's suffrage movement, in England as in Ireland, has concentrated on the militant campaign of the suffragettes. Consequently, there is an impression conveyed, particularly in the Irish situation, that the non-militant Irish Women's Suffrage and Local Government Association (IWSLGA),[4] founded by the Haslams in 1876, was somewhat overshadowed by the young militant Irish Women's Franchise League (IWFL) founded in 1908. The reality was that both worked contemporaneously, the IWSLGA was at its strongest numerically in 1912 and some prominent suffragists were simultaneously associated with both organizations. However, the militant activism and vibrancy of the IWFL has resulted in an undervaluing of the achievements of the nineteenth-century suffrage movement. While the ultimate victory of the vote was not won until 1918, the earlier campaigns, spearheaded by Anna Haslam, had enjoyed no little success. The question of votes for women was brought firmly into the public arena. Anna had barraged MPs with petitions, and had liased with and achieved recognition from the international women's movement. She was responsible for recruiting many prominent men to fight for the cause of women's equality, albeit in a law-abiding and perhaps unexciting way. Her efforts helped to win the right of Irish women to stand for election as poor law guardians and as members of rural and district councils. She was above all an expert lobbyist, but that is not exciting stuff. The suffragettes, on the other hand, broke windows, barracked political leaders, and got themselves imprisoned. They were of a different generation who had been empowered by the earlier campaign of the Haslams and their co-workers. The very impatience of these younger women with the methods of the older generation was an acknowledgement of how well that first generation of active feminists had succeeded in its educative goal. The Irish situation was further complicated by the fact that the young militant movement was overwhelmingly nationalist. Although publicly associated with unionism, Anna Haslam succeeded in attracting influential support from those who were on opposite sides in the Home Rule debate.

The Haslams' lives spanned a century of momentous happenings in Ireland. They witnessed the Great Famine, disestablishment of the Church of Ireland, Fenianism, the Land War, decades of Home Rule agitation, the Celtic Revival and, of course, the 1916 Rising. We know that Anna was active in famine relief organized by Youghal Quakers, but the evidence points to Thomas being out of Ireland for the duration of the famine. While Anna, and presumably Thomas, had many friends in the Irish Parliamentary Party, she was vehemently opposed to Home Rule. There is no evidence of their reaction to events of 1916 but I think it fair to say that they would have opposed both the aims and the methods of the rebels.

This work aims to reveal the importance of the lives of Anna Haslam and her husband to the history of nineteenth- and early twentieth-century Ireland. The history of feminism in Ireland is an integral part of the social, political and intellectual history of the country. While one might argue that Anna is the more significant figure of the pair, this study of them both, acknowledges the influence of Thomas on her public life, and attempts to demonstrate that her husband's writings and his practical support were important factors in her successful efforts to improve women's status in the political, social and educational fields. It puts forward the hypothesis that the Haslams not only played a major part in the early years of the feminist movement in Ireland, but also contributed to the evolution of feminist thought in the United Kingdom; the writings of Thomas Haslam on sexuality were significantly earlier than those of British writers who are regarded as pioneers in the field. It is hoped the study demonstrates how Anna, and more particularly Thomas Haslam, exploited the stereotype of the asexual Victorian woman in order to testify to her moral superiority, thus confirming her incontrovertible right to full legal and political equality.

This reconstruction of their lives was challenged by the discovery that, contrary to available information, the Haslam papers were not in the National Library.[5] Perhaps this discovery should have been taken as a portent, a warning to abandon this project, but by this stage I was deeply committed to both Anna and Thomas and, convinced that the project was worthwhile, soldiered on. This book is, in essence, an attempt to uncover their histories, an attempt which is obviously hampered by the lack of a conventional archive. While there is documentation on their early lives, there is little information on them as young adults. The public lives of their middle and later years are well enough documented, particularly from 1876 when the Dublin Women's Suffrage Association was founded; however, while the archives of the various associations for which the Haslams worked give us a detailed picture of their political activities, the reconstruction of their private lives is more problematic. Despite the paucity of personal papers, however (there are no diaries and few letters extant), a portrait emerges of a deeply happy, yet childless marriage which exemplified their principles and beliefs. Their public and private lives were inextricably interwoven. The circle in which they moved was composed of people who shared their convictions and their passion for reform. When the sources for a work that contains a biographical element are official rather than personal it can be difficult, if not impossible, to present the reader with a 'feel' for the personalities involved. One can, however, piece together a picture of the Haslams' lives in the Dublin township of Rathmines, organizing pressure groups, writing letters and pamphlets, hurrying to meetings, lobbying, chivvying others to rally to the cause. Their fingers were on the pulse of everything relevant happening in Dublin and Westminster. The personality of Anna – outspoken, open-minded, valiant in old age – emerged from the small number of letters that survive. The official papers reveal her as a strong and authoritative personality, skilled in argument, adept in the use of propaganda, with high expectations of others and with an enormous capacity for hard work. It is obvious also that she was a woman of great charm who inspired affection in those who knew her. Thomas is a more enigmatic character but, despite his undoubted *gravitas,* he was ever open to new ideas and retained a youthful enthusiasm for the causes in which he believed into his old age. I hope their personalities emerge from these pages as they emerged for me from Thomas's writings and from the archives of the associations with which they were involved.

The structure of this work is thus dictated by the available archive. In the opening chapter the lives of Anna and Thomas are described and contextualized in the milieu in which they lived, and the factors that influenced them are discussed. Chapters 2 and 3 examine the writings of Thomas on birth control and sexual morality and use his theories to explore his life and marriage. Chapter 4 describes the campaign against the Contagious Diseases Acts. The pivotal role played by the Haslams in that campaign marked the start of their long careers as public lobbyists and organizers for reform. Chapters 5 and 6 examine their sustained campaign for votes for women. The book demonstrates how Thomas and Anna Haslam combined their talents and energies to achieve their joint aim of equal rights for women.

1

'Let us meet together':[1] A biographical sketch of Anna and Thomas Haslam

Anna Haslam was born Anna Maria Fisher in Youghal, Co. Cork in 1829. Her birth into a family imbued with the values of the Society of Friends was a significant factor in the development of her social conscience and in her deeply held belief in the equality of men and women. To members of the Society of Friends, man is basically good and has within himself the seed of his spiritual growth. They believe that God speaks to the listening soul and that each attentive soul can make deeply satisfying contact with God. This capacity, the 'Inner Light', gives Quakers independence from hierarchical structures and empowers them to challenge certain man-made traditions. Inner light renders each person capable of ministering to his or her fellows and gives each member of the Society significance in its ordering and service. There are no ministers, no hierarchy, no sacraments. God speaks directly to the listening soul – a religious meeting is simply a gathering of Friends waiting in silence for the guidance of God. Any man or woman moved by God might address a meeting. With spiritual ability as the only criterion, Quaker ministry has been open to women throughout the Society's history.

The recognition that every human being has the 'Inner Light' within means that Quakers believe war is wrong; members were pacifists from the start, often at considerable cost to themselves. Belief in the divine seed in all men and women also means that Friends constantly challenge injustice and cruelty in others. They do not believe in class distinction and as a matter of principle refused to doff their hats to any man or woman irrespective of rank. Anna Haslam's lack of obsequiousness, obvious in her letters to leading politicians, was doubtless due to these egalitarian principles.[2]

The first Friends who came to Ireland in the seventeenth century were predominantly small farmers, craftsmen, merchants or professional people.[3] Despite some restrictions imposed by the penal laws, Quakers managed to avoid political and armed conflict, and they prospered. By the eighteenth century, they were prominent traders in the towns of Munster, Leinster and Ulster. They were bound to one another by family networks through intermarriage and by the structure of the Society's administration. Honesty or 'truth' for Quakers was not an abstract concept but a living inward spiritual perception expressed outwardly in plainness of dress and language. The adherence to truth was such a basic tenet of the Society that the taking of oaths was forbidden to members as to do so was to imply the existence of a double standard of truth. This strict adherence to truth was beneficial in that it helped them gain a reputation for honesty in their business dealings with people of other denominations.[4] In addition to this reputation, their success in business was also due to the quickly established network of useful contacts within the Society. Friends guarded their reputation for fair trading jealously; members of the Society who were bankrupt, or who were shown in any way to have been guilty of less than honourable business practice were disowned by the Society until such time as they discharged all their debts.

As well as meetings for worship several times a week, Quakers attended constant rounds of monthly, quarterly, and yearly administrative meetings at local, provincial and national levels. Such meetings facilitated the formation of networks outside immediate communities, which in turn encouraged business and increased opportunities for marriages between members. Quaker women had their own administrative meetings where they ran their affairs and dealt with various matters such as poor relief, marriage, female dress and the education of children. They settled questions such as 'marriage practices, the care of the sick and poor, and community responsibilities . . . in terms favorable to women's participation and leadership'.[5] In the last quarter of the seventeenth century, Margaret Fell, wife of the Society's founder, George Fox, and her daughters settled questions of the community responsibilities of women. A letter was circulated to all Quaker communities setting out theological justification for the participation of women Friends: 'We are all children of God by faith in Christ Jesus, where there is neither male nor female.' The letter provided instructions for the running of women's meetings, which followed a similar programme to men's meetings:

> Also let Care be taken that every particular womens monthly meeting have a booke to set down, and record their businesses and passages that is done or agreed upon . . . that collections be set downe in the booke; and that the Receipts, and disbursements of every particular meeting be set down . . . that every particular meeting may see and know, how their collections is disbursed. And that some faithfull honest woman, or women friends, that can Read, and write, keep the Book and receive the Collections.[6]

Having adopted 'a common philosophy women's meetings for business on both sides of the Atlantic followed remarkably consistent programs of action'.[7] It is noteworthy that this was done without the development of a bureaucratic structure. Women's meetings managed their own agendas and selected their own priorities. In Ireland the first National Women's Meeting was held in 1678 and continued annually until 1903, after which men and women always met together.[8] London women Quakers succeeded in obtaining the right to hold their own yearly meeting only after 1753 when the American Quaker, Susanna Morris, spoke to the London Yearly Meeting demanding that women have their own gathering.[9] This suggests that Irish Quaker women were networked on a national scale within the Society earlier than their English sisters. Quaker women, particularly those who were involved in monthly, quarterly (provincial) and annual (national) meetings, gained important practical skills. They were practised in addressing meetings, writing reports, keeping accounts, chairing committees and in ensuring that a meeting arrived at a consensus. They shared a commitment and common purpose to take care of one another, their children, the poor and the sick, and to extend their care to others outside their circle who were in need and also to minister outside 'if it were to come to them'. They were also free to set their own priorities. They were obliged to aid a fellow member to 'formulate her witness' even if they did not, in conscience, share it.[10] Such tenets fostered tolerance, evidenced in the attitudes displayed by Anna Haslam in her public life. Her understanding of the point of view of those who opposed her, and particularly her justification of the motives of the militant suffrage women whose methods she deplored, were true to the spirit of her early training at women's meetings. Her remarkable organizational and administrative skills had their basis in Quaker practice.

If moved to do so, Quaker women frequently travelled distances to visit other communities of Friends. 'Peripatetic women Friends bound their sisters together in . . . a web of interlocking ties' from the eighteenth century onwards.[11] The apparent freedom of women to travel far afield unchaperoned, at a time when the movement of middle-class women was constrained, is remarkable.[12] Visiting women spread the word of reform causes such as the abolition of slavery with the result that Quaker women were active in most of the reform and progressive movements in the United States, Great Britain and Ireland. The commercial success and subsequent enhanced social status of the Quakers also lent respectability to the causes they espoused. The stance of Quakers against slavery, particularly in North America, was often against economic self-interest and was recognized and respected as such.

Obviously there was often a conflict between perceived duties to husbands and children and the desire to minister at meetings. An examination of their roles *within* the Society, however, goes some way to explain why 'Quaker women transcended the stereotypes of their time and place to play effective, and often transforming, roles in the world'.[13] Anna Haslam was such a woman. She explained: 'I was brought up a member of the Society of Friends and was accustomed to see women working side by side with their brothers as Ministers, Elders and Overseers[14] upon the footing of undisputed equality.'[15] She could not 'remember any time when she was not a believer in women's equality. It came to her naturally, and was always taken for granted in her household – a Quaker household.'[16] One must, however, question the extent to which true equality of gender existed within the Quaker community in Ireland. The minute books and other documents in the Dublin Friends' Historical Library (DFHL) reveal that women's autonomy was confined to what could be called female concerns and that men wielded the ultimate authority; yet women's part in the running of their own affairs and particularly in their right to minister, gave them inherent advantages over non-Quaker women. It is not coincidental that so many Quaker women were involved in the first wave of feminist activism. In her work on Victorian feminism Philippa Levine has written that 'many of the best known feminists of the period were the daughters of small but active communities of Quakers . . . known for their radicalism and interest in social conditions and welfare'. She also identified exposure to anti-slavery agitation in childhood as an experience typical of those who became active feminists.[17]

The Fisher family was descended from Reuben Fisher (1669–1723), the second son of a chirurgeon (surgeon) from the London Borough of Southwark. He came to Youghal to visit his sister Martha Dobbs, a Quaker, who lived in the town. Reuben too became a Quaker and moved permanently to Youghal in 1701. Martha Dobbs lived on an estate that was afterwards forfeited for the non-payment of tithes. Many testimonials brought by Reuben from Friends in London are copied in the books of the Youghal Meeting. He married Margaret Shute who for many years was the clerk[18] of the Youghal Women's Meeting. Reuben's son Joseph (1718–91), only four when his father died, was apprenticed to William Richardson of Limerick, druggist and apothecary. Eventually he returned to Youghal where he started a hosiery business. He was appointed an elder by the provincial meeting at Cork. His son Reuben (1753–1806), married Jenepher Abell (1757–1807), daughter of a prominent Cork Quaker family. They had eleven children, including Abraham, their second son and fourth child, father of Anna Haslam. Abraham (1783–1871) was a successful miller and a noted philanthropist. He married Jane Moor (1789–1877) and Anna Maria, born in 1829, was the sixteenth of their seventeen children. Effectively she was the youngest child as Rebecca, born in 1830, died in 1832.[19]

The Fishers at the time of Anna's childhood had been a successful merchant family for generations. Joseph Fisher (1778–1816), who described himself as 'Being concerned with the Corn Trade', elder brother of Abraham, wrote to Lord Liverpool in 1815 to convey to him the alarming state of the country. The letter revealed Joseph's ability to gather information from the network of Friends. It also expressed concern for the feeding of the poor and was prophetic concerning the fate of the 'lower classes . . . particularly should the Potato crop prove defective'. Fisher provided details of conditions in the north of Ireland, Liverpool, the north of England and most of all in Youghal where 'the crops are in a deplorable state after the almost incessant wetness of the last two weeks'. He feared that 'the deficiency in Flour will be very great'. His suggested solution was 'the stoppage of distillation' which would allow grain onto the market to be used as a food substitute for wheat or potatoes. The letter is remarkably free of obsequiousness.[20] It suggests the public spiritedness of Joseph Fisher, manifest in his concern for the poor, and particularly by his concern that scarcity of grain would drive up the price, a factor that would have benefited him as a corn trader. It may also reveal his adherence to the cause of temperance. The writing of such a letter to the Prime Minister is revealing of the confident self-image of this senior family member.

The Fisher family had considerable business interests in Youghal's North Main Street. In contemporary trade directories Abraham, whose chief occupation was milling, was also listed as an insurance agent. (Quakers were popular insurance agents because of their reputation for honesty and the assumption that 'their wide business contacts [were] likely to encourage business and add to the respectable image of the company that they represented'.)[21] His eldest son, Peter Moor Fisher (1809–99), may well have taken over the milling business by 1846. He is listed as a baker, butter merchant and miller, with an address at 71 North Main Street. Another son, Joseph, was a bookseller and stationer, oil and colourman and tallow chandler. Fisher & Moss, ironmongers and trimming dealers, operated from Peter Moor Fisher's premises at North Main Street.[22] Abraham Fisher and his family no longer lived 'over the shop' but in Springfield, a large house on the outskirts of the town.

Anna's mother, Jane Moor Fisher, would appear to have been an exemplary member of the Society of Friends. She was the only daughter of Peter Moor, who left his home in Yorkshire, eventually arriving in Youghal after a journey that reads like a *Boy's Own* adventure story. *En route* he was forcibly taken by a press gang on board a man-of-war, but said he was a Quaker and would not fight. He was then robbed and set down on the coast of Kerry where 'Irish peasants treated him with great kindness'. In Cork he found kind Friends ready to help and employ him. He subsequently married an Irish Friend named Sarah Chamberlain and settled in Youghal where their daughter Jane was born in 1789. She lived to be a great age and was married to Abraham Fisher for over sixty-five years. She was a lifelong supporter of the temperance movement and was a noted philanthropist. 'She took a lively interest in all benevolent efforts in her native town especially in the education question. She was a kind and sympathetic neighbour, friend to her poor neighbours, very skilful in the use and application of herbs, active in relieving suffering and attending to the wants of those in distress.' She was a zealous supporter of the anti-slavery cause and as an old woman recalled how her young family gave up the use of slave produce, including abstaining from sugar for some considerable time until 'free grown goods' arrived in Ireland. There was sometimes tension between her busy life as the mother of a large family and her call to the service of the Society:

> She often left her bed of sickness to attend her Quarterly Meeting and it was her practice to attend such meetings when held at a distance to leave her young family under the care of her elder children whom she was careful early to educate in the leading doctrines of our Religious Society's practices and discipline.

For Jane Fisher, attending quarterly meetings meant travelling to Cork by horse drawn transport. During her lifetime she was pregnant for a cumulative period of at least twelve years.

Jane Fisher's attire was simple, neat and 'never conspicuous. She ever bore a faithful protest against adopting the changing fashions of the world.'[23] There is little information available on Anna's relationship with her mother. Discussing her husband Thomas Haslam's *Duties of Parents,* in which he recommended limiting the number of children born to a family, Anna referred to the reaction of her 'old mother aged over 80 who had 17 children' to the book: 'To our astonishment [she] said generations unborn would welcome and bless such a pure wise book.'[24] This response suggests, perhaps, that Jane Fisher may have regretted having borne so many children. Travelling to meetings, no matter how onerous the journey, and despite the crisis of conscience about leaving children, must have provided Quaker women with a welcome respite from domestic cares and also opportunities to socialize and exchange ideas.[25] The records of the Youghal meetings reveal the constant participation of Jane Fisher in the running of the Women's Meeting in Youghal and her frequent attendance as a delegate at the quarterly meetings in Cork. Anna Haslam's grounding in beliefs of equality, the example of her mother's active ministry, her Quaker birthright of administrative skills, and her resolve to dedicate her life to the service of others, were all inculcated as a child in Youghal. At her eightieth birthday party she said that 'she would take no credit to herself for her work in various spheres because from the first it was in her blood'.[26]

Her mother's busy life suggests that Anna was frequently left in the care of others. While one would imagine that in a prosperous family like the Fishers, the small children would be in the care of nursemaids, the evidence points to Anna being left in the care of her older siblings.[27] There are no details of the childhood of the Fishers – an occasional glimpse is all we get. It is safe to surmise, however, that they were simply dressed in the Quaker fashion and that they attended religious meetings from an early age. Anna's eldest brother Peter was twenty years her senior and was more than likely in full-time employment in the family business when she was born. Her sister Deborah, with whom she did famine relief work, was nine years her senior and appears to have been the sister closest to her in age.[28] The Fisher children went to boarding school in Waterford and there, and at home, were educated in Quaker principles.

Anna's lifelong commitment to education for women was another legacy of her membership of the Society of Friends. In the first half-century of its existence, the Society founded fifteen schools and it was noteworthy that 'many of their schools were for girls as well as boys'.[29] Schools concentrated on character formation, striving to cultivate honesty and truthfulness and a charitable disposition towards others. Although the primary aim of Quaker education was religious, schools also supplied a practical vocational grounding in subjects that would prepare pupils for occupations in trade, business or the professions.[30] By the end of the eighteenth century, there were many Quaker schools in Ireland, including co-educational provincial boarding schools at Mountmellick, Lisburn and Waterford. Anna Haslam attended the Munster Provincial School at Newtown, Waterford from 1840 to 1842. The curriculum for girls included 'Spelling, Reading, English, Grammar, Writing, Arithmetic, Sewing, Marking, Knitting', while boys were, in addition, taught geography and 'some useful branches of Mathematics' but were not offered sewing or other female skills. However, a pupil who started at Newtown in 1844, revealed that the education for girls was wider than the above curriculum suggests: she had been 'grounded in English Literature, Grammar, Geography, History of the World in general and of England Scotland and Ireland. French was taught by a French master.' In 1898 at the centenary celebrations at Newtown, Anna and Benjamin Fayle, the oldest 'old scholars' present planted an American oak tree. Anna, called upon to speak, 'gave some interesting particulars of school life . . . in the olden times'. Her niece Margaret Fisher, daughter of her eldest brother Peter Moor Fisher, also gave an account of her schooldays in Newtown which were almost contemporaneous with Anna's. She said that twelve of Anna's generation of the Fishers had been at Newtown.[31]

From 1842 to 1845 Anna was a pupil at Castlegate (The Mount) School in York. This Quaker school, founded in 1831, offered a wider curriculum than Newtown, including literary and classical studies. At the Mount there was less emphasis placed on ladylike accomplishments than in contemporary girls' schools and more on 'intellectual culture'.[32] It is likely that for some of her time at the Mount, Anna trained as an apprentice teacher. The school admitted a small number of girls at lower fees in order to train them as teachers. They remained at school for an extra year and then were engaged as junior teachers. This system proved so successful that 'the children so trained were in demand for The Mount staff and for the staffs of other schools'.[33] Anna served as an assistant teacher at Ackworth, also in Yorkshire, from 1847 to 1848 and here she met Thomas Haslam from Mountmellick and presumably fell in love with him. She left Ackworth and teaching in 1848.[34] She returned home and did not teach again although she always maintained an active interest in education and campaigned for many years for increased educational opportunity for women. She was a founding member of the Central Association of Irish Schoolmistresses and Other Ladies Interested in Education (CAISM) and served for many years on its executive committee.

The provision of relief during the Great Famine by members of the Society of Friends was a practical manifestation of the Quaker commitment to philanthropy. The Society's Central Relief Committee in Dublin organized the ongoing work of relief. Twenty-one 'corresponding' members, one of whom was Abraham Fisher, were appointed throughout the provinces to inform the Central Committee of local conditions. An auxiliary committee was formed in Cork of which Abraham Fisher was one of the three Youghal representatives. Joseph Fisher, brother of Anna, was the secretary of the Youghal Poor Relief Committee.[35] Another brother, Peter Moor Fisher, 'set up several food kitchens in his district' on the Waterford/Cork border some miles east of Youghal.[36] Between 1847 and 1849 he imported Indian corn 'showing the people how to use the meal for food'.[37] Anna, on her return from Ackworth, was surrounded by family members deeply involved in famine relief. A profile in the *Irish Citizen* described her 'as providing employment to mitigate the horrors of the Famine'. It credited her and her sister Deborah with 'teaching girls knitting and lace-making' and with establishing the 'lace-making industry of Youghal' later taken over by the Presentation nuns.[38] In the next issue Anna demurred that 'it was not lace-making but knitting and crochet which my sister and I taught the girls during the famine years. The subsequent development of the lace-making industry . . . was entirely due to the initiative of the nuns.'[39] She wrote that 'they at first met in her father's kitchen at Springfield in the evenings until the girls & the consequent orders got too numerous and in the future they worked in their own homes'. The enterprise was very successful and many girls were helped to emigrate.[40] This home industry was a considerable undertaking and continued until Anna's wedding in 1854 when the nuns of the Presentation convent in Youghal took over some of the 'best girls' and taught them lace-making.'[41] Anna and her sister Deborah generated signifi-cant employment; in 1852 they had 'over 100 females at work' and did not 'require any assistance in supplying material' but stated that they would be glad of 'some help in supplying coal and candles'.[42] It would appear from the available evidence that the Fisher sisters efficiently organized an enter-prise of considerable scale that lasted for a number of years and was probably the nucleus of what eventually became the famous Youghal lace industry. In a short autobiographical piece [this is a MS page in Anna Haslam's hand in IHA Archive] Anna said that she had also helped in the soup kitchen started on the occasion of the potato famine in Youghal.

During the period between her return from Ackworth and marriage, Anna was involved in the International peace movement. In a speech recall-ing her early life, she mentioned that she was 'Honorary Secretary of the first "Olive Leaf Circle" established in Ireland for the promotion of univer-sal peace. In 1849 she had stood on the platform with Elihu Burritt'[43] the 'learned blacksmith' from Connecticut who worked for a 'multiplicity of good causes which included anti-slavery, temperance and peace'. His arrival in Britain 'brought an added sense of purpose and a set of more lively tactics to the peace movement'.[44] He launched a League of Universal Brotherhood which by July 1848 had almost 30,000 members in 400 branches scattered throughout the Anglo-American world. Burritt recruited female support to his peace movement by means of his Olive Leaf Circles which were formed of women of 'various Christian denominations'. Olive Leaf Circles were essentially discussion groups for peace whose members also corresponded with like-minded women abroad. 'By the early 1850s there were 150 local Olive Leaf Circles with an impressive membership of 3,000 in Britain alone.' Members inserted 'Olive Leafs' (short peace messages) in for-eign papers.[45] Burritt's peace group was 'an active Anglo-American pressure group which helped to launch the Peace Congress movement of the late 1840s'. This was a venture 'to by-pass governments by rallying public opinion in support of policies based on international arbitration and disarm-ament.'[46] Peter Moor Fisher was a delegate at a series of 'well-publicized congresses at Brussels, Paris, Frankfurt and London.'[47] These peace confer-ences were led by delegates from Britain, the United States, France, Belgium, the Netherlands and Germany. Several delegates 'were members of the legislature of their respective countries; others were prominent clergymen and philanthropists'. The Paris conference was chaired by Victor Hugo.[48] Quakers played a prominent part in the peace movement and the leadership was also associated with temperance, corn-law repeal, complete suffrage and penal reform. 'Women were enrolled in the Olive Leaf Circles a parallel network of British and American female societies.'[49] The *Olive Leaf*, a magazine for children, contained morally uplifting tales on such diverse topics as slavery, the exploitation of the 'Red Indians of North America', and on the evils of war. In 1847 'a tale of suffering ... of unmitigated distress' of the famine in Ireland featured in the *Olive Leaf*.[50] The involvement of members of the Fisher family with the international peace movement shows them as actively sharing in the major concerns that became defining characteristics of nineteenth-century Quaker reform.

The minute book of the Youghal Women's Preparative Meeting for these years lists Anna Maria, Deborah and Jane Fisher as frequent representatives to the Cork meeting. The years between Anna's return from Ackworth and her marriage in 1854 were characterized by her involvement with famine relief, with the organization of employment for young women, with the international peace movement and with the running of the Youghal Women's Meetings. She was now an educated young woman with administrative and organizational skills, who had received training that would render her capable of earning her living.

In his history of the Irish Society of Friends, Maurice Wigham has divided members into two categories, the first, which included the Fishers, consisted of 'well-to-do Quaker families, which formed an interrelated series of clans each based on some business or industrial enterprise'. The second category was 'unconnected with the large families and probably less well off, some small traders or farmers, some craftsmen or workers often employed in Quaker businesses'.[51] The Haslam family of Rosenallis, Mountmellick was such a family. Unlike the Fishers in Youghal, members of the Haslam family do not feature prominently in the records of the Mountmellick meeting. They are not mentioned as delegates nor is there any account of their philanthropy. They appear in Quaker registers over three generations from the late eighteenth century onwards. The youngest generation mentioned, the children of Thomas's brother John, are registered as 'non-members'. The Haslam family, therefore, was not part of the well-to-do network of Quaker families, distinguished both for their commercial success and for their public manifestation of the Quaker virtues. Members of another branch of the family were Church of Ireland parishioners in Rosenallis. Thomas Haslam of Clonaslee, Queen's County was married in the Church of St Brigid, Rosenallis in 1828 and his children were christened there. This family had 'very strong roots' in the Church of Ireland.[52]

Thomas Joseph Haslam was born in 1825 to John Haslam of Rosenallis and his wife Mary (nee White of Templemore, Co. Tipperary). Thomas had an elder brother John born in 1822. His parents John and Mary had been married in 1821 at a relatively elderly age for a Quaker marriage, Mary being thirty-six and John, fifty-two. The graveyard at Rosenallis has only two Haslam gravestones, neither of which appears to belong to Thomas's immediate family. His mother Mary is buried in Dublin where she moved after the death of her husband.[53]

The Mountmellick Quaker records for 1840 devote much space to Mary Haslam, mother of Thomas. This is not because of her increased participation in the Society, but rather to censure her. Mary was accused of 'having withdrawn herself from friends' and meeting with 'members who separated themselves from us'.[54] She was visited on a number of occasions by overseers and eventually saw the error of her ways, wrote an abject letter of apology and was welcomed back into the fold. It is very likely that the 'withdrawal' referred to was an association with the 'White Quakers'. This schismatic movement, which lasted a little over ten years, was distinctly puritan, its members were obsessively clean, and advocated extreme simplicity of life, sometimes even casting off their clothes and running through the streets.[55] In 1840 the White Quakers (so called because they wore only white), opened meeting houses in Dublin, Mountmellick, Waterford and Clonmel. The language of censure applied to Mary Haslam – that she had attended 'another place of worship' and had sown 'discord in families . . . separating the nearest and dearest relations' – describes the realities of defection to the sect.[56] The White Quakers were notoriously divisive within the Quaker community and 'caused great hardship among families of Friends'.[57] Wigham described the 'distress and bitterness brought about' by individuals embracing White Quakerism as 'largely personal affecting the families concerned'.[58] What Mary's defection and her censure meant to the young Thomas we are not privy to; it may have been a contributory factor to his later leaving the Society of Friends.

The Friends Provincial School, Mountmellick, founded in 1786, admitted Thomas J. Haslam as a pupil in 1835, his brother John having enrolled in 1831.[59] Thomas attended the school's centenary celebrations of 1886 where he read *Mountmellick Revisited – A Centenary Ode by a Schoolboy*. He talked about 'the depth of feeling with which he had revisited the scenes of his boyhood'. It is not clear if he wrote this pleasant piece of doggerel, but line three of the stanza quoted below seems to bear his stamp:

> To those, who in our school-time hours
> Once taught us day by day
> Developing our latent powers,
> We grateful tributes pay.[60]

If the poem is his, then presumably he was asked to write it for the occasion, which suggests that his literary skills were recognized. Alternatively, if he was merely asked to recite it, it means that, at least, his skill in public speaking was known. An account given by an 'Old Boy' who was at the school at the same time as Thomas, describes how 'boys and girls met in the dining rooms for meals, and to hear the Scriptures read'. Although 'no further intercourse was allowed . . . little messages of love frequently passed between amateur lovers'. Pupils were encouraged to go for long rambles in the countryside, a fact attested to also in the poem read by Haslam. As was the practice in all Quaker schools at the time, there were no holidays: 'Parents and children seldom met, I was only home for two nights in three and half years.' A four-week holiday was granted in 1853 for the first time, 'a time of recreation being considered necessary for teachers and scholars'.[61]

Thomas attended Mountmellick School for five years; on leaving in 1840, he enrolled as an apprentice teacher at the Friends School, Lisburn.[62] His apprenticeship was typical of the Quaker teacher training system. Apprentices were trained for their teaching careers by part-time teaching and supervision. They were articled for six years and received free board, lodgings, clothes and a small monthly stipend. They 'provided most of the teachers of elementary subjects in Quaker schools until about the middle of the [nineteenth] century'.[63] Thomas went to Ackworth as a fully trained teacher where he had charge of the sixth class.[64] On the retirement of William Thistlewaite in 1847, Thomas was appointed to the temporary office of 'Master on Duty' and the school records claim that 'by his resolute will and keen sense of order and obedience, [he] converted a tangle of confusion into a perfect machine'. The Committee testified its appreciation of his work by voting him a gratuity 'in acknowledgement of his efficient services'.[65] The wages book of Ackworth School has a record of a gratuity of £10 paid to Thomas on 30 June 1848. His salary for the first half of 1847 was £48 per annum, increased to £50 in July 1847. His salary was paid to 13 July 1848 when he left teaching forever. The records reveal that Anna as assistant teacher was paid £28 per annum and that she too left her position on 14 July 1848, one day after Thomas.[66] It seems a remarkable coincidence that Anna and Thomas left Ackworth within a day of each other. There were no reasons for their leaving given in the Ackworth records, nor was there any hint of scandal. Perhaps Anna told her parents of her relationship with Thomas and was summoned home. Thomas may have found it impossible to continue teaching in a Quaker environment as he became disillusioned with religion. Alternatively he may simply have desired a change of career or may have wished to find a more lucrative calling in order that he might marry. Anna may have felt the need to return home to help her family in its famine relief efforts. Several bereavements suffered by the Fisher family in the 1840s may well have been the reason. James Abell Fisher, aged twenty, the sibling nearest in age to Anna, died in 1848. Two sisters, Sarah and Susanna, had died in 1847. Jenepher, the oldest member of the family, had died in 1844 aged thirty-six.[67] It would be understandable had Abraham and Jane summoned their youngest child home after such a spate of tragically young deaths within the family. There are no details of the cause of death of any of the family members. If any of these deaths had been caused by disease connected with the famine, it is likely that details would have survived. Whatever the reason for their leaving teaching within a day of each other, Anna and Thomas did not marry until six years later.

Thomas appears to have gone to London from Ackworth. Anna refers to a 'friend of my husband's in the London 50s when they read together in the B. Museum – *he* [indecipherable] worked for Thackeray, G. Reid, Carlisle +

other literary gentlemen'.[68] It is not clear from the letter whether Thomas Haslam or his friend from the British Museum worked for the literary luminaries. Thomas either knew those who researched for the great, or perhaps did so himself. Either way he was engaged in scholarly pursuits in the British Museum Reading Room. We know from his suffrage writings that he read Herbert Spencer in the early 1850s. There is a mention of Thomas devoting himself 'firstly to journalism in London' when he left Ackworth at the end of his teaching career'.[69]

At the time of his living in London, Thomas repudiated Quakerism. The Mountmellick Monthly Meeting reported with 'much regret' that a visit paid to Thomas J. Haslam 'had not produced any change in his sentiments' and consequently he was 'no longer considered a member of our religious society'. The information is tantalizingly scanty. The visit paid to Thomas was obviously in Mountmellick but the fact that Benjamin M. Wood and Thomas J. Pim were 'directed to write to Westminster Monthly Meeting to inform it' of this conclusion and to request that 'Thomas Joseph Haslam may be informed' suggests that he was back in London. The resolution was recorded on 19 February 1851. The minutes of the Westminster Monthly Meeting yield disappointingly little; the resolution of the Mountmellick letter was recorded but there was no further information on what 'sentiments' Thomas was unwilling to change. The family connection with Mountmellick ceased in 1851. Thomas's brother John had moved to Dublin in 1843. His father John died in 1850, following which his mother Mary joined John and his family in Ranelagh in Dublin.[70]

The fact that Thomas was now a non-member meant that Anna Maria Fisher, daughter of a prominent Quaker household, could not marry him within the Religious Society of Friends. In order for a Quaker marriage to take place, the man had first to obtain the permission of the woman's family. It was also necessary to obtain approval from the Quaker meetings to which the man and woman belonged. The couple had to present themselves before the meetings where the matter was openly discussed.[71] Theoretically Anna and Thomas could still have enjoyed a Quaker marriage provided they obtained parental and community approval and married at a Quaker meeting, 'where the actual wedding ceremony was often deeply moving' consisting of the couple standing up 'in their own time . . . [to] make their declaration unaided'.[72] It is extremely unlikely that Abraham and Jane Fisher would have encouraged their daughter to marry someone who had been disowned for his 'sentiments', and equally unlikely that Thomas would have been prepared to testify that he changed those sentiments in order to be readmitted as a member. Although the conditions of Quaker marriage appear stringent, it is fair to say that most middle-class marriages in the mid-nineteenth century did not take place without parental approval.

We do not know when Thomas returned to Ireland from London, but in 1854 when he married Anna Maria Fisher, he was a resident of the Parish of Inisloughnaught, Clonmel. Anna was residing at Great Georges Street, Cork, probably a temporary measure to satisfy the residency qualification, when they were married by the registrar, David Hill, at the Registrar's

Office in Cork on 20 March 1854. The witnesses were Reuben and Julia Fisher.[73] Anna was aged twenty-five and Thomas was four years older. There is no further information available regarding the wedding, nor is it possible to ascertain the reaction of Anna's parents. There is evidence in the minute book of the Clonmel Monthly Meeting that the couple lived in Clonmel after their marriage in 1854. The Clonmel Meeting received a letter from Cork in April 1854 within three weeks of the wedding of Thomas and Anna stating that 'Anna Maria Fisher had been married in a manner contrary to our rules to a person not a member of our religious Society'. It was stated that Anna was residing in the 'compass' of the Clonmel Meeting and Clonmel Friends were asked to visit her. Anna was subsequently visited by two women Friends and 'acknowledged having been married by a public marriage register to a person not in membership'. She was said to have received the Friends in an agreeable manner. The Cork Monthly Meeting, after various visits to Anna had been reported from Clonmel, concluded in August 1854 that she had 'forfeited her right to membership of our religious society'.[74] She was formally expelled from the Society of Friends and never rejoined, nor did Thomas. Because they continued to be associated with Quakerism, and were always identified as Quakers, it is difficult to ascertain the effect of disownment on Anna. There is no evidence of any resentment on her part at her treatment by her co-religionists. Of course she would have known that expulsion was the inevitable outcome of her marriage. It is obvious that she continued to approve the Quaker ethos; she always spoke with approval of her Quaker upbringing and of the benign influence of Quakerism on her life. She kept up contacts with members of the Society of Friends, particularly those engaged in reform movements and she and Thomas are buried together in the Quaker Burial Ground, Temple Hill, Dublin. It is likely that by continuing to be associated with the Society they gained an entry into reform circles on their arrival in Dublin. Such association also reveals the lack of animosity to the Haslams from members of the Society. In the 1850s there was much criticism of Quakerism from within, including a recognition that the inflexibility of the rules on marriage was losing many members of high calibre to the Society. Rules on 'marrying out' were relaxed in 1859 just a few years after Anna's disownment.[75] The *Annual Monitor*, which printed obituaries of noteworthy Quakers, published obituaries of Thomas and Anna:[76] 'They had both ceased to be members . . . many years before but they continued their association with the Society though they never rejoined in membership.'[77] Thomas, of course, had been disowned some years prior to their marriage for his expression of unknown 'sentiments' obviously alien to the Society. There are suggestions in his correspondence, discussed later in this chapter, that he was no longer a believer in aspects of Christian teaching. Anna's beliefs are not known but there is a hint that she was, at very least, doubtful of the existence of an afterlife.[78]

There is no information available as to why Thomas Haslam moved to Clonmel. There were many Quaker enterprises in the town in which he may have found employment. From Anna's correspondence we know that his income was less than £100 per annum, a sum they considered insufficient to rear a family. At the start of their married life they dedicated themselves and their lives to the service of others: 'The first night in our new house we prayed that we might have neither poverty or riches, that we would help others to the best of our ability & this we always endeavoured to do.'[79]

The Haslams' sojourn in Clonmel was brief and by 1858 'they were resident in Dublin where Thomas was employed as an accountant or book-keeper in the firm of Jameson Pim & Co. brewers of porter, ale and beer' with an address in Aughrim Street.[80] Pim was a Quaker name; the family was one of the leading Quaker families in Mountmellick. Thomas and Samuel Pim of Mountmellick were brewers.[81] Despite Thomas having been disowned by the Society of Friends, he obviously secured employment in Dublin through Mountmellick Quaker connections. The Haslams moved to Rathmines in 1862 and lived at 91 Lower Rathmines Road until 1898. In the 1860s, their lifestyle was altered by the breakdown of Thomas's health. Charles Oldham, who knew them well, dated the illness from 1866 when 'his health broke down completely, so that he had to abandon work of every kind'.[82] Henceforth Anna was the family earner, supporting them both by running a small business from their home. Thomas was proud of his wife's ability to earn a living, stating publicly that during the greater part of their marriage Anna 'had maintained not only herself but also an invalid husband by carrying on a business which requires her almost undivided attention'.[83] There is a suggestion that Anna's business venture preceded her husband's illness and was, in fact, started 'to supplement their slender income'.[84] The earliest evidence of the enterprise is from 1863 when it was described as a 'stationery and toy warehouse'.[85] The 1870 Dublin Trade Directory lists Anna M. Haslam as 'Stationer and Fancy Repository' at 91 Rathmines Road.[86] From correspondence with John Stuart Mill and F.W. Newman, we know that Thomas discussed his health in letters of 1868. Mill was glad to hear that Thomas was better, while Newman was sorry to hear of his grievous illness.[87] Anna's ability to support Thomas and herself is testament to her Quaker upbringing and training. She was remarkable in that she was not only a multi-cause campaigner, but was simultaneously the family breadwinner.

The marriage of Thomas and Anna Haslam was very happy, a fact frequently attested to by friends and colleagues. It was 'an example of an ideal happy union, a perfect idyll'.[88] They were described as being 'lovely and pleasant in their lives . . . Each advanced and stimulated the devotion of the other. Their ideal marriage, the admiration sometimes the envy of their friends was a factor in their longevity and in their power of endurance. They were childless but each was a child to the other.'[89] A poem, written in their honour on their diamond wedding anniversary called them 'A pair of lovers, as they were / In youth upon their bridal morn.'[90] Professor Charles Oldham wrote that 'no more ideal, mutually-helpful and happier marriage has ever been made or endured longer'.[91] Anna and Thomas each spoke of the other lovingly and appreciatively on public occasions and in private. Anna wrote to Marie Stopes:

I do not think there could have been a happier & more united couple who had lived in such close intimacy for over 62 years – alas I have now to live alone – the memory of the past is with me day & night & the longing to be re-united if there be a future life is always present.[92]

Thomas called Anna his 'dear wife'; she called him 'my darling'. His public acknowledgement of her support and care for him in his lifelong invalidity is touching. Thomas was proud of his wife's achievements including her ability to support them both. He never claimed equal credit with Anna but generously acknowledged that she was the prime mover and he was the helper: 'For myself, the most that I can say is that, from time to time, I have rendered my wife some little help in her various efforts to raise her sex out of the many disabilities from which they are everywhere suffering.'[93]

Anna, in her old age after the death of Thomas, wrote to Marie Stopes letters of astonishing frankness about her marriage. The correspondence was mainly concerned with birth control about which Thomas had written a pamphlet in 1868 advocating a form of the 'safe period'.[94] He followed this with a longer work called *Duties of Parents* published in 1872 in which his preferred method of family limitation was sexual abstinence. From the correspondence with Marie Stopes, Anna emerges as both informed and curious about female sexuality. She was an avid reader of Marie Stopes's works on marriage and parenthood.[95]

In a reference to birth control within her own marriage she wrote: 'We practised what we preached and I do not think there could have been a happier or more united couple.' If practising what they preached means their usage of the safe period as advocated in *The Marriage Problem*, Thomas's work on birth control, it is likely that one or other of the Haslams was infertile, as the safe period recommended by Thomas was, in fact, the most fertile time of the female cycle. However, the message preached in the *Duties of Parents* was one of sexual abstinence. A later and less ambivalent letter suggests that Anna and Thomas were involved in a relationship of happy celibacy. She wrote that 'a great deal' of people confided in her of their various birth control practices:

I know several who practised 'Safe methods' satisfactorily – And some with whom it failed – owing we believed to their *not* keeping to the *middle of the month* indulging *too near* the monthly period – I know many who have only *one* child – and often wished to ask the wife *why* – *we* my husband and myself *never* tried it – we preferred abstinence – after the first week we were married – *never after that* – we slept together for over 50 years – and were a most loving couple – every one thought us an ideal pair – we had decided *before we were married* that we were *too poor* – had *less* than £100– a year and unsuitable to be parents.[96]

This aspect of the Haslam marriage is discussed in Chapter 3, in the context of Thomas's writings on sexuality. Despite the restraint practised in their marriage, neither Anna nor Thomas was prudish in writing about sexual matters. In her letters to Stopes Anna was remarkably frank, possibly because of Stopes's authorship of *Married Love,* a book about which Anna wrote approvingly: 'I liked *Married Love* (and have ordered a copy to lend to my Dr. & others) because it explained so much that must be dark and obscure to the average wife.'[97] She discussed ovulation and orgasm and was morally non-judgmental when writing about various methods of birth control: 'The *"withdrawal"* is not satisfactory . . . "French letters" have been used by some and quinine etc. Injections – to me next to *abstinence* – the *mid month* has always appeared the best. I have always been deeply interested in these questions & have helped many women.'[98] In a letter written when she was ninety-two, Anna complained of the narrow-mindedness of 'a niece by marriage and other ladies who think me real indelicate when dealing with such questionable matters [birth control]. I tell them they are very old fashioned.'[99] Although open-minded and informed regarding contraceptive methods she thought that abstinence was 'the highest and best . . . the *desire* grows on being yielded to as much as gluttony & alcohol drinking'.[100] The concept of abstinence being 'higher and better' was perhaps the same idea expressed 'implicitly at least' in William Godwin's *An Enquiry concerning Political Justice* (1793) that sexual desires would lessen as society advanced.[101] This belief in the moral evolution of society is central to Thomas Haslam's *Duties of Parents* (1872).[102]

Phyllis Rose, in *Parallel Lives*, a study of the marriages of five Victorian notables, Carlyle, Dickens, George Eliot, Mill and Ruskin, has written that 'at least two of them, and possibly a third, were sexless'. In her discussion of the phenomenon of celibate marriages, Rose has argued that such marriages should not be seen as 'bizarre'. The advent of 'popular Freudianism' in the early twentieth century 'by sexualizing experience . . . had the moralistic result of limiting possibilities'. Rose sees 'sexless marriages' not as non-marriages, but as 'examples of flexibility rather than of abnormality' – as another 'model of marriage'.[103] Sheila Jeffreys, too, has argued that 'The idea that a fulfilling love relationship which excluded sexual intercourse could exist between men and women' while 'unfamiliar if not incomprehensible' to those brought up after the twentieth-century 'sexual revolution', may have been perceived differently in an age which did not define '"sex" specifically as sexual intercourse'.[104] While there has been an amount of revisionism on the subject of Victorian sexuality it is undeniable that 'many cultural circumstances worked against the likelihood of sexual satisfaction within Victorian marriages'.[105] Margaret Cousins, the twentieth-century Irish suffragist, implied that her own happy marriage to a committed feminist was celibate after an initial unhappy experience. She 'grew thin and white during her first married year'. This was 'due to the problems of adjustment to the revelation the marriage had brought me as to the physical basis of sex . . . My new knowledge, *though I was lovingly safeguarded from it,* made me ashamed of humanity and ashamed for it' (my italics).[106] There are suggestions too that the marriage of feminists Hanna and Francis Sheehy Skeffington was sexually unfulfilling, although unlike the Cousins, the

Haslams, and the Mills, there was a child of the marriage. A biography hints at difficulties in their sexual relationship: 'both had received a rigid, Catholic upbringing in a puritanical era, which resulted in ignorance, misconceptions and fears with regard to sex'. It is stated also that 'There is substantial basis for the belief, that she [Hanna], like so many of her contemporaries, felt that procreation was really the only excuse for intercourse.'[107] Rosamund Jacob's diaries also reveal that Hanna confided in her 'about her upbringing & the prudishness that she was trained in & will never get rid of'. Hanna told her also of how she and Frank had occupied separate bedrooms as she thought 'that the most civilized way'.[108]

It is likely that the espousal of feminist causes by men rendered them more likely to endure, or enjoy, celibate marriage. Nineteenth-century feminists objected to the prevailing notion, enshrined in law, that a woman's body was the property of her husband. In the event of a woman being repulsed by the sexual advances of her feminist husband, or even by the discovery of what was entailed, as in Margaret Cousins's case, he would be unlikely to force his attentions upon her. Mill wrote, two months before his own marriage, that he objected to the 'legal power and control' marriage granted to one party 'over the person, property and freedom of action of the other party'. He put on record his 'solemn promise never in any case or under any circumstances to use them'.[109] Harriet Taylor, for whom Mill was the second husband, said that her relationship with her first husband, John Taylor, and with John Mill was that of 'Seelinfreundin'.[110]

Despite the confidently proclaimed expertise of Thomas on the subject of birth control, his knowledge of the so-called safe period was not gleaned until he read Dr Trall's work, Sexual Physiology, which was published in 1866. Thus the decision of the Haslams not to have children was predicated on their choice of abstinence as a birth control method. Thomas did have knowledge of alternative methods, such as the sheath, in 1868 but found them distasteful. Until he read Trall, with its 'natural family planning' advice, the absence of an acceptable birth control method made it impossible for the Haslams to separate sex from the threat of unwanted pregnancy. Can the decision not to have children, and the resolution to abstain from sexual intercourse, have been adhered to without emotional cost to them both? There is certainly no evidence of any emotional dysfunction or unhappiness in Anna, and from her letters to Stopes it is clear that she considered her marriage exceptionally happy. One could speculate that their celibacy may not have been unconnected with Thomas's subsequent breakdown. We cannot know. We do know, however, from Thomas's later writings that he saw sexual self-control as essentially 'manly' and 'chivalrous' rather than as diminishing masculinity. This perception was echoed in the teachings of men's chastity leagues in the 1890s, which suggested that 'in place of maleness connoting a physical expression of male sexuality was a sense that masculinity could be expressed by restraint'.[111]

The Haslams' marriage was untypical; the gender roles were reversed in that Anna supported Thomas financially and in her public life he was her helper. He does not appear to have been a weak or ineffectual man, however, but speaks through his writings in a strong and authoritative voice. There is no information available as to the nature of his ill health; despite his having to stop working he led a fruitful and busy life of writing and public speaking and exhibited great stamina when a very old man in the amount of travelling and speech making that he undertook. It is possible that his breakdown may have been mental rather than physical. One can, perhaps, detect a hint of hypochondria in the bulletins on his health included in letters written to J. S. Mill and Francis Newman. Whatever the facts regarding his health, Thomas Haslam was nevertheless a popular figure. Those who wrote of him described him with affection. Charles Oldham in particular painted a picture of an attractive personality: 'His youthful enthusiasm for new ideas and . . . his vivacity in conversation . . . his gentle and winning personality . . . sweet good-heartedness; he never said an unkind word of anybody, and all who knew him will themselves feel kindlier whenever they think of Thomas Joseph Haslam.'[112] Together they were a formidable team – Anna intensely practical, efficient, a capable organizer; Thomas 'a small, active, spare figure' mindful of his delicate constitution, yet ever ready to compose a pamphlet, to write a letter to the newspapers, to propose or second a resolution, to deliver a paper which complemented his wife's active endeavours. It appears that Anna was no orator. In an article praising her for her devotion to the 'political and social advancement of women' the writer stated that 'she was not endowed with any great oratorical gifts'. Her husband, 'who had considerable literary skills, backed her up by reading papers at public meetings and writing articles for the newspapers'.[113] There are, however, many accounts that suggest that she was, at the very least, a competent speaker. Nor does she appear to have been reluctant to speak. On occasions when her husband replied to addresses of good wishes on behalf of them both, when it would not have been necessary for her to speak, we are told that 'Mrs. Haslam . . . also replied [and] was received with great enthusiasm', or that 'Mrs. Haslam also replied to the address in a very touching manner'.[114] Other accounts describe Anna's speeches as 'charming' and 'bright' delivered with 'spirit' and 'vivaciousness'.[115]

Obviously Thomas Haslam was not unique as a nineteenth-century male supporter of female franchise; the introduction of suffrage bills in the House of Commons was, after all, dependent on male members of parliament. His writings reveal his conviction that discrimination against women was based upon man-made injustice that could be righted only when men acknowledged the inequity of women's lot. As the male partner of a campaigning female suffragist he was in distinguished company. Millicent Fawcett's husband Henry was a pro-suffrage member of parliament. The Pankhursts, the Pethick Lawrences and, in Ireland, the Sheehy Skeffingtons and the Cousins were all marriages in which both partners advocated and worked for women's rights. The Haslams' suffrage principles were instilled in each of them prior to marriage. Anna Haslam has already been quoted as never remembering a time when she did not take equality of women totally for granted. Thomas knew Anna from 1847 onwards but was converted to the cause by a Herbert Spencer epigram that he read in the early 1850s.[116] The evolution of Thomas's feminism is discussed in later chapters on suffrage.

Although Thomas in his writings constantly challenged patriarchal attitudes, he also appealed to the chivalry of male readers: 'We ask you if you have any true chivalry of feeling to come forward manfully, and assist them in their uphill battle.'[117] It has been noted that there was a tendency in pro-suffrage men to counter

> potential opposition by reappropriating the language and claims made by those who attacked them. Thus the smug statement by the opponents of women's suffrage that they were the chivalrous protectors of the female sex was subverted by male supporters who stressed that it was *they* who really cared for women.[118]

Male supporters of suffrage used the Victorian vocabulary of female virtue and sweetness of character to argue that if women were allowed to enter the political arena their stereotypical female qualities would enhance and elevate political life. Male political leadership was castigated for 'social chaos, war turmoil, and poverty'.[119] Keir Hardie, leader of the Independent Labour Party, asserted that 'unchallenged male dominance, arrogant armaments, harsh and unfeeling administration of law, industrial conditions ... are proving fatal to the race. With the incoming of the mother element into politics this would be gradually changed.'[120]

It would be unfair to Thomas Haslam to see his suffragism as an inevitable feature of his life as husband of Anna. His feminism was grounded in his intellectual conviction of the inherent right of women to equality. John Tosh has pointed out that 'men do not decide to work for a major change in the position of women without experiencing a modification in their own gender identity'.[121] Caroline Spring uses a quotation from Haslam's pamphlet *Women's Suffrage from a Masculine Standpoint* (1906) in which he castigated 'masculine statesmanship', to demonstrate her point that pro-suffragist men through their advocacy of women's suffrage could be a platform 'to express the contradiction between the dominant notions of masculinity and individuals' reluctance to pursue that notion'. She argues that 'Oratorical attempts to renovate masculinity embedded in a critique of the state not only functioned to promote a public distance from hegemonic ideologies of manliness but also operated to re-establish men's self-affirmation.'[122]

Thomas Haslam was a Victorian and possessed that most Victorian of virtues – earnestness. Life for Haslam was a constant search for improvement not only for himself but also for mankind. His writings reveal him as full of purpose, convinced that he had the solution for the eradication of poverty in his teachings of temperance and restraint, resolute in his determination to convince his male readers of the need to develop and foster within themselves the so-called female virtue of chastity, and dedicated to the removal of all discriminatory legislation against women. His life was dedicated to the improvement of mankind – the building of the Kingdom of Man. His polemical writings on birth control, parental duties, and prostitution, preached self-denial as the means by which mankind could progress to an ever more civilized future. He shared the Victorian passion for self-improvement and in addition to his writings on moral improvement, wrote *Good English for Beginners,* a well-received work that provided examples and exercises designed to improve writing skills.

In his own way Haslam was a 'Victorian Sage' – one who tried 'to express notions about the world, man's situation in it and how he should live'.[123] In the nineteenth century, before the age of specialization, thinkers and scholars could presume to have an overall view of their times. 'The polymath, sage or seer could not only pronounce oracularly about the state of the world and of civilization, but also ... could communicate his message to others in a language intelligible to most literate people.'[124] Haslam's method of reaching an audience was to dash off a pamphlet, to write to the newspapers, to address a meeting. Today such men have been replaced by 'academic experts, mass media pundits, cultural functionaries'.[125] He spoke with a magisterial voice; his supreme self-confidence when writing on birth control, where his theories were wrong, and on parental duty, where he can only have been theorizing, is breathtaking. Victorian atheism and agnosticism had a high moral tone. Its ethic was the pursuit of good for its own sake without the hope of eternal reward or the fear of everlasting punishment. While there is no explicit example of Haslam's agnosticism surviving, he never declares his credo nor do we know the 'sentiments' that caused his expulsion from the Society of Friends, there are clues that point strongly to his doubts. His circle of correspondents included noted agnostics such as John Stuart Mill, Francis Newman and Thomas Scott. Newman, described as anti-sex and pro-woman was, like Haslam, a dedicated suffragist and a campaigner against the Contagious Diseases Acts. He saw himself as dedicated to saving the world 'from Pantheism, Selfishness and Sensuality'. He wrote defending his rejection of Christianity: 'Our highest ideal is (whether we know it or not) a God to us ... He who worships no ideal at all, but lives for self, is the real atheist.'[126] Mill wrote in denunciation of Christian teaching on the afterlife: 'I will call no being good, who is not what I mean when I apply the epithet to my fellow-creatures; and if such a being can sentence me to Hell for not so calling him, to Hell I will go.'[127] Haslam wrote to Newman 'of false training at an early age, the results of which (like the dread of hell)' he would 'never be able altogether to shake off', which suggests a rejection of Christian teaching.[128] In another letter he uses the following analogy to repudiate a theory as strongly as possible: 'It appears repugnant to my common sense as the Athanasian Creed.'[129] Victorian agnostics 'were caught in an impossible dilemma'. To publicly defend one's agnosticism was to run the risk of 'undermining the moral foundation of society'; to remain silent on doubts was to feel a hypocrite. Mill wrote of the 'painful position' of the 'cultivated mind' drawn 'in contrary directions by the two noblest of all objects of pursuit, truth, and the general good'.[130] There is a caution present in Haslam's work regarding religion; only in his letters to correspondents such as Newman is there honesty about his beliefs, or lack of them. Haslam was innately cautious. His works on moral questions were anonymous. While he doubtlessly shared Mill's fears regarding the moral foundation of society it is very likely that he did not want to weaken the causes for which he worked by exposing them to the possible criticism that their advocate was godless. His continued association with the Society of Friends would have given an air of respectability, countering his reputation as the author, albeit anonymous, of works on controversial subjects.

Haslam was a member of the Statistical and Social Inquiry Society of Ireland from the 1860s. The statistical movement was concerned with the 'ideology of improvement' and was with 'the moral effects of the physical environment' and the problem of poverty. Statistical societies advocated public health reform and education as answers to crime.[131] The Irish society 'analysed the major changes that have taken place in population, employment, legal and administrative systems and social services . . . The founders of the Society believed that statistics and economic analysis would provide scientific answers to the major problems of the time.'[132] It 'can be seen as an Irish variant of the many moral and social reform movements that were so typical of mid-Victorian England'. Membership included 'a small group of politicians and senior officials based in Dublin Castle'.[133] Many of those in membership of the Society in 1864 were subsequently interested in the campaign for women's suffrage. Membership included Sir Robert Kane and Sir John Gray who were both on the platform when Mrs Fawcett came to Dublin in 1870 to address a large public meeting on women's suffrage. David Sherlock, QC, for many years a member of the Dublin Women's Suffrage Association (DWSA), was also a member of the Society. Quakers were well represented and included members of the Webb and Pim families. John Stuart Mill was an honorary member.[134]

Women were eligible to become associate members of the Society and were allowed to present papers. Thus the Society, unusually for the time, provided a platform where women could speak in public on a chosen topic to a (presumably) interested mixed audience. In the early days a male member often read such papers, demonstrating that despite the recognition of the ability of women to produce papers to the required standard, there was unwillingness on their part to speak in public to a mixed audience. In 1863, Charlotte Stoker, mother of Bram, was the first woman to address the Society when she read her paper 'on the need for state provision for the education of the deaf and dumb'. Isabella Tod, campaigner with Anna Haslam in many causes, addressed the Society in 1878, and Anna herself read a paper on women and children in workhouses. The paper was not her own, however, but was written by Mrs Morgan John O'Connell.[135] The associate members included Miss Corlett, a signatory in 1866 of the first petition to parliament for women's suffrage and founder of the Queen's Institute in Dublin in 1861, and Mrs Jellico, prominent in the founding of Alexandra School, both members of the Society of Friends.[136] The question of women's suffrage exercised the Society as early as 1864, when Alfred Webb, a Quaker, read a paper entitled *Propriety of Conceding the Elective Franchise to Women*. In 1872 and 1873, W. G. Brooke delivered papers on the higher education of women, and on the law as it applied to the protection of women.[137]

The annual membership fee of the Society was one pound, a sum that must have represented a considerable outlay to the Haslams. Thomas Haslam did not address a paper to the Society but, in 1865, produced a pamphlet entitled *The Real Wants of the Irish People*. Authorship was not acknowledged – the pamphlet was by 'A Member of the Statistical and Social Inquiry Society of Ireland'. The copy in Dr. Williams's Library, London is inscribed in Thomas Haslam's hand, 'Professor Francis Newman with the author's kind regards. Thomas J. Haslam'. The pamphlet consists of fifty pages of closely argued solutions to Ireland's ills. His recommendations included Church disestablishment, 'an enormous reduction' in farmers' rents, the principle of tenant right and the granting of proper leases to tenants (in effect the 'three Fs' demanded by the Land League in 1879), emigration for labourers and unsuccessful farmers, and the ending of sectarian education. He objected to Irish labourers who were unable to find employment being forced 'to barter every sacred privilege of manhood for the miserable stipend of the British soldier'. He is cynical of the necessity of the 'evil' of a standing army in an 'imperfect world like ours' and does not want to see his 'fellow-Irishmen enrol themselves amongst its victims'.[138] Membership of the Statistical Society provided Haslam with stimulating ideas on social policy which he subsequently developed in his writings, particularly in *Duties of Parents*. He met there with a circle of like-minded people, many of whom were subsequently connected with the suffrage movement.

There is little solid information on the Haslams before the 1870s. There is an account of Anna having been at a public meeting in Dublin when she

> was present in the Library of the Friends' Meeting House, Eustace Street in 1861 when Miss Bessie Rayner Parkes,[139] Mrs. Lloyd,[140] Mrs. Jellicoe[141] and Miss Corlett[142] urged the need for providing employment for educated women ... [F]rom these meetings came the Queen's Institute, and subsequently the Alexandra College and Alexandra School.[143]

The Queen's Institute was established in 1861 with the purpose of training girls for employment opportunities as machinists, law writers, telegraph clerks, office clerks, ornamental writers, engravers and lithographic workers.[144] As will be seen throughout her life, Anna was concerned with equal employment opportunities for women. Her presence at this meeting, five years before the first petition for women's suffrage was presented to parliament by J. S. Mill and fifteen years before she founded the Dublin Women's Suffrage Association demonstrates her perennial interest in any issue that forwarded the cause of women. It also places her, as early as 1861, in a network of mainly Quaker women involved in reform and innovation.

Having signed the petition of John Stuart Mill in 1866 for the enfranchisement of women, Anna commenced her lifelong commitment to the cause of women's suffrage. In the decade following the production of the *Real Wants of the Irish People*, Thomas came into his own as a pamphleteer. In 1868, using the *nom de plume* Œdipus, he wrote *The Marriage Problem*, which recommended the limitation of family size by the use of what he understood to be the 'safe' or infertile period. This pamphlet and his more substantial 1872 work, *Duties of Parents*, are the subjects of Chapters 2 and 3. His writings provided the theoretical framework for his own and his wife's lives of activism. His pamphlet *A Few Words on Prostitution* published in 1870 was a powerful polemic that coincided with the campaign against the Contagious Diseases Acts, while three issues of his *Women's Advocate* produced in 1874 marked the beginnings of their fight for suffrage. In 1892 Thomas produced *Good English for Beginners*, a work on literary composition. He produced three pamphlets on women's suffrage in the early twentieth century. The scope and scale of the Haslams' involvement in reform movements is impressive.[145] She was simultaneously involved in the leadership of the suffrage movement, the campaign against the Contagious Diseases Acts and the movement for the advancement of educational opportunities for women. Amazingly her own perception of this period suggests that her energies and those of her husband were principally engaged in the Anti-Home Rule movement to which, she said, they turned all of their attention.[146]

Despite the limitations imposed on the Haslams by their straitened circumstances, they appear to have enjoyed their lives in Victorian Dublin. They moved in a circle that included politicians and business people many of whom were Quakers. They were inveterate attenders at lectures and meetings and were connected with myriad reform movements. Thomas enjoyed the lively discussions at the Contemporary Club, the Friends' Institute and the Ninety Club. From the very small amount of correspondence surviving we learn that they welcomed callers to their home and were constantly busy.

Anna was released from the necessity of supporting Thomas and herself, when in 1895: 'A very substantial testimonial . . . [was] presented to Mr. and Mrs. T. J. Haslam by their numerous friends and well wishers in Great Britain and Ireland in recognition of their long-continued service in the cause of various social and other reforms.'[147] Thomas may have been alluding to this gift when, at the celebrations for Anna's eightieth birthday in 1909, he said her business was no longer necessary 'owing in part to the generosity of some warm-hearted friends'.[148] There was a perceptible increase in Anna's suffrage activities from the time it was no longer incumbent upon her to make a living. This is not to suggest that she did not carry out a prodigious amount of voluntary work while engaged in business.

Thomas died in 1917; his death was widely reported and many obituaries were written. Anna lived until late 1922, and, as will be seen in Chapter

6, she was active to the end of her life. While she did not discuss the political upheaval involved in the birth of the Irish Free State, there is a sense of displacement and isolation in her final years. She wrote to Marie Stopes in 1921: 'I am very dull and uncomfortable, *no servant*, have to do more than I like – can't be helped – it is miserable. Strikes innumerable . . . What will become of us all? Ireland is a puzzle.'[149] She made a will in August 1922, a few months before her death in November, which included some small legacies to the Irish Women's Citizens' Association (IWCA), Irish Women's Patrols and the Dublin Friends' Institute.

There is extant a short biographical piece, written in the third person, on Anna Maria Haslam. As it is her own handwriting, it can be safely assumed that she composed it herself. She gave some details of her campaigns and stated simply: 'Was greatly interested in social questions.' She 'had a most valuable helper in her husband. She never could have undertaken what she did in latter years if it were not for his sympathy and help.' She called herself 'a strong unionist' and summed up her life as assisting 'all movements to help and forward the interests of women'.[150]

2

'Alas! the practice fails':[1] Thomas Haslam's writings on birth control

Thomas Haslam was forty-three years old in 1868, when he wrote a pamphlet, *The Marriage Problem*, on birth control which he published privately.[2] This pamphlet of fifteen pages was written with almost evangelical zeal, and offered those who wished to 'regulate the number of their offspring . . . an easy, inoffensive, and practical solution'.[3] In the pamphlet, Haslam stressed the economic, social and moral desirability of birth control. His recommended method, which he explained in great detail and in uneuphemistic language, was the use of the 'law' of the safe or infertile period. The language of the pamphlet conveys a palpable sense of urgency – its message must be 'speedily disseminated amongst all classes'. In order to facilitate 'the dissemination of important truths set forth', readers were 'at liberty to reprint' and privately circulate the contents. Despite the loss of income due to his early retirement from business on grounds of ill health, Thomas seemingly bore the cost of publication as the pamphlet was 'printed for gratuitous circulation amongst Adult Readers only'.[4]

The Marriage Problem has to be examined in the context of the English birth control movement. There is no evidence of any corresponding movement in Ireland; indeed Haslam seems to be unique as a nineteenth-century Irishman writing in favour of birth control. His correspondence shows that he was in touch with Englishmen who were involved in secularist and reforming movements, and also reveals his own secularist approach to the question. Thomas kept abreast of the available literature on birth control and Anna saw herself as mentor to young women on the subject. The birth control movement in England arose from the development of the philosophical doctrine of utilitarianism and of the economic doctrine of Malthusianism. Thomas Robert Malthus (1766–1834), fellow of Jesus College, Cambridge, and Church of England curate in Albury, Surrey, has been described as 'a timid bird in the sociological aviary and . . . an inappropriate person to have a euphemism for birth control, Malthusianism or Neo-Malthusianism fathered on him'.[5] His theory propounding the nation's duty to limit population appeared in 1798 in his *Essay on the Principles of Population*.[6] His thesis, that population tended to increase faster than the means of sustenance, was not original but he was the first to treat the subject of population theory systematically.

The only barriers to population increase, in the opinion of Malthus, were limited food and limited space and the natural checks of disease, famine, plague and war. His solution to the problem of over-population was that the poor must marry late in order to limit family size. Ironically, as he never advocated any artificial check on conception, the name of Malthus became inextricably bound in the public mind with the advocacy of birth control, yet he went little further than to suggest the raising of the age of marriage as a solution to the problem of over-population. Malthus specifically repudiated artificial birth control in the 1817 edition of his *Essay* where he wrote: 'Indeed I should always particularly reprobate any artificial and unnatural modes of checking population, both on account of their immorality and their tendency to remove a necessary stimulus to industry.'[7] The theory of Malthus was essentially pessimistic and was an antidote to the dreams of progress occasioned by the French revolution, and, specifically, to William Godwin's argument in *An Enquiry Concerning Political Justice* (1793), which suggested a more equitable sharing of property. Malthus believed that a child born to a man of no property 'has no claim of right to the smallest portion of food . . . At Nature's mighty feast there is no vacant cover for him. She tells him to be gone, and will quickly execute her orders.'[8] It must be stressed that Malthus saw the population crisis as being caused by the reckless breeding of the poor. His critics accused him of class bias, 'of inculcating the prudential check' upon working men only.[9]

The earliest of the nineteenth-century birth control advocates were adherents of the philosophy of utilitarianism who adopted the demographic theories of Malthus but allied them to a belief in the logical necessity of contraception. Utilitarians looked upon happiness and well-being as an end to which man should aspire. They did not see the conception of children as the sole purpose of sexual intercourse and they were inhibited neither by religious qualms nor by an unrealistic faith in the so-called moral restraint of the poor. They were, however, prevented from setting forth their philosophy plainly because of the horror with which the subject was regarded by popular opinion. Middle-class radicals were not prepared to ruin their reputations by speaking out openly on such a controversial topic and thus we find the first arguments in favour of the social necessity of birth control couched in allusive language. James Mill in his 1824 *Supplement to the Encyclopaedia Britannica* hinted that there were ways of maintaining a balanced population if 'the superstitions of the nursery were discarded'.[10] Mill hardly practised what he preached as he fathered nine children despite his straitened circumstances. Those who allied the population theory of Malthus with a belief in the desirability of the use of artificial checks on conception became known, however inappropriately, as Neo-Malthusians.

It is virtually certain that Thomas Haslam was aware of the considerable birth control literature that was available when he wrote his pamphlet in 1868. Books on the subject written in the 1830s, 1840s and 1850s continued to be reissued in new editions for decades. Francis Place (1771–1854) is credited with being the first birth control propagandist to attempt to educate the masses in the advantages of family limitation. Place is untypical in that he was not middle class but a self-educated working man who rose to prominence in English political life through his own 'heroic effort'.[11] He published, in 1822, *Illustrations and proofs of the Principles of Population*, the first treatise in English to propose contraception as an alternative to the 'moral restraint' of Malthus. By moral restraint Malthus meant, not the restriction of sexual relations within marriage, but the postponement of marriage until the contracting parties were in a position to support potential offspring. Place was much less cautious than his middle-class colleagues and courageously disseminated handbills which advocated birth control, and included suggested methods. He alluded to the support he enjoyed from those 'who were themselves afraid to encounter the certain obloquoy (sic) of such allusions'.[12] It is has been estimated that tens of thousands of these handbills were distributed in London and in the industrial cities of the north of England between 1823 and 1826.[13] He addressed the bills *'To the Married of Both Sexes of the Working People'* and sought to reveal to members of this class the law of supply and demand in relation to their labour. 'When the number of working people in any trade or manufacture, has for some years been too great wages are reduced very low, and the working people become little better than slaves.' The inevitable result of this state of affairs was that 'working people can no longer maintain their children as all good and respectable people wish to maintain their children'. The solution to this was 'short and plain: the means are easy. Do as other people do, as to avoid having more children than they wish to have.' Place described clearly how to use a 'piece of soft sponge tied by a bobbin or a penny ribbon . . . as large as a green walnut or a small apple'. This, he promised, would prevent conception and limit the number of children; the subsequent reduction in numbers of the working class would result in a consequent increase in wages. Young men would no longer fear to take a wife: 'all will be married while young – debauchery will diminish – while good morals and religious duty will be promoted.' Although the appeal of the handbill was essentially economic, Place also pointed out that the 'pleasures of married life' need not be 'diminished' by the sponge method of family limitation.[14] Haslam shared Place's aim of improving the lot of the working classes by reduction in family size and was familiar with the use of the sponge as a contraceptive. However, he judged that its use was 'somewhat revolting to the feelings of highly refined and conscientious women'.[15]

The writings of Place influenced Richard Carlisle who published *What is Love?* in 1825. It was reprinted as *Everywoman's Book; or, What is Love?* in 1826. In the 1838 edition Carlisle wrote that 10,000 copies had been sold, claimed that it had become a 'standard work' and anticipated that it would become 'one of the most valued books in the English language'.[16] Haslam's claims for the importance of his own work are remarkably similar to those made by Carlisle,[17] but there the resemblance between the two works ends. Carlisle, an outspoken freethinker, was of the opinion that contraception would be of great advantage to '[t]hose women who chose to have lovers [as they] would neither be degraded nor brutalized'. He believed that women were capable of enjoying sex and advised them to take the initiative: 'Young women assume an equality, plead your passion when you feel it.'[18] He described three methods – the sponge, the 'glove' or *baudruche* (condom), and partial or complete withdrawal.[19] In 1831 Robert Dale Owen published *Moral Physiology,* the frontispiece of which portrays a visibly distressed young woman in the process of abandoning a baby and bears the legend 'Alas! That it should ever have been born.'[20] The contraceptive advice offered in *Moral Physiology* is virtually confined to *coitus interruptus.* The 'glove' or condom Owen thought inconvenient – 'disagreeable on the score of cleanliness and very expensive', although he conceded that its efficacy was 'certain' and it was a 'check' against syphilis. If the sponge could be 'ascertained to be infallible' he would consider it 'a great gain to mankind' but he has heard of 'several cases' where it failed.[21] *Coitus interruptus* or 'complete withdrawal on the part of the man immediately previous to emission . . . *is in all cases effectual'.* This method, he judged, would involve sacrifice and self-control but such sacrifice would be insignificant compared with the resultant benefits.[22] Sixty-five of the pamphlet's seventy-two pages were devoted to a justification of the morality of contraception. The book was intended for 'uncorrupted' if 'ignorant' young men and women and was not for 'libertines and debauchees'. Owen castigated 'prudes and hypocrites' in a memorable sentence: 'You who at dinner, ask to be helped to the bosom of a duck, lest by the mention of the word breast, you call up improper associations . . . I do not address.' To him the 'instinct of reproduction' was designed 'to give, even while receiving pleasure; and, among cultivated beings, the former power is ever more highly valued than the latter'.[23] Owen praised those who had previously disseminated the birth control message as 'men of unimpeachable integrity, and of first rate moral character, many of them known as the first political economists and philanthropists of the age'.[24] Utilitarianism was Dale Owen's creed: 'Let UTILITY be our polar star.'[25] It would be reasonable to assume that Haslam had read *Moral Physiology,* as it went through several editions within a year, and in Britain alone, sold an estimated 800 copies a year for the next forty years.[26]

The works of Place and Carlisle influenced the American birth control movement and American authors in turn had a considerable influence upon the social diffusion of contraceptive knowledge in England.[27] Dr Charles Knowlton, an American physician, published *The Fruits of Philosophy* in New York in 1831 and in London soon afterwards.[28] It is estimated that 1,000 copies of Knowlton's work were sold each year in England between the 1830s and the 1870s. His recommended method of birth control was female douching. Knowlton advised the purchase of a 'female syringe' from 'an apothecary for a shilling or less', which was to be used 'in connexion with a solution of sulphate of alum, zinc, pearlash or any salt that acts chemically on the semen and at the same time produces no unfavourable effect on the female'. The practical advantages of this method were that it was safe and cheap, 'used *after* instead of before connexion', and was in the control of the woman.[29] Although in the literature of birth control there was a tendency to favour methods controlled by women, there was also continuing mention of *coitus interruptus.*

Dr George Drysdale's *Physical, Sexual and Natural Religion* was published in 1854, and an enlarged edition entitled *The Elements of Social Science* appeared in 1861. Drysdale, who wrote under the pseudonym 'A Student of Medicine' (later editions were by 'A Doctor of Medicine'), challenged mainstream Victorian opinion on religion and sexuality. He was opposed to the teaching of Malthus and asked rhetorically 'IS IT POSSIBLE TO HAVE BOTH FOOD AND LOVE?' He answered that he firmly believed 'it is perfectly possible'.[30] His preferred method was the sponge as it was practical and safe and was the responsibility of the woman: 'Any preventative means to be satisfactory must be used by the *Woman* as it spoils the passion and impulsiveness of the venereal act if the man have (sic) to think of them.'[31] Haslam would not have agreed with Drysdale that sexual abstinence was 'itself an evil and one of the very greatest of evils'. Drysdale deplored that the 'preventative check, in the shape of sexual abstinence is operating at this day with so tremendous a power as was probably never before known in this world'.[32] This is an interesting observation in the light of the Haslams' preferred birth control method of sexual abstinence – decided upon in 1854, the year of the first edition of Drysdale's work. Drysdale does not tell us where he gets his evidence for this statement but writes 'nothing could be of greater interest to mankind' than the availability of solid information on 'preventative sexual intercourse' which could 'only be brought about by an ample experience . . . freely laid before the public'.[33] Owen, too, regrets that there was not more effort devoted to 'collecting and collating the *actual experience* of human beings'. He regretted that it was not thought 'fitting or decent' for people to supply details of 'personal experience'. Hence 'even medical men' were ignorant of the 'power which men may possess over the reproductive instinct'.[34]

From Haslam's pamphlet, and from his correspondence, it is clear that he was greatly influenced by the work of Dr Russell Thacher Trall (1812–77) from whose *Sexual Physiology* (1866) he quoted extensively and a copy of which his widow bequeathed to Marie Stopes on her death. This copy, now in the British Library, is copiously glossed by Haslam.[35] *Sexual Physiology* was something of a best seller; there were three editions in 1866 alone and by 1884 the book had sold 40,000 copies.[36] Its recommended method of birth control was the use of the 'safe period'. Trall's theory of the 'safe period' was 'that the ovum usually passes off in a few days after the cessation of the menstrual flow, and that if intercourse is abstained from until ten or twelve days after the cessation of the menstrual flow, pregnancy will not occur'. He believed that 'from that time until the commencement of the next menstrual period' women 'will not be liable to impregnation'.[37] This, we now know, was completely wrong. Trall was not alone, however, in his misunderstanding of the link between menstruation and conception. The mistaken ideas of the latter part of the nineteenth century when 'a great deal of scientific effort was directed towards a formulation of a biological theory on the probable time of conception', were based on the 'erroneous views' that menstruation and ovulation coincided.[38] In contrast, Knowlton in his *The Fruits of Philosophy* (1831), displayed some understanding of the function of menstruation although his tone was tentative: 'The use of the menstrual discharge seems to prepare the uterine system for conception.'[39]

Almost seventy years after Trall's work was published, the findings of Knaus and Ogino, 'two scientists who did not collaborate in their work but ... [whose] conclusions were practically identical' revealed that 'Human conception can occur in a limited period between two menses (from the twelfth to the nineteenth day before the subsequent menses) and this conception period can be predicted practically in most cases.' This calculation is based on 'the time of ovulation in the menstrual cycle, the life span of the sperm and the life span of the ovum'. If one allows for a maximum life for the sperm of forty-eight hours after entering the female reproductive tract and a probable four consecutive days on which a woman may ovulate – thus allowing for variations of cycle – and also allow for two days for the maximum lifespan of the ovum 'a fertile period of approximately eight days is set up within the menstrual cycle'.[40] This scientifically researched fertile period is precisely that identified by Trall as the *infertile* period.[41]

Thus, Trall's, and subsequently Haslam's, contraceptive advice, which ensured that those who practised it abstained from sex during the *infertile* period and resumed relations precisely at the stage of the cycle when conception was most likely to occur, ironically must have been responsible for pregnancies rather than preventing them. Trall claimed that the rule 'has been relied upon by thousands of married persons with very few failures'. He went on to discuss the failures. In a passage clean of Haslam's markings, he wrote: 'All of the failures which I have known (and on this subject my correspondence has been very extensive) occurred in those who had suffered of leucorrhœa, displacement, constitutional plethora, or torpor of the uterine system.'[42] The mention of 'extensive' correspondence suggests extensive complaints from dissatisfied practitioners of his theory. Rather than question his theory, however, Trall was at pains to discover extenuating circumstances which would explain why it did not work: 'In one case wherein I had the opportunity to investigate the patient's condition and history, pregnancy occurred sixteen days after the cessation of the monthly discharge' (i.e. within the fertile period as defined by Knaus and Ogino). Trall's belief in his system was not shaken, however; rather he finds an explanation for this failure: 'She had long been the subject of uterine disease, the uterine system was exceedingly weak and torpid, and so feeble was the muscular tissue that it required nearly the whole month for the egg to be transported from the ovary to the outside world.'[43] Trall did not tell us if she survived childbirth. Himes, in his work of 1936, is doubtful of Trall's right to be 'genuinely ranked among the birth control pioneers of the nineteenth century'.[44] Marie Stopes, however, writing in 1923, judged that *Sexual Physiology* 'gave not only an exposition of the necessity for [birth control] ... but practical ... information of a kind not bettered until two or three years ago, when the subject was taken up again in a more scientific way'.[45] Although *Sexual Physiology* contained advice for the avoidance of conception, Trall added the stern rider: 'Let it be distinctly understood that I do not approve any method for preventing pregnancy except that of abstinence.'[46] By abstinence he obviously meant abstinence in the fertile period of the reproductive cycle.

In 1868, then, when *The Marriage Problem* was published, there was in existence a number of works on contraception to which it is reasonable to assume Haslam would have had access. As he was in correspondence with J. Burns of London who stocked and sold birth control material from his Progressive Library in Camberwell, he would not have been dependent on procuring such literature in Ireland.[47] His own addition to the corpus of material did not, however, achieve a wide circulation. Michael Mason judges that *The Marriage Problem* was one of four pamphlets published on the subject 'in the years between 1840 and 1870 which do not appear to have achieved any circulation at all'.[48] This assertion of Mason's is difficult to check as there is no information available regarding the extent of the print run or the method of circulation of *The Marriage Problem*. Burns, however, distributed copies of the pamphlet.[49]

Thomas Haslam's pamphlet argued for the necessity of family limitation on various grounds. A happy marriage to a congenial partner was one of the 'most exalted joys which can dignify humanity' – it was the 'crowning felicity' of life. This state of happy domesticity should be available to all and fear of being unable to provide for offspring should not be allowed deter 'so many men and women from incurring the responsibilities of married life'.[50] Neither should those of feeble health or those whose 'organization is so diseased, that the danger of transmission of their defects to an unfortunate posterity would be a very heinous transgression' be prevented from enjoying 'the joys and consolations of married life'. Abstinence was, of course, an option, but 'It would be a cruel sentence which would exclude all of those for ever or even for the larger portion of their vigorous manhood, from the joys and consolation of married life.'[51]

Haslam mentioned the use of the contraceptive sponge which he described as 'the introduction of a small piece of soft and elastic sponge into the Vagina immediately before the act of copulation, and its withdrawal immediately afterwards'. However, as mentioned above, he judged that women would find it 'somewhat revolting'. He avoided 'the debated question of the morality of adopting any *artificial* preventives' but observed that 'large numbers of our most elevated women have an invincible repugnance to their employment'.[52] Trall recommended the sponge, albeit as a last resort in 'exceptional cases dependent on constitutional peculiarities or local derangement to whom no general rules will apply'.[53]

Haslam stressed the need for 'the discovery of some expedient which is so simple, so natural, so inoffensive in every way, that the most sensitive and pure-minded woman who has ever lived might avail herself of it without any feeling of impropriety or degradation'. His venture into the field of contraceptive advice was to publicize just such an occurrence, the discovery of the 'law . . . by which the conception and birth of offspring are regulated'. This discovery was as important and as timely as the discoveries of 'The Printing Press, the Steam Engine, the Electric Telegraph'. The 'intelligent apprehension' of the law, he claimed, would 'enable every married couple . . . with very rare exceptions, to regulate the number of their offspring'. The 'practical application' of the 'law' was simple and 'involved nothing more difficult . . . than entire *abstinence from sexual intercourse during a certain lim-ited portion of every month'* (his italics).[54] His theory was grounded in his understanding of female ovulation, based on Dr Trall's 'admirable and exhaustive treatise'.[55] He summed up: 'Women generally are liable to impregnation for one or two days before the appearance of the menstrual flux, during the whole period of its continuance, and for about six or eight days subsequently to its cessation.' Haslam wrote that those who used this method would 'only have to abstain inflexibly from sexual indulgence dur-ing one half of every month' and 'can amply compensate themselves during the remainder of the month, subject only to the restrictions of temperance and mutual comfort'.[56] He was convinced that the knowledge he was imparting would ensure 'efficient . . . check to that dreadful scourge of civi-lized communities, prostitution'. It is from 'the hosts of our compulsory celibates that the ranks of the seducer and the seduced are alike everywhere recruited'. Those who would most benefit from this knowledge included 'innocent victims of congenital disease' (who presumably would not be born, or, who would not transmit disease to a succeeding generation), 'ardent' young men who would be safely married and consequently 'obtain a virtuous sphere for the satisfaction of their sexual instincts, without con-demning themselves to the misery of cheerless pauperism'.[57]

In *The Marriage Problem* Haslam included a footnote: 'The subject [the safe period] has been made the subject of special inquiry by M. Raciborski who affirms that the *exceptions to the rule that conception occurs immediately before or after menstruation, are not more than six or seven per cent'*. See Principles of Human Physiology, Sixth ed., p. 759.' This extract, Haslam tells us, is 'from the eminent pen of Dr. Carpenter' and 'is evidence that our English physi-ologists are becoming aware of this important fact'. Despite Raciborski's claims for such a small error margin for the method, Haslam hastens to reas-sure the reader: 'I may observe here that these exceptions appear to be confined to cases of irregular menstruation, or serious uterine disgorgement of some kind.'[58] Making all possible allowances for Haslam's errors in knowledge of the safe period, it is difficult to excuse his confident assertion of the virtual infallibility of the method. It is extremely unlikely that he can have attempted any research on the topic. Trall, whom he cites as his author-ity is much less extravagant in his claims for the method as he asserts that the 'rule' was not infallible.[59]

Haslam, a committed feminist of impeccable credentials and an admirer of the writings of Mill, did not seek to forge a connection between his femin-ist ideals and birth control. Mill had not yet written the feminist classic, *The Subjection of Women* (1869), but in his *Political Economy* (1848) had stated that 'Among the barbarisms which law and morals have not yet ceased to sanc-tion, the most disgusting surely is, that any human being should be permitted to consider himself as having a *right* to the person of another.'[60] Trall's *Sexual Physiology,* which undoubtedly influenced *The Marriage Problem,* was unambiguous about its author's feminist commitment. His chapter on 'Regulation of the Number of Offspring' opened with a resound-ing declaration of the cause of 'Women's Rights': 'No truth is to my mind more self-evident, no rule of right more plain, no law of Nature more demonstrable, than the right of a woman to her own person. Nor can this right be alienated by marriage.'[61]

Trall's defence of the right of woman to the integrity of her person is impressive. He argued, in passages marked by Haslam, that 'It ought to be understood by all men and women that the sexual embrace, when either party is averse to it – when both parties are not inclined to it – is an outrage.'[62] He used what must have been a novel argument in the age in which he lived:

> Would it not excite the just indignation of a *man* to be told. . . . that he must beget children when he did not desire them? or that he must perform the act of sexual intercourse when he did not feel inclined to? . . . it is . . . [a woman's] absolute and indefeasible right to determine when she will, and when she will not, be exposed to pregnancy . . . the health of a majority of women in civilized society is seriously impaired and their lives greatly abbreviated by too frequent pregnancies.[63]

The passage above was marked and underlined by Thomas Haslam who would undoubtedly have agreed with its sentiments. Trall's approach to the question is unambiguously woman-centred, but in *The Marriage Problem* Haslam's approach is problematic and difficult to reconcile with his strongly held feminist beliefs. One is reminded of St Paul's stricture, 'Better to marry than to burn', in his assertion that 'young men of fiery temperament' could marry early thus being saved from 'moral destruction if not from early graves'. Using the method of birth control recommended in the pamphlet, such men could 'sow their wild oats' in 'the protecting care of a loving wife' while avoiding having children too young. It would, of course, be preferable if such young men 'could control their passions during the critical period of dawning manhood' rather than contract an early marriage. However, in the case of those unfortunates who are '*unable* to control their passions' an early marriage and use of the information contained in the pamphlet 'may not infrequently be a matter of life and death'.[64] The suggestion that birth control would allow a man unlimited access to his wife's body without fear of impregnation was anathema to feminists. The feminist argument against contraception was that it made it more difficult for women to refuse husbands' unreasonable demands for sexual intercourse if the threat of unwanted pregnancy were removed. Feminists believed that men should learn to control their appetites, and that artificial contraception reinforced the coital imperative and the patriarchal model of sexuality.[65] Members of the radical discussion group, the Men and Women's Club, were of the opinion that birth control subjected a wife to 'her husband's every sexual whim'.[66]

Haslam's suggested method was the 'natural' one of abstinence during the fertile period, a method that demanded some restraint from husbands. Nonetheless, his suggestion that young men who could not control their overwhelming sexual desires should marry young rather than contract 'vicious temporary unions'[67] gave credence to the feminist view that birth control could reduce a wife to a 'virtual prostitute'.[68] In correspondence discussed later in this chapter, he justified this stance as the lesser of two evils. In the pamphlet he admittedly expressed concern for the 'unbearable hardship' suffered by women through bearing excessive numbers of children, and for those whose strength was insufficient for the rigours of childbirth. He believed that their 'existence might be replete with joy and brightness' with the relief of the 'burden' of childbearing.[69] In the event of couples being unable for 'whatever cause' to abstain from intercourse during the 'fertile period' they should decide for themselves whether the 'emergency' justified 'the adoption of some preventive expedient like that of the sponge, as the smaller and less objectionable of the two evils'. It is difficult to deduce what emergency Haslam can have been talking about. Was it uncontrollable mutual passion or the threat of the male partner rushing out into the night in search of a prostitute? He urged such couples 'to discuss the matter unreservedly with their medical adviser'.[70]

Haslam was at pains to point out that he had medical endorsement for the views put forward in *The Marriage Problem*: '*Every medical* opinion that I have obtained so far has been most favourable.'[71] The citing of medical authority was a feature of those early works on birth control that were not written by medical men. Robert Dale Owen quoted French physicians as authorities on the efficacy of the sponge, and Richard Carlisle wrote that 'where a state of health will not justify a pregnancy, it is common in London for the physician to recommend the means of prevention, it is well understood that abstinence and domestic happiness cannot coexist'.[72] Charles Knowlton, George Drysdale and R. T. Trall were, of course, medically qualified.

If birth controllers sought to claim medical authority for their theories, however, the medical profession stoutly repudiated them. In the nineteenth century the profession assumed an increasingly important role in the shaping of official definitions of sexual and moral behaviour. It saw itself as responsible for public morality and its members adopted a 'sanctimonious attitude' to the sexual life of patients.[73] Foucault, in his work on nineteenth-century sexuality argued that medical discourse was set apart from other discourses through its authority as science and its associated connotations of objectivity and truth. It was 'a science subordinated in the main to the imperatives of a morality whose divisions it reiterated under the guise of a medical norm'.[74] The *Lancet* responded to Place's handbills by stating loftily that the 'things', i.e. the handbills, 'are beneath our notice'.[75]

In the 1860s the medical profession's seeming indifference changed to vociferous opposition. In the year after the publication of Haslam's pamphlet the pages of the *Lancet* contained virulent criticism of the 'beastly contrivances for limiting the number of offspring', citing the President of the Royal College of Physicians of Ireland, Dr Beatty of Dublin, in his address to the British Medical Association, during which he castigated the 'Malthusian philosophy' of family limitation. He went on to link contraception with infanticide. He concluded his address 'amid loud cheering'.[76] The report goes on to praise Dr Beatty for having discharged the 'unpleasant task' of pointing out 'the way in which those views are regarded by the great bulk of the medical profession . . . so courageously'.[77]

The public reaction to early birth control propaganda was exclusively male; it was obviously too controversial a topic to be discussed in public by women. The campaign against the Contagious Diseases Acts in the 1870s was the catalyst that empowered some women to speak publicly about sexual matters. While it is difficult to know to what extent, if at all, Thomas Haslam was influenced by his wife in his writings on birth control, there is evidence that she agreed with the sentiments he expressed. In her correspondence with Marie Stopes she explained: 'I have always been deeply interested in this question & have helped many women.'[78]

Early birth control literature was practically women-centred in that there was a tendency to favour methods controlled by women.[79] Lucy Bland writes that female contraceptive devices 'had their own disadvantages; they were expensive, difficult to obtain, and douches necessitated access to running water'.[80] However, Place suggested a homemade sponge, while Knowlton was conscious of cost and also careful to suggest easily available materials. In Bland's book there is an illustration of 'The Improved Vertical and Reverse Current Syringe', sold as a 'Malthusian Appliance', which clearly shows that running water was not used, rather one end of the syringe was immersed in a large container of water.[81] Robert Dale Owen, however, was happy to put the onus on the male for the success of *coitus interruptus* as a method of birth control. Haslam's recommended method would have relied on the cooperation of the male partner while the woman was responsible for the calculation of the safe period. In *The Marriage Problem* Haslam gave detailed instructions to women for identifying the physical signs of ovulation in order to enable determination of 'the law of her own constitution with sufficient accuracy for practical guidance'.[82] Although this information was acquired from Trall, it is noteworthy that Haslam did not shrink from a description of intimate female bodily functions in a remarkably unprudish manner.

Although the word had not yet been coined, Haslam's eugenic tendencies are obvious to today's reader of the pamphlet.[83] The eugenics movement was in the tradition of Victorian reform movements which were responses of the middle class to the perceived growth of social problems among the urban poor: 'The tradition of middle-class meliorism, together with the new ideas about heredity . . . and the Malthusian concept of the dangerous fertility of the poor, provided the elements that came together . . . to form the eugenics movement.'[84] From the 1870s onwards there were increased calls for action to prevent people with mental or physical afflictions from having children. Those who proposed what came to be called 'negative eugenics' were 'worried by increasing evidence that serious mental and physical disorders were hereditary'.[85] Allied to this was the growing conviction of the 'inheritance of . . . negative moral as well as physical qualities'. Thus, if 'the prolific breeding of this class were not controlled . . . undesirable qualities must necessarily keep increasing until the direction of the evolution of the human race was reversed'.[86] Haslam subscribed to the belief that moral defects were inherited: 'I hold it to be a well authenticated fact that the offspring of the drunken & the sensual are likely to be themselves sensual.'[87] In 1868, some months after Haslam's pamphlet was issued, W. R. Greg, renowned for his work on prostitution, said that he thought it 'conceivable' that at some future date only those with a 'pure and vigorous and well-developed constitution' would 'be suffered to transmit their names . . . to future generations'.[88] Haslam's pamphlet pre-dated Charles Darwin's *The Descent of Man*, published in 1871, which stated that 'the weak members of a civilised society propagate their kind. No one who has attended the breeding of domestic animals will doubt that this must be highly injurious to the race of men.'[89] Although Haslam's interest in the question of heredity predated the first eugenics meeting in Ireland by over fifty years,[90] a paper read in 1858 at the Statistical and Social Inquiry Society of Ireland suggests that the topic was being aired among the membership.[91] Haslam's proto-eugenicism is discussed at greater length in the next chapter.

There is no record of any public response to Haslam's pamphlet; the private nature of its publication and circulation would have precluded it. There is, however, an interesting private correspondence extant from some prominent people interested in the question, to whom Haslam had sent his pamphlet. Three of the five surviving letters in response to *The Marriage Problem* were from prominent secularists. Birth control propaganda flourished in freethinking and secularist circles, and 'it was in these circles, that it became so much a part of the general philosophy of life without religion that the two movements seem to have become identified in the public mind'.[92] The English authors of birth control material, Carlisle, Place and Drysdale were associated with 'anti-Christian scepticism'.[93] That being said, of the three known secularists who responded to Haslam, only one was enthusiastic, while another was downright hostile.

John Stuart Mill's letter in response to receipt of the pamphlet was written with the utmost tact, but in essence was non-committal and did not offer any practical encouragement: 'Nothing could be more important than the question to which it relates, nor more laudable than the purpose it has in view.' Mill cannot have agreed with Haslam's suggestion that the method would help young men to 'sow their wild oats' with a loving wife rather than avail of prostitution, but he offered no critique of the contents. He made it clear that he, for one, would not be availing of the author's permission to reprint the contents for 'private circulation': 'About the expediency of putting it into circulation, in however quiet a manner, you are the best judge.' It is obvious that Mill did not consider the material suitable for dissemination in a pamphlet; he suggested, rather, that the 'morality of the matter lies wholly between the married people themselves and that such facts as those which the pamphlet communicates ought to be made known to them by their medical advisers'. This, he thought, was not likely to happen 'at present' and 'in the meantime every one must act according to his own judgement of what is prudent and right'.[94]

Norman Himes is of the opinion that Mill's short letter was important in that it threw light upon the vexed question of his stance on birth control. His reference to the purpose of the pamphlet as 'laudable' is thought by Himes to be 'interesting in view of the fact *publicly* Mill always wrote and talked as if he wished to exceed Malthus' demand for self-denial, and apply *within* the marriage bond the restraints which Malthus dared insist upon only *up* to the threshold of the married state'. The use of the word 'laudable' was taken by Himes to suggest that Mill 'was definitely in favour of the artificial check'.[95] However, the claims made by Himes for the letter were exaggerated; had he read *The Marriage Problem,* he would have seen that Haslam was advocating not 'artificial checks' but abstinence for part of every month – in effect, the application of restraint within marriage.

Haslam had an extensive correspondence with Francis W. Newman, the brother of the cardinal, which gives insight into the way both men thought on sexual matters.[96] Newman, a feminist, was a true eccentric and greatly admired by Haslam. This correspondence predated the campaign for the repeal of the Contagious Diseases Acts, for which both Haslam and Newman campaigned actively. Newman, who had rejected conventional religion, 'went so far as to reject the Bible and conventional Christian morality as a guide to present day life; he wanted it superseded by public legislation founded on scientific investigation and inspired by belief in moral progress'.[97] It is likely that Haslam sent his pamphlet to Newman because of his position as a prominent secularist. He cannot have been unaware of the latter's determined opposition to birth control. Although Newman did not publish his well-known treatise, *The Corruption Now Called Neo-Malthusianism,* until 1889, he had written a number of works condemning birth control prior to 1868.[98] Haslam may well have seen his natural method as the answer to those who opposed the use of 'beastly contrivances' and have hoped that Newman might have endorsed the discovery of the 'law'.

As in the case of the Mill letter, this correspondence with Haslam has been used to illustrate Newman's opinions on birth control, in this case his perceived change of heart on the subject. As an example of the change in attitudes of even committed anti-birth controllers, Marie Stopes cited the opening sentence of Newman's first letter to Haslam: 'It has gradually broken upon me that too large and earnest a body of men hold doctrines such as you promulgate, to discard them as I once did, with a simple revulsion of disgust.'[99] She is being disingenuous, however, as Newman's next sentence reveals: 'The difficulty of reasoning them down is this, that a public argument may be depraving, and one's book may be scouted even by those whose convictions one is maintaining.'[100] Newman was also on James Burns's mailing list: 'I have lately had sent to me Mr. James Burns's periodical called *Human Nature,* in which I found Dr Trall's book advertised for the edification of all who will buy it & I perceive that he announces that it contains drawings of the secret parts of men & woman & what not beside.' Such is Newman's distaste for the subject that he was reluctant to challenge Haslam's ideas: 'I suppose we now *cannot* evade the discussion, and however great our reluctance & misgivings & disgust we shall have to go through it.'[101]

Newman was extremely critical of Haslam's pamphlet. He did not believe in the Malthusian argument of overpopulation and argued that Haslam's theory was self-defeating as it would 'never take large effect on any but the more educated. Not but that the views of this doctrine may chance so to damage the whole character, that such classes will deserve to waste & wane.' Newman aired his pet theories of temperance and vegetarianism as solutions to the problems of poverty: if 'humble artizans' 'abstain from intoxicating drink' and are 'satisfied with mainly or solely vegetarian' diet, they will be enabled 'to raise families of children in high health with superior or intellectual refinement'.[102] He was prominent in the temperance movement and president of the Vegetarian Society: '"Oh! I am anti-slavery, anti-alcohol, anti-tobacco, anti-everything," he once told an amused dinner-party.'[103] Newman totally rejected as 'morally vicious & physically ruinous, the doctrine that we are to exercise any of the animal instincts for the sake of the pleasure accompanying them.' He admitted with disarming candour: 'The physical pleasure from the marriage union, is in my judgement, contemptibly small . . . The real great rapturous pleasure of married love is moral not physical.'[104]

Newman saw the establishment of 'Women's Rights' as a 'proper restraint' to male immorality: 'Chastity in man is Justice to Woman. Self-control in a husband is Justice to a Wife. Our law infamously refuses to a woman right over her own person.' He suggested legal adoption as an aid to large families. He tempered his criticism with 'Accept this kindly, I pray you', which ends his letter.[105] Despite the ten closely written pages, however, he appended a two-page postscript, in which he challenged Haslam's 'astonishing sentence' that accused parents who generated offspring they were 'not in a position to maintain' as 'one of the most brutal selfish enormities which man or women can commit'. Newman argued that 'Every honest worker adds more to world's wealth than he takes from it.' He turned Malthus's theory on its head by declaring: 'If we resolve not to raise families until we have realized means of supporting them, the earth will become depopulated . . . Woe will befall the state which . . . supposes children to be *of no value* to the country.'[106]

Haslam immediately responded to Newman's critique of his pamphlet. He was deferential in disagreement: 'If I venture to differ from you it is only because my mind is unable to resist the weight of evidence to which my own conviction has been determined.' He alluded to his ill health; in his 'existing condition' he 'dare not subject [his] brain to the stress of close and detailed reasoning'. He continued: 'It is very probable too that I shall have to suspend this letter for days coming to a conclusion.' Despite this plaintive tone, however, Haslam managed to dash off a letter of impressive length and fluency. He 'fully shared' Newman's 'repugnance at the discussion of sexual matters'. However, he saw such repugnance as a fault, a result of early training. Haslam objected, however, to the 'spurious delicacy which now prevails . . . [it] is not from knowledge but from ignorance or half knowledge' that 'enormous evils' spring. While he shared Newman's 'feelings of disgust at pictures of the organs of men and women', he believed this to be 'a morbid prejudice, the result of false training – a remnant of the contempt which an ascetic Christianity has lavished upon some of the most wonderful parts of the human frame'.[107]

Haslam's theory would, in Newman's opinion, have greater effect on the educated classes, thus, of course, increasing the ratio of the coarse and ignorant to the educated and refined. Haslam cautiously replied: 'If I agree in the sentiment that it is desirable that the higher races & higher organizations should replace the inferior ... it cannot be the duty of the refined to abandon restraint. It is the duty of the coarse and sensual to practice it.' Newman, in fact, bitterly opposed the proto-eugenicists and had written critically of Herbert Spencer who had coined the phrase 'the survival of the fittest': 'He denounces the vicious poor, seems to inculcate that we ought to let them die out, overlooks the fact that children reared to vice, or tempered to vice in early years, deserve pity and aid, not cold contempt.'[108]

Haslam questioned Newman's belief in the supremacy of instinct:

> That passion ought as a rule in the first instance, to inspire the wedded embrace, I do hold. . . . Its demands must be endorsed by reason or they are not to be obeyed. Most married men imagine that their natural instinct demands coition far more frequently than is good for either themselves or their wives. In many cases they practice it nightly as a rule, not infrequently to the dreadful injury of both . . . yet they plead instinct as their justification.[109]

Where, one must ask, does Haslam get these facts? Hardly from questioning acquaintances, as he admits that he cannot easily talk on sexual matters. It is likely that he is summarizing Trall who gave details of patients 'who had for years indulged in sexual intercourse as often as once in twenty-four hours and some who had indulged still oftener. Of course the result was premature decay and often permanent invalidism.'[110] Haslam, however, felt that in such matters it was impossible to prescribe any absolute rules of duty or propriety: 'Married people ... must decide for themselves.' He justified the most controversial theory propounded in his pamphlet: 'In the abstract it is a degrading thing for a wife to surrender her person to her husband when she herself does not reciprocate the passion & nevertheless it may be her duty to submit to that degradation rather than drive her husband into the arms of prostitutes.' Haslam added a comment which is further evidence of his secularism: 'I believe there is no higher authority than enlightened human judgement to pronounce on such matters ... And after all human life is only a series of more or less fallible experiments.' He does not allow for any authority other than 'enlightened reason' in matters of sexual morality. Despite the didactic tone of the pamphlet Haslam claimed that he believed that people had freedom of conscience: 'Every married couple must be a law unto themselves. Provided they love each other sincerely & provided their intellect is enlightened on those subjects they will not go far astray.' What was really needed in Haslam's opinion was the 'widespread diffusion of sound knowledge upon these subjects. To this imperious necessity all scruples, however respectable in their origin, must be taught to give way.'[111]

Haslam was at his best when arguing against Newman's claim that the 'safe period' was 'against nature'. He argued: 'Provided *mutual desire* dictates it is perfectly natural . . . [to enjoy] the connubial embrace when the wife is not liable to impregnation.' He acknowledged that '*abstinence* when mutual passion exists may in a certain sense be stigmatized as unnatural but it is not so in married people any more than in that of the unmarried and in *that* sense all restraint of the lower propensities in obedience to the moral sentiments may be branded in the same way'.

He asked Newman to reconsider:

> If two unmarried people of the opposite sex feel passion for each other & do not yield to it because they know by so doing they may inflict some injury upon each other and upon society, & if this unnatural restraint be right, how can it be wrong for married persons to practice a similar restraint in cases where they feel that a similar injury would be the result of their indulgence . . . If all restraint of mutual passion be unnatural & if everything unnatural be wrong, then unlimited free love is the only condition in society.[112]

Actually Newman did not in his letter place any emphasis on mutual pleasure but argued: 'The expedient which you propose of confining connubial embraces precisely to the times at which (you believe) they will be barren is . . . [to] act precisely against nature.'[113] Haslam, on the other hand, repeatedly allowed for the possibility of mutual passion:

> I think I have not said enough . . . on the vital point that indulgence in mutual passion (even when the female is not liable to impregnation) can in any fair sense be stigmatized as an *unnatural* act. So long as the act is governed by genuine passion on both sides it is perfectly natural. The passion wh.[ich] justifies the act has no knowledge respecting impregnation, it is enlightened reason alone wh.[ich] possesses them & reason so far as I can perceive does not withhold her sanction from the act provided it be hallowed as I have said by passion & provided no injurious consequences are likely to be the result.[114]

Trall allowed for mutual passion; he believed that the sexual union 'should be pleasurable to both parties' otherwise 'unless generation be intended' it is 'mere lust' presumably for one of the two.[115] Haslam had underlined this passage. Although Haslam did not 'recommend any artificial expedients for preventing impregnation except in special cases', he went on to say, 'unquestionably I hold that a wife whose health would not justify her having offspring & who finds herself solicited by a *passionate* husband is morally justified in adopting some such expedient rather than drive her husband to the still more baneful indulgence of prostitution or of some form of self pollution'. He shared the prevailing Victorian horror of masturbation that he appears to couple with prostitution as a 'baneful indulgence'.[116]

In the light of Haslam's celibate marriage his remark to Newman that he believed that 'popular doctrines' gave rise to *'unnatural* Christian asceticism' is interesting. It is likely that the popular doctrine to which Haslam referred was the conviction that abstinence was the morally acceptable method to avoid conception. On the theme of unsatisfied desire, he told Newman that 'the craving for indulgence which cannot be gratified is a far more ... demoralizing state of mind than anything that will result from such expedients [artificial birth control]. I cannot enter at any length into this painful side of the question.'[117] Was it 'painful' to speak on the subject owing to the circumstance of his celibate marriage? Did his opinion that prolonged abstinence was possible only for men of 'peculiar organization' apply to himself?

Haslam considered the right of woman to her bodily integrity, as argued by Mill and Newman, secondary to the dangers inherent in refusing a husband his conjugal 'rights': 'To sum up, artificial expedients are undesirable, prostitution is infinitely worse, & there are other alternatives wh.[ich] are worst of all.' He claimed however, in his letter to Newman, that he had 'always been an advocate' of women's 'extremest rights. The right of their own person is one of the prominent doctrines enforced in Trall's book wh.[ich] I think you ought to read.'[118]

Haslam's perception of male sexuality as difficult to control was commonly held Victorian opinion. He had 'no doubt that there are multitudes of men whose constitutions are the slaves of animal passion', whereas Newman averred that such men 'have weaker moral principles & will'.[119] Haslam subscribed to the theory that such natures are hereditary: 'I hold it to be a well authenticated fact that the offspring of the drunken & the sensual are likely to be themselves sensual. I am not a thorough going phrenological but there are certain men whose organs *of* amativeness – destructiveness etc. are preternaturally large. When it is said that such men can control their passions, if they will, I can attach no meaning to the words.' It is hard to follow Haslam's line of reasoning here. The word 'amativeness' is certainly Trall's. He can scarcely be suggesting that such men are candidates for the 'safe period' method of birth control. He allowed for the rehabilitation of the 'reprobate' and the 'fallen': 'It is only Christian Pharisaism wh[ich] brands such errors as awful irrepressible guilt ... When youthful errors are treated simply as errors & that in women as well as men, there is some probability that those who have fallen into them will rise above them instead of being enslaved to them for life.'[120]

Haslam did not think it necessary to reiterate his 'lesser of two evils' arguments regarding young men 'sowing their wild oats' in the marriage bed. He 'cannot modify a word' regarding 'the selfishness of men having large families while unable to maintain them ... [M]en have large families not only at the cost of their wives' health ... they are persons of notorious selfishness of character.' He summed up the advantages of 'a discovery which will enable men to satisfy their sexual appetites within the bounds of reason without either destroying the health of their partners or sacrificing the well being of their posterity & with no greater price than that of partial abstinence (itself good for their own health)'. He was at pains to point out that he has received 'testimonies of approval (already) from numbers of refined and educated men & women'. Newman's long and detailed letter notwithstanding, Haslam again appealed to him: 'May I ask the favour of a *few* final remarks or reconsiderations.' He was not finished yet, however, but embarked on a lengthy postscript: 'On humbly casting my eye over the preceding sheets, I see that there are some of the most prominent features of my views on these subjects that I have failed to bring into adequate relief.' These views were concerned with his theories of those who are unfit to breed and could be said to reveal Haslam's beliefs as a negative eugenicist. 'Let them [the criminal classes and those of 'feeble health or impaired organization'] marry by all means, but let them take all necessary precautions not to inflict the curse of vicious or enfeebled organization upon an unfortunate progeny.' Haslam went on to state that 'the less coition is practised . . . the better as a general rule. Most married persons injure themselves by excess . . . [T]hey also destroy mutual self respect & they degrade marriage to a mere arrangement for sexual satisfaction.' This is much more dogmatic then Haslam's earlier statement that 'Married people (whose reason is enlightened) must decide for themselves . . . Every married couple must be a law unto themselves.' Perhaps the reason for this is revealed in the letter's second ending: 'there are very few people to whose view and character I look up to [sic] with such reverence & I do not wish that you should evidently set me down as an advocate of any unnatural or debasing practices'. [sic][121]

Unfortunately Newman's reply is unobtainable. Haslam's response to this missing letter, dated 8 May, however, is terse and, though polite, revealed that Newman's reply had displeased him greatly. No thanks are expressed, rather he launched straight into a chilly rebuttal:

> I regret to find the more I understand of your position on the population problem the more strongly I am compelled to dissent. The doctrine that 'all pursuit of pleasure' (social, intellectual, aesthetic . . .) is unlawful does not awaken a response in either my conscience or my intellect. It appears repugnant to my common sense as the Athanasian Creed or . . . [indecipherable] primitive religion . . . Trall's recommendation is practically nothing more than a deduction from Mill's 'Political Economy & Utilitarianism' . . . [S]o far as I can see no refutation of either of them has yet appeared.[122]

Newman's response, too, dispensed with the niceties and started: 'J. S. Mill has not yet gone to the exaggerated censure that you have; but take whatever support you can get from him. I have sometimes wished to know whether the events of Ireland since 1848 have modified Malthusianism. I regard them as demonstrating, beyond reasonable denial that the theory is either a useless truism or a mischievous falsehood.' Newman went on to state that 'if men were actuated by no principle but prudence, hardly anyone would rear children'. He regarded it as 'the opposite of selfish' that 'a poor man . . . marries and raises children'. He ended by insulting Haslam roundly: 'But I think nearly everyone, if your theory were publicly communicated would say, that Chinese infanticide is far more honourable & manly & immeasurably less tending to general depravity.'[123] Newman's question to Haslam regarding the relevance of Malthus's theory of population to Ireland is surely a valid one. For an Irishman to discuss the population question without referring to the Great Famine and its aftermath seems bizarre. In *The Real Wants of the Irish People*, which Haslam wrote within twenty years of the start of the famine, he referred to the 'four-fold' increase in Ireland's population between 1731 and 1841. His opinion that prudence on the part of the poor would have averted the disaster of the famine seems naive in the extreme. He argued that had the poorest labourers, whom he conceded had an 'equal right to the comforts of family life with the wealthiest capitalist', accumulated a 'few years savings to provide for contingencies' before marriage, 'Ireland would never have been visited with the awful calamities of 1846 and 1847'.[124] While Haslam appears compassionate to the plight of the poor his message is essentially the same as the Malthus doctrine of moral restraint. It points to ignorance on his part of the reality of the lives of the 'poorest labourers' prior to the famine. Landless labourers lived in conditions of utter deprivation and destitution and were the most unlikely candidates for accumulating nest-eggs for the future. Haslam lived outside of Ireland for the duration of the famine. However, there is evidence to suggest that he had visited Mountmellick in 1851.[125] His wife had been actively involved in famine relief and surely would have spoken to him of the horrors she had witnessed. Despite the dramatic reduction in population in the aftermath of the famine he argued that 'So long as there is one industrious man in Ireland who cannot find employment sufficient to maintain himself and his family in comfort & independence, Ireland is overpeopled in the only sense in which I employ the words.' He was conscious of the difficulties in Ireland of educating the 'lower classes . . . so long as they are taught that prudence is a vice & that large families are a proof of manhood . . . Hitherto all teaching on these subjects has been left in Ireland to the priests & we know they are professionally in favour of large families.'[126] Fifty years on Anna made the same point to Marie Stopes.[127] Haslam's works on social theory suggest that his main concerns are with the urban rather than the rural poor.

Haslam's letters to Newman are a valuable insight into his thoughts on male sexuality where he clearly subscribed to the theory of the biological imperative. His abhorrence of prostitution, and his belief in the inevitability of celibate young men resorting to it, was such that he argued against his beliefs as an 'advocate' of women's 'extremist rights'. His desire to spread the gospel of birth control was predicated on his aspirations for the improvement of society. The birth control movement was concerned with 'improving the economic well-being and welfare of the lower classes by inculcating such solid virtues as prudence, foresight and self-restraint'.[128] Haslam appears to have been typical of that movement as his concerns were with the poor, the unhealthy and those young men 'who are *unable* to control their passions'.[129] His optimism regarding the message of his pamphlet was unrealistic but conveys a palpable sense of the excitement he felt at the importance of his message. It also places him firmly in the mainstream of those reformers who saw birth control as an important instrument for the improvement of society:

> When working men of every country have obtained an adequate knowledge of these momentous facts, and have made up their minds to act upon that knowledge in their daily lives, it is not too much to predict that pauperism everywhere will have received its death-blow, and that the problem of the moral and social elevation of mankind universally will have accomplished the more important half of its solution.[130]

Haslam had a warm response from the publisher Thomas Scott[131] of Ramsgate who wrote: 'I have read your "Marriage Problem" with great pleasure for it is one of these steps in the right direction, the consideration of which is being forced upon us.' However, Scott, while praising Haslam's effort, is unambivalent in his opinion of its efficacy: 'Your theory and intention are both most excellent – but – alas! the practice fails.' Scott had heard of the 'plan' suggested by Haslam when 'a student of medicine in Paris forty-two years ago and afterwards repeated to me when again a student in a lying-in hospital in Philadelphia', and had recommended it 'to a clergyman friend who tried the experiment *carefully*, and signally failed'. Scott recommended the French plan, the *bonnet de nuit* to another clergyman, a relation of his, 'pointing out to him how comparatively seldom it was that more than two children were found in the better class (i.e. a class most likely to be exempt from foolish or superstitious prejudices)'. The clergyman 'afterwards got over his scruples and adopted the French plan of *bonnet de nuit* (I enclose you one) and never after was his wife with child'. How Thomas reacted to receiving a condom in the post we do not know. Despite the success of the 'French plan' Scott favoured the withdrawal method, the success of which he conceded was dependent on the man being 'master of his passions, and carefully thoughtful for his wife's comfort'. Scott knew many clergymen who had used this method and it had never failed. For an avowed secularist Scott seems to have given contraceptive advice to many clergymen. His secularism is revealed in his closing paragraph: 'One little bit of criticism I must make on your pamphlet. You say "marriage is the moral safety valve which *Providence* has established etc." . . . Please tell me my friend where you find authority for your assertion that *"Providence"* established it?'[132] Thomas Scott was a friend of the Haslams. Anna wrote to Marie Stopes: 'He and his wife were with us for a week and we were with them in Margate, he was a most remarkable man.'[133] Haslam's acquaintance with Scott, the fact that they visited each other, the tone of the letter with its gentle rebuke on Haslam's use of 'Providence' all suggest Haslam's interest in free thought and secularism. Scott's letter is totally non-judgemental on the morality of the subject.

Haslam's pamphlet also provoked a positive response from one J. E. George of Hirwain, Aberdair, Wales, who had received a copy from 'Mr. J. Burns of London' and was obviously a customer of Burns's Progressive

Library. George, a chemist and druggist, was the inventor of the 'notorious George's Pile and Gravel Pills'.[134] Untypically for one obviously interested in birth control, he was a prominent member of the Baptist Chapel in Hirwain. He was renowned in church circles for his wide reading particularly on scientific subjects and had donated many books to the Sunday school library.[135] Did he attempt to spread the birth control message among church members, one wonders? George accepted the message in Haslam's pamphlet without question: 'This comparatively new discovery will be the salvation of millions of our countrymen from poverty vice etc.' The circumstances of his own family being 'extremely prolific' weighed 'heavily upon his mind'. Until he was 'acquainted with these preventative measures' as explained in Haslam's pamphlet, celibacy had been his 'only refuge'. There is a biblical resonance to George's acceptance of Haslam's message: 'All situated like me will hail the glad tidings with great joy.' George told of a magistrate to whom he lent Haslam's pamphlet who would appear not to have needed it, but,

> He was highly pleased with it. He also told me that he has regulated the number of his family for the last 25 years – his method however is not mentioned in your pamphlet. He has done it by 'partial withdrawal of the penis at the time of emission.' I have been told that this practice is inconsistent with sound health – he is however one of the firmest, most robust & muscular that I have ever seen.[136]

George ordered twenty copies of the pamphlet and asked the cost of having two hundred and fifty sent. He advised Haslam to get his 'excellent pamphlet translated into the Welsh language: it would be the means of doing much good as there are amongst us a great number who do not understand the English language.' On 14 August 1868, George acknowledged the receipt of six pamphlets with the words: 'It is to be regretted that we have not more men of the same caste of mind in the world – men able & willing to benefit their race.' George had read Trall's book' and considered it 'an excellent work'. He stated his intention of reproducing extracts from Haslam's work for a Welsh readership:

> I greatly admire the disposition displayed at the commencement of your pamphlet, viz. that of allowing those who are willing to assist in the dissemination of these truths, to reprint the whole or any portion of your pamphlet, I will thro' your kind permission extract a few of the ideas there set forth for the Welsh pamphlet which I intend publishing in a few weeks time.

He planned to distribute 'a few thousand copies of these tracts' amongst the 'large portion of our working class [who] do not understand English'.[137] There is no record of extracts from Haslam's pamphlet having been published in Welsh translation.[138]

J. Burns wrote from his Phrenological and Physiological Consulting

Room, which incorporated the Progressive Library, Camberwell, praising Haslam's pamphlet 'as well written to the point . . . a very fair essence of the question'. Burns was glad to avail of Haslam's kind offer to disseminate his 'little work'. He suggested advertising it as 'The Marriage Problem solved and the Increase of population controlled by moral measures in accordance with the Laws of Nature, a Physiological discovery of great importance'. George's letter from Hirwain is proof that Burns did indeed send on the pamphlet to those on his mailing list.[139]

Armed with the knowledge of the circumstances of his married life, discussed in Chapter 1, one is compelled to look again at Thomas Haslam's discussion of celibacy in his pamphlet. Statements such as: 'It is from the compulsory celibate that the ranks of the seducer and the seduced are alike everywhere recruited' appear in a different light; one could, of course, argue that Thomas's celibacy was voluntary.[140] It is to be regretted that he was not moved to give an equally frank personal assessment of the 'physical pleasure of the marriage union' as Newman had. There are hints that Haslam is at times speaking personally rather than theoretically: 'I cannot enter at length into the painful side of the question.' Is it personally painful for him to discuss such matters? Is it again personal experience that spawned the opinion that 'the craving for indulgence which cannot be gratified is a far more demoralizing state of mind than anything that will result from such expedients'?[141] Had he perhaps hoped that the 'discovery' might transform his own life?

Important correspondence between Anna Haslam and Marie Stopes has survived in which Anna revealed that she subscribed fully to her husband's theories on birth control. It is also interesting in that it is a record of the considerable help given by Anna to Stopes in her compilation of two histories of birth control. The first letter, dated August 1918, was in response to an article on 'Proper Parentage' written by Stopes in the *Sunday Chronicle.*

In her first letter to Stopes, Anna Haslam enclosed a copy of her husband's *Marriage Problem.* Obviously she saw herself as an adviser on the subject of contraception as she told Stopes that she kept a copy 'for *lending* to newly married couples'. The letter is important also in that it contains the only reference to Anna's belief or lack of it in the hereafter: 'The memory of the past is with me day & night & the longing to be re-united if there be a future life is always present.'[142] This suggests, at the very least, that she had doubts about Christian teaching on life after death. In her next letter she told Stopes: 'When Home Rule was started by Gladstone we turned all our attention to combating it & the C. D. Acts & latterly he [Thomas] was more taken up with literary matters.' Surprisingly, she did not allude to his works on suffrage. However, Anna herself had not lost interest and would appear to have run an informal advisory service. 'I had a great deal of convidences [sic], I know several who practised 'safe methods' satisfactorily & some whom it failed indulging too near the monthly period.' Obviously she believed in the efficacy of the 'mid-month' system, as did the scientist Marie Stopes. Her observation that she 'knew many now who have only one child & often longed to ask the wife *why*', is revealing of her desire to learn about successful methods. The context of the comment shows clearly that she meant *how* couples had managed to limit families rather than *why* they had done so. She was typical of the early advisers on birth control in that her main concern was with the poor: 'Oh if we could only reach the poor.' She revealed her familiarity with methods in current use; she mentioned 'French letters' and douching, but to her, 'next to abstinence, the mid-month has always appeared the best'.[143] Anna did not pass judgement on the use of 'artificial expedients', nor did she agonize about the morality of the question. For her, abstinence was best, and also, she revealed 'Mrs. Josephine Butler[144] . . . preferred abstinence'. She told Stopes that Butler had written praising Thomas's *Duties of Parents*.[145]

Marie Stopes sent Anna a copy of her *Married Love* which the latter thought 'a deeply interesting & most important book'. She had 'never read so much before about the 'orgasm'. Despite claiming that 'of course there is little in it [*Married Love*] that is *new* to me', she confessed that she had not seen the word 'orgasm' before.[146] Stopes next sent Anna her *Wise Parenthood*, a work she found disappointing. She felt that the I. R.[147] cap which Stopes had recommended as a method of contraception was unsuitable as 'the chars and other poor women . . . could not afford to get the I. R. cap . . . I don't understand it & could not have used it.' Quoting the reaction of 'one lady' to whom she had lent both of Stopes's books, Anna wrote: 'I liked *Married Love* . . . because it explained so much that must be dark and obscure to the average wife, it told me for one that sexual intercourse between man & wife need not always be just the expression of the physical needs of the male.' This remark came from the mother of three fine children, 'who tried to use the I. R. cap – it was no use to her – she is going to show me one'. While these remarks were attributed to an acquaintance one cannot help wondering if perhaps Anna shared the perception that sex was an 'expression of the physical needs of the male'. Had she believed otherwise she surely would not have continued to consider abstinence as 'the highest and the best.'[148] Having abstained from sex for over sixty years of married life, perhaps she had to believe that to have done so was a positive virtue rather than a deprivation. Despite her belief in abstinence she never lost 'an opportunity to talk about it' [contraception].[149]

Anna continued to lend Stopes's books to acquaintances including '3 of our M.D.'s'. Her own doctor, who was a '*Homeopathist*' had read from the books to 'six medical students of Trinity'. He too greatly approved 'of the mid month + knows of its success when judicially attended to'. She was satisfied that 'the knowledge has been spreading in spite of the Bishops'. She was ever mindful of the need to educate on the subject and was very supportive of Marie Stopes's clinic for mothers:

> Admirable idea, please send me a few copies [of leaflets] for distribution . . . It is the commencement of what I trust may be a great movement to help the poor – *it is they who need the teaching now*. The middle and upper classes know what to do more or less – but the poor!!! Oh dear their clergy preach *plenty of children the more the better*!!![150]

Anna suggested to Stopes that she occasionally got into hot water for her opinions on the subject – 'I have frequent fights with some women' – but did not elaborate.[151] In a later letter she wrote that she had 'great discussions with a niece by marriage and some other ladies who think me real indelicate when dealing with such questionable matters'. She defended herself robustly: 'I tell them the world is moving and that they are very old fashioned.'[152] She was ninety-two when she wrote this letter.

The letters to Stopes reveal that Anna Haslam shared the conviction of her husband regarding the desirability of the widespread dissemination of information on birth control, particularly among the poor. She was convinced that abstinence was the best method of limiting the number of children born to a marriage. However, she obviously realized that for the poor, with whose welfare she was very concerned, it was not a realistic one. She did not have any moral problems with the use of artificial birth control and liked to be informed of all developments in the field. Unlike her husband, who admitted to Newman how difficult he found it to discuss such matters, Anna was not embarrassed to talk about sex and reproduction. She appears to have set herself up as an adviser on birth control matters and, even when a very old woman, was engaged in disseminating literature and information. Her stance on birth control was very typical of the time in that she sought its use in order to alleviate the plight of the working classes by reducing their family size. Although her major concern was with the poor she was also anxious to educate members of the middle class in the possibilities of limiting their family size. Richard Soloway has written that birth control 'transformed gradually from a humane and useful gift to be taught to the poor by their compassionate, far-sighted betters into a fundamental natural right of all who wished to exercise it'.[153] She could be said to have exemplified both features of Soloway's definition.

Marie Stopes, in her correspondence with Haslam, was anxious to obtain information of the early days of the birth control movement. In her manual on contraception, published in 1923, Stopes wrote that in 1868 'contemporary pens were active ... at least two pamphlets of practical advice were published and circulated'. One was *'The Power and Duty of Parents to Limit the number of their Children* [which] contained advice on physiological means of limitation by the safe period, by coughing, sneezing, jumping, violent exercise'. Thomas Haslam's pamphlet was simply described as *'The Marriage Problem* privately printed and circulated by "Œdipus" [which] also contained contraceptive advice'. Anna Haslam had given her both pamphlets. Stopes also cited 'some personal letters written in the same year (1868)' which are 'most valuable and illuminating, as indicating the general interest then taken in the root of the subject'. The letters cited were those addressed to Thomas Haslam regarding *The Marriage Problem*, and these had also been given to her by Anna Haslam, a fact which she did not acknowledge. She cited the letter to John Stuart Mill in full and quoted extensively from the letter of J. E. George.[154] Nowhere did she reveal that Haslam had written *The Marriage Problem* nor did she acknowledge the help she received from Anna Haslam in her researches. She also cited Newman's first letter to Thomas Haslam in *The Early Days of Birth Control*, published in 1922.

Stopes praised Dr Trall's *Sexual Physiology*: it 'gave not only an exposition of the necessity for it [birth control], but practical "birth control" information of a kind not bettered until two or three years ago when the subject was taken up in a more scientific way'. The book 'dealt profoundly with matters of sex and marriage, and was packed with extraordinarily valuable deductions from the author's own cases'. She judged the book to be 'of real use to the general public, and in such a spirit of sympathy, understanding and reverence that it could revolt none but the prurient minded'.[155] Anna Haslam had introduced Stopes to Trall: 'If you have not seen "Sexual Physiology" by Dr. Trall of America, 1866, from which my husband derived his information, I will send it to you with other pamphlets registered to return.'[156] Stopes borrowed the book, then over fifty years old, from Anna Haslam on a number of occasions and offered to buy it: 'I am so glad to see Trall again and wish that I could possess this book. I would gladly give you £5 for it and as you know treasure all its marks. I have tried in every way to get an early edition.'[157] Anna was not willing to sell it: 'I quite intend to leave you *eventually* my Dr Trall – in the meantime I have many requests for it. I shall be glad to have it back when you have done with it.' She gave Stopes a list of 'pamphlets and little books which I have and would be very glad to send you if you have not got them or care for them. We were married in 1854 so we had not literature before that time.'[158]

The list included only one item published before 1868, *Hints to Husbands* by George Morant (1856), and *The Power and Duty of Parents to Limit the Number of their Children* (Anon.),[159] published in 1868, the same year as Haslam's pamphlet. Anna sent Stopes these two works. Stopes 'felt sure' that the latter work was written by Thomas and asked: 'Could you let me have any idea what number were ultimately circulated of it?'[160] Anna replied 'I have no idea of the number of the leaflet. . . . It was *not* written by my husband.'[161] From Stopes's description of this pamphlet cited above, it is obvious that the writer was using ideas already expressed in Trall's work. Stopes must have seen similarities between the pamphlets to have prompted her query. A possible answer to the puzzle is that some person, possibly Burns, availed of Haslam's offer to reproduce 'the whole or any part of the pamphlet'. Anna wrote for the last time in June 1921, 'I have not *seen a line* or heard from you . . . On looking over my letters there is nothing about birth control that would interest you.'[162] On 12 December 1922, Leonard Webb of Webb & Webb, Solicitors, 1 Suffolk Street, Dublin, wrote to Dr Marie Stopes:

Mrs. Anna Maria Haslam of Dublin who died on the 28th November last, informed me some days before her death that she had promised to you on her death a certain book, which she was unwilling to sell to you during her life time. As Mrs. Haslam did not leave any written directions on the matter, I should be glad if you will let me know the name of the book and its author.[163]

Stopes replied:

> I learn from your letter with great sorrow of the death of Mrs. Haslam.
> The book which she always told me she would leave to me was the
> original edition of Dr. Trall's 'Sexual Physiology.' She promised me
> also that I should have the original correspondence with her husband
> and her friends about the population problem and Birth Control in the
> early days. If these can be found I should very much value them as the
> President for Constructive Birth Control and in my private capacity.[164]

As the correspondence cited above shows, Anna had never promised Stopes
anything other than the copy of Trall's *Sexual Physiology*; indeed the correspondence reveals that she had sent Stopes all relevant material before her
death. Webb replied on 2 January 1923: 'I send you herewith Trall's Book
and two phamplets (sic) bearing on the same subject. I regret to say I have
not found the correspondence to which you refer.'[165] On 4 January Stopes's
secretary wrote to Webb acknowledging receipt of the books 'from Mrs.
Haslam's estate which were left to her'. The letter further stated that 'if by
any chance the letters came to her later that she would be very glad to have
them'.[166] There is no mention in any of the correspondence of the names of
the two other pamphlets which were not, of course, 'left' to Stopes. Despite
the unethical nature of Stopes's claim to the Haslam birth control correspondence, one can understand her wish to procure such items, which
would cast light on the early history of birth control. One can only wish that
her ruse had succeeded as so much of the Haslam correspondence has disappeared without trace. In the case of the birth control correspondence,
however, it appears that Anna Haslam had indeed, as she had claimed, forwarded all available material to Stopes, as there are several letters addressed
to Thomas Haslam in the Stopes archive. One feels that Stopes might have
acknowledged Haslam's authorship of *The Marriage Problem* and given him
his rightful, if minor, place in the history of birth control. Perhaps she felt
that his anonymity, obviously desired when the pamphlet was written,
should be maintained. Anna Haslam was in her nineties when she
responded generously and promptly to all of Stopes's requests for material,
requests which must have demanded considerable effort on her behalf. She
was by this time in poor health and, it seems, in poor circumstances. She
wrote to Stopes in June 1920: 'I am very dull and uncomfortable, *No servant*,
have to do more than I like – Can't be helped it is miserable.'[167] On 13 May,
Anna wrote: 'I have not been very well and the weather is trying, hot & cold.
I tried to do without a fire had no coal – have just got two bags 10/- they
will last me until the real hot weather comes.'[168] In May 1921 in the covering letter she sent with the copy of Trall and 'a few old letters 14', Anna
wrote, 'I am still in Dr.'s hands can't walk much, he says he can't perform
miracles on me.'[169] However, Stopes had paid Anna a compliment in her letter of 22 March 1921:

> As you will understand my husband and I are running this Clinic
> absolutely on our own, but at the same time we want to have associ-

ated with us a body of people such as yourself to whom we can turn for counsel and sympathetic advice if the need should arise. Would you be one of our Counsellors?[170]

Again on 19 April Stopes wrote: 'You will be pleased to hear that I am convening a meeting at the large Queen's Hall in London on May 31st on Birth Control and I have some very distinguished speakers. How nice it would be if you could be on our platform.'[171]

Hints to Husbands, the only pamphlet in Anna's list sent to Marie Stopes which predated Thomas Haslam's own pamphlet, is now in the Marie Stopes Collection in the British Library. The full title of this work is *Hints to Husbands: A Revelation of the Man-Midwife's Mysteries* by George Morant, published in its third edition in 1857. The copy is inscribed with Thomas Haslam's name. The work is a polemical tract of 155 pages devoted to exposure and amendment of a 'vast social evil'. Morant resolved 'to probe to the very core, and fearlessly unveil and drag into the light its indecent mystery', namely 'the practice of man-midwifery'. This is a very eccentric work, couched in extravagant language and written in histrionic style:

> [Male-midwifery] is one among the noxious weeds which the rank luxuriance of civilization has produced and since its introduction it has thriven with unrestrained vitality . . . and treacherously, mysteriously, and silently distils the poison of its presence, deep into the sanctuary of domestic life.[172]

Presumably Morant was railing against obstetrics as a branch of medical science. His diatribe is based on the indecency of men assisting at childbirth. Childbirth is 'a purely natural process so wisely ordered that it rarely demands any other aid than experienced mothers can safely give'. Morant did not allow for the necessity of medical intervention in difficult childbirth but based his objections on the grounds that 'it is an insult to virtuous women', whose 'modesty' was sacrificed 'to passion, her person to indignity, and her husband's honour to the sneers and contempt of her male midwife'.[173] There is no mention at all of birth control in this curious work, the author of which is cited on the title page as 'late of the Grenadier Guards' in a manner which suggests that this gives him authority to write on childbirth. There are no passages marked by Haslam in this work, nor can Anna have been familiar with it as she sent it to Marie Stopes as a birth control book. The title suggests that the work is a marriage manual for men and may have been purchased by Thomas Haslam on the strength of that. The books sent to Stopes by Anna Haslam included Dr Allbutt's *The Wife's Handbook*, published in 1885, which cannot have influenced Thomas Haslam's work but is interesting in that its author was struck off the medical register.[174]

Ironically, Haslam's correspondence resulting from *The Marriage Problem* has attracted more attention than the work itself. As mentioned previously, Marie Stopes and Norman Himes both used letters received by Haslam to illustrate attitudes on the subject of birth control. While Stopes presumably read the copy given to her by Anna, it would appear that Himes had not read it.[175] Michael Mason merely mentioned it as one of four pamphlets 'advocating birth control' published between 1840 and 1870, and gave no evidence of having read it. F. H. A. Micklewright, while noting its publication gave Stopes's work as his reference.[176] In 1995, however, a sizeable extract was published and Haslam was credited with the authorship.[177]

The period in which *The Marriage Problem* was published was dubbed the era of 'quiet percolation' in terms of birth control.[178] The desire of Haslam for anonymity is understandable when one considers that birth control was inextricably linked in the public mind with the 'philosophy of life without religion'. Open discussion of the topic 'was inhibited by the fear that those who were engaged in it would be branded as adherents to . . . militant, anti-Christian scepticism'.[179] The 'particularly malevolent review of Mill's career' printed in *The Times* on the morning of his funeral which referred to his 'carrying out the Malthusian principle,' is but one example of public hostility to the question.[180] Haslam saw the practice of birth control as ameliorating the economic distress of the poor while simultaneously inculcating in them the virtues of prudence and thrift. Although the plight of the poor in Ireland was aired in his correspondence with Newman, his pamphlet was not written in an Irish context, nor was there any recorded Irish response.

Thomas Haslam's pamphlet is not of great significance in the overall history of nineteenth-century birth control propaganda. It is not a truly original work, as he drew heavily on the writings of Trall. It was, however, a courageous and innovative enterprise for a mid-Victorian Irishman. While the modern reader deplores the advice which was confidently, and wrongly, guaranteed to prevent conception, it must be reiterated that others more qualified than he gave the same advice, albeit not quite so confidently. Like Dr Johnson's dog walking on its hind legs, the wonder is not how well it was done, but that it was done at all.

3

'Connubial temperance': Thomas Haslam as sexual moralist

In 1872 Thomas Haslam published *Duties of Parents*, a prescriptive manual that encouraged 'exemplary' parenthood. Despite the childlessness of his own marriage, Haslam confidently ladled out advice on all matters pertaining to conception, child rearing and education. The *Duties of Parents* is a work of 160 pages and, although divided into fourteen sections, tends to repeat its major themes of suitability for parenthood, development of character, moral purity and sexual temperance. While Haslam returned to topics aired in *The Marriage Problem*, his approach was different; in *Duties of Parents* his emphasis was on positive procreation. He was adamant that those who are unfit to bear children should not marry. While readers of *The Marriage Problem* were advised to practice the 'safe period', if they wished, or needed, to avoid conception, *Duties of Parents* recommended abstinence from sexual relations as the ideal method of birth control. The book may have been the result of Haslam's growing realization that the crusade for birth control was having little impact among the poor and those whom he judged unfit to have children. In *Duties of Parents* there is a decided emphasis on social engineering as a means of achieving the moral improvement of society. The ideas he promulgated reveal his knowledge of contemporary theories of sexuality, heredity and environmentalism.

Haslam seemed ever willing to pronounce on matters about which he may not have had any particular expertise. This was not unusual in the nineteenth century when, before the age of specialization, thinkers and scholars were wont 'to express notions about the world, man's situation in it and how he should live'.[1] Such men, and they were invariably men, were capable of disseminating their ideas 'to others in a language intelligible to most literate people'.[2] Haslam's voice was confident and authoritative. The ideas propounded in this work, and the authorities cited, reveal his adherence to Lamarckian theories of heredity and also to the prevailing discourse of sexual morality. Collini's remarks seem particularly apposite when applied to Haslam's influences:

> Those mid-Victorian psychologists and physiologists who obtained a wide non-professional readership, such as Bain, Spencer, Carpenter, and Maudsley, all toyed with the notion that habit could modify or leave a deposit in the nervous system itself. This needs to be seen in the context of that more general appeal of a diluted Lamarckianism to

a scientifically semi-educated audience, which nurtured a fascination with the idea that in properly exercising the muscles of the will the individual might be acquiring a new capacity that could operate instinctively on future occasions and, through the related Lamarckian belief in the inheritance of acquired characteristics, could determine the behaviour of future generations.[3]

The theories of Jean Baptiste Lamarck, an eighteenth-century biologist, that 'organisms evolved by acquiring characteristics and then passing them on to their offspring in the form of altered hereditary (later called genetic) information', were used to explain how transgressions, including sexual excesses, became implanted into men's beings.[4] Herbert Spencer, whose writings were recommended by Haslam as essential reading, believed in the 'inheritance of acquired characteristics'.[5] Despite Spencer's coining of the phrase 'survival of the fittest', his theories were Lamarckian rather than Darwinian.[6] Haslam too attached great importance to biological determinism. His concern for the 'moral purity' and sexual temperance of parents was predicated on his conviction that such traits would be inherited by offspring. He was convinced that the immorality and 'connubial intemperance' of parents ensured that their children would ultimately behave equally badly and would, in turn, bequeath their immoral characteristics to future generations.

Haslam attached great importance to the formation of character; an ideal 'which enjoyed a prominence in the political thought of the Victorian period that it apparently had not known before and that it has, arguably, not experienced since'.[7] He believed that good habits could be acquired and in turn passed on to progeny. Haslam's ideal of inherited good character being combined with its optimal development may have been influenced by the 1867 writings of Henry Maudsley: 'The strong or well-formed character which a well-fashioned will implies is the result of good training applied to a well-constituted original nature; and the character is not directly determined by the will, but in any particular act determines the will.'[8]

Haslam's message was similar to that of Maudsley, and was basically optimistic regarding the potential of positive heredity and character formation: 'Provided we are endowed with healthy, happy natures at the hour of birth; provided we are reared vigorously; and provided we receive an adequate mental and moral preparation for the tasks of life; in a vast majority of cases that life will be a prosperous one.' This, of course, was dependent upon the traits one inherited from one's parents and on the rearing one received. The breeding of the physically or morally 'unfit' meant that progeny were 'born into the world with diseased and vicious natures as a primary endowment'.[9] He acknowledged that

large numbers of parents *are* faithful in the performance of their duties; are doing all they can to inaugurate this era of universal well-being . . . The proof of this we see in the large percentage of vigorous, exemplary young men, and of healthy, virtuous young women, who are to be found in every social grade, and who could not exhibit those noble traits if they did not inherit them from a righteous ancestry.

Thus he saw the moral and healthy as contributing to 'universal well-being'; conversely the immoral and unhealthy detracted from the possibility of social harmony in the future. Examples of the negative effects of bad and unsuitable parenting were to be found

> in our gaols and work-houses, in our gin-palaces and haunts of infamy, in our hospitals and lunatic-asylums, in our vast percentages of preventable mortality, in our hydra forms of incurable disease ... wherever there is constitutional infirmity, wherever there is ingrained natural depravity, and wherever there is brutal ignorance, parental negligence may be inferred.[10]

Haslam devoted a chapter of *Duties* to 'Moral Disqualifications for Parentage' in which he admitted the difficulty of passing 'sentence of exclusion from the joys of parentage upon our fellow-men'. He considered those who were 'afflicted with scrofula or consumption, with paralysis or epilepsy, with insanity or idiocy', unfit for parenthood. Despite the understandable instinct of such persons 'to be surrounded by innocent *fac-similes* of themselves', Haslam considered that society had a moral duty to teach them that such longings must be restrained:

> We are bound to impress upon them, with all possible tenderness, but with unmistakable firmness that they are morally debarred from the exercise of this responsible function ... The time is possibly not remote, when society will recognise the duty of enforcing this lesson of self-restraint, by firm, but judicious legislative enactments.[11]

He was unambiguous regarding the hereditary nature of the criminal personality: 'There is not a shadow of doubt that evil propensities are transmitted from father to son; that the children of the profligate have a natural tendency to vice.'[12] His often repeated strictures on the undesirability of those with criminal or diseased 'organizations' begetting children are similar to those of Herbert Spencer: 'There is no greater curse to prosperity than that of bequeathing an increasing population of imbeciles and idlers and criminals. To aid the bad in multiplying is, in effect, the same as maliciously providing for our descendants a multitude of enemies.'[13] Although he did not develop the point, Haslam seemed to suggest that if children were removed from the baneful influences of unfit parents they might overcome the influence of heredity: 'children of the profligate have a natural tendency to vice, which, unless they are subjected to the best of moral discipline from a tender age, they will always have great trouble in controlling.' It is unlikely that he thought it possible that such children would receive this 'moral discipline' from the parents who had passed on the undesirable characteristics in the first place. Whatever Haslam really meant, he was open to the possibility of training and education overcoming inbred criminal or dissolute tendencies. He was not optimistic, however, that such an eventuality was likely, and considered that 'society will soon be compelled to grapple with the problem; will be forced to devise some efficacious measures to avert the propagation of an everlasting race of criminals'. He realized the difficulty of trying to persuade such criminals to desist from breeding by 'considerations of ethical propriety'. The state must intervene; 'this enormous evil' must 'be checked by legislative action'. We are given no hint of the nature of the proposed 'legislative enactments' that would ensure that the criminal did not propagate. It is difficult to envisage how Haslam thought such legislation could feasibly prevent criminal types having children. Can he have meant compulsory sterilization? Perhaps he intended that some form of sanction be applied in the event of children being born to those who were 'unfit'. In the event he fudged the question and referred the problem to 'our social reformers'.[14] His ideas may not have been original; a comment printed in *Nature* in 1869 suggested that 'judicious legislation' should be introduced 'to multiply the conditions *favourable* to the development of a higher type'.[15] Irrespective of where Thomas Haslam derived the ideas that prompted his prescriptive writings on reproduction and heredity, they reveal him as keeping abreast of the latest theories in social thinking. However, he did not share 'the deep ... cultural and social pessimism accompanied by the sense of impending decadence and decline'[16] which later characterized those interested in eugenics. His message is optimistic for the future of mankind:

> When these disqualifications are practically observed, one enormous obstacle will be rolled from the path of human advancement ... The strong, the healthy, and the virtuous will be all the more free to multiply and replenish the earth; disease and vice and crime will die out for lack of sustenance; a manly self-reliant race will overspread the world; and happiness and virtue will become the universal heritage.[17]

Haslam was, of course, not only interested in the welfare of individuals; his message was dedicated to the improvement of society. His desire to discourage, and, if possible, prohibit those of bad character and 'imperfect organization' from breeding would seem to have the same object of improving society. His indefatigable correspondent Newman identified the essential weakness of this theory when he trenchantly asks how the unfit are to be persuaded not to breed.[18]

Although Haslam's work predated the organized eugenics movement by almost thirty years, he was not the first to suggest social engineering: eugenics was rooted in a belief in perfection which could be traced back to Rousseau and Condorcet.[19] Robert Owen, industrialist and socialist, had speculated on the state's supervision of births to attain 'improvements of the organization of man'.[20] Haslam's eugenic theories show that he shared this ideal of the perfectibility of society and that he also possessed the paternalistic philanthropist's desire to improve the lot of the working classes. He saw the plight of the poor as being caused by their exploitation, their lack of

foresight and education, and his message was the need for responsible parenthood. He did, however, repeatedly stress the need to prevent the
mentally and physically unfit and those of criminal tendencies from breeding. Lindsay Farrall has written that in the 1870s and early 1880s a number
of works were published which 'called for action to prevent people with
varying afflictions from having children'. The activism of the later organized
eugenics movement, however, 'was a sign . . . of a new fear of the lower
classes . . . The poor were not demoralised, they were degenerate.'[21] While
the older liberal interpretation, of which Haslam's work was an example,
focused on the irresponsibility of the poor, it also allowed for the possibility
of their improving their lot by their own efforts. The eugenicists' attitude
was more brutal; if the problems of the poor were caused by heredity 'the
state could only limit the problem by restricting their breeding'.[22] By the
turn of the century 'the fear of lower-class degenerates swamping civilised
society by simple force of numbers precipitated a deluge of books and articles . . . calling for policies to check their breeding'.[23] Suggested methods
included the prevention of marriage, the discouragement of preventative
medicine, withdrawal of charity to the insane, the epileptic, the criminal,
segregation of 'incapables' and the prevention by the state of the breeding
of the unfit.[24] Haslam does not appear to have shared the eugenicists' desire
to promote the fertility of the middle and upper classes nor was he class specific in his condemnation of the breeding of the unfit. He claimed that ' in
every social grade' there was a 'large percentage of exemplary young men
and of healthy virtuous young women'.[25]

From the mid-nineteenth century onwards, the plight of the poor tended
to be viewed, not as an economic problem, but as one of demoralization and
degeneration. Thomas Haslam, however, believed in the capacity of the
poor for self-improvement and in the possibility of the improvement of their
living and working conditions. He wrote that for good health children
needed: 'nutritious food, substantial clothing, proper bathing-apparatus,
pure water, free ventilation, thorough drainage, means of disinfection etc.'[26]
The importance of sanitation and clean water supply had been a matter of
public debate since at least the middle of the century. By the time Haslam
was writing, Sir Edwin Chadwick had published *The Sanitary Condition of the
Labouring Classes*, in which he argued for the provision of a piped system for
the supply of clean water in urban areas. The connection between lack of
adequate sanitation and disease had already been acknowledged. In 1842
Chadwick wrote: 'The great preventatives [to diseases are] drainage . . .
cleansing by means of supplies of water and improved sewerage and especially the introduction of cheaper and more efficient modes of removing all
noxious refuse from the towns.'[27]

Haslam stipulated that 'intending parents' should not marry until they
are provided with a healthy home of at least 'three or four lightsome rooms'.
He was very concerned regarding the provision of adequate bedrooms: 'The
huddling together of a whole family of children and adults, irrespective of
sex, in one sleeping apartment, is a deplorable barbarism, whether on the
score of health or morals.'[28] His stipulation on suitable housing predated the

Royal Commission on Housing by some thirteen years. This Commission followed an extended debate on the government's role in the solving of the housing problems of the poor.[29] Bad housing, as well as bad sewers and drains, was recognized as a contributing factor to ill-health and disease.

Haslam was concerned that 'there should be a reserve fund in some Bank, or other safe investment, of some two or three years income, to fall back upon in case of illness, so that the family may not be driven into the poor-house under any probable contingency'.[30] This seems very impractical especially for the poor at whom the advice is obviously aimed. Haslam nevertheless thought it possible although he conceded that 'it will often demand self-denial and self-sacrifice'. He believed, however, that the practice of economy and temperance might realize the fulfilment of these conditions 'in a good degree'.[31] He concluded his financial advice in full Malthusian spate castigating 'premature marriage' which condemned people to lives of misery: 'there is no prospect of improvement until they are taught that, by their reckless and improvident marriages, they are not merely hanging a millstone about their own necks, but they are entailing ill-health and most probably untimely death upon their little ones.'[32]

Had Haslam, by 1872, realized the difficulty, or the impossibility, of the dissemination of the birth control message? He had, after all, recommended the 'safe period' as an alternative to the cycle of deprivation in *The Marriage Problem* where he stipulated that it would allow young men to marry before they could afford children. In *Duties of Parents*, however, there is not the merest hint of such a solution and early marriages are 'reckless and improvident'. He referred only briefly to the use of the advice of 'some physicians' who had proposed restricting intercourse to times when 'impregnation would not be likely to ensue', although he conceded that the 'adoption of this precaution would certainly be preferable to the generation of a diseased or vicious progeny; it might even be safer than a state of unsatisfied longing'. He warned of the 'grave moral objections to all such expedients. At best they are mere palliatives; they do not lay the axe at the root of the evil. That evil consists in the supremacy of the carnal desires; – the inability to control the lusts of the flesh in obedience to the moral law.' Where is the Thomas of the *Marriage Problem* who so cogently argued for the morality of the 'safe period' four years previously? 'What our epoch demands is not a cunningly-devised method by which we can revel in sensuality whilst evading its natural consequences; but a power of self-command which will enable us to abstain from indulgence where parentage would be wrong.'[33]

It is difficult to understand how Haslam had moved so radically from his warm recommendation of the 'safe period' in *The Marriage Problem* to the rebuttal contained in his calling it a 'cunningly devised method'. While one could argue that in *The Duties of Parents* he was writing for a different audience, one for whom he felt the message of the advantages of the 'mid-month method' would be unacceptable, the reality is that both publications were essentially concerned with the theme of responsible parenthood. Had Newman's arguments convinced him in the end? There is no possibility that in *The Marriage Problem* he proclaimed the virtues of something of which he inherently disapproved. The pamphlet is patently sincere, a sincerity that is reiterated in the correspondence with Newman. Haslam would appear to have been convinced that he was spreading important news of the wonderful discovery made by Trall and others. In *Duties of Parents* he calls for 'the diffusion of that noble endowment which has characterised the best and purest of our race in all ages: – the power of trampling under foot the seductions of sense; the power of self-renunciation in the interests of true manhood'.[34] When Anna wrote to Marie Stopes she grouped together the two works, *The Marriage Problem* and *Duties of Parents,* and did not remark on the essential difference between them. She was concerned that the poor be educated in easily understood, feasible birth control methods, not that they be taught the virtues of abstinence which, of course, she believed in herself. Abstinence *was* a commonly practised method of birth control. Nearly fifty years after the publication of *Duties of Parents*, 'correspondence poured in' to Marie Stopes from readers of her *Married Love*, documenting their sexual difficulties and describing the contraceptive methods which they employed: 'For many couples total abstention had been the only reliable method known to them.'[35]

In *Duties of Parents* Haslam was concerned with the need for moral purity: 'It is hard to find language sufficiently strong to express the stringency' of the 'obligation' of the 'preservation of our moral purity, spotless and unsullied'. For such preservation it was essential that parents did not transmit 'organic impurity' to the next generation; to do so was 'an evil of unspeakable magnitude'.[36] He would appear to have subscribed sincerely to the prevailing code of sexual morality of his time. Michael Mason is of the opinion that for most of the nineteenth century 'Sexual moralism was a mass movement . . . [with] tremendous ascendancy in respectable public discourse . . . nineteenth-century anti-sensualism had a very broad base.'[37] Haslam shared the horror and fear of the 'terrible practice of self-abuse' as exercised by young boys, 'and a few even of our girls . . . long before they have any suspicion of its deadly consequences'.[38] While some of the theories of anti-sensual moralists were questioned, most notably by small numbers of medical men, there was virtually universal condemnation of masturbation. George Drysdale, whose work on birth control was discussed in the previous chapter, described as 'the one declared sexual liberationist of the nineteenth century in Britain. . . took as bleak a view of the evils of masturbation as anyone'.[39] In the notorious and explicit account of his sexual exploits, *My Secret Life*, in which experiences are salaciously recorded, the author, 'Walter', informed the reader that he refrained from masturbation because of the dangers it posed to health.[40] Masturbation was the subject of religious tracts and of medical discourse; horror of the practice was exploited by quacks and vendors of patent devices. 'In a climate of sexual ignorance, guilt and fear' propaganda against masturbation gave 'shape to inchoate male anxieties'.[41] The warnings of Haslam against the dangers of masturbation were the common currency of his time: 'Every physician knows that a frequent cause of premature death on the part of our young men, is the violation of this [reproductive] instinct during adolescence by the practice of self-pollution.'[42] This statement, absurd to the modern reader, was corroborated by contemporary medical opinion: 'Victorian doctors . . . commonly were convinced of the physical as well as the moral evils of masturbation . . . threatening a string of ailments ending in insanity as the inevitable outcome of onanism.'[43]

Haslam warned against the 'seductions which await . . . upon the threshold of early manhood'. The list included 'the gin-palace . . . the smiling wanton . . . the concert-hall, the theatre, the betting-house, the race-course . . . poisonous literature . . . with its glowing pictures of successful vice'. He urged young men to avoid such 'pitfalls'. He was concerned, not only for the sake of the young men themselves, but for the sake of their wives and offspring: 'If they ever mean to enter into the holy bonds of marriage: to ask a pure confiding woman to become the angel of their firesides; if they ever hope to surround themselves with children . . . they must religiously abstain from every vicious practice.'[44] Here Haslam echoed Coventry Patmore's epic poem, 'Angel in the House', which celebrated the chaste wife in her eponymous role. The dangers of habits of vice being transmitted to progeny must be 'solemnly impressed upon our young men'. Haslam argued not only for education in the avoidance of vice but also positively in the teaching of noble virtues:

> We must cherish a spirit of truthfulness, of singleness of heart, of moral courage, of inflexible probity, of loyalty to every pure and holy principle. We must raise ourselves above all petty slavery to money . . . We must be prompt to sympathise with every righteous cause with every movement that has for its aim the elevation of mankind.[45]

This would seem to be how he himself tried to live. He urged his readers to cultivate their intellects and considered it vital that within a marriage each partner was dedicated to the development of the other. 'It is not sufficient that we cultivate our own nature to the highest possible perfection, we must demand as severe a standard from our partners.'[46]

Haslam devoted a chapter to the 'difficult topic' of 'connubial temperance'; 'spurious delicacy' would not deflect him from broaching the subject. He acknowledged that: 'The transition from the restraints of celibacy to the unrestricted licence of wedded love is so sharp, and the stimulus which it imparts to the sexual appetite is so urgent, that it not infrequently suspends the power of self-control, and leads to excesses of a most disastrous character.'[47] Dr Acton[48] and Dr Miller[49] are cited in support of this theory. The primary function of 'the reproductive element in our physical economy' was 'the continuation of the species'.[50] Whereas in his defence of *The Marriage Problem*, Haslam argued for the morality of 'natural' birth control, here he appeared to have abandoned this stance. While he conceded that nature had ensured that the human reproductive instinct was 'clamorous', he claimed that experienced medical practitioners were in agreement that 'connubial intemperance is not uncommonly the cause of premature decay in the prime of manhood'. Nature exacts 'retribution' for the 'systematic perversion' of the reproductive urge for the sake of 'animal pleasure'. He listed a terrifying catalogue of the effects of 'connubial intemperance' which includes 'consumption and paralysis', a statement which he assured the reader will be corroborated by 'every experienced practitioner'. Haslam believed that 'sexual indulgence is an exhaustive tax upon our energies', causing diminution of 'muscular force', irritability, loss of memory, failure of the digestive system, acute disease, etc. The finale of this misery is risible to the modern reader, but the sincerity of Haslam's belief in his theory is patent:

> the seeds of death accumulate until we drop into the grave, worn out before our time, a victim to our own debasing self-indulgence. It may be in a fit of apoplexy that our final summons reaches us; it may be paralysis or epilepsy which is our allotted recompense; the still more dreadful sentence of insanity may cast its rayless shadow over the scene; but, whatever may be the form of our special chastisement, premature decay is its unfailing characteristic.[51]

Haslam was not unique in linking sexual intercourse and debilitating diseases. The dangers of over-frequent sexual activity to the male was a favourite topic of Victorian writers on sexuality. William Acton, an authority cited by Haslam, believed that 'the waste of vital spermatic fluid (even in legitimate marriage) itself could lead to debilitating disease'.[52] Haslam frequently cited Acton as his authority for medical opinions expressed in *Duties of Parents*. For Acton all sexual activity was full of danger. He stressed the danger of too frequent intercourse; he felt that the sensation of orgasm was so intense that it was unsafe to experience too frequently.[53] There has been much historical debate challenging the writings of Acton as the definitive Victorian voice on sexuality.[54] His work, however, was 'issued in three editions in its first five years and continued to be reprinted well after . . . [his] death'.[55] While there are some dissenting medical voices regarding Acton's theories, it is fair to say that his 'views on men typified the medical profession of the period'.[56] Dr Miller's theory that 'the material which goes to generate a new being is so refined, so intensified in its vitalising powers, that one ounce of it is equal to forty ounces of blood in any other part of the body' was also cited by Haslam to buttress his argument on the dangers of 'connubial intemperance'.[57] Dr Trall, too, believed that to have sexual intercourse more frequently than once a week led to the risk of 'serious detriment to health and a premature old age'.[58] Haslam's recommendation that within marriage the frequency of sexual intercourse should be limited to 'what is required for the creation of offspring', is a total rejection of his arguments in his correspondence to Newman where he eloquently defended the 'natural law' of sexual satisfaction: 'Indulgence in mutual passion . . . is perfectly natural', and, 'The doctrine that "all pursuit of pleasure" . . . is unlawful . . . appears repugnant to my common sense.'[59] While Haslam cited the recommendations of Drs Acton and Trall regarding the frequency of sexual intercourse, once in 'seven or ten days' and 'once a week' respectively, his own suggestion that sexual relations take place for 'procreation' only was predicated on the 'judgement of some of our highest ethical teachers'.[60] He did not, however, name these authorities. Can he have been thinking of Newman?

One of the most notable features of the *Duties of Parents* is Haslam's volte-face on his theories of wifely duty expressed in *The Marriage Problem*. His opinion that: 'Numbers of women who, in their self-sacrificing devotion to their husbands, are nightly persuaded to accept endearments which their natural instincts do not solicit, could bear a melancholy witness to the indifference which has long replaced the original delight',[61] contradicts the stance of *The Marriage Problem* in which such devotion is recommended as an antidote to the husband resorting to prostitutes. Why had Thomas reversed his opinion? Was it a realization that his former stance was totally inconsistent with a woman's right to bodily integrity, and made nonsense of his assertion that he was an 'extremest advocate' of women's rights?

In *Duties of Parents,* he was convinced that excessive sexual demands on a wife 'drains the life-springs of that rapturous sentiment which first attracted the youthful couple to each other with an irresistible magnetism. It is this excess, which, probably more than any other cause, induces the proverbial disenchantment of the honeymoon.'[62] Anna Haslam's revelation that their sexual relationship ceased after the first week of their marriage does not enlighten us on whether her own honeymoon was 'proverbially disenchanting'. One does, however, assume that Thomas is speaking from experience when he praises 'mutual respect, which next to love itself, is the brightest jewel in the crown of wedded bliss'. This he warns 'can seldom long survive the contraction of this baneful habit [sexual excess] unimpaired'. Connubial temperance, however, would ensure that 'the tenderness of courtship' would survive 'all through life, and shed its romantic influence over our declining years'.[63]

Women forced to overindulge in sexual relations were also prone to 'an endless catalogue of maladies peculiar to themselves'. Haslam stated that 'more miscarriages result from this excess than from any other cause'. Dr Miller was cited as the authority for the list of female diseases caused by sexual excess: 'The long train of diseases and sufferings consequent upon these excesses . . . such as inflammations, ulcerations, displacements, tumors, cancers, etc. most commonly have their origins in sexual abuses . . . Very much of the nervousness and hysteria so common among women arises from abuses of the sexual function.'[64] Dr Churchill's 'sterling treatise', *On the Diseases of Women,*[65] is cited by Haslam as enumerating: 'amenorrhæa, dysmenorrhæa, menorrhagia, hypertrophy, inflammation, erosion, vaginitis chronic and acute, languor of mind, nervous incapacity, not to speak of consumption, amongst the diseases which, within his own sphere of observation, he has traced to overindulgence'.[66] Haslam believed that 'there are thousands of wives who are never well except during isolation from their husbands'. This was the reason for the popularity of the spa, frequented by women 'whose only chance of recovery consists in withdrawal from this source of injury'.[67] Dr Miller's rather purple prose revealed a perception of woman as noble, self-sacrificing and asexual:

I know the heart-history of many noble, high-toned women, whose whole being revolts at the use to which they are put. Yet their ideas of domestic peace are so exalted that, loyal and true, they submit themselves to a constant sacrifice, and by the mere force of will, keep alive the fire of love within their tortured souls . . . Our grave-yards, could they speak, would send forth a sad and sickening wail from the young wives and mothers who have been placed there, the victims of matrimonial abuse of the sexual function.[68]

Haslam conceded that the rule of sexual intercourse for propagation purposes only was difficult and 'centuries will probably be needed to educate mankind to so high and self-denying a standard'. As a guideline in the meantime he suggested that 'no indulgence which does violence to the natural instinct of pure and healthy women can be right'.[69] Why pure *and* healthy one wonders? Surely there are pure women of delicate constitutions whose wishes on the subject are even more important? The coupling of 'pure' with 'healthy' may have referred to 'moral' health. The dire warnings of the physical and mental dangers of sexual excess and of masturbation suggested that if one were healthy one must be pure. Where did that leave Haslam himself? The eugenics movement tended to associate 'unfitness' for parenthood with immorality, particularly in the case of 'feeble-minded' women. Mary Dendy, a leading campaigner for the care of the feeble-minded in the early twentieth century, believed that 'if a woman comes into the workhouse with an illegitimate child, it should be considered evidence of weakness of mind; there is certainly evidence of lack of moral fibre'.[70]

Haslam subscribed to the notion of women as 'naturally finer and purer in their organization than our coarser sex . . . In all matters respecting connubial indulgence, it is time that the principle should be universally recognised that pure women are the final and authoritative judges.' He did not seem to envisage a scenario in which the woman might actively solicit or enjoy overindulgence. Although he did briefly concede the possibility of 'mutual delight', he is much more concerned with the male 'blind and selfish appetite' being satisfied at the expense of women.[71] Haslam's theory must not be dismissed merely as a manifestation of a Victorian's perception of female passive sexuality. It should, rather, be seen as a belief in a woman's right to control her own body. Mill had argued for this right in *Principles of Political Economy*. In *The Marriage Problem*, while not approving of the double standard, Haslam saw women's submission to male sexual demands as the lesser of two evils; he now demanded of men that they control sexual desire. He no longer accepted the stereotype of overwhelming male desire that must be assuaged. His implicit belief in woman's moral superiority was one shared by feminists. His suggestion that within marriage woman should be the arbiter of the frequency of sexual relations was typical of feminist writers on sexology such as Elizabeth Blackwell, who believed that 'male sexuality could and should be attuned' to women's needs and desires. This implied a potentially radical shift in the balance of power within marriage.'[72] The perception of women as having a greater capacity for sexual self-control was a positive one that empowered them to speak with authority in the campaign against the Contagious Diseases Acts.

Feminist theory was essentially Lamarckian; man had transgressed the 'natural law' of sexual continence and consequently women's experience of the dangers and pain of repeated childbirth had acted as an inhibitor of women's sexual urges. This reduced desire was also inherited by future generations. Tendency to excess of male sexual desire was due to inherited habit and could be countered by new habits of continence which in turn could be passed on to future generations.[73] This belief is evident in the writings of Haslam. If one accepted the biological determinism of male sexual excess, one had also to accept the inevitability of women being forced to continue as its victims. Man's excessive desire was believed by theorists to have been caused by overindulgence in the past. Lamarckian theory allowed the argument that sexuality was transformable by the learning of new habits of continence. This would be a step towards the elimination of the sexual subordination of women. The aversion of women to sexual intercourse would presumably disappear once the practice of self-control by men became the norm. Unwanted pregnancies would decrease and sex would be transformed from being solely a physical phenomenon into something with a more spiritual dimension. This possibility of the transformation of the sexual urges of men and the consequent improvement of society, an underlying theme of Haslam's work, is evident in the work of medical and feminist theorists.[74]

Dr Trall, who, as already mentioned, adopted an unambiguously woman-centred stance in his *Sexual Physiology,* was convinced that 'in the good time coming' it would be possible for 'a single act of coition . . . to beget a single child'. Consequently acts of intercourse will then be 'limited to the number of offspring. Such is the legitimate result of the theory carried to its ultimatum.'[75] The Irish feminist Margaret Cousins was profoundly shocked and suffered many 'problems of adjustment to the revelation that marriage had brought [her] as to the physical basis of sex'. She wrote that she 'and many men and women of like nature including . . . [her] husband' would not be satisfied 'until the evolution of form has substituted some more artistic way of continuance of the race'.[76] Herbert Spencer believed that 'progress towards higher social types is joined with progress toward higher types of sexual relations'.[77]

The advice on 'connubial temperance' was directed at men; Haslam would appear to have subscribed to the Victorian stereotype of woman as the pure and unsullied creature of little sexual appetite. He cited Dr Acton's dictum that there were 'many females who never feel any sexual excitement whatever.'[78] He believed that in 'pure and healthy women the desire for the connubial embrace does not arise frequently and is easily appeased'.[79] Haslam considered it indispensable that: 'Every bride should, if possible have her own separate sleeping apartment.' He did not, however, suggest that 'as a rule husband and wife should habitually sleep apart'.[80] Anna wrote that despite the non-sexual nature of their union, 'we slept together for over 60 years & were a most loving couple, everyone thought us an ideal pair'.[81]

Virtue had its own rewards in the chaste marriage:

> Daily and hourly communion with a loving partner, of purer, chaster, nature than themselves; the privilege of bestowing life, and health and education, upon a succession of innocents, fresh from Nature's mintage . . . those are the joys to which they should look forward with passionate yearnings and compared with which the indulgence of the flesh should be esteemed as nought.[82]

This elevating of the spiritual communion between a married couple to a higher plane was possible once sexual relations were confined to the procreation of children. In the case of the Haslams, where no children were planned, the romantic nature of their marriage, even in old age, was evident and commented upon. The suffragist Elizabeth Wolstenholme Elmy[83] was a correspondent of the Haslams and, indeed, her *Life to Women* (1896), was included in the list of books sent by Anna to Marie Stopes. She wrote under the pseudonym Ellis Ethelmer,[84] mainly on sexuality and reproduction. A major theme was the right of women to control their own bodies, and she was concerned with the ideal form of sexual relations between men and women. While 'Ellis Ethelmer' conceded that women and men might choose to engage in sexual relations for pleasure as well as procreation, and recommended the precarious 'safe period' for such couples, she proposed an alternative ideal that was strikingly similar to Haslam's ideas in *Duties of Parents*. Like Haslam, she suggested that the ideal relationship between husband and wife included sexual intercourse only for procreative purposes. In *Phases of Love* she described the development of the 'psychic character and attribute' of a loving relationship. Such 'psychic love' was possible only if its practitioners were educated to a 'realisation of justice, equality, and sympathy between the sexes'. 'Psychic love' could only be developed through the promotion of the ideal of sexual self-control.[85] 'Ethelmer' developed the argument further than Haslam, however, as she wrote that woman, when freed from sexual slavery, would be enabled to take her part in a world formerly the preserve of men only. She saw the sexual function of women as underlying their oppression, and testified to their right to control their own bodies. In *Women Free* she broke into bad verse on the subject:

> For but a slave himself [man] must ever be,
> Till she to shape her own career be free;
> Free from all uninvited touch of man,
> Free mistress of her person's sacred plan![86]

She detected that 'the growing emancipation and autonomy of woman' was enabling the development of 'the psychic emotion and impulse between two human beings of different sex, to which the name of "love" is specially and worthily applied'.[87] Ellis Ethelmer's work on 'psychic love' was published twenty-five years after *Duties of Parents*. We know that Wolstenholme Elmy had read Haslam's work, however, as in a letter written in 1873, she 'warmly' acknowledged the gift of the book and ordered three more for circulation: 'The book is valuable in every way and will be most useful if it can be largely circulated.' She deplored the law which decreed that: 'The husband has the legal right to compel her [the wife] to his desires even to the extent I believe of locking her up in a room in his house and feeding her on bread and water if she is refractory.' She connected the sexual subordination of women to their lack of property rights, a point not made by Haslam, and saw the reform of the Married Women's Property Act as the greatest priority. She thought that 'such works as Mr. Haslam's serve the very important purpose of maturing public opinion'. Her letter showed that she had read the book carefully:

> Have you ever noticed that all the analogies of nature are in favour of the view argued out on moral grounds by Mr. Haslam? The predominance of the female in such relations is the universal law throughout the whole animal kingdom except where the contrary has been artificially contrived by man.[88]

The Haslams' own marriage would seem to be a potent example of the advantages of 'psychic love'. He does not suggest how, other than by connubial temperance, the romantic element of a marriage may be retained into old age. While Wolstenholme Elmy's 'poetic and rather flowery descriptions were very vague and inexplicit ... there can be little doubt that it did include expressions of love and affection'.[89] Her central thesis, like Haslam's, was based on the principle of female sexual autonomy. She was not alone. Frances Swiney, suffragist and prolific writer, argued that male sexual incontinence was responsible for the sexual exploitation of women: 'The only being in civilised life from whom the human female has to be protected is the male of her own species.'[90] Elizabeth Blackwell, pioneer female doctor, twenty-three years after *Duties of Parents*, wrote with medical authority of her belief that male sexual desire was not uncontrollable, nor was its release vital to good health. She believed, like Haslam, that 'No physiological truth is more firmly established than the fact that we can modify the action of our physical organs.' No human being was dependent on the 'degradation of another human being for the maintenance of personal health'.[91]

Haslam's oft quoted authority, Acton, did not agree with the emergence of what may be called a feminist attitude to the frequency and timing of sexual intercourse. He wrote with disapproval of 'a lady who maintains women's rights to such an extent that she denied her husband any voice in the matter whether or not co-habitation should take place'.[92] Acton, like Haslam in *The Marriage Problem*, wrote approvingly of the loving wife who submits to her husband in an unselfish manner and who 'is willing to give up her own wishes and feelings for his sake'.[93] Acton's work was issued in several revised editions, and in later editions he deplored the 'spirit of insubordination' displayed in women 'who regard themselves as martyrs when called upon to fulfil the duties of wives'.[94] This may have been a tribute to the increased dissemination of the feminist message of sexual autonomy.

Haslam's strictures on the necessity of the moral and physical health of parents would have been standard in the 1870s: 'Vigor, manhood, intelligence and purity are the paramount conditions of perfect reproduction ... The primary condition, therefore, of pure and healthy parentage, is that we should ourselves be pure and healthy.'[95] Pat Jalland, in her *Women, Marriage and Politics*, remarks: 'There is ample evidence throughout the years 1860 to 1914 that the state of each partner's health was very seriously considered by the families before agreement was given to marriage.'[96] Marriage manuals argued, as did *Duties of Parents*, that those suffering from ill health had no right to marry and 'thus run the risk of entailing other diseases upon children'.[97]

Scholarship has challenged the stereotype of Victorian sexuality as prudish or repressed. Steven Marcus's *The Other Victorians* graphically depicts the seamy underside of Victorian life. Peter Gay, in *The Bourgeois Experience*, gives evidence, mainly from contemporary personal journals, that many women enjoyed a healthy sexual relationship. Michel Foucault demonstrates the potency and multifaceted reality of the sexual discourse of that era.[98] Evident from the work of revisionists, and indeed from contemporary writers who were avowedly anti-sensualist such as Haslam and his mentor Acton, is the potent image of sexuality that prevailed in public discourse in the Victorian era. Haslam saw sexuality, specifically male sexuality, almost as an inherent character flaw, which had to be overcome by the development of will-power and the cultivation of good habits. Although 'not all Victorian women closed their eyes, opened their legs and thought of England, nor did all husbands tell their wives that ladies did not move ... widespread sexual anxieties and inhibitions should not be minimised.'[99]

Phyllis Rose presents a convincing scenario when discussing the subject of sexual satisfaction within the Victorian marriage. She argues that many cultural circumstances worked against it:

The inflexible taboo on pre-marital sex for the middle-class women meant, among other things, that it was impossible to determine sexual compatibility before marriage. The law then made the wife absolute property of her husband and sexual performance one of her duties ... The legendary Victorian advice about sex, 'Lie back and think of England,' may be seen as not entirely comical if we realize that in many cases a distaste for sex developed from a distaste for the first sexual partner and from sexual performance which was essentially forced. In addition the absence of birth control made it impossible to separate sex from its reproductive function, so that to be sexually active meant the discomforts of pregnancy, the pain of childbirth, and the burden of children.[100]

Haslam was conscious of the possibility of disaster in the initial sexual experience of a marriage when he described the 'proverbial disenchantment' of
the honeymoon. In the catalogue above, Rose does not include the real dangers of death in childbirth, a point tellingly illustrated by Pat Jalland in her
discussion of marriage among the political elite: 'Among prominent politicians . . . Joseph Chamberlain lost his first wife in 1863, five days after the
birth of their second child. His second wife . . . Florence Chamberlain died
of shock or exhaustion during labour . . . Sir Charles Dilke's first wife,
Katherine, died . . . following the birth of a child.' The above are but a few
of the many examples given by Jalland who does not assert that 'the upper
classes suffered [maternal mortality] more than the masses'.[101] When one
considers that healthy well-nourished women, who would have enjoyed the
best available medical care, frequently died giving birth, one realizes how
fear of pregnancy must have affected sexual enjoyment, particularly for
women.

In *Duties of Parents* Haslam would appear to have accepted the patriarchal paradigm of marriage, where man is head of the household, which he
leaves to earn the means of support for his family, and to which he returns
to enjoy the love and ministrations of the wife who is the 'angel' of his
hearth and home. Haslam departs from this paradigm in one essential,
however, in that he recommends that the woman should enjoy the freedom
to stipulate the frequency, or infrequency, of sexual intercourse with her
husband. His arguments on the rights of the woman to bodily integrity
were an echo of John Stuart Mill: 'Among the barbarisms which law and
morals have not yet ceased to sanction, the most disgusting surely is, that
any human being should be permitted to consider himself as having a *right*
to the person of another.'[102] Haslam's own marriage did not, of course,
conform to the stereotype in that his wife was the breadwinner from the
mid-1860s.

Whether or not Thomas's remarks regarding the honeymoon period were
applicable to his own marriage and were instrumental in its evolution to
permanent celibacy, we do not know. It seems remarkable that Thomas, having discovered the so-called safe period and enthusiastically publicized it,
did not practise it in his own marriage. Perhaps by this time the celibate
habit had become so ingrained that there was no desire to resurrect what
may have been an unsatisfactory sexual relationship. Perhaps he felt it
would be a betrayal of his high ideals to abandon the self-control so successfully attained. He wrote in *Duties of Parents*: 'When once we have
accustomed ourselves to self-restraint for months together, it will become
easy to us; and every year will add to our power of self-control.'[103]

The marriage of John Stuart Mill and Harriet Taylor was also celibate.
Phyllis Rose's description of the Mills' relationship acknowledges the 'psychic' nature of that union:

To understand the story of Mill's affair with Harriet Taylor one must
appreciate the disgust for sex which marriage [to Taylor] had left her
with, the low estimation of sexual activity which they shared, and

their conviction that in each other they had found the highest companionship of which human beings were capable, a love compounded only of spirit and intellect, with no earthly dross, a love at the high end of the platonic ideal – the greatest goal life has to offer.[104]

In the *Early Draft* of his autobiography Mill wrote of Harriet and himself: 'We disdained, as every person, not a slave of his animal appetites must do, the abject notion that the strongest and tenderest friendship cannot exist between a man and a woman without a sensual relation.'[105] The ideal of sexual temperance within marriage must be viewed within the context of the prevailing sexual discourse of Haslam's day. Szreter argues that from the 1830s and 1840s onwards there was

> a consensus regarding the *normality* of self-control and moderation in sex as the sign of the properly adjusted spiritually healthy and civilised individual . . . Sexual self-control and sexual continence were now viewed as spiritually correct forms of conjugal behaviour, which incidentally implemented Malthusian prudence. Indeed, this was something which later in the century would come to assume the status of a grand social evolutionary goal.[106]

This theory elucidates Haslam's teaching and indeed his marriage. Having decided that no children were to be born to the marriage, the logical method of birth control was abstinence. The mystery is not the celibate marriage, but rather the closely argued and warmly defended birth control pamphlet which demonstrates that Haslam, at least briefly and timidly, saw fit to recommend the joys of sex for its own sake. As mentioned earlier, it may have been his work on prostitution and the Contagious Diseases Acts (CDAs) which caused him to re-evaluate his ideas on birth control. The objection of some feminists to birth control was based on the fear that women no longer had the excuse of possible pregnancy, 'they would be more than ever "a vehicle of men's pleasure".'[107] Readers of *The Marriage Problem* who held this point of view would have had their fears justified by Haslam's thesis. His suggested role for the young wife is that of a 'virtual prostitute' precisely because he appears to have subscribed to the notion of the stereotypical asexual woman. Josephine Butler insisted that the double standard of sexual morality, implicit in Haslam's solution for young men unable to control their passions in the *Marriage Problem*, had to go. The CDA campaign fought against 'the false idea that there is one code of morality for men and another for women . . . which has more or less coloured and shaped the whole of our social life'.[108] Repealers ultimately sought to purify the male. Josephine Butler argued that it was the male client 'backed by the medical lust of handling and dominating women', and not the prostitute, who was the source of moral and physical contagion.[109] Haslam's pamphlet on prostitution (1870) identified *'men's unchastity'* as the cause of prostitution.[110] His *Duties of Parents* demands chastity *within* marriage, giving credence to Anna's claim: 'We always practised what we preached.'[111] Haslam was no longer willing to preach that women should be sacrificed to male lust as 'the lesser of two evils'. Men henceforth were to subjugate and control such feelings and to endeavour to emulate the higher moral standards of women who 'are naturally finer and purer in their organisation', and 'in all matters respecting connubial indulgence ... should ... determine how frequently ... such indulgence is admissible'.[112] Haslam, in *Duties of Parents,* was still an advocate of family limitation. Now, however, small families were to be achieved by the 'power of self-command which will enable us to abstain from indulgence where parentage would be wrong'.[113] He gave advice on the optimal times for conception, which he gauged as the 'first three or four days after the cessation of the menstrual disturbance'.[114] Ironically, this work which eschews birth control and recommends intercourse for procreation only, is, by default, a much more accurate contraception primer than *The Marriage Problem.* If readers attempting to conceive obeyed Haslam's instructions on timing, and also his edict that intercourse other than for procreative reasons should be avoided, it is extremely unlikely that pregnancy resulted.

Duties of Parents also contains detailed advice on the moral and intellectual training of children that is high-minded rather than practical. Recommended reading for parents includes Mill's *Political Economy,* Trall's *Sexual Physiology*, Herbert Spencer's *Education* and *Social Statics,* Dr Miller's *Vital Force* and various volumes on child rearing. Although much of the advice in this manual is for the edification of the less privileged, the expected readership is middle class and educated. Haslam suggested the publication of a series of 'easy manuals' produced in 'simple language' published at one or two shillings per volume, as these 'would prove an invaluable boon to parents of small means and imperfect culture'.[115] While emphasis was placed on moral training Haslam was reticent about the need for religious education:

> In the present distracted state of the world in matters of faith, the question of doctrinal instruction is full of difficulty; but parents are bound to investigate the truth for themselves and to countenance no religious creed which does not command their entire conviction. 'Prove all things; hold fast to what is good;' is a maxim which should guide us in this sceptical era.[116]

Haslam was qualified to write on the education of children. His experience as a teacher, and indeed as pupil, obviously coloured his advice to dutiful parents. He was opposed to boarding schools:

> [W]here boys and girls are banished for the greater part of the year beyond the range of parental observation, there is no limit to the danger. Their health may be broken down through insufficiency of food or exercise; their faculties may be injured by unsuitable tasks; their affections may be chilled through want of sympathy; their conscience may be hardened by oppressive punishments; their standard of character

may be lowered through the inculcation of mean principles; or their morals may be corrupted through the example of depraved school-fellows.[117]

He had, of course, been at boarding school himself. A contemporary at Mountmellick wrote: 'Parents and children seldom met. I was only home for two nights in three and-half years. No vacations. In these times we did not think of them.' In Mountmellick, a four-week vacation was officially granted in 1853.[118]

Teachers were not necessarily to blame if children turned out badly. 'Injustice to the many admirable men and women who devote their lives to the scholastic profession ... the fault lies, not in the deficiencies of the teacher, but in the evil disposition which those children received at birth.'[119] There is evidence from Ackworth School that Thomas Haslam was an able teacher. The Ackworth Old Scholars' Association described his temporary appointment as 'Master on Duty' in glowing terms: 'Found school in great disorder', but in three months 'by his resolute will [he] converted a tangle of confusion into a perfect machine.'[120]

While Haslam did not 'underrate those elegant accomplishments' of a 'liberal education', he recommended as vital a knowledge of the 'rights and duties' involved in 'complex relations with our fellows'. An understanding of:

> [t]he relations of husband and wife, of parent and child, of employer and employed, of landlord and tenant, of the people and the government; the laws which regulate the production and distribution of wealth; the nature and use of money; ... the origin and cure of pauperism ... the influence of co-operation with trades unions in extending or reducing pauperism

was vital for people to ensure they were not unknowingly either victims of injustice or that they did not inflict it upon others.[121]

Some letters survive which reveal a positive response to *Duties of Parents*. As already mentioned, Elizabeth Wolstenholme judged it to be a 'most valuable' book.[122] Maria Tod, mother of Irish feminist Isabella, thought the topic discussed was of 'vital importance' and had been 'judiciously handled'.[123] Mrs Tod subsequently sent the book to her son James in Melbourne where it was passed around among a group of friends. One of them, a Mr Evans, wrote that, despite the opinion of two clergymen who thought the aim of connubial temperance 'impossible' and 'against nature', he thought 'so far as a man is a true Christian will his spiritual nature govern his animal nature & make its instincts subservient to their proper ends'. Haslam's 'little book' was responsible for the 'commencement of their real union of happiness', where husbands and wives having read the book had acted upon its 'principles'. Another acquaintance of Tod, Mr Featherstonehaugh, 'the English Church clergyman lately inhibited from preaching on account of his disbelief in eternal punishment', wanted a dozen copies sent to him.[124]

Isabella Tod forwarded this letter to Anna Haslam asking that copies of the book be sent to Australia. Isabella, friend and co-worker with Anna in many causes, expressed concern that the Haslams 'have had a great deal of expense with the book' and assured her that 'Mr. F.' wished to purchase it.[125] Another correspondent thought the book 'perfectly free ... from any religious expressions or rather dogmatic & sectarian expressions', but was saddened because the ideals laid down in the book were unlikely to be realized. However, she was aware that 'Mr. Haslam would not be writing to his "highest light" nor in accordance with his best principles' had he sought more attainable goals.[126]

Haslam had again sent a book to Newman with a covering letter that courageously accused him of not treating his 'Œdipus [*The Marriage Problem*] with fairness'. Newman, although he had not had time to read the book, immediately recognized the considerable difference between the two works: 'I never could have guessed the same person to have written the Œdipus and this new book ... At first sight I regard the two to have come from opposite sides.' He judged Haslam to be 'now *more ascetic*' than he was: 'if I differ from you now it is because I find you outran me in your claims of subduing instinct & passion.' He '*most warmly*' agreed with all he had to say 'about the wife being arbiter in this sacred matter'.[127] In a second letter, Newman had some advice for Haslam: 'If you wish your treatise to be effective, the more you cut off from it what is superfluous & what stirs up doubt or opposition, the better ... On matters so secret & sacred & little discussed premature dogmatism is very irritating to people.' Newman was anxious to avoid further correspondence: 'I will try and say nothing which shall require a new letter from you.' He challenged Haslam's suggestions that the unfit must not be allowed to breed: 'Indirect methods must be used ... To *forbid* their marriage would be a crime; to *forbid* their propagation, an insanity. To *dissuade*, seems to me a waste of labour.' He thought doctors had 'enormously' exaggerated the 'doctrine of hereditary weakness'. Bad rearing is 'worse by far than unfavourable parentage.' Newman was 'very glad' that Haslam had 'renounced Œdipus'.[128]

Haslam's *Duties of Parents* was written at a time when he had become involved in the campaign against the Contagious Diseases Acts. The campaign and the research for his pamphlet, *A Few Words on Prostitution* (1870), may have affected his thinking on birth control, abstinence and sexuality. One of the arguments against the CDAs was that the legislation facilitated promiscuity, prostitution and disease. The advocates of the acts believed prostitution to be a necessity. Haslam may have reconsidered his birth control pamphlet, which also suggested that prostitution, or a compliant wife, was a necessity for passionate young men. The CDAs and Haslam's pamphlet will be discussed in the next chapter.

Essentially Haslam's message in *Duties of Parents* was of the necessity of learning new habits of sexual continence, of thrift, hygiene and of moral and physical purity. Parents who succeeded by a combination of will-power and education in acquiring these admirable traits would in turn pass them on to their offspring, ensuring the ultimate perfection of mankind. He privileged motherhood, particularly the role of the mother as principal moral educator of the child. Lucy Bland has written that feminists of the late nineteenth century 'were in favour of the learning of new habits – new ways of thinking and behaving'. Her description of how these were to be learnt and transmitted could be used to describe the message of Haslam's book:

> Learning these new habits would entail an extensive programme of education – of children, men and women. Children were to be given a basic programme of sex education while men were to be taught the value of living by an equal moral standard. Women needed to be educated about human physiology and sexuality, both for their own protection, and also to equip them, as mothers, for the task of teaching their children.[129]

Haslam stressed the need for such an education programme. Parents who so educated themselves would pass on to their offspring the benefits of their learning and the character traits that it fostered. His message that women should have the right to negotiate how frequently, or better still, how seldom, sexual intercourse occurred within a marriage, was full of optimism for the eventual betterment of mankind. His beliefs were typical of mainstream feminist thought as explained by Bland: 'Armed with such knowledge [of human physiology and sexuality] . . . wives . . . would insist on the highest morality from their husbands . . . through the law of inheritance, women would pass on to their offspring the moral tendencies of their husbands and themselves.'[130]

While to the modern reader, Haslam's *Duties of Parents* may seem naive and impossibly high-minded, his ideas were typical of a strand of Victorian thinking. His cited authorities included respected medical men and social theorists. The work is typical of the Victorian marriage manual as described by Porter and Hall: 'What the young needed was not sexual knowledge but sermons in temperance and alternative mores, the pleasures of domestic affection and companionship and improvement, education, thrift, character building and piety. Sexual self-restraint now became a central virtue in a new kind of . . . anti sensualist matrimonial advice manual.'[131] Thomas Haslam's works on birth control and morality are important indicators of his growth as a feminist thinker. Although an advocate of the equality of women since the 1850s, he was influenced by contemporary beliefs in the stereotype of the asexual woman and in the 'coital imperative' of male desire. Between *The Marriage Problem* (1868) and *Duties of Parents* (1872), he underwent a change of heart regarding his theories of male sexuality. Henceforth he demanded of men what society had hitherto demanded of women. His commitment to the limitation of family size continued, but his suggested method was now predicated on male self-control. With his belief in the stereotypical Victorian passionless woman, his birth control pamphlet, for all its recommended 'natural' method, could only spell further exploitation of these women. Haslam now demanded from others the standards by which he had lived since his own marriage in 1854.

4

'Mrs Haslam has worked well in Dublin'[1]: An account of the Haslams' participation in the campaign against the Contagious Diseases Acts

The campaign against the Contagious Diseases Acts (CDAs) was enthusiastically supported by Thomas and Anna Haslam. Anna was a prominent member of the Ladies' National Association for the Abolition of Government Regulation of Vice (LNA); Thomas contributed a pamphlet[2] to the debate and, as a member of the National Association for the Repeal of the Contagious Diseases Acts (NARCDA), was present on the platform at many public meetings for the repeal of the legislation.[3] The Haslams' commitment to the repeal of the CDAs was sustained; Anna later said: 'That fight . . . took us eighteen years.'[4] The CDAs, introduced in 1864 in specified garrison towns in Great Britain and Ireland, were an attempt by the government to address the alarming prevalence of venereal disease among the military. The Acts allowed for the compulsory examination of suspected prostitutes for venereal disease and for their subsequent detention and treatment. The campaign was a watershed in the development of feminist activism; it enabled women to speak in public on what was hitherto unspeakable, to organize and to lobby. The LNA has been described as a 'political nursery in which women learnt to withstand male hostility, and acquired tactical skills'.[5] The campaign against the Acts also clarified feminist objections to the prevailing sexual double standard.

Foucault has defined the age of Victoria as an era in which 'sex was driven out of hiding and constrained to lead a discursive existence'.[6] The result was less a discourse on sex than a 'multiplicity of discourses produced by a whole series of mechanisms operating in different institutions'. Ironically, such discourses testify to a massive focus on sexuality, the ultimate area of privacy. It emerged as a major social issue and permeated political debate and public policy. Foucault called it an 'explosion of distinct discursivities which took form in demography, biology, medicine, psychiatry, psychology, ethics, pedagogy, and political criticism'.[7] Haslam, in his pamphleteering, was in his own, albeit minor way, a part of this discursiveness; he cited demographic, biological, medical and ethical authorities in support of his contribution to the sexual debate.

The 'multiplicity of discourse' defined by Foucault applies especially to the subject of prostitution; in the nineteenth century it became the target of scrutiny in a wide range of publications:

Parliamentary reports and state legislation, police statistics and
medical investigation, letters and articles in newspapers and periodicals, evangelical manifestos and religious sermons, novels and poems
. . . the prostitute was . . . the subject of social investigation and philanthropic concern and the focus of the developing science of moral
statistics.[8]

Medicine and the law assumed increasingly important roles in the construct
of the official norms of sexuality. As we have seen, the definition of norms
of sexual and moral behaviour was gender specific. The male sexual urge
was seen as active, 'inherent and spontaneous', while the female desire was
passive and responsive.[9] The perceived difference between active male and
passive female sexuality was encapsulated within a double standard,
producing a 'concept . . . of sexual mores which condones sexual activity in
men as a sign of "masculinity" whilst condemning it in women as a sign of
deviant or pathological behaviour'.[10] The domain of the sexually passive
middle-class lady was the private sphere of which she was guardian. She
was responsible for the construction and maintenance of domestic and
social order and her moral purity ensured that the home was a spiritual
haven for her husband and children. A contemporary journal summed up
the role and its rewards neatly:

High-minded, noble, delicate, trusting to her instincts and not
ashamed of the feminine quality of her brain . . . grateful for the
gracious duties of her home – grateful for the precious burden of
maternity – grateful that her path lies in sheltered ways.[11]

This definition of female sexuality and morality was class specific. Clear
boundaries were created between the 'respectable' lady's asexuality and the
prostitute's wantonness. The two types of women were seen to be diametri-
cally opposed and operating in separate spheres. Ironically, some opined
that the existence of the prostitute was essential to the preservation of the
purity of the lady in the private sphere.[12]

In Britain, between mid-century and 1870, when Thomas Haslam
published his pamphlet on prostitution, the recognized authority on the
subject was William Acton whose *Prostitution Considered in its Moral, Social
and Sanitary Aspects* was published in 1857 and reissued in a revised edition
in 1870. Acton, born in 1814, was a member of the Royal College of Surgeons
who had studied in Paris under one of the foremost men in the field of
venereology, Phillipe Riccord.[13] Haslam respected Acton as a medical
authority and quoted his theories in *Duties of Parents*. In the preface to the
1870 edition of *Prostitution Considered*, Acton acknowledged that in the
twelve years that had elapsed since the first edition, 'prostitution and its
attendant evil has been the subject of anxious inquiry', for which he could
'claim without vanity, to have in some measure, paved the way'.[14] The legislation to which Acton referred was the Contagious Diseases Acts of 1864,
1866 and 1869.

In 1864 the British parliament passed legislation that provided for the physical examination of alleged prostitutes for evidence of venereal disease.[15] This legislation permitted the apprehension of a suspected 'common prostitute' within ten miles of the major naval and military stations of eleven designated 'protected districts' including, in Ireland, the Curragh, Cork and Queenstown. (The 1866 Act allowed for an extra two designated districts with the addition of Chatham and Windsor.) The alleged prostitute was subjected to a compulsory medical examination by a naval or military surgeon. If she were found to be suffering from venereal disease, she became liable to detention in a lock ward for a period (by 1869) of up to nine months, during which she was compelled to undergo fortnightly inspection. Refusal to comply, or the leaving of the hospital without formal discharge, was a summary offence for which a gaol term could be imposed. There was no right of appeal and no recourse to habeas corpus. Only women were examined; no attempt was made to inspect their clients. The 1869 Act extended the provisions of the 1866 to a further six stations, lengthened the maximum period of incarceration to nine months and allowed for five days' detention of the women if they were 'unfit' for examination (i.e. menstruating).[16]

The CDAs highlight the confusion that underpinned the dominant sexual ideology of the period and they provided 'one of the major sites where conflicting Victorian views on sexuality were both expressed and generated'.[17] They were not designed to rid the protected districts of commercial sex but rather to ensure that the concomitant venereal infection was held in check.[18] The supporters of the Acts regarded prostitution as a necessary evil. Unlike Haslam, they did not see the prostitute as victim, but as vendor of commercial sex and, as such, a conduit of disease. Their concern was the provision of uninfected sex to military and naval consumers of the commodity. The theory that young men's health was dependent on regular sexual relations was also relevant to the formulating of the Acts. Because the marriage of enlisted men was restricted by army regulations to about six per cent of the total the '"bachelor army" was accustomed to turn to prostitutes, hordes of whom were to be found in dockyards and garrison towns'.[19] The obvious solution of allowing such men to marry was contrary to government thinking at the time:

> the government could not rely on the loyalty of the socially under-privileged, it had to prevent troops and citizens from acquiring common interests and common ties. Instead of creating a national citizen militia therefore, a bachelor professional army without family ties was assembled in large depôts and moved regularly about the country.[20]

To Haslam, soldiers were *compulsory* celibates', but he had little sympathy for their plight; he called them the 'dregs of our population' and advocated, as did many of the opponents of the Acts, that the men be allowed to marry. He questioned 'whether the reputed security derived from our army and navy is adequate compensation for the moral evils which they inflict upon the community'.[21] Many of those who opposed the CDAs 'were driven by the logic of the situation into becoming army reformers'.[22] Haslam called for change also: 'A higher class of men must be allured into the profession, must be remunerated in proportion to the intrinsic value of their services, and must be encouraged to marry in the interest of public morals.'[23]

The military débâcle of the Crimean War, where more soldiers died in hospital than had been killed on the field, profoundly shocked the people of the United Kingdom. Press reports revealed the bestial living conditions of the soldier in the field. The ensuing Royal Commission on the Health of the Army in 1857 acknowledged that there was a higher incidence of venereal disease among the armed services than in the civilian population. An army statistical department produced annual statistics that listed the incidences of venereal disease and ultimately led to the CDAs of 1864. The returns on admissions to hospital of military and naval men show a very high rate of hospitalization for venereal diseases. (In Limerick and Dublin 40 per cent; almost 35 per cent in Cork and 37 per cent in the Curragh.)[24] Acton, having analysed the Army Medical Department Report for 1868, wrote: 'It appears, then, from this and subsequent statistics that about one in three soldiers suffers from some venereal complaint.' The percentage among naval personnel was lower. A naval report for 1864 and 1865 revealed that over 11 per cent of the total force suffered from either gonorrhoea or syphilis: 'These diseases (venereal) appear as a certain sequence of leave ... Our men contracted the disease in Plymouth and Portsmouth and a few cases occurred after leave at Cork.'[25]

Haslam's pamphlet on prostitution was published within weeks of the start of the organized campaign for the repeal of the Acts. We do not know if the publicity attendant on the start of the campaign was the catalyst for the pamphlet, but it is clear that he meant it to be a contribution to the arguments against the Acts. It is interesting to compare his general remarks on prostitution with those of William Acton, who defined the prostitute as

> a mere instrument of impurity; degraded and fallen she extracts from the sin of others the means of living, corrupt and dependent on corruption, and therefore interested directly in the increase of immorality – a social pest, carrying contamination and foulness to every quarter to which she has access.[26]

He saw prostitution in economic terms of supply and demand: '[The] desire of the male is the want that produces the demand, of which prostitution is a result, and which is, in fact, the artificial supply of a natural demand.'[27] Haslam, in his pamphlet, defined economic necessity as one of the main causes of prostitution. The poverty of young men delayed marriage thereby creating a demand for prostitution. The lack of employment for uneducated women was a major cause of their becoming prostitutes.[28]

Acton did not support Lecky's thesis that the prostitute 'Herself the supreme type of vice ... is ultimately the most efficient guardian of virtue.

But for her, the unchallenged purity of thousands of happy homes would be polluted.'[29] He disagreed with the model of prostitute as the 'safety valve of society' and asserted that any 'diminution of the number of prostitutes' would not mean 'that the man who will use a harlot is prepared to insult or injure a modest woman'.[30] Haslam did not address this question, although we know from *The Marriage Problem* that he recommended birth control in marriage as a means of keeping young men away from prostitutes; in his later work, however, self-control was recommended.

Haslam's pamphlet is an unambiguously feminist tract. He was unequivocal in blaming *'men's* unchastity and *men's* injustice' (the italics are his) as being 'mainly responsible for this crying wrong [prostitution]'. He derided the theory 'that chastity is dangerous to the health of men and that therefore its violation is lawful, if not even praiseworthy'. He could not find any evidence for this, but even 'were it ever so true that chastity is incompatible with health . . . it is nevertheless our duty to sacrifice even our health, rather than commit a brutal outrage for its preservation. The virtue of our women is infinitely more important than the health of our male fornicators.'[31] Acton, as a medical man, was cynical that celibacy caused ill-health in young men: 'It is asserted by some writers that indulgence in sexual intercourse is necessary for the male as soon as he has attained puberty'; he wonders if this theory is 'not simply due to the imagination of prejudiced advocates of immorality and wickedness'. Even if such a theory were true, resorting to prostitutes was not the answer; rather 'the cure is to be found in the cricket-field, the river, or the racquet-court'.[32]

Haslam subscribed unambivalently to the stereotype of the prostitute as victim whose adoption of the profession was the result of seduction and subsequent abandonment and, simultaneously, to the stereotype of the asexual respectable woman. Acton and Greg shared this latter perception. Acton wrote: 'The majority of women (happily for them) are not very much troubled with sexual feeling of any kind.'[33] Greg also wrote of the absence of 'ready, strong and spontaneous desire in women'.[34] There were some dissenting contemporary voices; Dr Culverwell, member of the Royal College of Surgeons, asserted that female sexual desire was healthy: 'The best test of their healthy condition will be the presence of desire and the enjoyment of the orgasm simultaneously with the husband.'[35] Many late twentieth-century writers on the period disagree that the contemporary perception of the Victorian woman was of an asexual being. Revisionists argue that representations of repressive and repressed Victorian sexuality were based solely on the writings of a few 'experts' such as Acton and Greg. They challenge the notion that Victorian women were viewed as passionless by citing the range of nineteenth-century popular medical advice, literature and personal documents that acknowledge and affirm the presence of female sexual feelings.[36] Haslam, however, would appear to have subscribed fully to the stereotype as defined by Acton: 'so pure-hearted as to be utterly ignorant of and averse to any sensual indulgence, but so unselfishly attached to the man she loves, as to be willing to give up her own wishes and feelings for his sake'.[37] This is precisely what Haslam recommended in

The Marriage Problem when he suggested that 'loving' young wives, irrespective of inclination, should surrender to the sexual imperative of their husbands' desire.[38] Nowhere in his prostitution pamphlet did Haslam suggest that a seduced woman may have desired seduction or even been the seducer. Nor did he differentiate between the sexuality of the 'respectable' woman and that of her less fortunate sister. Generally, there was not the same expectation of chastity from women of the lower classes. A government report of 1843 contained evidence of a 'particular deficiency . . . as to chastity' in women employed as agricultural workers: 'they seem hardly to comprehend or value it as a virtue'.[39] Haslam was not class specific in his remarks. His stressing of '*men's* unchastity and *men's* injustice' illustrates the point; he clearly did not see the fallen woman as contributing to her own downfall. He defined male sexual behaviour to women who subsequently, through necessity, become prostitutes, as 'the unchastity which sacrifices woman to an animal lust, the cruelty which deserts her when that lust has been appeased.' He called such men 'the *immolators* of woman . . . their original *betrayers* and their *subsequent co-partners* in the sin of fornication'.[40] He considered that all prostitutes were originally seduced and then abandoned and that such seduction is a greater evil than prostitution:

> Fornication with prostitutes is no doubt a fearful transgression; it is unspeakably degrading to both the victim and the participant; nevertheless in a moral and social point of view, it is infinitely less criminal than the original act of seduction followed by the desertion of the victim.

His solution was enforced marriage: 'In the eye of true morality the man who persuades a virgin girl to surrender to his passion, is bound to make her his wife, and to concede her every privilege to which his legal wife would be entitled.'[41] Presumably he meant a seduced and pregnant young woman. Perhaps in an era when arranged marriages were not unusual, to condemn a couple to a marriage which was a legal punishment to one of them, was not as bizarre a notion as it appears today. It is, after all, a version of the clichéd shotgun wedding; in this case the agent of coercion is the state rather than the irate father of the 'ruined' girl. Marriage, even under duress, was perhaps a better option than the nineteenth-century version of single-parenthood for a young woman. The practicalities of proving seduction or of finding a seducer who had abandoned his 'victim' were not addressed. Interestingly, however, Haslam's agenda for reform includes full political participation by women: 'Whether such a measure will be speedily enacted it is impossible to predict; but it is certain to be enforced as soon as our women are allowed their rightful voice in the passing of those laws upon which the well-being of both sexes is equally dependent.'[42]

W. R. Greg, in his influential article in the *Westminster Review* published in 1850, presented seduction and abandonment as the precursors to a life of prostitution: 'For that almost irresistible series of sequences, by which one lapse from chastity conducts ultimately to prostitution.'[43] William Rathbone

Greg, a failed cotton manufacturer, earned his living by writing on a variety of topics. His work on prostitution was 'surprisingly direct for its time . . . it represented the first major penetration of this emotionally difficult discussion into the regular reading matter of the middle classes'.[44] Greg pleaded with his readers to regard 'these unfortunate creatures rather as erring and suffering fellow-creatures, than as the outcasts and Pariahs they are now considered'. He argued that the fallen woman 'is driven into prostitution by the weight of all society pressing upon her'.[45] Haslam echoed these sentiments; he regarded 'respectable' women as the main offenders in the ostracizing of fallen women:

> The *social ostracism* which condemns the victim of seduction to a life of perpetual infamy, is a serious blot upon the high character of the women of our country . . . Cast forth from the parental roof with scorn ineffable, refused admittance into virtuous circles . . . they have often no available choice except prostitution, starvation or suicide.[46]

Modern feminist writers challenge the stereotype of the young woman driven into prostitution by seduction and betrayal: 'The stereotyped sequence of girls seduced, pregnant, and abandoned to the streets fitted only a small minority of women who ultimately moved into prostitution . . . Difficult circumstances precipitated the move into prostitution, but for many, that move still constituted a choice among a series of unpleasant alternatives.'[47] For many, it is argued, it was a matter of a temporary career move rather than ruin, caused by 'occupational dislocation' rather than 'premarital sexuality and pregnancy':

> For most 'public' women prostitution represented only a temporary stage in their life . . . registered women appear to have stayed in prostitution for only a few years . . . [A]s long as prostitution represented a temporary stage in a woman's career, and as long as she could leave it at her discretion, she was not irrevocably scarred or limited in her future choices.[48]

Acton, in 1870, acknowledged that many prostitutes subsequently married: 'I have every reason to believe, that by far the larger number of women who have resorted to prostitution for a livelihood, return sooner or later to a more or less regular course of life . . . the better inclined class of prostitutes become . . . wedded wives.'[49] Greg identified most prostitutes as coming from a class 'who were born and bred in sin; whose parents were thieves and prostitutes before then . . . Such abound in London, in Dublin, in Glasgow.' He acknowledged that there were prostitutes who are 'poor women [who] fall in the first instance, from causes in which vice and self-ishness have no share'.[50] Haslam, like Greg, was convinced that poverty and the 'want of remunerative occupation by a very large proportion of our unmarried women is perhaps a . . . powerful agent in its production'.[51] Greg's opinion that they were 'born and bred' to prostitution found no echo in Haslam's writing. As we have seen, however, the theory of inherited 'vice' was addressed at length in Haslam's *Duties of Parents,* but even there he would appear to specify the users of prostitutes' services as transmitters of vice rather than the women themselves. His espousal of the feminist cause was all inclusive.

In December 1869 the National Association for the Repeal of the Contagious Diseases Acts was formed in response to a proposed extension of the CDAs. NARCDA had excluded women from its first meeting. Although they were afterwards accepted as members this temporary exclusion resulted in the formation of the Ladies' National Association (LNA); this was a parallel, but separatist, female association. Josephine Butler emerged as the charismatic leader of this group, which mounted a veritable women's crusade against the Acts. She was a woman of striking appearance, a compelling and accomplished public speaker with the power to move an audience. A contemporary account described her as: 'Elegant, refined . . . she gave quite an original piquancy. She expressed herself with great simplicity; but by this simplicity she reached irresistible oratorical effects.'[52] Her personal contribution to the campaign was crucial as her 'strength of personality swept others along with her'.[53] Anna Haslam said of her effect on a Dublin audience: 'Mrs. Butler moved to tears some of the people who would not listen to her at the first.'[54] Her background was philanthropic and she had previously helped prostitutes from the docks in Liverpool to give up prostitution.[55] She had set up a Home of Rest for 'desperate destitute women', many of whom were affected by venereal disease, and was a leading member of the English movement for the higher education of women.[56]

Prior to the campaign against the CDAs there had been little female activism, although the Matrimonial Act of 1857 engendered some organized protest and the suffrage campaign was already in its infancy. The blatant double standard contained in the CDAs was the catalyst that moved women to organize and protest. Keith Thomas has written that the Acts represented the 'high water mark' of the double standard because of 'their bland assumption that prostitution was a permanent and necessary evil and by their direct application of the double standard in that all regulations and medical examination applied to the women alone'.[57] The CDAs were concerned 'wholly with women as conduits of infection . . . men were never targets of direct police and judicial scrutiny'.[58] The use of the euphemism 'public woman' to describe prostitutes in the Acts, neatly illustrates the dominant 'separate sphere' ideology in which the woman was guardian of the private sphere with responsibility for the construction and maintenance of domestic and social order. The oxymoronic juxtaposition of the word 'public' with 'woman' signified the very antithesis of the feminine ideal. Ironically, the protest against the injustice of the treatment of these public women was to give women activists a voice in the public arena; thus they too became, in a manner of speaking, 'public women', for which they were much criticized.

By the end of December 1869, a general committee of the Ladies' National Association had been formed and a *Ladies' Protest* published in the

Daily News signed by 124 women, many of whom were Quakers. The *Protest*'s stated objections to the Acts can be summarized as follows:

(a) the secrecy of its passing; the removal of legal guarantees from women,
(b) the ill-defined nature of the laws,
(c) the punishment of one sex only,
(d) the easing of the path to vice,
(e) the violation of women's feelings,
(f) their brutalizing by the measures of the Acts,
(g) the inability of the legislation to eradicate disease.[59]

Opponents of the Acts recognized that they gave legal status to the double standard of sexuality by setting up a system to attempt to provide disease-free prostitutes for the army and navy. Previously 'soldiers and sailors had been inspected weekly or fortnightly ... for venereal disease until Florence Nightingale and Sidney Herbert, operating through their Army Sanitary Commission, stopped it in 1859–60 (or in about 1864 in the case of sailors) on the grounds that it was degrading'.[60]

The participation in the campaign by women was revolutionary. In 1870 society was unused to women speaking publicly. When the wives of Henry Fawcett and P. A. Taylor addressed a suffrage meeting in 1869, the men were criticized in parliament for permitting their wives to behave in such 'advanced' and 'unsexing' a manner. That women now spoke out on such matters as venereal disease, prostitution and internal gynaecological examinations was unprecedented. Josephine Butler quoted a member of parliament's perplexed response to the 'revolt of the women': 'It is quite a new thing; what are we to do with such an opposition as this?'[61] The campaigns against the CDAs raised questions on the nature of prostitution, and engendered debate on whether it was capable of ever being eradicated or was an inevitable result of the human condition which, in the public interest, should be regulated. Thomas Haslam's pamphlet of March 1870, completed within three months of the *Protest*, roundly condemned the CDAs. He called the Acts 'a dangerous piece of legislative bungling' and described them with palpable anger:

> Those Acts provide that in various naval and military stations, scattered over the Kingdom, any woman *suspected* of prostitution may be dragged before a magistrate, and condemned to a periodical inspection of her person by a male surgeon, under the penalty of protracted imprisonment; that where affected with disease she shall be secluded in hospital until restored to health; and that when thoroughly *disinfected* she shall be let loose upon society, under a medical certificate which proclaims to the world that she is once more free to ply her hateful traffic, and may now be abused without risk by the licentious sons and husbands of her district.[62]

The language of this passage is interesting. It is simultaneously angry and disdainful. The *suspected* prostitute is dragged rather than brought before a magistrate. She is subsequently 'let loose' when '*disinfected*' and thus is enabled to 'ply her hateful trade'; yet she is the victim, as she is abused by men of the district, albeit without risk to them as a result of her disease-free status. The men who used her services were licentious, she was not. Men, as abusers, were described in terms of the respectable women to whom they were husbands and sons. Although Haslam saw the prostitute as the victim of male lust, rather than the cause of it, his use of language suggests a parallel conviction that he saw her as dangerous and untamed. The 'certificate' which proclaimed their disease-free status sometimes led to the holders' claim to be the 'Queen's women', a point repeatedly made by anti-CDA campaigners.[63]

Haslam's repetition of points raised in the *Protest* suggests that he was familiar with it. He objected to the legislation being 'smuggled through the House of Commons ... without discussion or even the cognizance of the majority of the members'. It did not 'diminish vice', but by removing the 'natural penalties' it encouraged the prostitute in her 'profligate career' especially as it did not seek to reform the 'guilty sufferers'.[64] Haslam was not alone in thinking venereal disease a 'natural penalty' for immorality. Sir Samuel Solly, President of the Royal Medical and Chirusurgical Society, said that syphilis was 'intended as a punishment for our sins and we should not interfere in the matter'.[65] Such an opinion inevitably raises the question that if sexually transmitted disease were a 'natural' punishment for the sin of fornication, was it appropriate to cure it?

Haslam objected, as did the *Ladies' Protest*, to the 'compulsory introspection of the unfortunate women by male examiners' and called it 'a brutal and degrading outrage'. He pointed out the double standard employed in examining and treating only the women and called the 'exemption of their male associates from a like examination' a 'scandalous partiality'. He was convinced that the 'arbitrary powers which these Acts invest the Superintendent of Police are liable to flagrant abuse and opposed to the whole spirit of our constitution'.[66] Haslam dubbed the CDAs 'a disgrace to our statute-book'. Compulsory inspection must be abandoned or, at very least, be 'extended to the profligate of both sexes'. Thus, the double standard, which justified male access to prostitutes, but exempted them from responsibility or punishment for the spreading of venereal disease, would appear to have been a major factor in Haslam's objection to the Acts. He conceded, however, that the establishment of the 'free hospitals' was a good thing.[67]

The standard objections to the CDAs, aired by the *Ladies' Protest*, and reiterated by Haslam, appear to have been justified. Each of the Acts was passed without either public or parliamentary debate:

> The 1864 Act had its first, second and third readings at two o'clock in the morning in a thin House of Commons. There was no discussion. It was the product of a secret committee of Army, Admiralty and medical experts, and appears never to have gone before Cabinet. The 1866 Act . . . too was devised by a secretive committee of medical mili-

tary experts who took no evidence from witnesses likely to be adverse. The 1869 Act . . . also derived from a secret select committee.[68]

Indeed it was alleged that Queen Victoria herself supposed the 1864 Act to refer to veterinary rather than human disease.[69] An uncited reference in an early work on the women's movement reveals that earlier legislation had been considered but 'Lord Melbourne had not been able to face the thought of taking such an Act to the young Queen for signature'. It was possible to obtain her signature in 'the first year of her widowhood when she was giving less attention than usual to public affairs'.[70]

The charge that the Acts removed 'every guarantee of personal security which the law has established' appears to be sustainable. The Acts did not define 'common prostitute', and allowed women to be detained on the suspicion of the Metropolitan Police who were drafted into the protected districts in order to enforce the Acts.[71] In Cork, however, it would appear that the local constabulary operated the Acts: [T]he management of the matter is in the charge of one of the constabulary constables, who has been in Cork for the last 20 years.'[72] The police did not have to prove that the women engaged in sexual acts for money.[73] Although the question of police propriety was hotly contested between the proponents of the Acts and their opponents, it is undeniable that 'slack legal drafting and enlargement of the powers of a sole policeman acting behind closed doors with a sole magistrate seemed designed to breed persecution and corruption'.[74] Repeal campaigners frequently complained that women who were not prostitutes were challenged by police. The charge that the Acts punished one sex only was undeniable. Although sailors and soldiers had been inspected regularly until 1859–60, and some were inspected afterwards, this was a 'discretionary' ruling made by the particular regiment or ship. Prostitutes in the protected districts alone were subject to the inspection law. One could argue that for practical reasons, it was easier to identify a 'public woman' and to treat her, than it was to identify her clients. Undoubtedly, however, the laws' portrayal of men as innocent of all responsibility in the spreading of disease enshrined in law the double standard of sexual morality. [75]

It is likely that the Acts did ease the path to vice by seeming to make it safer, as men now had access to 'clean' prostitutes in the subjected areas. As women only were punished and regulated by the Acts, men were not only absolved from all responsibility for the spreading of disease but were also lulled into a false sense of security by the existence of certified prostitutes. It is difficult to ascertain to what extent women were brutalized by the physical examination, as there is conflicting evidence on this point. Inspection conditions were 'briskly coarse' and took place in 'uncurtained huts'.[76] The proponents of the Acts argued that, as the women were brutalized by their profession, it would not be possible to degrade them further. Opponents of the Acts provide most of the evidence of the women's reaction to 'the indescribable compulsory surgical atrocities of the examination room', and testimony from women of their ill-treatment became the standard stuff of repeal speeches.[77] There were, however, instances of prostitutes refusing examination, which supporters of the Acts claimed was the result of their having 'been put up to it' by ladies:

> They speak in tones of strong indignation of those people of good intentions, no doubt, but who have aided and abetted them in breaking the law . . . The girls told me they were ladies who go into their houses and advise them not to obey the law, and tell them that they will be supported in their resistance of the law, and that they have only to club together and in time the Act of Parliament will be altered.[78]

The charge that the CDAs would not diminish venereal disease was a valid one. 'Syphilis and gonorrhoea were *never* conclusively cured during the nineteenth century . . . [T]he only real preventative then, as now, was careful sexual practice or chastity.'[79] The disease could return after the disappearance of superficial symptoms. Complete cure was not possible until the availability of penicillin, almost seventy years after the CDAs were repealed. The repealers' theories were vindicated in that moral and economic improvements were more likely to ameliorate venereal diseases than inspection of prostitutes, particularly when their clients were not examined.

Many of the prime movers in the campaign in England were known to the Haslams. F. W. Newman, Haslam's indefatigable correspondent, was a prominent repealer and was also the first honorary secretary of the Bristol Suffrage Society founded in 1868.[80] J. S. Mill testified against the Acts to the Royal Commission in 1871, as 'infringements of personal liberty'.[81] Elizabeth Wolstenholme Elmy, who wrote to Haslam praising his *Duties of Parents*, is credited with asking Josephine Butler in 1869 'to organize a woman's campaign against the Acts'.[82] Isabella Tod from Belfast, a friend of Anna and Thomas Haslam, was prominent in the campaign; she frequently addressed meetings and was a member of the London Executive of the LNA.[83]

Although Haslam did not mention Ireland in his pamphlet, there were three Irish 'subjected districts': Cork, Queenstown and the Curragh.[84] The subject of prostitution in Ireland, as in Great Britain, was a high-profile media issue. The *Cork Examiner* frequently complained of the ubiquitous presence of prostitutes; in 1860 it was noted that great numbers of prostitutes were present on the streets of Cork, 'lurking in all the corners, flaunting throughout all thoroughfares, they make the night hideous with their riot and their shame'.[85] Mr James Curtis FRCS, senior surgeon of the Cork General Hospital and South Infirmary, in medical practice in Cork for twenty-three years, stated in evidence to the select committee:

> I believe there was no place so immoral as the city of Cork prior to 1869 . . . it was no unusual thing to see, at the end of the lanes, a lot of half-dressed prostitutes, drunk and going through the streets, even in the daytime . . . I believe when the Acts came into force there were some 500 or 600 registered prostitutes.[86]

A Cork citizen stoutly refuted Curtis's claims that, as a result of the Acts, prostitution had reduced dramatically in the city. The writer quoted Curtis's assertion that 'there now remains in the district but 181, of which latter there are usually in hospital, prisons, and workhouses 104, leaving . . . in Cork, Queenstown and an area around them of 10 miles, but 77 at large', and went on:

> If we might venture to believe our own eyes and ears, we should judge that the flaunting girls who throng the streets in the evening and by night and who sometimes add . . . the good-natured assurance 'I'll guarantee you' were prostitutes . . . encouraged in audacity and elevated in position by government guarantee.[87]

Reverend Thomas O'Reilly, who was, like Curtis, in favour of the Acts, stated that 'in or around' 1866, when playing cricket in the public park in Cork, he had seen 'scenes of gross immorality at five o'clock in the evening'.[88] An opponent of the legislation, Mr Henry Richardson, Register of the Court of Probate, also conceded that extensive numbers of prostitutes plied their trade 'openly in the streets'.[89]

It is impossible to know how many prostitutes operated in the 'subjected districts'. The 1861 census stated that seventy prostitutes operated in County Kildare, a figure very likely to be an underestimate. In 1855, within a few months of the occupation of the Curragh by the military, there were already complaints of 'the numbers of loose and impure' camp-followers. Naas Gaol was crowded with the 'abandoned prostitutes of Ireland'.[90] The women were described as 'poor wretches . . . in ditches and bush dwellings'. These dwellings, 'nothing but a furzy bush', were approximately nine feet by seven, and the roof was 'not more than four feet from the ground'. They were known as number 1 bush, number 2 bush, etc. Altogether there were ten bushes 'with about sixty inhabitants'.[91] The women suffered not only from hunger and cold in their makeshift dwellings but also from 'the brutality and recklessness of the soldiers. To be knocked down and kicked by fellows half mad with drink is an everyday occurrence.'[92] The women were known as 'wrens' as they 'nested' in the furze; the nests were actually 'makeshift huts along the perimeter of the Curragh army camp'.[93] In the Report of the Royal Commission in 1871, they were described as being 'in the most degraded and most diseased state . . . in the habit of burrowing into the ground like rabbits . . . in a constant state of filth and covered with vermin'.[94] The 'wrens' were all Irish, and 'almost all young'. Many were said to have 'followed soldiers to the camp from distant towns and villages – some from actual love and hope, some from necessity or desperation', in doing so, conforming to the stereotype of the seduced and ruined girl. However, there were others who chose the life of a 'wren' as an alternative to 'roaming for field work'. For those 'the free loose life there has . . . attractions superior to those of the virtuous hovel at home'.[95]

In Queenstown, Co. Cork another 'subjected district', the living conditions of prostitutes were strikingly similar to those of the Curragh. In evidence to the Select Committee Mr Curtis, FRCSI testified: 'The Bush is a place in Queenstown where there are trees and furze, a wild space, overhanging the shore . . . there were about 20 to 25 or 30 women who lived there all the year round under the furze, just like the "wrens of the Curragh" . . . like animals.' This description, however, was said to be 'quite true of the women within the precincts of almost all the barracks'.[96] Curtis also painted a picture of the camp followers on the move: 'They are always moving about from Fermoy to Kinsale and the garrison towns and here and there, and sleeping under the forts, and behind the barracks.'[97] He was of the opinion that neither the 'wrens' of the Curragh nor the women of the 'Bush' in Queenstown were controlled by police prior to the Acts. The women in Queenstown 'were in a sort of a wood, and the police never interfered with them . . . it was hidden up by immense brakes of furze, and there was no public road within 150 yards'.[98]

Dublin, though not a subjected district, was under discussion by the Select Committee. A reference was made to a letter from the 'General Commanding the forces in Ireland' recommending extension of the CDAs to Dublin.[99] The 80th Regiment, when garrisoned for ten months in Dublin, had 'over 43 per cent of the unmarried portion of . . . [the] regiment . . . incapacitated for duty by venereal disease' which they had contracted in Dublin.[100] The Superintendent of the Westmoreland Lock Hospital, Dublin 'was greatly surprised the Contagious Diseases Prevention Act was not made to extend to Dublin'.[101]

We are given further insight into official thinking on the subject of prostitution in Ireland by recent work on the rules and regulations governing the behaviour of the Royal Irish Constabulary. Brian Griffin has shown that constables had to fulfil stringent service and financial requirements before they could get permission to marry. However, '[i]t was not uncommon for an R. I. C. man to get married with permission and to be dismissed when his wife gave birth less than nine months after the marriage'.[102] Such a birth was considered proof of 'criminal intercourse' and such intercourse was a dismissible offence. There was a much more lenient attitude to those who contracted venereal disease, or even to those 'found drunk and in uniform in brothels'. Such offences were punished 'merely by a fine'.[103] The rules concerning marriage had their origins in concerns for the image and security of the force; the fiancée's background was examined to ensure that her family was respectable. It would appear that evidence of premarital sexual intercourse, simultaneously rendered the *woman* unrespectable and unsuitable to be the wife of a police officer, and acknowledged that the man was guilty of the crime of premarital sex with a 'respectable' woman. Lenient punishment for consorting with an acknowledged unrespectable public woman would appear to have been predicated on the assumption that 'some bachelor policemen at least were going to pay prostitutes for their services', and that this was understandable.[104]

There was evidence that the CDAs were perceived by some prostitutes to have conferred a status upon them. Mr Kingston, honorary secretary of the 'Cork Midnight Mission and Female Temporary Home for more than 20 years,'[105] gave evidence to the Select Committee that since the legislation he had noticed a marked difference in the attitude of women to his 'friendly ministrations'. 'They are now Queen's women and do not want me . . . the Queen looks after them.'[106] In evidence to the Commission Mr S. Wolferstan explained the term as evolving from the description of soldiers as 'Queen's men': 'I think they now look upon it that the State keeps them clean for the use of soldiers and sailors, and therefore recognises them and gives them a sort of *status*.'[107] The *Shield* printed a letter from a Cork reader which stated: 'My friend Mrs. — of – Cork has an old servant who was walking home lately at about eight o'clock in the evening, when one of the town prostitutes pushed her off the flags rudely saying: "Make way for the queen's woman."'[108]

The 'Return of Women Committed to Cork Female Prison under the CDAs from June 1869 – May 1882 for Neglecting to Attend for Periodic Examination', comes to a total of eighteen, seventeen of whom were admitted once, and the other, three times. No dates are given and women are identified by initials. In age they ranged from twenty to forty-three with the majority in their twenties.[109] Evidence was given of the prevalence of gonorrhoea in Dublin which was not a subjected district. In 1881 Rawton Macnamara, senior surgeon of the Westmoreland Lock Hospital, Dublin, gave evidence to the Select Committee of a 'most extraordinary outbreak at the present moment of gonorrhoea; I never saw gonorrhoea so virulent as it is in the female patients at the present time.'[110] Significantly, Macnamara revealed his own prejudices in his statement that 'we only admit women to the Lock Hospital but amongst the private male patients who do me the honour of consulting me, I never saw anything so severe'.[111] His language suggests that he attached no blame to men who had contracted venereal disease. He testified that, of the 874 patients in the Lock Hospital in the year 1878–9, some were 'married women, and I would not call them prostitutes, girls that have been seduced and almost on the very first act have been diseased . . . and then we have the *habitués*' of whom he estimated 'professional prostitutes would number about 60 per cent'.[112] Statistics show that in 1880 the strength of the garrison in Dublin was 4,357, out of which there were 940 hospital admissions with primary syphilis and 605 admissions with gonorrhoea. This rate of admission amounted to 213.44 per 1000 admissions with syphilis and 138.82 per 1000 with gonorrhoea.[113] A table from Cork would appear to show a considerable reduction of first time admissions to Lock Hospital. These had fallen from 322 women in 1869 to 50 women in 1880.[114] However, a 'Table Showing the Average Fall per Cent in Primary Venereal Sores before and since the Acts in the Fourteen stations under the Acts, and the Gain or Loss of Improvement since the Acts' shows that of the fourteen areas analysed only Cork and Windsor

exhibit the special feature of having a higher average of primary venereal sores ever since the Acts have been applied to them. In Cork the fall had been fairly continuous for six years previous to the Acts, and the increase since amounts to 4.4 per cent of the amount of disease

existing when applied; and in Windsor the increase amounts to 9.8 per
cent of the amount existing when the Acts were applied.[115]

On the other hand 'The Curragh ... exhibits an improvement out of all
proportion to the English Stations of corresponding size.'[116] Analysis of the
statistics included in the official reports is difficult as tables frequently
appear contradictory. Published statistics included in the reports were
compiled by military statisticians and by medical experts on behalf of the
repeal organizations who challenged the official statistics. Repealers were
doubtful of the veracity of the published medical statistics on the incidence
of venereal disease among the armed forces in the subjected districts.[117]

An account in the *Shield* of an 'energetic appeal' by the Roman Catholic
Archbishop of Cork for 'the purpose of establishing Homes and
Reformatories for the poor fallen women of the subjected district', stated
that 'the prevalence of vice in Cork, and its public manifestation' was 'worse
than at any former period'. Obviously 'the Acts had confessedly not
produced in Cork even an outward semblance of improvement'. An anonymous 'gentleman' who was identified as a 'physician' was also quoted at
length. He forged the connection between the embryonic suffrage movement and the campaign for repeal: 'This Act is a powerful argument for the
enfranchisement of women ... [H]ad women a vote such a measure as this
... would never ... have disgraced the laws of England.'[118]

The *Shield*, organ of the repeal movement, was not an impartial journal,
but one is struck by its repeated assertions of the inefficacy of the Acts in
Cork:

> The intelligence as to the moral condition of Cork, gleaned from the
> columns of local newspapers, bitterly hostile to our movement, leads
> us to imagine that the spirit, energy and wonderful statistical inge-
> nuity shown by Inspector Anniss, are sadly needed to give a coat of
> whitewash to the operations and results of the Acts in this subjected
> city ... We have for a long time received convincing testimony that the
> condition of the streets in Cork is a public scandal.[119]

Inspector Silas Anniss, stationed at the subjected district of Devonport,
provided statistics showing 'a precipitous decline in the number of brothels,
pimps, prostitutes, and promiscuous juveniles' since the introduction of the
Acts.[120] Such statistics were thought by repeal campaigners to be exaggerated: 'In England ... we have had quires of foolscap wasted by police
returns as to the moral results which the Contagious Diseases Acts are said
to have achieved, and there has never been a dispute ... as to the accuracy
of or falsehood of those returns.'[121] Most evidence on the extent of prostitution in Cork reported in the *Shield*, is in the form of letters signed with a
pseudonym. 'A Resident' wrote that Winthrop Street and Pembroke Street
'from 11 p. m. to 3 a. m. form a promenade for a number of prostitutes of the
lowest class, together with their male companions'.[122] There is evidence of a
concentrated effort to clear the area south of the Lee of brothels by Father

Shinkwin, a curate of the parish of St Finbarr. He was reported to have been successful in closing a large number of brothels between June and August with the help of two plain-clothes Contagious Diseases constables.[123] From evidence given to the Commission, the Catholic clergy of Cork appear to have welcomed the CDAs, presumably as a deterrent to prostitution, as they surely would not have been in favour of them as a means of providing clean 'harlots' for the British army.

Anna Haslam spoke in her old age of her commitment to the campaign for the repeal of the CDAs: 'That fight . . . threw the suffrage movement back for ten years; we were all so absorbed in it.'[124] It could be argued, however, that the CDA campaign transformed women repeal workers from passive objects of ideological prescription into active agents in a political campaign to transform male sexual mores. Susan Kingsley Kent has written that the suffrage and CDA campaigns were 'all of a piece; they aimed at a redefini- tion of the roles and relationships between women and men'.[125] The CDA campaign, therefore, while it may have lessened the time available for the suffrage campaign, actually enhanced the ideological commitment to suffrage; it was an integral constituent of a movement that challenged the status quo. A male legislature had voted for the CDAs which enshrined the double standard of sexual morality in law; to prevent discriminatory legis- lation against women, not only must they have the parliamentary vote, but, as Thomas Haslam pointed out, seats in cabinet.

The archives of the Irish branches of the National Association for the Repeal of the Contagious Diseases Acts (NARCDA), and the Ladies' National Association (LNA) do not appear to have survived but their activ- ities were reported in the London based newspaper the *Shield*, which was the organ of the repeal movement. Accounts of the Irish campaign were also included in the LNA and NARCDA annual reports. The first issue of the *Shield* on 7 March 1870 mentioned the formation of a 'local association' on 21 February and also reported 'a meeting of ladies, convened by the Belfast branch of the LNA'. The agitation was reported to be 'progressing vigor- ously' in the north of Ireland and spreading to Waterford, Limerick, Clonmel, 'and many other places'.[126] On 23 March 1870, the *Shield* included Thomas Haslam's pamphlet on prostitution in its 'Publications Received' column.[127]

There was a 'splendid demonstration' in Belfast on the 28 April 1870. The report published in the *Shield* reveals evidence of an impressive organizing ability of the newly formed repeal movement. Publicity for the meeting had been handled well: 'thousands of small hand-bills had been extensively circulated, as well as large posters and advertisements, employed to inform the inhabitants of the atrocities of the law, and the intended demonstrations against it.' The Ulster Hall 'was completely filled'. The demonstration was composed entirely of prominent men, including aldermen, justices of the peace, clergymen and doctors. Although the meeting opened with a prayer and was addressed by various clergymen, it was not overtly religious in tone. While the immorality of the Acts was deplored, it was pointed out that the act discriminated against the poor, and that it was 'contrary to all precedent . . . that protection should be withdrawn from the sex which stood in the greatest need of it'. Among the many resolutions passed, Revd Chadwick moved that the meeting 'objects to the Acts as unfair in their operation, exposing one sex to penalties from which the partners of their guilt are exempted'. In a powerful polemic against the double standard, Chadwick stated that while women were subjected to 'scandalous outrage . . . the man, viler far, who sins for lust, not bread . . . is allowed to escape without a hair of his head being touched'. A speaker felt the Acts were 'wholly inapplicable in Ireland'.[128]

The inaugural meeting of a Dublin Local Association 'to promote the Repeal of the Acts' was held on 6 May 1870.[129] 'Petitions numerously signed' had been sent from Dublin 'and a strong feeling of indignation has been manifested. No fewer than 26 medical men have signed the petition of Repeal, some of them being men of decided eminence in their profession.'[130] Initially, Belfast would appear to have been the major Irish centre of the repeal movement:

> From Belfast a running line of petitions have been sent to Parliament, due to a great extent to the labours of Mrs. Porter, Miss Tod, Mrs. Lindsay and other Committee ladies. It appears that the inhabitants of Belfast have been almost unanimous in the subject, and distinguished members of the Queen's College have notably espoused your cause.[131]

Although the report states that 'Early in the Spring powerful committees of ladies were formed in Dublin and Belfast', the account of activity in Dublin is, in contrast to Belfast, laconic, demonstrating, perhaps, the relative inactivity of the committee. It does, however, acknowledge the importance of Anna Haslam to the embryonic movement. 'Mrs. Haslam has worked well in Dublin.'[132] Mrs Haslam and Miss Tod each contributed 2s 6d to the cause.[133] Isabella Tod was, of course, a leading campaigner for women's rights in Ireland and worked with Haslam on many feminist campaigns.

The annual reports of the Ladies' National Association reveal how the activities of the association inevitably led to an increased demand for votes for women. While the first report acknowledged the support of prominent women such as Harriet Martineau and Florence Nightingale, it also proclaimed the potential of all women as political campaigners. Committed and energetic campaigning by 'women everywhere' would force the House of Commons 'to surrender the Acts sooner or later'.[134] The writer of the first annual report also had a complete understanding of the emergence of the medical profession as powerful arbiters in sexual matters. It called for the 'purification of the medical profession' and for the 'defeat of those deadly materialist doctrines respecting the . . . necessity of unchastity . . . which together with the dogmatism and despotism of doctors, have begun of late years to exercise so undue and fatal an influence on our legislative councils'. Here is an implicit critique of the sexual double standard and of the principle of the regulation of 'vice' by the state. The report continued with a clever scriptural analogy comparing the 'conditions of the womanhood of our country with that of the afflicted woman . . . in the Gospel of whom it was said: "She had endured many things of many physicians."' It ended with a powerful feminist polemic against 'the medical lust for handling and dominating women . . . physicians, who, in the supposed interests of the body, trample underfoot . . . the unalienable rights of every woman, chaste or unchaste, over her own body'.[135]

Maria Luddy has commented that the Ladies' National Association in Ireland was 'a very localised and small affair' and that few, if any, members were Catholics.[136] In evidence before the Commission in 1871, a Catholic priest, 'the Reverend Mr. Maguire' from Cork stated that there were 'a great many ladies who exert themselves very much, and we do not approve of their putting placards before young females inviting them to read these Acts, of which women never heard before'. His description suggests an active campaign conducted by 'a certain portion of the community – of course I would not wish to give names, but they are composed chiefly of persons who are Nonconformists in religion'. The 'placards' were described as bringing into the public domain 'a subject that ought not appear before the public. I think it is a subject which any girl passing can read.' He added that invariably when a 'woman sees a thing which she should not read, she is almost sure to read it'.[137] While he was in favour of the Acts, he obviously felt that the subject was a matter to be kept from respectable women. While opinion in Cork on the Acts was divided, Catholics left matters to the clergy: 'Our people leave it more in our hands . . . I do not think they care about discussing them; of course we do not dream of discussing such things with a lady; we object entirely to these things being placarded about the streets, and we fancy it has done great mischief.'[138] Obviously priests would not approve of parishioners being active in the repeal campaign; such disapproval would in the nineteenth century have ensured non-participation of Catholics.

The vulnerability of women who were not prostitutes to apprehension under the Acts was a major theme of repealers. There are many instances of such events recorded, and understandably these occurrences were exploited by repeal campaigners for their propaganda value. A 'correspondent at Cork' complained 'that in order to facilitate the action of the C. D. Acts' the identification numbers of policemen 'have been taken away from the policemen's caps' thus rendering redress in the case of wrongful arrest 'out of the question'.[139] Revd McNaughton in Belfast declared that 'the mill girls, servant girls, milliners' apprentices' were now subject to the power of the policemen.[140]

The branches of the repeal movement in Ireland appear, from the pages of the *Shield* and annual reports, to have been part of the English movement, rather than forming a coherent Irish movement, which perhaps explains the lack of an archive for the Irish campaign. However, the 1870 meeting in Belfast did acknowledge the Irish dimension when Revd G. A. Chadwick made the point that Ireland had always been subjected to 'special Acts for the Church, the land, the Press', and asked why 'we might not for once have had special immunity'.[141]

A Cork 'Ladies' Committee' was in place by 1871, and on 21 February of that year there was 'a great public meeting' held in that city which forwarded a petition to the Chief Secretary. The Revd Hugh Stowell Brown said, in the course of a long speech, that the purpose of the Acts was not to reclaim prostitutes but to 'provide harlots for the troops'.[142] Nor had the Dublin committee been idle. They sent 'influential deputations which waited upon the country and city members' and obtained variously promises of support and consideration of the matter. Some members condemned the Acts outright 'both on constitutional and moral grounds'. The delegation included the President and Vice-President of the College of Surgeons, physicians, clergymen, Quakers and Thomas Haslam.[143] In May, Revd Stowell Brown, lately in Cork, addressed a meeting in Dublin. The meeting was chaired by James M. Wharton, FRSCI, and present were Sir William Wilde, the prominent Quakers Thomas and Alfred Webb, Charles Eason and Thomas Haslam. In May a petition signed by a quarter of a million women was presented to parliament and three memorials were presented to Mr Gladstone.[144] Mrs Haslam sent £5 1s 0d which she had collected in Dublin, while £2 4s 0d came from Belfast, and £3 3s 6d from Cork where Mrs Addey, also a Quaker, was secretary.[145] The annual reports for 1872, 1873 and 1874 have little to say about Ireland, although Mrs Haslam's participation is noted and subscriptions from named persons who would later be loyal members of the suffrage association are listed.[146] Miss Tod succinctly summed up the causes of prostitution as 'a question of education and *bread*'. She charted the evolution of her political awareness: 'It was the danger of respectable women being mistaken for women of bad character which first overcame her reluctance to meddle with so painful a subject.' However, her understanding of the situation grew to a conviction that 'as the laws of God, [are] the same for men and women, human laws must be so too'.[147] Isabella Tod's increasing prominence in the movement is documented in the sixth annual report (1875) where she is listed as a member of the executive committee.[148] In late 1874, perhaps as a result of her presence on the executive committee, a determined effort was made to further the campaign in Ireland by the arousal of public opinion. Mr Burgess, the organizing secretary, visited Dublin. In Cork, Burgess addressed a conference and public meeting; subsequently he went to Belfast.[149]

There is evidence of a crisis of confidence in the Dublin committee in 1875:

> Our agent Mr. Bligh has recently been in Dublin. He reports that at first our friends there were not at all hopeful, but a meeting was called and Edmund Jones, President of the Working Man's League, was announced to speak, the result being that the hall provided was far too small to accommodate those who flocked to hear.[150]

Mr Bligh then went on a tour of urban centres which included Carlow, Wicklow, Wexford, New Ross, Waterford, Cork and Limerick where 'he excited great interest by placing large posters on the walls'. Mr Bligh attempted to bring his message to the Irish peasants; his main difficulty was getting them to believe that such laws existed. He recounted how they displayed 'horror and disgust' when he 'succeeded in convincing them of the reality of the Acts'.[151] There is no evidence of any working-class response to the visits of the organizers for the association to Ireland. From the beginning the LNA had tried to forge an alliance with working-class men. It welcomed the formation of the English Working Men's National Alliance as it felt that the combination of 'cultivated ladies' and working men would bear fruitful results. The message was full of condescension and class superiority, as one would expect from the class divisions of the time. Working men were willing to accept the

> gentle guidance of a grave and educated lady in a crusade which concerns so deeply the interests of women and the homes of the poor, and they are found to be willing to devote their brief hours and leisure and the whole influence of their vote and character to the cause, when the right chord in their hearts and consciences is touched by a delicate hand.[152]

Paid agents, such as the two who visited Ireland, 'constituted an important working-class presence with the repeal camp . . . [They] . . . were frequently veterans of earlier radical causes like moral chartism . . . Some like William Burgess . . . were skilled organizers'.[153] In 1876, Mr Bligh was again in Ireland when he visited many urban centres in Ulster. Despite the upbeat tone of the report one senses that the visit did not achieve the desired result: 'Some of the meetings which Mr Bligh promoted in Ireland were of a most encouraging character, and had it not been for the insufficiency of funds, which caused this important work to be suspended very substantial results in the influencing of Irish votes would, we believe, have accrued.'[154] The report goes on to stress the importance of influencing Irish MPs and the desirability of winning over the Irish people 'whose well known character for chastity and domestic fidelity would make them a true moral aid to our cause'.[155]

The annual reports chart the evolution of feminist thought for which the movement was the catalyst. In 1877, when it was noted how many petitions were sent to parliament from the Belfast and Dublin committees, the significance of the women's campaign was emphasized:

> The uprising of women during these last years must be regarded an absolute necessity for the saving of society; and the best and noblest men at the present moment have begun to acknowledge this. The principle we have to maintain is the absolute equality of men and women in all obligations to chastity, purity, justice and mercy, and then equal rights as citizens before the law.[156]

The double standard of sexuality had to go. Chastity was demanded of men, as it had always been demanded of women. Women were entitled to equal treatment 'as citizens' before the law. Equal treatment 'as citizens', of course, implied the right to vote. The LNA, after all, was concurrent with the setting up of suffrage associations. Mr and Mrs Haslam had founded their Dublin Women's Suffrage Association in 1876.

In 1878 the Ladies' National Association appears to have concentrated on the campaign in Ireland. In January its representative, Mrs Goulder, visited Ireland and held meetings in Dublin, Cork and Limerick. Mrs Haslam presided over the drawing-room meeting in Dublin at which 'very interesting and earnest addresses were delivered and petition-sheets in favour of Sir H. Johnstone's bill taken by several ladies'.[157] The meetings in Cork and Limerick were judged successful. In Cork the attendance of thirty-five ladies included many 'of high social position and influence'. The Limerick meeting was held in the Mission Rooms, and a Wesleyan Minister, the Revd W. Gorman was 'most helpful'. Members of the Society of Friends were also mentioned as helping the cause.[158] A second meeting arranged for Mrs Goulder in Dublin was convened by Presbyterian ministers, and addressed by Mrs Haslam who also read from Mrs Butler's writings. At another meeting, convened by Wesleyan ministers, Mrs Haslam spoke 'very earnestly'.[159]

Josephine Butler's writings and speeches attacked the premise, implicit in the Acts, that prostitution was 'a necessary and inevitable portion of Christian civilisation'. She argued that they were based on 'a belief that purity is impossible or unhealthful and that man cannot be any other than the slave of sin'. In all her speeches she stressed the lack of parliamentary representation for women and she complained that women had been 'drilled into silence' on the topic of prostitution. 'Men have demanded of them an affectation at least of ignorance on the subject, albeit it is one which more intimately and terribly concerns the whole of womankind than any other.'[160] The ideas expressed by Butler are similar to those of Thomas Haslam in his 1870 pamphlet. However, Butler's speeches and writings were imbued with religious sentiment, a characteristic totally lacking in the work of Haslam. Anna was an admirer of Butler, as is evident in her letters to Stopes.[161] A manuscript, which is described as 'Private copy of Extracts of a letter from an Irish "Friend"', in the Mary Estlin Collection, recounts the visit of an anonymous Irish 'Friend' to the home of Josephine Butler. The writer recounts how Josephine Butler, herself a member of the Anglican church and married to an Anglican clergyman, confided in her that she wished she had been born a member of the Society of Friends as 'the world would have recognized the right of a Quaker woman to speak in public, there would not have been the uphill work'. It is unlikely, however that the original letter was written by Haslam; she would be unlikely to describe herself in those terms, nor was she wont to seek anonymity. The document is interesting in that Butler's opinions on Quaker workers for repeal are quoted by the writer:

[Josephine Butler] had come to appreciate the vantage ground on which 'Friends' stood for aiding any crusade against evil, not merely by their own general morality, but from their habitual tone of thought & word; not looking lightly upon immorality nor speaking lightly of it – but these 'Friends' who have aided her – and they are her aids in every town – have, as a matter of course looked on the moral side of the question – they have never had to be educated to that.[162]

There was a preponderance of Quaker women in the LNA executive. The LNA annual reports reveal that of those involved in Ireland, the majority were Quaker. In Dublin, the names of subscribers read like a roll-call of the Society of Friends: Webb, Edmundson, Shackleton, Wigham. The Cork movement was led by Mrs Addey, a Quaker, herself a member of the Webb family. Of the twenty-one Cork persons named in 1878, it was possible to confirm that nine were definitely 'Friends' and a further three were likely to have been. In Clonmel and Waterford the few named subscribers, the Misses Grubb, and Strangman, were Quakers.[163]

The LNA movement in Ireland was obviously confined to a small number of middle-class women and, after eight years of campaigning, would appear to have had little success in reaching a wider public. A breakdown of the signatures of the 1878 petition 'from women of the United Kingdom' reveals that from a total of 115,132 signatures, 5,572 came from Ireland.[164] Of the Irish total, however, 3,528 signatures were obtained in Belfast and only 375 in Dublin.[165] The Dublin total is surprisingly low when one considers that the main activity of that branch was the collection of signatures for petitions against the Acts. Cork produced 247 signatures, a respectable number when compared with Dublin, but unremarkable when one considers that there were two subjected districts in the county. The figures perhaps illustrate the apathy of the population to the question. From 'other places' in Ireland, 1,170 signatures were collected. There is no breakdown for signatures collected from the vicinity of the Curragh.[166] As 'places from which more than 200 names were received' were listed separately, obviously fewer than 200 were obtained from County Kildare. In the English campaign the organizing of repeal movements in the subjected districts presented difficulties: 'The population of those districts were largely either naval or military ... Their prejudices were too strong to make it an easy matter to hold meetings, or obtain a fair hearing in these districts.'[167]

In 1878 the annual meeting of the Ladies' National Association was held in Dublin. A meeting for women was held in the 'ancient Concert-room' on 31 October. 'The room was crowded with a most respectable audience, and great interest was manifested in the cause.' Josephine Butler does not appear to have been at the women's meeting, which was addressed by Isabella Tod. In a passionate speech she appealed to those present on behalf of the 'women who are oppressed and degraded by the soul-crushing machinery of State regulation of vice'. Tod echoed the genetic theories mooted by Haslam in *Duties of Parents*: 'The ignorance, the hopeless poverty, the feebleness of mind and body inherited from debased parents ... leave these women without a chance of leading any other life.' She saw the work of the LNA as twofold: 'to get rid of this legislation of despair ... to remove the

evils social and economic, which leave so many women ready for a prey.'
She attacked the philosophy on which the Acts were predicated: 'that men
must sin, and that . . . women, who have fallen . . . may lawfully be seized
and sacrificed for it.' She appealed to the 'Christian women' present to do
their duty irrespective of the 'angry and contemptuous words which some
people fling at every woman who comes forward actively to care for, or
plead for, those whom society chooses to ignore'.[168] Mrs Haslam moved the
resolution pledging the meeting to 'renewed efforts for the abolition of the
Contagious Diseases Acts'.[169] On the following day a conference was held in
the Pillar Room of the Rotunda at which there was large attendance
including Thomas Haslam. It was judged by the compilers of the annual
Ladies' National Association report as 'perhaps, a more interesting and
successful Conference than we have ever yet had'. The chairman, Professor
Stuart of Cambridge, said that the 'Conference had been called by the
Ladies' Association . . . [which] had come from the sister country to take
counsel with those in Ireland who were interested in the question and . . . to
give information and to answer objections, and to see what aid could be
obtained in Ireland towards the special aims of the Association'. The
meeting was also addressed by Mr Henry J. Allen of Dublin, 'who has
laboured energetically for our cause', and by Miss Tod and Mrs Butler. A
resolution was passed which recognized 'the duties of the Irish people' to
cooperate in the campaign to repeal the Acts.[170]

The public meeting held later that evening in the Round Room of the
Rotunda 'was of a very disorderly character'. This was judged not to represent 'any very passionate hostility to our cause, still less had it a cynical
character'. The reasons given for the uproar betray some racial stereotyping
of the Irish audience: 'The presence of several hundreds of Dublin medical
and other students, whose character for insubordination is well-known, and
the equally well-known excitability of an Irish audience are almost sufficient
in themselves to account for the scene of confusion and uproar which took
place in the Rotundo (sic).'[171] The *Shield* described the constant interruptions
to speakers 'by disturbances in the body of the hall of a character so disorderly as to eclipse anything of the kind that for many years has taken place
in the Rotundo (sic)'.[172] Dr Thomson of Dublin, who claimed medical
expertise, put a resolution to the meeting that: 'The CDAs, although capable
of improvement, are calculated to effect great physical and moral good and
deserve the approval of this meeting.'[173] Thomson appeared to have many
vociferous supporters in the hall. Accounts of what happened next varied.
The LNA report stated: 'Some misunderstanding and confusion having
arisen . . . with respect to the voting on the resolution and amendment, the
uproar in the meeting increased, and noisy demonstrations continued to be
made in favour of the opposite propositions.'[174] *The Times* suggested that Dr
Thomson's resolution was ignored by the chair.[175] Seats were overturned
and those sitting in the front rows were forced to seek refuge on the platform. During Mrs Butler's subsequent speech, the disturbance was such that
'the chairman was finally obliged to appeal to the police to clear the hall'.[176]
Anna Haslam spoke of these events in a 1914 interview:

Mrs Butler came to Dublin to speak in the Rotunda; she was refused a hearing, and the platform was stormed by medical students and others. Mrs Butler was going back to England in chagrin; but Mrs Haslam would not allow it. She declared that a meeting must be held, and Mrs Butler must get a hearing in Dublin. And she did. In a couple of days Mr and Mrs Haslam alone, organised another meeting, and Mrs Butler moved to tears some of the people who would not listen to her at the first.[177]

The annual report did not mention the Haslams' part in the reconvened meeting; it mentioned 'an earnest request proffered by our friends in Dublin that our Association would immediately hold another meeting'.[178] At this meeting, which was uneventful, Mrs Butler called the Irish 'a chivalrous people . . . chaste, domestic and home-loving'. She continued: 'It is well that you love purity; but how do you express your love of purity? Too often by harshness to the woman who errs and to the woman only.'[179] She stressed the unity of women involved in the cause – a unity that levelled distinctions. 'We no more covet the name of ladies; we are all women.'[180] Her speech confirmed that, despite the efforts of Irish members in the lifetime of the association, they had achieved little impact on the general public:

> The reasons that induced her and those who were with her to come to Ireland were – because they went everywhere with their message, but they had not yet been to Ireland; because the system they opposed was already in force in Ireland, and was already exercising a corrupting influence upon their country though they might not know it; and lastly, because of the well-known character of Ireland for chastity and domestic morality . . . which led them to expect a very hearty response to their appeal in this country.[181]

Much of the meeting was devoted to a refutation of Dr Thomson's claims for the beneficial results of the Acts at the previous meeting. James Stansfeld MP, an erstwhile member of Gladstone's cabinet, challenged Dr Thomson's claims and concluded that 'the principle of these Contagious Diseases Acts was, in fact, to propagate and stimulate disease by engendering vice and establishing a system of State doctors and police to facilitate its exercise'.[182]

Those at the reconvened meeting judged the abandoned meeting as beneficial to the cause. T.W. Russell said that 'the most enthusiastic meeting held in the interests of the movement could not be more effective in drawing public attention to their proceedings than the row which had taken place'.[183] At this remove it is difficult to judge whether or not the disturbance was an organized protest or merely the result of youthful high spirits. Certainly Dr Thomson's claims for the beneficial results of the Acts would appear to have had some support from the body of the hall. His assertion that an 'unholy and impure crusade has been started in Dublin and carried on for the last three weeks' suggests a possible reaction to the extensive advertising of the public meeting.[184] Mrs Butler alluded to a writer in the *Freeman's Journal* who acknowledged the courage of Englishwomen in the campaign but 'could not regret if Irishwomen did not follow their example'.[185] That the writer did not realize that there were Irishwomen who had participated with the 'courageous' Englishwomen virtually from the beginning reaffirms the very low profile of the Irish branch of the LNA.

Press coverage of the Irish meeting reveals great unease with the involvement of 'ladies' in the movement. The *Irish Times* was especially disapproving: 'The entire course of conduct of the people who have been thrusting this unsavoury subject upon the inhabitants of Dublin is in the highest degree reprehensible.' Matters once the preserve of medical men, which even in the House of Commons were discussed 'behind closed doors', had 'for days been debated openly and unabashed in this city by some ladies and a small retinue of gentlemen'.[186] The *Freeman's Journal* was less critical and in an editorial admired the 'courage' of the campaigning ladies. The leader writer, however, appeared to have had his head firmly buried in the sand regarding prostitution in Irish garrison towns:

> The truth is we know little here about these Acts . . . the necessity for them . . . is happily not as great in Ireland as in England . . . If they are in force in Cork, and Queenstown as well as at the Curragh, it must be in a very modified form . . . While according our most respectful admiration to those ladies who have identified themselves with a subject which is generally tabooed we think that they will not . . . find Ireland a good field for their labours and we . . . will be very glad if we are spared the further consideration of a matter which is a little too strong for our Hibernian tastes.[187]

The account in *The Times* implied that the disturbances at the public meeting were justified because the protesters were 'shocked at witnessing ladies taking part in the discussion of so unpleasant a subject'.[188]

Critics were especially censorious of the posters displayed to advertise the meetings and of unsolicited material delivered to private houses. Dr Thomson, at the abandoned meeting, objected to the pollution of the walls of the city 'by placards in which statements grossly and fearfully slanderous were circulated (loud applause)'.[189] The *Irish Times*:

> had reason to believe that . . . for some times past the homes of respectable people have been flooded with the abominations of an impure literature circulated in tracts and pamphlets by a handful of zealots who really retail vice in the language of sham virtue . . . no one can deduct the effect of the polluted placards which have been staring from every dead wall in Dublin.[190]

Evidence given to the Royal Commission, as mentioned above, was critical of campaigners in Cork 'putting placards before young females inviting then to read these Acts, of which women never heard before'.[191] It is likely that the paid agents of the LNA, rather than the 'lady' members, were responsible for the placing of posters on Irish walls. In his study of the repeal movement, Paul McHugh has written: 'A travelling agent's primary responsibility was simply to visit as many areas as possible, spreading the word and attracting support . . . putting up bills, distributing literature and generally arousing interest.'[192] LNA annual reports mentioned agents working in Ireland. Bligh, a paid agent, toured urban centres in Ireland in 1875, when he excited great interest by placing large posters on the walls.[193] William Burgess and Mrs Goulder also visited Ireland to spread the word of the repeal movement.[194]

The annual report for 1878 announced the formation of 'An Auxiliary Committee of Ladies comprising thirty members' to act with the 'mixed committee', and Mrs Haslam, 'who has so long and earnestly served our cause in Dublin', already 'local secretary and correspondent' of the Dublin Branch of the LNA, was appointed treasurer of the auxiliary committee.[195] One can see from Josephine Butler's Dublin speech how the campaign inevitably strengthened the demand for votes for women. She called the legislature: 'A Parliament composed of men only, making the laws which are to influence family life in the whole future, while women are sitting silently in their homes and forbidden to speak.'[196]

The leadership of the LNA initially encouraged rescue work, but by 1878 'had grown wary of the rescue impulse'.[197] The 1878 report's conclusion stressed that, however necessary and praiseworthy the work of rescue of prostitutes,

> we regard with regret and even alarm the strong diversion of our forces which has taken place in some localities . . . from the all-impor-tant aim of combating the State regulation of vice, which means the *public recognition of the necessity of vice for men,* to the almost exclusive object of gathering up the poor broken fragments of the womanhood sacrificed to that impious doctrine, and restoring them to an honest life. This latter work is . . . necessary . . . but there are a hundred women who will engage in it, for one who will take up the more unpopular and laborious and difficult work of carrying on a well-sustained crusade.[198]

There is no record of any attempt by the Irish LNA to involve itself in rescue work. The emphasis on the campaign in Ireland in 1878 would appear to have led to greater activity by the Dublin committee. Mrs Haslam appeared as a member of the London executive committee in the eleventh annual report.[199] The Dublin committee was reported to have met every month at the houses of members, with an average attendance of about forty. It organ-ized five meetings 'on a larger scale' in the drawing rooms of hotels, Friends' meeting houses and rooms attached to churches at which 'earnest and powerful addresses were delivered.' 'A greatly increased interest was excited amongst ladies' which resulted in an increase of membership. The Dublin association now numbered over one hundred women. A pamphlet, *Immoral Legislation,*[200] 'was compiled by a member'; addressed to the Irish clergy it was funded by the Provost of Trinity College, the Reverend H.

Lloyd. Two hundred copies were sent to ministers of the 'different denominations' and Mrs Lloyd distributed a large number amongst the 'clergymen of the Irish Church'. The 'mixed committee' of men and women was reorganized and also held meetings. Thus the campaign would appear to have been stepped up considerably. There is, however, evidence of the public unpopularity of the cause in the recounting of difficulties experienced in organizing 'another series of mass meetings'. Clergymen were reported as being unwilling 'to lend their rooms for this purpose or to persuade their members to attend', suggesting a fear of a repeat of the disorder at the 1878 public meeting in the Rotunda.[201]

The 1881 report recorded a trip by Mrs Haslam to London to represent the Dublin association. Many meetings were held in Dublin, some of which resulted in the recruitment of new members. The list of subscribers from Dublin, however, does not reflect this increase in membership. 'Thirty-six petitions have been presented by members [of parliament] during the last session from various meetings and religious bodies in the city and suburbs; also memorials to Mr Gladstone, and our city, county, and university members.' An account of peripheral events in Dublin reflects the Haslams' allied interests and were also perhaps included to supplement a rather meagre report. The committee had been addressed on the duties of mothers; an account was also given of a speech delivered in Dublin on 'the necessity for making the law as stringent in Ireland as in England to secure the liability of fathers of illegitimate children for their support', and of a talk on the 'Evils surrounding the present law of seduction'. These subjects had been addressed at length by Haslam in *Duties of Parents* and *Prostitution*, both of which reflected the ethos of the repeal associations' insistence on the 'moral purity' of men. It was thought worthy of mention by the writer (Anna Haslam) that 'several ladies as well as gentlemen' joined in discussions following the above talks.[202]

The 1882 report suggests that even among the converts to the cause, interest had waned. The committee 'has tried to keep up the interest of friends here by circulating papers, canvassing for signatures to petitions and holding a few meetings'. Among the meetings mentioned was an address to 'a little company at the Friends' Meeting House, Monkstown, and a meeting in the small hall Christian Union Buildings'. The tone of Anna Haslam's report seems dispirited, the use of the adjectives 'few', 'little' and 'small' emphasize the modest extent of the Dublin effort, and the hope that 'many ladies . . . will help us more vigorously in the future' seems a vain one.[203]

By 1883 the sustained campaign inside and outside the House of Commons, began to reap positive results. On 12 April 1883, the National Liberal Federation supported the repeal of the Acts. Eight days later James Stansfeld MP, veteran campaigner, made a powerful speech in the House during which he confessed that he loathed having to speak on the subject of the 'hygiene' campaign:

What I have done I have done for conviction and for duty's sake, and never will I abandon a duty which I have once undertaken to fulfil, nor will I cease until I have proved the hygienic failure and imposture of the Acts . . . I have never admitted the possibility of any dissonance between the moral and hygienic law. The law of morals and the law of physical health are but parts of the harmonious whole – that great, that supreme providential law under which we hold our human lives.[204]

Stansfeld moved a resolution that 'the House disapproves of the compulsory examination of women under the CDAs'. 'Twenty members of the Government, including the Premier, either voted or paired in favour of the Resolution and it was carried by a majority of 72.' The long awaited victory took everyone by surprise, including the members of the LNA in the gallery. The compulsory clauses of the Acts were suspended immediately.[205] The Bill for 'the total and unconditional repeal' was introduced in the House of Commons in 1886, again by Stansfeld, and was passed without division on its second reading.[206] The great contribution of Stansfeld, 'whose faithful advocacy of this unpopular cause in the House of Commons has been crowned with so great a moral victory', was gratefully acknowledged. The LNA, in its triumphant editorial, claimed equal credit with the male NARCDA for the successful outcome: 'As an Association of Women we desire to thank all the good men who, with unwearied devotion and zeal, have shared the work of Repeal in Great Britain from the beginning to the end of the prolonged conflict.'[207] There is no suggestion, here or elsewhere, that the LNA considered itself in any way as a subsidiary female association; the acknowledgement, if anything, suggests that the women were to the fore.

The confident editorials of the reports from the post-repeal period illustrate the inevitable evolution of the movement into a full-scale campaign for the parliamentary vote for women: 'When our work began, nearly twenty years ago, few, if any, of us realised that we were laying an axe to the very root of political despotism and social wrong as well.'[208] Women who had experienced the heady elation of successfully lobbying to overturn legislation enacted by the British Parliament, were unlikely to continue to accept the denial of democratic participation in electing that parliament. The overlap between activism in the CDA and suffrage campaigns has been already mentioned in relation to the Haslams; they were not unique. Although Millicent Fawcett, the British suffrage leader, distanced herself from the prostitution issue for fear of bringing her suffrage work into disrepute, many early suffragists involved themselves in the campaign. Walkowitz called the repeal campaign the 'first exposure to political activity' for women. [209] In Ireland the leaders of the LNA, Isabella Tod and Anna Haslam, were also active in the infant suffrage movement. The overlap was significant in that the repeal campaign evolved into what Levine has called 'a more cohesive and consuming perspective on women's rights' on the part of activist women who 'were now conceptualizing and vocalizing palpable connections between these various campaigns in a concrete manner.'[210]

The successful outcome of the long campaign against the CDAs did not result in the disbanding of the Ladies' National Association. From 1884 onwards, the reports reveal an alignment with the social purity movement. Ironically this alignment caused the libertarian defenders of prostitutes of the CDA campaign to become allied with what eventually became a repressive movement. The repealers believed that men, not prostitutes, were the 'source of contagion and moral corruption'.[211] The social purity movement initially sought to reform male sexuality and the morals of the working class. It eventually sought to regulate working-class behaviour, especially that of working-class women, by methods which ranged from philanthropic 'rescue' work to vigilante activities. While Anna Haslam does not appear to have become actively involved in the movement, she approvingly recorded the visit of Miss Ellice Hopkins, the social purity campaigner, in May 1885. Her meetings were very well attended, and she appears to have been a compelling speaker: 'Miss Hopkins' powerful and touching addresses excited considerable interest, and resulted in the formation of a Men's Social Purity and Vigilance Committee with the Archbishop of Dublin at its head; the Dean of the Chapel Royal and leading ministers in various denominations taking part.'[212] Ellice Hopkins 'provided impetus and direction for the new interest in sexual politics. She was central in forging an inter-denominational social-purity movement.'[213] She had by the mid-1880s organized 'hundreds of male chastity leagues and female rescue societies'.[214] She was noted for her power to move an audience; the Archbishop of Dublin wrote: 'her tender, pathetic, and touching words went through like winged arrows into the hearts of those who heard her.'[215] Anna Haslam also mentioned the formation of the Union for the Care and Protection of Young Girls 'under the Presidency of The Lady Plunkett ... It included various Committees working under the following heads: Preventative, Educational, Legislative, and Petitioning, Workhouse and Magdalen, Vigilance and Rescue Work.'[216] Anna wrote years later to Marie Stopes concerning the visit of Hopkins to Dublin and recounted that at a meeting in Dublin in October 1918, she had given an account of the CDA campaign that included a mention of Hopkins's visit.[217]

Although the social purity movement was repressive in tendency, it initially attracted many LNA supporters, including Josephine Butler herself (but who later resigned). Ellice Hopkins's campaign was directed at men; it sought to inculcate in them moral purity comparable to that evinced by pure women. The doctrine of sexual restraint, already embraced by women, at least according to the prevailing stereotype, and now preached to men, laid the foundations for a more egalitarian code of sexual relations within marriage. It also implicitly proclaimed the moral superiority of women, thus strengthening their cause of equal rights. 'In feminist hands, desexualisation could empower women to attack the customary prerogative of men.'[218]

The White Cross Army, Ellice Hopkins's male social purity society, was dedicated to the single standard of morality and chastity. Early feminists demanded the raising of male moral standards and by so doing refused to countenance the stereotype of the Victorian male unable to overcome his passions, and thus forced to use the services of a prostitute. Anna Haslam included 'Social Purity' in the list of associations to which she was affiliated, but there are no details available of the extent of her involvement.[219] Although Anna appears from her 1918 letter to Stopes to have been uncritical of the social purity movement, Josephine Butler eventually disassociated herself from it; she disapproved of its 'fatuous belief that you can oblige human beings to be moral by force, and in so doing that you can promote social purity'.[220] It appears that 'A Dublin White Cross Vigilance Society' employed vigilante-like methods when it 'fielded a midnight patrol of two-dozen young men who kept customers away from the city's brothels by accosting them in the dark with identifying lanterns'.[221]

The Dublin branch of the LNA also sent resolutions 'thanking Mr Stead for his brave and noble advocacy and also petitioning Her Majesty for his release'. Stead, a crusading journalist, had published in the *Pall Mall Gazette* in 1885, an exposé of child prostitution in London that electrified public opinion. The response to Stead's revelations in 'The Maiden's Tribute' that it was possible to purchase a child prostitute for five pounds, and to his subsequent imprisonment, united people of diverse beliefs in outraged reaction. A huge rally in Hyde Park, attended by a quarter of a million people, including Michael Davitt, reminded Josephine Butler of the 'revolution days in Paris'. Walkowitz has written: 'For one brief moment feminists and personal-rights advocates joined with Anglican bishops and Socialists to protest the corruption by aristocrats of young innocents.'[222] The extent of the reaction to 'The Maiden Tribute' ensured the passage of the Criminal Law Amendment Act of 1885, which raised the age of consent for young girls from thirteen to sixteen and was regarded as 'a substantial triumph for feminists and puritans. They looked to the events of the year as a turning point in the history of morals and as an example of how women might cleanse society.'[223] Anna Haslam knew William Stead: 'The last time W. T. Stead was in Dublin he ... exclaimed "Mrs. Haslam, I have known you for the last forty years."'[224] Isabella Tod gave a talk on Stead in Dublin in 1886.[225] The later reports of the LNA show concern with state regulation of prostitution in British colonies and chronicle Anna Haslam's continued involvement as a member of the executive.

Although the Irish campaign against the CDAs did not involve large numbers, and was confined to members who were not Roman Catholic, the nucleus of campaigners, in which the Haslams were to the fore, was involved from the beginning and persevered until the Acts were repealed. Anna Haslam's own admission that the extent of her involvement interfered with her suffrage work, demonstrates the time-consuming extent of her repeal activities but may underestimate the ultimate importance of the CDA campaign to the suffrage question. Thomas, too, played his part in the repeal movement as a member of NARCDA; his pamphlet on prostitution demonstrated his feminist stance on the subject and reiterated his revulsion, shared by the LNA, of the double standard of sexuality that underpinned the legislation. He saw the Acts as a manifestation of the powerlessness of unenfranchised women and stressed the necessity of their obtaining the vote. That the repeal movement in Ireland fought an uphill battle against apathy, and occasionally vociferous protest, is clearly demonstrated by the annual LNA reports to which Anna Haslam unfailingly contributed. The Irish campaigners do not appear to have involved themselves with the subjected districts, but to have engaged in meetings, petitions and general consciousness-raising. There was no successful alliance with the working class, which was a potent feature of the English movement. Although there is evidence of public advertising campaigns in Dublin, Cork and other urban centres, it appears that such campaigns emanated from London. The hostility engendered by the 1878 public meeting in Dublin reveals the Irish members as willing to expose themselves to opprobrium; the tenor of the speeches at that meeting, however, reveals the lack of impact made by the campaign on the press and public. Nor are there any reports of activists visiting the subjected districts to examine the working of the Acts on the ground.

In the LNA, feminists challenged the sexual double standard by demanding an end to state-condoned male 'unchastity'; women became activists in the attempt to transform behaviour, rather than, as hitherto, passive subjects of prescriptive ideology. Millicent Fawcett, the pioneer of the English suffragist movement, pragmatically separated herself from the campaign, as she feared 'confusing an already unpopular question with a new, much more controversial one',[226] but she acknowledged that it had been invaluable 'in shedding light on the wider aspect of women's place as responsible citizens in the body politic'.[227] Anna Haslam, however, founded her suffrage society while an active campaigner for the repeal of the CDAs. The public identification of respectable middle-class women with those whom society saw as fallen, depraved and degraded was a remarkable phenomenon; active political campaigning by women even more so.

The Irish campaign for repeal was contemporaneous with the start of the campaign for the enfranchisement of women. Many of its supporters also supported repeal of the CDAs. While some feminists in England remained aloof from the campaign as they were fearful that allegiance to it would jeopardize the suffrage cause, the Haslams, particularly Anna, worked simultaneously for suffrage, for the repeal of the Acts and for the extension of educational opportunities to women. The involvement of Thomas, and the writing and researching of his pamphlet on prostitution, may well have been responsible for the development of the doctrine of moral restraint with its total rejection of the moral double standard, so compellingly championed in *Duties to Parents*.

Ray Strachey, in an early history of feminist activism, claimed that the LNA campaign

> changed the whole basis of sex morality and swept away a multitude of shams. When Mrs. Butler came forward in the cause, a double moral standard was not only tolerated but widely upheld; before she had been working a year that comfortable assumption was upset . . . its hold on thoughtful and serious people was destroyed.[228]

Thomas and Anna Haslam were typical of the membership of the repeal movement in that their background was Quaker and they were part of a 'reform tradition'.[229] Many repealers came from an anti-slavery background.[230] Thomas, like many husbands of women in the LNA, was himself involved in the campaign and, of course, he penned his pamphlet in opposition to the Acts. Frank Mort has written that 'in their private lives many of the repealers sought to live out the ideal of companionate marriage. This was seen as an equal union between husband and wife . . . cemented by the power of human love.'[231] This description neatly fits the Haslam marriage. It is likely that the public discourse on the sexual double standard was instrumental in the formulation of the Haslams' feminist theory. The agitation for the repeal of the CDAs was important in the shaping of a feminist discourse against the inequity of the double standard of morality. The influence of the CDA repeal movement in the struggle was recognized by suffragists. In 1912 the non-militant National Union of Women's Suffrage Societies re-issued Josephine Butler's *Reminiscences of a Great Crusade* in a deluxe edition. The militant suffragettes credited the work with sowing 'the seeds of a mighty harvest which others are about to reap'.[232]

5

'Full of perseverance and buoyant energy'[1]: The Haslams' nineteenth-century suffrage campaign

While Anna Haslam and her husband Thomas were the founders of the suffrage movement in Ireland, their overall contribution to the cause of votes for women is, more often than not, treated as a mere prologue to the suffragette campaign of the early twentieth century. Rosemary Owens's seminal work on suffrage, *Smashing Times,* deals with the period 1889–1922. While she acknowledges that Anna and Thomas 'formed the first suffrage society in Dublin', she argues that 'it would appear that up to 1896 the Haslams and their colleagues were preaching to the converted'. Although Owens's account describes the methodology of the Dublin Women's Suffrage Association (DWSA)[2] she argues that, 'despite the flurry of letters and petitions, very little was achieved until 1896, when the society was twenty years in existence'.[3] Louise Ryan states that the DWSA's 'main tactics included writing letters and petitions to Parliament as well as holding small meetings, usually in the drawing rooms of members' houses'.[4] Margaret Ward writes: 'A Dublin Women's Suffrage Association had been formed as early as 1876 by the Quaker couple, Anna and Thomas Haslam. This held few public meetings, concentrating most of its activities in the drawing-rooms of the influential.' However, she concedes that while 'such a genteel plea for the franchise' was not attractive to young women, 'the Haslams' group would be an important first stage for many young militants. It served an invaluable function in providing a forum where like-minded people could meet.'[5] Cliona Murphy's work on the Irish suffrage movement in the early twentieth century credits the Haslams with 'working quietly but steadily' in the course of lives devoted to 'the promotion of women in local and national government'.[6] Hanna Sheehy Skeffington, however, called Anna a 'Quaker rebel, one of the most consistent and ardent feminists I have known of the old school', and acknowledged that the DWSA (later IWSLGA) 'did much educative spadework'.[7] There seems to me to be a serious undervaluing of the sustained efforts of the first wave of suffragist activism spearheaded by the Haslams. I have, of course, been lucky enough to have access to the minute book of the DWSA, not available when the above-mentioned works were written. Accounts of early Irish suffrage meetings, however, were copiously reported, with occasional editorial comment, in Irish newspapers and frequently mentioned in contemporary English suffrage journals.

Anna was that oxymoronic animal – a genteel revolutionary, but recent commentators see only the gentility and overlook completely the radical

nature of her campaign's demands. Hanna Sheehy Skeffington emerged as
the leader of the early twentieth-century feminist movement in Ireland. The
activism and militancy of this later movement should not be seen as belit-
tling or erasing what Anna Haslam had achieved.[8] David Rubenstein has
stated that in England 'the suffragette decade before the outbreak of war in
1914 . . . is often treated as if it were unrelated to movements of opinion
which preceded it, or at least as an exaggeratedly sharp break with the past'.
He goes on to argue that the earlier nineteenth-century period, 'fascinating
and important in itself, formed an essential background to a new, stronger
and better organised movement which . . . increased the effectiveness or at
least the prominence of the women's cause in the new century'.[9] The same
argument can be advanced for the Irish movement.

From the perspective of the twenty-first century, an age sometimes called
post-feminist, it is difficult to appreciate the radical nature of the original
feminist discourse. Nineteenth-century feminists had to challenge the view
that citizenship was possible, and preferable, only for male heads of house-
holds – an idea entrenched in European classical education. They had to
couch their demands in the contemporary language of male political
thought and to overturn the precept that the subjection of women by men
was natural. They had to challenge the dominant Victorian ideology of the
woman as belonging only to the private sphere – the Angel in the House
syndrome. Anna Haslam represents an almost textbook case of the development of feminist consciousness. Feminism is firmly rooted in Enlightenment
ideas of individual natural rights. This was very evident in the convention
at Seneca Falls* in 1848 where one of resolutions passed declared that it was
self-evident that men and women were created equal. Once that credo was
accepted, then obviously and logically women were entitled to equal educational, legal and social opportunities. Anna Haslam was educated; the
quality of her moral education was manifest in her philanthropic work; she
was engaged in the improvement of society, and most importantly the
reality of education and self-improvement empowered her to argue logically the cause for equality in the political sphere. Her philanthropy and her
Quaker upbringing had also ensured that she was adept in the work of
administration.

In the first thirty years of Irish suffragist activity, Anna Haslam and her
co-workers may have achieved no more than propaganda victories in the
campaign for the parliamentary vote. But at local level they had achieved
significant gains. The passing of the *Women's Poor Law Guardians (Ireland)
Act* in 1896 had been achieved by the parliamentary efforts of the 'indefatigable friend' of the DWSA, W. Johnston MP, who had introduced the bill
and safely carried it through all stages. This act allowed women in Ireland
to stand for election as poor law guardians. There was an immediate and
enthusiastic response in the Dublin organization, ably orchestrated by Anna
Haslam. Women candidates were elected to office; a drive to register women

* Seneca Falls was the site of the first public meeting of women activists in the United
States.

voters all over the country was undertaken, and Anna produced pamphlets containing practical advice to women wishing to stand for election. A sustained campaign for the employment of women as sanitary inspectors, as instructresses in the newly formed Department of Agriculture and Technical Instruction, as workhouse and poor law officials, met with no little success. Women graduates, whose access to education had been the subject of campaigning by Haslam and her fellow members of the Central Association of Irish Schoolmistresses, joined the DWSA. Their awareness of the cause of suffrage was heightened by their education and informed by the long and painstaking, if unexciting, endeavours of the DWSA. The very impatience of these younger women with the methods of the older generation was an acknowledgement of how well that first wave of feminism had succeeded in its educative goal, at least where young educated women were concerned.

David Rubenstein has written that by the 1890s, 'the pages of newspapers and literary journals confirm the topicality of the "women question" . . . Publicity arose from and reinforced self-confidence on the part of increasing numbers of women.'[10] This self-confidence, acquired by dint of sustained effort in the face of frustration and discouragement on the part of original feminist campaigners, benefited the new generation and, ironically, resulted in their dismissal of the pioneers as ineffectual and timid. The first wave, interesting and innovative in itself, formed the bedrock on which the new, vibrant, militant movement was built.

While there are many similarities between the suffrage situation in Ireland and Great Britain, the Irish campaign was complicated by the 'national question'. The younger suffragists who emerged to form the Irish Women's Franchise League (IWFL) in 1908 were mainly nationalist and pro-Home Rule. Anna Haslam was a staunch unionist, and the DWSA, while having members with Home Rule aspirations, was largely unionist in sympathy. The nationalist wing of suffrage was engaged in the second decade of the century in a vigorous debate with activist separatist women on the question of priorities. Suffragists argued that, without the vote, women were powerless and, in the event of independence, would have no input in the formation of the new state. Separatists, on the other hand, felt that that it would be invidious to accept the vote from a Westminster government; they worked for independence, confident that once it was achieved, their efforts would be rewarded by the granting of full equality by the rulers of the new state. This debate is well documented and will not be discussed at length in this work, as it did not engage Anna Haslam or her suffrage association. However, the spadework of Haslam and her cohorts influenced not only younger suffragists, but also the separatist women, who, on the whole, were suffragist also. Without the emergence of women into the public sphere in the nineteenth century, the activities of young women in suffrage and nationalist causes in the twentieth century would have been unthinkable. The suffragette women of the early twentieth century could be said to have taken the justice of their cause so much for granted that they undervalued the achievements of those who succeeded in bringing the question successfully into the public domain. They took for granted the issues, raised by women's rights campaigners in the past, which had been resolved in their favour. The Married Women Property Act gave women greater control over their property; the Contagious Diseases Acts had been repealed; greater access had been gained to education, at both second and third level, and a number of professions had been opened to women.

Undoubtedly the new women of the new century contributed to the increase in prominence of the women's cause. One could argue that the nineteenth-century women's movement was over-cautious and too timid in its methods to achieve its goal of pushing the cause of women's suffrage to the forefront of practical politics. A counter argument suggests that the unorthodox methods of the suffragettes harmed the cause and alienated vital parliamentary support. There is some truth in both arguments. The nineteenth-century movement *was* moderate when compared with the suffragettes, and voting patterns of parliaments in the suffragette era show a decline in support for the cause on the floor of the house. Fenner Brockway wrote that there was little doubt that the suffragettes lost support for their cause by militant actions and correspondingly: 'The Parliamentary majority for women's suffrage, reflecting public opinion, disappeared.'[11] Previously when the moderate suffrage associations were to the fore, repeated parliamentary majorities were achieved for first and second readings of suffrage bills, all ultimately unsuccessful. Had their campaign been more forceful, perhaps their cause would have been espoused by a political party rather than by individual members of parliament. The movement for suffrage was, even at its height, a minority cause, but there was a steady increase in numbers both militant and non-militant up to the outbreak of the First World War. Although the moderate and militant movements coexisted, not always harmoniously, in the early twentieth century, militancy did not suddenly appear from nowhere; it evolved from the moderate movement. Anna Haslam uniquely spanned both eras, literally from start to finish. A study of the later period of her activity reveals the similarities, as much as the differences, between the old movement and the new. The Great War and the War of Independence muddy the waters somewhat when trying to apportion credit for the achievement of the vote. The argument developed in this chapter is that Anna, and to a lesser degree Thomas Haslam's contribution to the successful outcome of the suffrage campaign is significant and without it it is unlikely that there would have been a 'second wave' of activist feminists in Ireland in the early twentieth century. In the early days of the suffrage movement – and the Haslams were involved from the start – it was daring and innovative for women to speak in public, and those women who addressed meetings often encountered considerable hostility and were considered to have disgraced themselves. By the end of the century women speakers had become acceptable and mundane, which, of course, meant that as propagandists they were to a certain degree less effective. Rather than such women being criticized for stale tactics, they should be praised for their ground-breaking activities, which enabled those who came after them to confidently enter the public sphere.

While Anna Haslam's feminism was grounded in her upbringing in a

Quaker household, her marriage to a feminist theorist was a significant factor in her emergence as activist for the cause. One of the defining moments of Anna's life was the appending of her signature to the petition of John Stuart Mill in 1866; this fact was always mentioned whenever she was interviewed or written about. It is very likely that had the petition not been confined to women, Thomas too would have signed. The Haslams of necessity looked to Westminster for reform, and in his letters to Thomas, John Stuart Mill mentioned the need for a suffrage campaign in Dublin.

The petition presented by John Stuart Mill marked the start of the public campaign for votes for women. Mill had been elected to represent the City of Westminster in 1865 despite his pre-election stipulation that he would not canvass for election and, if elected, would not undertake any constituency business. He promised, however, to work for women's suffrage. The embryonic English women's suffrage movement enthusiastically supported Mill's candidature; a carriage was covered with placards urging votes for him, earning him the doubtful accolade of the 'man who wants to have girls in Parliament'.[12] Mill's election, and the imminent Reform Bill, were the catalyst for the formation of the Women's Suffrage Association that collected approximately 1,500 signatures to a petition for votes for women. The petition claimed: 'That the participation of women in the Government is consistent with the principles of the British Constitution inasmuch as women in these islands have always been held capable of sovereignty, and women are eligible for various public offices.' The petition further sought 'the representation of all householders, without distinction of sex, who possess such property or such rental qualification as your honourable House may determine'.[13] Mill considered the completed petition something he could 'brandish with effect'.[14] His success in bringing about the first debate on women's suffrage was, in his opinion, the most important public service which he performed in the House of Commons. In May 1867, during the debate on the Reform Bill, he moved that the word 'man' be replaced by the word 'person', thus ensuring 'that the question of a woman's right to vote was heard for the first time in modern history in the legislative assembly of a civilized country'. After a short debate a division was taken and Mill's amendment received 73 votes, or almost a 'third of the thin attendance'.[15] He was pleased that the introduction of the topic had given an 'immense impulse to the question'.[16]

The successful petition was the catalyst for the formation of a 'provisional' London committee, the membership of which included the Dean of Canterbury. In January 1867, a committee was formed in Manchester for the 'promotion of the enfranchisement of women'.[17] In the autumn of 1867, the 'provisional' London committee became the London National Society for Women's Suffrage.[18] In August 1867, Mill wrote to Thomas Haslam acknowledging receipt of Haslam's 'valuable letter' which was obviously 'not encouraging as to the immediate prospects of the Women's Suffrage movement in Dublin'. Mill conceded that although 'it might not yet be time to organise a Society' in Dublin, 'it is all the more desirable to obtain as many adherents as possible from Ireland to the Society'. He enclosed details of the membership of the Women's Suffrage Society and further stated: 'If the Society might have the benefit of your name and Mrs Haslam's . . . it would give me a very great pleasure.' Mill gave Haslam details of Irish members of parliament who had joined his 'General Committee', among whom were John Francis Meagher MP, founder of the *Cork Examiner*, and Sir John Gray, MP, proprietor of the *Freeman's Journal*. Mill also assured Haslam that he was 'very well acquainted' with the latter's pamphlet, 'which is very good as it is, though I have no doubt that any addition or alteration which you would now make would still further improve it'.[19] T. P. Foley has written that this pamphlet is 'not identified' and speculated that it is the *Marriage Problem*,[20] but this was not published until 1868 and was the subject of a later letter from Mill to Haslam. The pamphlet mentioned here is most probably *The Real Wants of the Irish People*. This work, 'by a Member of the Statistical and Social Inquiry Society of Ireland', was published in Dublin in 1865.[21]

Thomas never demurred from including a bulletin on the state of his health to his correspondents, however eminent. Mill wrote: 'I regret extremely that the state of your health is such as you mention, and I hope that rest and abstinence from unnecessary nervous and cerebral excitement will in time reestablish it.'[22] One month later in a letter to John Eliot Cairnes,[23] Mill is again concerned with the Irish suffrage campaign.[24] He is pleased that Alfred Webb[25] of Dublin has become a member of the suffrage society. Webb, however, 'modestly declines being on the Committee'.[26] Webb obviously shared Haslam's pessimism, as Mill wrote that he was 'not sanguine about gaining much support in Ireland at present, but it will come in time. A good many Irish liberal members of Parliament both Catholic and Protestant have already joined the Committee.'[27] Mill presumably received more positive intelligence of the state of the cause in Ireland in the following year. In a letter written to Haslam in 1868, Mill was 'very happy to hear . . . of the progress of the movement for women's suffrage in Dublin'.[28]

Despite this correspondence, however, there is little evidence of organized suffrage activity in Dublin before 1870, although there were petitions for suffrage presented to parliament from Ireland in 1869. Signatures came mainly from Dublin and environs although there were some also from Cork, Waterford, Queen's County, and twenty-one signatures from Bruree, Co. Limerick.[29] In April 1870, Mrs Millicent Fawcett addressed a large and very successful suffrage meeting at the Molesworth Hall. The theme was 'The Electoral Disabilities of Women', and the distinguished audience included Sir Robert Kane, Sir William and Lady Wilde, Provost Lloyd of Trinity College, Sir John Gray MP, member of Mill's suffrage society, and Revd Mr Mahaffy FTCD. [30] The *Freeman's Journal* reported the meeting in full but did not mention the presence of Anna or Thomas Haslam. However, in the scrapbook of newspaper cuttings compiled by Anna, the names of Isabella Tod, Mr and Mrs Haslam, Miss Corlett, Miss Gough, and Mr and Mrs Eason were added to the printed account in her handwriting. Barbara Corlett, and three members of the Gough family, all with addresses in Dublin, had signed the Mill petition in 1866.[31] In an interview in 1914, Anna talked about her memories of this meeting: 'I well remember seeing Mrs Fawcett, a mere girl leading her blind husband on to the platform. That was the best meeting that was ever held in Dublin – no such names have been got together for any meeting since.'[32] Lady Wilde (Speranza) was very interested in the question of suffrage. She wrote to feminist friends in Sweden: 'There is to be a lecture ... next week in Dublin by Mrs Fawcett, wife of an eminent member of parliament – and there is to be a meeting also at *our* house where she will speak and explain what female liberty means.'[33]

Perhaps due to the presence of Sir John Gray, the Fawcett meeting received extensive coverage in the *Freeman's Journal*. The Molesworth Hall was said to have been crowded 'with a large and influential gathering'; not only was 'the body of the Hall' crowded, but the reserved seats and the platform were 'also completely occupied'. Mrs Fawcett's speech is impressive even to the modern reader. She listed the arguments commonly put forward against votes for women and effectively demolished them. Miss Annie Robertson, 'who was loudly cheered', proposed a vote of thanks to Mrs Fawcett. It is interesting in that she performed this function despite the presence of high-profile male supporters. Also her remarks reveal the existence of a suffrage campaign of sorts in Dublin, but they underline the lack of a public or organized movement. Miss Robertson was gratified to be granted the opportunity of addressing a Dublin assembly. While she had 'already spoken to many thousands of the inhabitants of Dublin, individually and separately in their own houses, upon the question of the enfranchisement of woman', she had never before done so in public. She went on to discuss developments over the previous two years:

> I am glad to be able to testify to the great intelligence of the people of Dublin and to the strong feeling which I know to prevail generally among them in favour of granting the suffrage to women who are householders and ratepayers. When the movement in favour of the enfranchisement of women commenced in Dublin more than two years ago ... I canvassed for signatures among great numbers of the people and in this way found out what an intelligent interest they took in the question when it was explained to them – men and women signed the petition with equal alacrity and in 1868 we sent to Parliament two petitions from Dublin in favour of the enfranchisement of women, signed by nearly three thousand persons of all classes, of different creeds and different political opinions. In 1869 there were ten petitions sent from Dublin and other parts of Ireland, and in the present year, 1870, we have already sent sixteen petitions in favour of the enfranchisement of women and are preparing more.[34]

Miss Robertson's reference to 'many thousands' of Dubliners whom she had addressed individually is surely an exaggeration. Nonetheless, her words reveal the existence of some form of proto-suffrage group as early as 1868 and corroborate the mention of progress in Dublin referred to in Mill's 1868 letter to Haslam. Robertson stated that the progress in Dublin had been mentioned by Jacob Bright 'at the last meeting of the London Society for Women's Suffrage'.[35] She claimed that, after London and Manchester, Dublin had sent most petitions to parliament in the last session. She was unambivalent in her assertion that 'the rapid progress made in this movement during the last two years is altogether owing to the persevering and energetic efforts of women themselves (applause)'. The movement also had among its 'numerous supporters . . . some of the most eminent men in the kingdom'. From her many references to the situation in England and Scotland, it is evident that Miss Robertson saw the Dublin movement as an integral part of the campaign in the United Kingdom.[36] She complained that in Dublin, 'the work has fallen heavily and expensively on one or two persons and it would be well if any ladies or gentlemen who are interested in the cause would come forward and assist it'.[37] We do not know the identity of the 'one or two' persons active for the cause in 1870. It is unlikely that Anna Haslam was one of them as she surely would have referred to this period of activity when discussing her campaigns in later interviews. Moreover the reference of Miss Robertson to the expense borne by 'the one or two' activists would seem to exclude Anna. While Thomas was employed their income was one hundred pounds a year, their relative poverty, after all, was the reason they decided not to have children; when he was forced through ill-health to give up work, their circumstances were presumably even more straitened. It would be unlikely that either Anna or Thomas would have been in a position to bear heavy expense. In the *Irish Citizen* article of 1914 Anna recalled the 1870 meeting: 'It was got up by Miss Robertson who worked alone in the suffrage cause for some years. Petitions were her chief form of activity.'[38] This supports the view that she was not a co-worker but rather that Robertson was her precursor in activism. Helen Blackburn also credits Robertson with the organization of the meeting, and mentions that she had written to Irish candidates in the election of 1869 to elicit their stance on women's suffrage.[39] In a list of those involved in the very early days of suffrage, between 1866 and 1869, there is an entry for 'Robertson, Miss Annie, Dublin, 14th April '68' – presumably the date she joined. The list included Mrs J. T. Haslam, which almost certainly refers to Anna (Mrs T. J. Haslam). The photograph of her in the volume is similarly labelled and there are other typographical errors – e.g. F.W. Newman is listed as T.W. Anna never called herself Mrs T. J. Haslam, however, but was always known as Mrs Anna Maria Haslam.[40]

In April 1871 a notice 'summoning Women's Suffrage workers to a Conference' was signed by 'Hon Secs.' of the movement from principal cities in the United Kingdom. Annie Robertson's name was attached to this notice as 'Hon Sec. Dublin'.[41] The annual report of the National Society for Women's Suffrage (NSWS) London for 1875 acknowledged a subscription of 5/– from Mrs Haslam, Dublin, but also named Miss A. I. Robertson as President of the Dublin Central Committee.[42] Evidence of the existence of a committee in Dublin also appears in the *Englishwoman's Review* of April 1870, which names the members of 'The Dublin Branch of Women's Suffrage Society' as Miss Sharmon Crawford, Mrs Robertson, Miss Robertson, Rev.

W. Handcock, Mr Richards, Honorary Secretary, Miss A. Robertson;[43] furthermore there is a note in Anna Haslam's hand which reads: 'Mrs Fawcett's Meeting 1870; Miss Robertson's Committee 1871, Mrs Haslam's 5/– Subscription to London Feb. 1872 and ever since'.[44] Blackburn's account does not acknowledge the existence of a committee prior to the Haslams'. She wrote of a date in February 1873: 'This was to be the last time on which it could be said that there was no Committee in Dublin. In Mrs Haslam the Women's Suffrage cause had by this time found a worker full of perseverance and buoyant energy.'[45] Blackburn mentions also that by 1872 'there was a London Committee, a Manchester Committee, a Dublin Committee, a Bristol Committee and so on'.[46] A pamphlet, *Women's Need of Representation*, by Miss A. I. Robertson, published in Dublin in 1873, identified the writer as President of the Irish National Society for Women's Suffrage.[47] This pamphlet was the text of a lecture delivered in Dublin and in Portrush in 1871 and 1872. The attendance in Dublin included Lady Wilde and Lord Talbot De Malahide who expressed 'his sympathy with the movement'.[48]

Isabella M. Tod, with whom Anna Haslam worked for the repeal of the Contagious Diseases Acts, 'established the Northern Ireland Society for Women's Suffrage in 1871 and linked it to the London Suffrage Society'. In the early 1870s she 'travelled the country tirelessly speaking at public meetings on the suffrage issue'. As well as addressing meetings in towns all over Ulster, she spoke in Cork, Limerick, Bandon, Clonmel and Waterford.[49] These meetings were reported in the *Women's Suffrage Journal*, an English publication. A useful account of the Cork meeting, which reveals the barracking endured by the female speakers at suffrage meetings, survives in the private journal of Charles Ryan:

> A Woman's Rights meeting was held in Cork but it was very disorderly. When Miss Beed[y] MA came forward a ruffian called out: 'Hurrah for the Venerable Bede.' Miss Downing was requested to 'Speak up darling.' ... 'What's women's rights without women's charms' said another when a particularly ill-favoured lady, Miss Todd [sic] came forward. Singing and disturbance made the meeting very lively.[50]

This account illustrated the lack of seriousness with which the subject and the speakers were treated. The considerable ordeal undergone by a woman speaking in public must have been exacerbated by the unruly nature of meetings and the heckling which had to be endured. Isabella Tod did not complain about difficulties experienced at meetings; on the contrary she wrote to London that 'everywhere they received good local support and met with much cordial sympathy, and nowhere opposition'.[51] Her speaking tour for suffrage also took her to Dublin, where 'some friends ... especially Mrs Haslam, Mr Eason and Miss Corlett', had asked her to hold the closing meeting of the series. Isabella Tod's mention of Miss Robertson's committee is intriguing: 'There is no Committee in Dublin and Miss Robertson who has done much for the cause in other ways, was unfortunately, I believe in

Scotland. The meeting, however, was very good indeed.'[52] Why did Tod and Blackburn ignore the existence of Miss Robertson's committee, which had been detailed in the *Englishwoman's Review* of April 1871, a publication edited by Helen Blackburn. As late as 1875, a report of the NSWS Central Committee listed Miss Annie Robertson as the President of the Dublin Committee.[53] The membership included Lord Talbot De Malahide, Very Reverend Dean of Waterford, the Earl and Countess of Mount Cashell, and other influential and titled persons. Why were Mr and Mrs Haslam, already so interested in the cause, not members? Was membership perhaps confined to the wealthy and influential? At this remove we can only speculate, but it seems remarkable that at a time when support was being actively canvassed, 'Miss Roberston's committee' seems to have counted for naught. Of course, Miss Robertson may not have welcomed Miss Tod's meeting, and her absence in Scotland might well have been diplomatic

We are indebted to Miss Robertson for an interesting glimpse of Dublin's cultural life in a report sent to the *Englishwomen's Review* in 1871. Signs of 'women's progress' in Ireland were detailed; ladies had attended a Royal Dublin Society meeting in the Kildare Street boardroom where a paper was read on 'Recent discoveries in molecular physics'. This was the first time that ladies were 'admitted . . . to a scientific meeting of this society'. There was also evidence cited of 'ladies taking the chair at meetings', including the Lifeboat Bazaar Committee. She also praised Mrs Cusack (the Nun of Kenmare), for her *Life of St. Patrick.* The work had been praised by no less a person than Pope Pius, 'who found time' to send an apostolic letter to the author 'in the midst of his troubles'.[54]

The speakers at Miss Tod's meeting included three clergymen, representing the Church of Ireland, the Presbyterian and the Catholic Churches; the latter was represented by a Father O'Malley.[55] Marie O'Neill has written that after this meeting, 'Mrs Haslam formed a Dublin committee which was to be the forerunner of the Dublin Women's Suffrage Association'.[56] This fact is reiterated by Blackburn: 'This meeting now opened out opportunity for an organized cohesion of friends of the movement and . . . [Anna Haslam] took up the work as Honorary Secretary of the Committee in Dublin.'[57] Although Anna Haslam and her husband Thomas are invariably credited with starting the suffrage movement in Dublin, it is clear that Anne Isabella Robertson was involved in some form of organized suffrage activity as early as 1869 and that there was at least a nominal committee in place in Dublin. An entry in the minute book in the very early days of the Dublin Women's Suffrage Association records the formal proposal that Miss Robertson 'be asked to join the General Committee'. Miss Robertson, it was reported, did not reply to the invitation.[58]

While there is no other record of organized suffrage activism by the Haslams before 1876, a short-lived but interesting periodical appeared in 1874, in which Thomas Haslam penned his ideas on the rights of women to a 'more positive legal status'. There were only three issues of this journal, which might be more correctly called a series of pamphlets, which they resembled in layout and content. The first issue of the *Women's Advocate* published in April 1874 was implicitly addressed to Irishmen. In it Haslam challenged the perception that women 'degrade themselves by stepping out of their natural sphere of unobtrusive modesty' in seeking political equality. He trenchantly countered criticism of women's public agitation for the vote: 'If you are grieved to see so many of our best and noblest women "unsex themselves" – as you affect to call it – what have you done to prevent the necessity for their so demeaning themselves?'[59] It is difficult to know whether Haslam was referring to the situation in Ireland or whether his use of the term 'our country' meant the United Kingdom of Great Britain and Ireland. Ray Strachey has synopsized contemporary (1873) arguments against granting of votes to women, using uncited quotes: 'It would "unsex" women, "contaminate" them, "drag them down to our own coarse and rough level," and "defile their modesty and purity".'[60]

A perusal of newspapers for the month before the first issue of Haslam's periodical reveals that he was in correspondence with the editor of the *Freeman's Journal* regarding an editorial on the subject of the enfranchisement of women published in the issue of 10 March 1874. The editorial was a comment on the sixth annual report of the Manchester National Society for Women's Suffrage. The leader writer argued that 'women suffer many disabilities which have their origins not so much in male selfishness and tyranny as in the belief that men care and can care for the best interests of women much better than women themselves.' This thesis was based on the ideology of separate spheres with its emphasis on the 'angel in the house', pure *Sesame and Lilies*:[61]

> There is work for both sexes, and each has its sphere distinctly marked. Man is made for the outer world in all its ruggedness and encounter; woman for the house, with all its sweet influences and charming solace . . . We think it may be safely advanced that, even if the suffrage were extended womanward tomorrow, i[t] would be void almost altogether in deference to husbands and brothers and lovers . . . So far as we can learn the majority of those ladies who advocate what they call equality have no home ties, or are outside the sweet slavery of marriage vows.[62]

The editorial warned against rushing into 'extravagances such as mark the utterances and writings of the Manchester folk – utterances often unwomanly and almost always unreasonable'.[63] Thomas Haslam immediately wrote to the *Freeman's Journal* in response to this editorial. Perhaps prudently on this occasion he ignored the separate sphere ideology and the charge of 'unwomanly' utterances and challenged it on a point of fact:

> Will you allow me to correct an error into which you have as I am sure *inadvertently* [his italics] fallen in your quotation of the Parliamentary statistics of the Women's Suffrage movement. The number of petitioners to the House of Commons in 1872 in favour of our bill was not 79,000 but 355,801 . . . It is quite true the question is not one of very

pressing interest in Ireland; still even here it is making satisfactory way. [64]

Another correspondent challenged the editorial, 'which must be distasteful and discouraging to all . . . readers who are friends of the women's suffrage movement'. The writer claimed that there was much support for the cause in Ireland: 'Some of the best, if not the very best speeches in support . . . were made by Irish members . . . One hundred and forty-six petitions, if not more, went to the House of Commons from Ireland in support of the bill last year.'[65] Haslam again featured in the *Freeman's Journal* of 24 March, in a letter that was a pragmatic response to criticism from within the ranks of suffrage supporters, to the Women's Disabilities Removal Bill. This bill proposed that in all acts pertaining to the registration of voters 'wherever words occur which import the masculine gender the same shall be held to include females'. The bill, proposed by Mr Forsyth MP, included a clause 'excluding married women from the operation of the Act if passed'.[66] This proviso, which caused a split in the English suffrage movement, was included because Forsyth believed it increased the chances of the bill being carried. In a second letter Haslam defended the bill, while remaining noncommittal on the principle enshrined within it: 'Rightly, or wrongly, it is popularly assumed that married women are fairly represented by their husbands.' His letter was in support of the 'women who are not so represented . . . women of independent means – spinsters and widows who have to support their families'.[67] His letter provoked the ire of J. T. Hoskins[68] who, writing from the Reform Club, declared himself 'one who has . . . practically evinced his devotion to the cause of female emancipation', but who regarded the proposed bill an insult to married women.[69] The correspondence does not appear have progressed beyond this and in the event the bill was defeated on a second reading when eventually it came up for discussion.

Haslam's attitude as revealed in this correspondence is cautious. He does not allow himself to be drawn into the controversial question of the right of married women to the vote, rather he defends the rights of the women who are the subject of the bill. This caution, or perhaps, pragmatism, is a constant feature of Haslam's propagandizing; his methodology consisted of attempting to avoid controversy, and of concentrating instead on topics that he tried to show in as reasonable a light as possible. There is no doubt that Haslam would have wanted the vote for married as well as for single women of 'independent' means. His attitude, presumably, was the same as that of Forsyth, 'who believed that his proviso [the exclusion of married women] would increase the chances of carrying the Bill'.[70] It would also be the thin end of the wedge. Suffragists claimed the vote on the same terms as men, but in practice, they were prepared to support any bill, no matter how limited, that would overcome the sex barrier.[71] David Rubenstein has argued that the enfranchising of any women, no matter how limited the category, 'would have established a vital principle and held out the hope that the franchise would subsequently be extended to women on terms of complete equality with men'.[72]

Haslam does not challenge the 'separate sphere' ideology inherent in the criticism he is addressing in the *Women's Advocate;* on the contrary he appears to deplore that inequity forces women to emerge into the public arena: 'These ladies have been drawn – may we not say *dragged* – from the privacy of their firesides by an overpowering sense of duty, not merely to themselves, or their own sex, but even to the very men who scoff at their want of delicacy.' He wants men to assist women's release from their restrictions including access to 'an equitable share of our educational appliances'. Practical help included 'vigorous support' for the forthcoming Women's Disabilities Removal Bill that would extend suffrage to the very small number of women who were householders and ratepayers. His spirited defence of the 'womanliness' or otherwise, of those who petitioned for the vote is, perhaps, predicated on his perception of his own wife, who was by this time the family breadwinner. He asked: 'Is it womanly to pay rates and taxes ... to conduct the operations of a complicated business, purchase goods; provide for bills when due ... with a hundred other details which women in this position cannot evade if they would maintain their families in honest independence.' Thomas also reminded his readers that 'Englishwomen who are ratepayers possess the *municipal* franchise'; Irishwomen did not. He entreated his readers to write to their representatives to ask them to have this anomaly corrected.[73]

The *Women's Advocate* carried under its title the words of Herbert Spencer: 'Equity knows no difference of sex. The law of equal freedom applies to the whole race – female as well as male', a quotation that had been used by Millicent Fawcett in her 1870 speech in Dublin. Haslam attributed his allegiance to the cause of women's suffrage to his having read this quotation in 1851.[74] Haslam's analysis of the rightful place of women is complex. While he is unambiguous in his claims of the rights of women to equality, there is in his early writings on suffrage, evidence of an ambiguity in regard to the vexed question of campaigning women leaving themselves open to charges of 'demeaning themselves' by being forced into the 'field of controversy'. There seems to be in his writing at least a tacit acceptance of the doctrine, or perhaps more correctly, an ability to argue from an angle of acceptance. It must be remembered that his arguments were addressed to men in an effort to persuade them to become advocates of women in their search for the vote. There is, I think, a degree of sophistry in these arguments. In addressing his entreaties to men, he exploited the common perception of the indelicacy of women being forced to enter the public sphere. He used this ploy in order to persuade men that they should campaign on behalf of women, thus removing the necessity of such women behaving in what might be deemed an 'indelicate' manner. In practice, Haslam enthusiastically supported his wife's entry into the public sphere, and was a regular attender at suffrage and CDA meetings addressed by women. He was above all a pragmatist, who acknowledged the possible prejudice of his audience and sought to persuade within its constraints, rather than risk alienating it by attacking dearly held opinions. His later writings, as I will discuss, reveal his unambivalent disapproval of an attitude that claimed women needed to be 'protected' from participation in public life.

The May 1874 edition of the *Women's Advocate* dealt with methods of political action. Activists were urged to form themselves into local societies of three or four and to communicate with one of the 'central' associations. They should subscribe to the *Women's Suffrage Journal* or *Englishwoman's Review* and petition parliament. Although petitions may be 'over-rated; if they do not wield the magical power with which they are sometimes credited; still they have weight with Members of Parliament and when the numbers swell to an aggregate of several hundred thousand, they exercise a potent influence on the public mind'. He pointed out that in 1873, 300,000 inscribed their names on behalf of the Disabilities Removal Bill in 900 separate petitions. This did not, of course, succeed, but Haslam was right in that the question was now firmly in the public domain. His advice was an admirable example of practicality and reveals him not only as a theorist, but as someone with experience of organizing protest, albeit of the most law-abiding and constitutional nature. He stipulated that signatures must be obtained only from those committed to the cause; otherwise, 'a spirit of unscrupulousness' will be fostered, which is a 'source of weakness'. A steady stream of petitions must be produced; if they fall away 'observers infer that the cause is losing ground'. Sustained efforts to convert individual members of parliament by private letters was judged worthwhile; such members will realize that 'there is a reality in a cause which inspires such enthusiasm . . . sooner or later the justice of your claims will fall upon their minds'. Haslam gave much advice on the organizing of public meetings; he stressed the importance of engaging high quality speakers. He deemed public meetings effective in 'rousing up the zeal of despondent sympathisers' and in stimulating interest in the subject. He advised the penning of letters to newspapers by those who could employ 'a quick eye and fluent pen' with use of brief practical illustrations, rather than 'pages of faultless arguments'. Above all the campaign must never be allowed sink into oblivion.[75] Anna revealed in an interview in the *Irish Citizen* that his advice was considered so useful that 5,000 copies of this leaflet were ordered by Lydia Becker,[76] the English suffragist pioneer, for distribution to English activists.[77] The *Women's Advocate* was not produced in June 1874, and in July the third and final number contained a brief rebuttal of the *Spectator*'s hostile attitude to suffrage entitled, 'Woman Suffrage *versus* 'The Spectator'.[78]

The minute book of the Dublin Women's Suffrage Society shows the first recorded meeting to have taken place on 21 February 1876 in the Leinster Hall, Molesworth Street. Charles Eason chaired the meeting.[79] The account of the first meeting does not include a list of attendance, but a partial list can be reconstructed from resolutions passed. Abraham Shackleton (treasurer), Miss Corlett, Miss McDowell and Mrs Haslam were present. A resolution passed confirms that a committee had been in place before this meeting: 'That Mrs Haslam and Miss McDowell be requested to act as secretaries for a short time longer.'[80] The report of the second meeting of 6 March includes a list of the attendance: Henry Allen (chairman), Mrs McCarthy, Lady

Murray, Miss E. Webb, Miss Geoghegan, Miss Russell, Miss Corlett, Miss Laffan, Mrs Butler, Miss Helen Webb, Miss McDowell, Mr and Mrs Haslam. An executive committee was formed which included Mr Eason, Mrs Haslam, Miss Corlett, Miss McDowell, Miss Emily Webb and Miss Helen Webb.[81]

A suffrage meeting held in Dublin on 26 January 1876 in Exhibition Palace Hall, Earlsfort Terrace (now the National Concert Hall) would appear to have been the catalyst for the formation of the DWSA.[82] Among the speakers were Lydia Becker, Lilias Ashworth,[83] Eliza Sturges of Birmingham and Isabella Tod. They were supported by Mr W. H. Allen and Sergeant Sherlock MP, both of whom were subsequently DWSA members. The meeting was constantly interrupted by disturbance 'from the lower part of the room' and 'hisses' during the speeches. When the motion 'that the exclusion of women otherwise legally qualified from voting in the election of members of Parliament is injurious to those excluded' was put to the house, there were 'cries of aye and some confusion at the end of the hall'. The chairman, Maurice Brookes MP, asked that 'any person . . . of opinion it should not pass . . . say no. There was no response . . . and the resolution was carried unanimously.'[84]

The formation of the DWSA executive committee at the February meeting marked the start of a formal movement dedicated to the campaign for equality for women. Mrs Haslam proposed that an annual subscription of one shilling per annum 'shall constitute membership in the association'. Mrs Haslam and Miss Rose McDowell were appointed secretaries. Initially the meetings were irregular, usually about four a year, and mainly concerned with the presentation of petitions to parliament. The involvement of influential men in the suffrage society is striking. Among regular attenders at meetings were members of parliament including T.W. Russell,[85] Maurice Brookes,[86] Colonel Taylor[87] and William Johnston.[88] The Sergeant-at-Arms, David Sherlock, was a frequent participator.[89] The DWSA was proud of the male input to the society: 'co-operation with men has been a distinguishing feature of the policy of the Association from the first'.[90]

Many of the association's founding members had Quaker connections. In Europe and the United States Quakers were associated with the cause of suffrage.[91] Dora Mellone, suffragist and journalist, wrote that the Society of Friends was 'as prominent in the history of suffrage in Ireland as it is in every good work . . . to the Friends almost alone has it been given to win the trust and love of the Catholic South and the Protestant North, and so we find the name of Mrs Haslam in . . . suffrage work'.[92] Abraham Shackleton was a member of the Kildare family that had founded the Quaker school at Ballitore in 1726. The Webbs were a Quaker family 'remembered for the self-sacrificing work of its members in anti-slavery, prison reform, anti-capital punishment, peace and many other practical concerns'.[93] Henry Allen came from a prominent Quaker family one of whom had died of smallpox contracted while administering relief in Metz in the aftermath of the Franco–Prussian War.[94] Barbara Corlett, a Quaker, was a signatory of the Mill petition in 1866. She was involved in the Queen's Institute established in 1861

as a training centre and employment agency for young women.[95] Helen
Blackburn, in a discussion on advances gained by women in the categories
of 'Systematic Training Professional or Technical' wrote: 'Who ever thought
of such things until women had begun to realize their need of an equal
status as ratepayers? Then it was that . . . a Barbara Corlett could uphold the
need of such a systematic training as should give higher value to the work
of women, whether within the home or outside the home.'[96] Anna Haslam
was at the preliminary meeting of the Society for the Promotion of
Employment for Women.[97] Charles Eason was at different times a member
of Baptist, Presbyterian and Church of Ireland congregations and was
known as a holder of radical opinions. He shared with his wife feminist
views that were considered advanced for the times.[98] Eason was also
involved in the campaign against the Contagious Diseases Acts (CDAs).
Clergymen were prominent in the early days of the DWSA. In 1878,
Reverend T. Carmichael addressed a meeting in Baggot Street on 'women's
rights', and Reverend W. A. McDonald spoke on 'women's position' to
Trinity Church YMCA in Gardiner Street.[99] Clergymen regularly attended
committee meetings and also supported public meetings. David Sherlock
QC, First Sergeant at Arms, member for King's County and regularly chaired
DWSA meetings was, unusually for the DWSA, a Roman Catholic.[100]

The essentially middle-class nature of the association, a fact invariably
remarked upon by historians, is not surprising. The feminist socialist Helena
Moloney remarked that the Irish women's movement 'which aroused such
a deep feeling of social consciousness and revolt among Irish women of a
more favoured class, passed over the head of the Irish working woman and
left her untouched'.[101] Education was a vital element in the development of
feminist consciousness, and while there is evidence of working-class
involvement in England, particularly among the textile unions, there was no
similar involvement in Ireland, a fact regretted by Anna Haslam.[102]
However, in 1880 on the occasion of the Trades Union Congress meeting in
Dublin, 'a successful meeting was held, Jessie Craigan[103] [sic] being the chief
speaker, the first instance in Ireland of the effort to enlist the sympathies of
Labour'.[104] In the later suffrage era Helena Moloney enjoyed some limited
success in unionizing and politicizing working women.

Accounts of DWSA meetings contained in the minute book of the society
are perfunctory but reveal that much effort was invested in the obtaining of
signatures to petitions that were subsequently forwarded to Westminster. In
1877, there were '13 petitions containing 2,912 signatures . . . forwarded to
the House . . . presented by Sir A. Guinness and Colonel Taylor.'[105] One year
later we learn that '15 petitions were forwarded during the 1878 session'
which contained 3,191 signatures.[106] There was a veritable deluge of petitions presented to parliament in this period, particularly whenever a private
member's suffrage bill was being introduced. In the decade of the 1870s
there was a bill introduced every year except 1875. In the early days of the
DWSA there is occasional evidence of petition fatigue. In September 1876, it
was first proposed that a 'reliable man' be engaged at a pound a week for
four weeks to collect signatures to petitions. The minute book does not

record the outcome of this initiative despite the intention of the secretaries to 'report results to Committee'.[107] In March 1877, it was reported: 'Collection of signatures being proceeded with but great difficulty is found in getting people to sign.' It was particularly difficult to obtain signatures from women householders. 'Prevailing ignorance' was given as the reason for the poor response.[108] In April 1879, it is noted in the minute book, that 'a young person' was employed for a couple of weeks collecting signatures. Four hundred and twenty-five signatures were obtained by this method at a rate of five shillings per hundred.[109] The employment of paid procurers of signatures suggests a paucity of voluntary resources; it seems at variance with the spirit of Thomas Haslam's remarks in the *Women's Advocate* where he warned of the lack of 'moral value' in obtaining signatures of those who were indifferent to the cause. Nonetheless, Thomas had seconded the proposal that a paid canvasser be engaged to gather petition signatures.[110] One would imagine that a payment per signature might well lead to abuse of the system. The desirability, or otherwise, of the employment of professional canvassers as a method of collecting signatures does not appear to have engendered any lengthy discussion. This could, of course, be the result of the laconic style favoured by the compiler.

Other than collecting signatures for petitions, the main work of the Dublin Women's Suffrage Association in its early stages consisted in striving to overcome the 'prevailing ignorance' of Dubliners regarding the cause of votes for women. The committee placed emphasis on the educational role of the society. It strove to spread the message by circulating periodicals that advocated suffrage for women. At a meeting in September 1876, the secretaries were requested 'to obtain leave from the various reading rooms in the city to permit copies of the *Women's Suffrage Journal* to be laid on their tables'.[111] In January 1877, it was reported that the DWSA had arranged that the reading rooms of Trinity College, the Chamber of Commerce, the Royal Dublin Society, Mechanics' Institute, Coffee Palace and the Friends' Institute 'now receive the *Women's Suffrage Journal*'.[112] By 1879 the following establishments were included in the list of venues to which 'suffrage journals were sent': the Free Libraries in Thomas Street, Capel Street and Kingstown; the Workman's Club, Charlemont Place; Law, Historical and Philosophical Societies of Trinity College, and the Constitutional Club.[113] A great number of the above reading rooms were male-only preserves.

Drawing-room meetings in private houses were a favoured method of getting the message across to small numbers of invited guests. The minute book frequently mentions that such meetings had taken place, e.g.: 'Successful drawing-room held at Mr Eason's',[114] and, 'Two drawing rooms were held ... excellent addresses'.[115] The committee did not neglect self-education. It was regularly addressed by visiting activists from London. The committee instructed Mrs Haslam to 'purchase *The Women's Question in Europe*' for eleven shillings to lend to members. The DWSA members were aware of contemporary social and intellectual movements, and on at least two occasions held meetings in conjunction with congresses in Dublin. In September 1880 the Trades Union Congress held in Dublin was the subject of a debate at a DWSA committee, when it was decided 'after much discussion that it was not considered expedient' to hold a meeting for Miss Craigen.[116] It is likely that Miss Craigen was initially considered a bit off-putting for a Dublin audience. Helen Blackburn called her a 'strange erratic genius' who planned and carried out her tours alone, 'accompanied only by her little dog'. She appears to have devoted herself to spreading the suffrage message to workingmen, 'now miners . . . now fishers . . . or agricultural labourers', from whom she gathered petitions 'which in their grimy condition bore token of their genuineness'.[117] However, at the next DWSA meeting the secretaries reported that

> notwithstanding the determination come to at the last committee meeting they had taken upon themselves after consulting some of the Committee to hold a meeting in the Coffee Palace during the Trades Union Congress for the purpose of hearing Miss Craigen. The meeting was a perfect success and the Committee expressed their approval of the action of the secretaries.[118]

The meeting was reported in the *Englishwoman's Review* where we are told that it was addressed also by other women attending the Trades Union Congress.[119] Why did the secretaries decide to overturn the decision taken by the attending committee? This entry reveals, I think, the force of Anna Haslam as the true mover of the committee. Of course, without knowing how Anna contributed to the original discussion, this is speculation. Her fellow secretary for many years, Rose McDowell, appears to have been a backroom person. One comes across her only as a joint signature. Most of the minute book entries are in Anna's handwriting. This occasion of Jessie Craigen's address was referred to in the preface to the published collection of the committee's reports as an important occurrence in the history of the association, albeit that Miss Craigen's name was misspelt.[120] Jennie Craigen was a supporter of Anna Parnell's Ladies' Land League and visited Bodyke, Co. Clare, the scene of infamous evictions, in the summer of 1881.[121]

The DWSA has been described as 'preaching to the converted'[122] at 'small meetings, usually in the drawing rooms of members' houses'.[123] In reality, in the first years, the major resources of the committee were expended on large public meetings to which prominent speakers were invited. The first arranged by the fledgling association was in the Antient Concert Rooms on 6 April 1877. This was judged not 'so successful as we had wished . . . especially owing to the determined hostility of a small knot of disturbers'[124] – obviously not a case of merely preaching to the converted. Financial trouble also ensued as there was a deficit of £5 12s 1d and Mr Webb's printing bill had not been paid. Eliza Wigham, visiting from Edinburgh, gave 'a few words of encouragement in the full conviction that though the work is uphill and the opposition at present envenomed, eventual victory is certain'.[125] Despite the optimistic tone of this rallying call the impression gained is that the committee was battling against the odds. In October 1877 'Members of the Committee were asked to raise from 5/– to 10/– among their friends before the close of the year'.[126] Undeterred by this discouraging start, another public meeting was held in Leinster Hall on 19 August 1878. 'Much good has been done by this meeting' with which Lord Talbot De Malahide was associated.[127] The Lord Mayor presided at the DWSA public meeting at Leinster Hall in 1879.[128] A 'large and most influential' gathering was held in Leinster Hall in October 1881, which was 'crowded . . . [M]any people had to be turned back as there was not even standing room to be had.'[129] The publicity for this meeting, held in conjunction with the Social Science Congress, was impressive: '750 cards and 1,000 fly leaves' were printed and distributed; the 'usual' advertisements were placed in the newspapers, and placards placed in the tram cars.[130]

The embryonic Dublin suffrage movement had been affiliated to the English movement from the beginning. Mrs Haslam attended the 'Great Manchester Demonstration' in February 1880 for which she claimed expenses of £2 10s 0d. When asked to give an account of the meeting she demurred that she was no speaker; rather than speak from memory she had taken the precaution of preparing notes. Her account highlights the excitement of the occasion and conveys the impression that women present had a sense of being mould-breakers in the tradition of great reform movements of the past:

> The famous Free Trade Hall where in bye-gone times the voices of John Bright and Richard Cobden so often rang out during the Corn Law agitation was crowded by thousands of women who thronged the steps of the platform, passages and every available spot so that an overflow meeting had to be improvised in the Memorial Hall adjoining . . . [T]he meetings were managed from first to last by women – gentlemen, except the reporters were not to be seen in the body of the hall – they were relegated to the gallery on payment of 2/6 each (the entire hall being free to women).[131]

Although Anna Haslam's efforts for equal opportunity for women never included comments, nor suggested actions, which might be termed anti-male, there is in this account a rarely exhibited sense of glee in her comments of how, for once, when women were in control they neatly turned the tables on the male audience. Gentlemen who complained of the arrangements in the Free Trade Hall were reminded that 'in the most august assembly in the land, ladies were not only condemned to sit in a gallery perched up in the clouds, but were carefully caged in where they could not be seen and could very badly see and hear', whereas gentlemen at the Manchester meeting were offered 'their choice of seats in a fine spacious gallery where they could see and hear the ladies'.[132] These comments express familiarity with the purdah-like conditions to which women were condemned when they visited the Houses of Parliament. Female suffrage campaigners attended the debates of the many defeated bills, confined to quarters that effectively reinforced 'their unfranchised state in emphatic physical terms'.[133] Anna does not mention that she had addressed the Manchester Demonstration, a fact documented by Blackburn.[134]

Between the foundation of the DWSA in 1876 and the granting to Irishwomen of the right to become poor law guardians in 1896, there was a steady stream of unsuccessful suffrage bills presented to parliament. The DWSA lobbied assiduously for each bill. The modus operandi was simple but effective, and the campaign was not confined to Dublin. As well as initiating petitions, letters were sent to women all over Ireland by Anna Haslam as Honorary Secretary of the DWSA, asking them to organize local suffrage committees and to write to Irish members of parliament urging their support. Such letters, she argued, 'would have great weight with our Members; and the total expense need not exceed a pound at the farthest'.[135] Occasionally, an example of a suitable letter to members of parliament was included; recipients were asked to 'send a similar letter in your own language to all members in your town and county and any others over whom you can exert influence'.[136] In March 1884, when the campaign to include franchise for women householders in the forthcoming Reform Bill was at its height, a circular letter requested that the recipient 'not only write personally' to both 'Borough and County members', but that she 'induce the largest number of . . . friends and acquaintances, men and women to do the same'. The circular continued forcefully: 'Write to members; to Mr Gladstone; to other Cabinet members; to Mr Trevelyan; insisting and entreating that they will not deny to Women householders a measure of long withheld justice . . . But our action should be prompt and universal; we should not lose a day in pressing our claim.'[137] In April 1884, Anna mounted a newspaper campaign. She wrote to the *Daily Express* regarding the 'Household Franchise Bill'. She wished to 'solicit the kind support of the newspaper'. She argued that 'we have justice on our side as well as constitutional principle; our claim is a . . . reasonable one'. Her letter reveals her methods and also the other reforms to which she was committed:

> The only debatable argument is whether we shall be included in the present Franchise Bill or be compelled to go on agitating, petitioning, addressing public meetings, interviewing members of Parliament memorializing Cabinet Ministers . . . for another ten or fifteen years, to the exceeding waste of time of these energies which we might be devoting to the improvement of our educational, sanitary, licensing, poor law and other systems which greatly need reform.

She claimed supporters 'among all shades of opinion – Conservative, Liberal and Home Ruler'.[138] This letter was one of fifty-four sent to newspapers in Leinster, Munster and Connaught, thirty of which were published. A circular containing the history of Irish MPs' voting record on women's suffrage was 'largely distributed among friends of the movement requesting them to write to their members' and provoked a 'good response'.[139] Sixteen petitions were forwarded to the House of Commons, twelve to the House of Lords and 'numerous letters sent to members'.[140] Anna's obituary in the *Woman's Leader* praised her prodigious workload: 'No work appeared to her too great; no detail too small or tedious. To circularize every Irish Member, or to write thirty or forty letters to prominent public men with her own hand was mere child's play.'[141]

This 1884 Reform Bill was considered a 'great opportunity' for the introduction of the franchise for women householders.[142] In addition to the efforts described above, the DWSA in January had requested a meeting with Chief Secretary, G. O. Trevelyan, to plead the cause of Irishwomen. Trevelyan's reply regretted that his 'numerous engagements and the pressing nature' of 'duties before the meeting of Parliament render it impossible' to receive a deputation from the Women's Suffrage Association'. He would, however, 'be happy carefully to consider any statement which you may wish to make in writing'.[143] The draft of the response to this communication, penned in Anna Haslam's hand, reveals her as a consummate advocate of her cause, with a nice line in irony, and a distinct writing style as befitted her Quaker ethos. She regretted that Trevelyan could not 'find time to receive a Deputation from us', and continued rather wearily: 'We would gladly avail ourselves of your kind promise to consider any statement of our claim which we would wish to state before you, if we really believed that any formal statement of our claim was necessary.' Trevelyan was reminded that as a supporter of their cause he understood 'the bearings and merits of our case as perfectly as we do ourselves'. (Trevelyan was a supporter of votes for women and had voted for Mill's amendment in 1867.)[144] She told him that 'there is nothing to distinguish our case in Ireland from that of our sisters in Great Britain, except that we have not yet been conceded even the minor privilege of the Municipal Franchise – nor are we eligible to become Poor Law Guardians.' The letter argued that the 'prejudice with which our claims were almost universally regarded when first advanced by John Stuart Mill, has almost totally disappeared', and correspondingly, support for the movement had grown. In 1883 the majority of Irish members 'voted or paired in the affirmative' (twenty-four for, seventeen against); this 'faithfully mirrored the state of public opinion here'. Trevelyan was reminded that 'up to the present time it cannot be said that we women have urged our claims . . . in any fractious, impatient or unreasonable manner'. However, unless the 'extremely moderate, equitable and expedient measure of enfranchisement be conceded to us we shall smart under a sense of injustice, if not indeed of contumely such as they have never felt before'. Uncharacteristically from this source, there seems here an implicit threat of fractious, unreasonable behaviour to come if the vote went against them. Trevelyan was told bluntly what was expected of him:

> I do confidently expect that whenever the question may come up for discussion, whether it be in the Cabinet, or in the House of Commons you at least will be found amongst our champions, and that not even your many onerous duties will prevent your raising an earnest influential voice in our favour.

Anna revealed herself 'operating individually' as a Liberal supporter: 'If it were a Liberal Government with Mr Gladstone at its head . . . which should inflict this injury upon us and if we should be compelled to look at a cabinet, presided over by the Marquess of Salisbury . . . to redress this wrong . . . we should bitterly deplore it.' However, she continued: 'I will not for a moment believe that our present enlightened Government will stultify itself by so dishonourable a breach of its cherished principles.' The tone of this letter is confident; the Chief Secretary is addressed as an equal. He is gently chided for the typically bureaucratic brush-off, the request to 'put it in writing', and reminded that he understands the rightness of their case only too well, both as a declared supporter in the House and as 'one of the highest living authorities on the subject of our present elective system'.[145] There is not a trace of importuning in the tone of the letter; rather it is suggested that Trevelyan and his party do the decent thing or allegiance will be transferred to those who will. This letter could, of course, have been produced by committee, but its appearance suggests that it was drafted by Anna herself. It is possible that Thomas may have put his writing skills at her disposal but I think this unlikely; his style is different, less direct, more conciliatory. Anna's letter is compelling, direct, convincing and unapologetic, and reveals her as a lobbyist of no mean skills. A similar letter from 'seventy-six representative women of the day' to Members of Parliament is much less impressive, more cliché-ridden. It purported 'respectfully' to represent 'the claim of duly-qualified women' and 'earnestly begged' support.[146]

In the event, the Reform Bill did not include a clause enfranchising women householders. Strachey wrote bitterly: 'Party loyalty was stronger than promises to non-voters, stronger than conviction itself, and when the division came 104 of the Liberal Members who were pledged supporters voted against the Women's Suffrage amendment which was thereby roundly defeated.'[147] Blackburn was equally disillusioned: 'Liberal members known to be favourable to the inclusion of women householders in the Bill were informed, by the usual official channels for conveying the mind of the Government, that they were not to be free to exercise their judgement, nor to vote according to their honest convictions.'[148] Mr Gladstone explained that as much had 'been introduced into the Bill as . . . it can safely carry'.[149] Finally, the attempt to introduce a clause to extend parliamentary franchise to women householders was defeated by 271 votes to 135. The *Women's Suffrage Journal* summed it up:

> The true significance of the division may be estimated by an examina-tion of the number of known friends of Women's Suffrage who voted on this occasion in the Government majority. The number is no less than 104. If these 104 members had voted according to their previous wont and their avowed convictions they would have been deducted from the 271 who voted against the clause – leaving 167 opponents – and, added to the 135 supporters, which would have raised the vote in favour of the clause to 239.[150]

The defeat of the clause for the enfranchisement of women was a bitter disappointment. The sums had been done and victory seemed assured. The provisions of the Act, when passed, meant that 'the male population was now very fully enfranchised, and the impetus for pushing democracy farther appeared to be spent'.[151] Simultaneously the provisions of the Corrupt Practices Act (1883) resulted in the recruitment of women as unpaid party workers, as it was no longer legal to pay professional canvassers. Strachey has stated that activities of women in party politics did a great deal for the suffrage cause, as it could no longer be argued that women were unfit for the 'rough and tumble' of politics: 'They proved their utility; and by so doing they broke down the ancient belief that politics was exclusively a man's job.'[152] An acrimonious split occurred in the English suffrage movement between those who wished to include party political associations as affiliates and those who wished to keep the suffrage movement free from the 'intrusion of party spirit into the neutrality hitherto so carefully preserved'.[153] The DWSA were firmly behind Mrs Fawcett, who wished to remain independent of any party-political affiliation. She subsequently formed the National Society for Women's Suffrage (NSWS), established on the old non-party lines, and Mrs Haslam was appointed to the London executive.[154] The acrimony in London was replicated in Dublin, as at the meeting at which the committee's support for Mrs Fawcett was approved, 'Mr Shackleton and Mr Webb withdrew during the proceedings and . . . Mr Wigham resigned his membership from the Committee.'[155] The Dublin committee remained independent and non-party. Perhaps this dissent was the reason for the long gap between the meeting of 4 January 1889 and the next one on 26 February 1890. The reason given for the delay in convening a meeting was that they had been advised that 'there was no necessity for much agitation at present'.[156]

The determination of Anna Haslam to retain the non-party nature of the DWSA was, perhaps, based on pragmatism as well as principle. The argument for party-political affiliation was that it enabled suffragists to work for change from within a political party. What was meant in reality was affiliation to the Liberal Party, 'the obvious and traditional Party of reform'.[157] The defeat of the Liberal government on the Home Rule question and the ensuing split, the increasing strength of the Irish Parliamentary Party and the coming to power of the Conservative Party, would suggest that, in Ireland, the obvious thing to do was to remain politically neutral. Among the DWSA membership there were Liberals, Irish Parliamentary Party members and some Conservatives. Although Anna was vehemently anti-Home Rule, she worked happily and fruitfully for suffrage with those who were its enthusiastic supporters. She constantly reiterated the non-party, non-sectarian nature of the DWSA. In 1900 the association's non-party stance was repeated in a statement that '*as an Association*' it 'could take no part in Party politics – but that individually . . . [members] retained full liberty of action'.[158]

There is no documentary evidence extant of the attitude of the DWSA towards the Ladies' Land League that operated in Ireland from January 1881 to August 1882. One might have expected an organization that demonstrated that women were capable of operating a countrywide campaign under the most difficult of circumstances to have elicited comment from the executive committee of the DWSA. The women of the Ladies' Land League displayed the same organizational efficiency as the DWSA. It famously compiled 'The Book of Kells', a detailed register of all land rentals in the country, and also efficiently administered the Land League's considerable funds. The feminist press in England was opposed to these ladies' 'illegal' activities, however, and greeted news of the arrest of members with satisfaction. The seeming leniency of the constabulary towards the ladies prior to the arrests was deplored, as the principle of men and women being equal before the law was one of the basic tenets of the feminist movement. There is no evidence of the attitude of the Haslams to the Ladies' Land League. They would, however, have been bitterly opposed to what they would have perceived as the illegal nature of its operations, although they might well have been sympathetic to its work to alleviate distress caused by evictions. Dublin was a small city. Anna Parnell walked home to Hatch Street every evening from the League's offices in Sackville Street. It is extremely likely that members of the DWSA were acquainted with Ladies' Land League executive members – they may even have been friends. The actions of the Ladies' Land League were given much press coverage. However, the minutes of the DWSA never mentioned them, but they rarely dealt with anything other than suffrage matters. I think it fair to say that women of the calibre of the Parnell sisters and their co-members would have believed in female suffrage, despite the evidence of the embryonic Ladies' Land League in America being careful to point out that it had no connection with the suffrage movement.[159]

From an anti-Home Rule speech delivered by Anna on 22 June 1888, it is evident that she felt considerable animosity towards the National League, the association which replaced Land League and worked for Home Rule, and its methods. She argued that: 'no country in the world ... enjoys a greater amount of reasonable liberty than Ireland does at the present time – with indeed one melancholy exception – the tyranny of the National League – the most unscrupulous body of men, I suppose that ever attempted to seize the reigns of power in our land.' The language of this speech is most untypically heated and intemperate:

> The danger which now threatens us is – that the whole government of our country, legislature and administration, may be virtually handed over to these men to plunder and boycott and tyrannise over us as they like, unchecked by the wisdom, the common sense of the remainder of the Kingdom. What they are capable of doing in the prosecution of their wicked schemes, we all know from that atrocious system of boycotting which they not only invented but carried out ... with unrelenting savagery. A parliament in College Green ... simply means that Ireland should be handed over in perpetuity to the brutalities of these men ... It is impossible, ladies, to exaggerate the seriousness of the danger.

She appealed to the women of Dublin to stand 'formost [sic] in the defence of the movement', as Dublin Unionists would have the most to lose if Mr

Parnell were 'installed as a virtual sovereign in the Castle'. Despite the many disappointments visited on the women's movement by successive governments, Haslam saw Ireland as governed by the 'intelligence, the energy, the practical wisdom of the United Kingdom as a whole'. The Westminster government, she said, had given Ireland Catholic emancipation, national schools, the Poor Law system, the Royal University, and the intermediate education system, and had 'recently conferred privileges upon our tenant farmers, which competent authorities tell us are not enjoyed by the farmers of England'.

Surprisingly, she praised the Liberal government for the 1884 Reform Act which had so disappointed all the suffrage groups in the United Kingdom, but 'which extended the principle of a vote, if I cannot say to every householder in the Kingdom, I can at least say virtually every *Male* householder in the Kingdom'. She does not speculate how the women's franchise campaign might fare in the event of Home Rule; rather she is concerned that the 'Loyalists of Ireland will be politically extinguished ... they will be outvoted on every possible question; indeed for practical purposes, they might as well be disenfranchised for once and for all'. The main purpose of delivering this speech was to shake loyalist women out of their apathy and to form 'at least some little nucleus for united action'. Not surprisingly, Anna seems at this juncture completely disillusioned with Mr Gladstone; she refers to his 'illusory devices' and warned her audience that if women did not make their influence felt 'in some effective way in the great struggle' they need not express any surprise 'if Mr Gladstone should succeed in working his way back into power'.[160] Despite her disenchantment, however, she was a committee member and a co-founder of the Women's Liberal Unionist Association, formed 'after the cleavage of the great Liberal Party' caused by the Home Rule crisis. Thus, within a few years of the Reform Act 'which had refused them the rights of citizenship, women were justifying their claim, by the practical object-lesson of actual political work, on the lines of each of the great parties in the State'.[161] She was also a committee member of the Rathmines Unionist Society and a member of the Central Unionist Committee. A report of the Irish Unionist Alliance Executive Committee states that the Ladies' Committee of the Alliance was formed in 1893 and that Mrs Haslam was a member. The committee had met forty-one times in 1894 and Mrs Haslam had undertaken to write to women in Carlisle and Berwickshire as part of the campaign to educate interested women in 'certain English and Scottish constituencies'.[162] From this speech, Anna's unionism seems predicated on her certainty that Ireland was well governed by England and that successive governments were 'pledged to the removal of every remaining grievance under which our people, or any section of them, are still wrongfully suffering'.[163] She averred that if ample justice were not effected in legislative and administrative matters there were one hundred members in the House of Commons to set them right. There is nothing in this speech of blind loyalty to queen and country. There is, however, a strongly expressed antipathy to Parnell, the National League and by implication, the Irish Party. Her loyalism was based on her wishes for the welfare of Ireland, as she perceived it. (Parnell supported the suffrage movement; when in 1877 he forwarded a petition to the Commons.) Politically, she was convinced that Home Rule would result in a diminution of personal liberty.

Paradoxically, she numbered among her parliamentary suffrage supporters many pro-Home Rule members, proof of the independent non-party philosophy of the DWSA. In the above speech she does not address the question of how women might fare under Home Rule. In 1908, Hanna Sheehy Skeffington, a committed nationalist, addressed this question and concluded that 'Ireland was a conservative rural based society, heavily influenced by religion, where women suffered immense social and economic disadvantages'. She argued that nationalism did not transform people into new beings, nor did it free them from cultural prejudices. She accused the Irish Party of having 'steadily ignored' the claims of Irishwomen. She was sceptical that women's voices would be heard in the new Ireland without their first having gained the vote.[164] Anna Haslam's hostility to Home Rule must have been reinforced by the behaviour of the Irish Party in 1912, when their votes helped to kill the Conciliation Bill that would have granted a limited franchise to women. The avowed non-party stance of the DWSA effectively prevented her from pronouncing on the Home Rule question as it applied to suffrage, but it is reasonable to assume that she would have agreed with the Sheehy Skeffington analysis. When her averred hostility to Home Rule is set against her ability to work with professed Home Rulers for the suffrage cause, it reveals her as a pragmatist who could compartmentalize her various activities. There is no evidence of any tension in the committee caused by her stance on Home Rule nor is there any reference to resignations of those committed to Home Rule from the committee.

Thomas does not appear to have spoken out on Home Rule in the 1880s. In 1865 he had written a pamphlet, *The Real Wants of the Irish People,* which anticipated the government policy of 'killing Home Rule by kindness'. The pamphlet is a cleverly written, closely argued polemic which initially deplores the status of the Irish as a 'conquered people', then shows this to be inevitable and even desirable, and, in effect, suggests a form of constructive unionism. Properly and justly ruled, protected from the avarice of rapacious landlords, with development projects funded by the British taxpayer, the Irish will rejoice in their 'union with the land of Alfred and of Shakespeare, of Milton and of Newton'.[165] While his remarks on landlordism demonstrate sympathy with the aims of the National Land League for fair rent, fixity of tenure and freedom of sale, it is likely that Thomas, too, would have objected to its tactics.

Blackburn's summing up of the dispirited mood of the suffrage movement in the years following the 1884 defeat is applicable also to the DWSA: 'The suffrage workers had to reconcile themselves to days of dull, patient plodding – the bright hopefulness of the earlier times was gone out of the movement.'[166] The novelty value of the campaigning women was gone. The press and public were tired of an agitation that had been going on for over twenty years. 'Nothing was happening in Parliament ... the arguments were the same as they had always been.'[167] Despite the failure of successive bills in the 1890s, the Irish movement had cause for rejoicing when in 1896 'W. Johnston MP, undertook to introduce a Women's Poor Law Guardian (Ireland) Bill which was subsequently enacted.'[168] This legislation was the catalyst for a resurgence of the association. At once the committee focused upon the election of women as poor law guardians. A letter was sent in March 1896 to eighty 'leading ladies . . . urging them to look out for suitable women who would be prepared to offer themselves as candidates at future elections'.[169] The DWSA decided that

> while not neglecting any kind of reasonable effort to obtain the Parliamentary vote as soon as possible . . . [members] should in the meantime direct their more immediate action to the obtainment of the Municipal and other local Franchises, not merely for their own sakes but also largely for their education value in preparing for the Parliamentary.[170]

The election of Miss Martin as first female poor law guardian was felt to be 'the cause for much congratulation'.[171]

Although Anna Haslam did not herself stand for election as a poor law guardian, preferring to spearhead a campaign to persuade other women to go forward, she involved herself with standards in workhouses, a key issue for guardians. She visited Holyhead, Bangor and Caernarfon workhouses, 'some of the arrangements in which are decidedly superior to those adopted in our Dublin environs'.[172] When attending the Conference of the Women's Suffrage Association in Birmingham, and a conference of women workers in Manchester, she availed of the opportunity to visit workhouses and children's homes in the Birmingham, Manchester and Kettering areas.[173] She saw the advantages gained there by the presence of women as guardians. Her remarks reveal her as having a strongly compassionate nature; her perception of the workhouse was as a place that should be made as comfortable as possible for the poor whom she clearly saw as deserving the best treatment it was possible to provide within the constraints of the system. She was struck by the facilities provided by Welsh and English institutions, including swings and playrooms for children and superior sanitary facilities. Children were no longer dressed in workhouse uniforms, the old had armchairs, and the 'infirm old women' were provided with afternoon tea. These facilities she attributed to the 'womanly element' in the management of the institutions.[174] Haslam addressed many election meetings where she exhorted her audience to vote for women as poor law guardians.

The 1897 DWSA[175] report rejoiced in the election of twelve women poor law guardians 'fulfilling their most sanguine expectations'. It was noted that the women's election had been to the 'entire satisfaction of the great body of ratepayers but also to the acknowledged advantage of their respective boards'.[176] The importance of Irishwomen standing for election as poor law guardians was recognized as a powerful stimulus 'to the willingness of our more capable fellow country women to take their legitimate share in the public work which our social needs require'.[177] Local committees were formed in Strokestown, Skibbereen, Tralee and Milltown Malbay with the intention of 'moulding public opinion ... bringing electoral influence to bear upon such of our Representatives as are either hostile or indifferent to women's claims'. Women poor law guardians were subsequently elected in these four towns, demonstrating the effectiveness of the DWSA strategy.

The death of Isabella Tod in December 1896 was the cause of 'poignant grief' and a sense of 'irreparable loss' to the committee. The second reading of the Parliamentary Suffrage Bill in February 1897, which was carried by 230 to 159 votes, was 'exceedingly encouraging', and Irish members' voting had been 'satisfactory'. Michael Davitt was one of the Irish members who voted for the bill.[178] Despite continued disappointment in the search for the parliamentary franchise, 1898 was a 'red letter year for Irishwomen', as the government 'honourably redeemed their pledges, in the passing of the Local Government Act'. The practical result of this, announced the committee, was that qualified women in Ireland

> now enjoy all the franchises possessed by their English sisters together with the lodger franchise not yet conferred upon the latter. They now also enjoy all the franchises possessed by their fellow countrymen except the parliamentary; and if they have not yet obtained seats upon the County and Borough Councils, there is every probability that these will be thrown open to them at no very distant date.[179]

Once again Anna had worked closely with sympathetic MPs, most notably William Johnston of Belfast, to secure amendments to the bill that would enhance the position of women. Qualified Irishwomen were now entitled to vote under the act, and to stand for office as district councillors and as poor law guardians. She 'had reason to sound a triumphant note since she had played a leading role' in ensuring that successful outcome.[180] Her political acumen was displayed in the campaign for the local government franchise for women. She was convinced that 'because of political causes' in Ireland, in single seat electoral divisions, women would have very little chance of heading the poll. The intervention of the committee, which addressed 'appeals and remonstrances to numerous Members of both Houses of Parliament', ensured the dual membership proviso, permitting of the election 'of not fewer than two members in each electoral division in the case of District Councils and Board of Guardians [which] was not in the original draft of the Bill'.[181] A letter from Anna to Mr Balfour in which she points out that the 'the single member principle ... will throw a serious obstacle in the way of Poor Law lady guardians especially in rural districts', elicited the reply that Mr Balfour 'thinks it not improbable' that the vote in the House of Lords 'will be in the direction you require'.[182] Because of similar representations, including a letter sent to the chief secretary of Ireland, a further amendment ensured that persons who were not local government electors were eligible to stand as candidates if they fulfilled the residence qualification. This provision was particularly important as it enabled many married women to stand as district councillors.[183]

By the end of 1898 there were eighty-five women elected as poor law guardians, thirty-one of whom were also rural district councillors. Mrs Maurice Dockrell had been elected as a councillor in the Blackrock township, and Mrs Rutter in Limavaddy, Co. Derry. These results furnished:

> a conclusive answer to those who affirm that Irish women are too exclusively wrapped up in their family concerns to take their rightful share in the duties of Local Government and it also conclusively proves that they will be well qualified to perform their duties as intelligent electors when the Parliamentary vote has been conferred upon them.[184]

Despite this upbeat account of victory the committee deplored that, 'strange to say', Cork was still without a woman guardian, nor was there a single woman elected in Galway, Waterford or Limerick.[185] The lack of an active feminist movement in Cork was a recurring cause for concern. This lack of an 'influential Committee' in the 'southern metropolis' meant that there was little progress in Munster. It was surprising that the existence of Queen's College did not bring 'enlightenment'.[186]

The DWSA committee regularly published lists of elected women poor law guardians and Mrs Haslam never lost an opportunity to publicize the advantages of women's contribution when elected. She saw them, not merely as administrators, but as compassionate philanthropists who brought a practical humanity to their role as poor law guardians. Above all she saw them as reformers who 'added to the inmates' comfort' by improving the 'diet', the kitchens and the clothing of the inmates.[187] Modern feminists might well deplore her perception of women poor law guardians' strengths as essentially the application of their domestic skills to the workhouse. Anna Haslam, however, saw such skills as uniquely equipping the women for the task of bringing much needed reform to the institutions they administered. She felt that, prior to the election of women, the voting of poor law guardians 'was carried out upon exclusively party lines and with . . . little regard for the well-being of our destitute poor'. Now when women voted for 'the lady candidate' they 'rose above all sectarian prejudices and gave her their vote . . . simply because she was well known for her deeds of mercy to the poor and can be absolutely trusted to do her duty by them'.[188] Thus women, as electors and elected, were presented as superior beings whose concerns were service to those who were the denizens of the workhouse. Anna was ever conscious of the need to convert those prejudiced against the election of women to public office and saw the perceived excellence of the service provided by these women as an important step in the inevitable, if lengthy, progress towards the granting of the franchise. She continually reiterated this point and although the parliamentary franchise obviously continued to be the main aim of the DWSA, its energies, and especially those of Anna herself, were henceforth also channelled into more immediately attainable goals.

In 1898, the DWSA, now calling itself the Dublin Women's Suffrage (and

Poor Law Guardians') Association published a pamphlet entitled *Suggestions for Intending Lady Guardians*, which offered practical advice to suitably qualified women on gaining support for their candidacy. It advised the formation of a committee 'of influential men and women of all shades of political opinion and of all religious denominations – to promote the election of two or more capable and judicious women ... in all the more important Unions in Ireland'.[189] Anna revealed herself as possessing considerable public relations skills in advocating the desirability of electing women as poor law guardians. In November 1900 she wrote a letter to the *King's County Chronicle* in which she commented on a recent meeting of the Roscrea Board of Guardians at which 'a laundry case' was discussed. She declined to comment on the particular case as she did not know the circumstances, but she asked to be allowed to make 'one obvious suggestion' that would provide 'true remedies for such disorders not only in your Union, but in all our Unions'. Her solution, of course, was the election of women as poor law guardians 'who would have the same power as the other Guardians and will meet them on equal terms on the Board'. From 'intimate personal knowledge' she could assure readers that elected women 'in their brief term of office, have already done invaluable service by their unfailing tact, good sense, discretion and undying vigilance as their brother guardians freely and generously acknowledge'. She enclosed reports of the conference of women guardians of April 1900 that revealed the 'sterling good sense' of the participants.[190] The DWSA also produced a pamphlet, *DWSA. Suggestions for Intending Women Workers Under the Local Government Acts*, with advice for 'philanthropic Irishwomen' who wished to avail of the opportunities afforded by the legislation of 1896 and 1898. Readers were given all relevant information on the categories of person eligible to vote in local government elections and detailed instructions on the mechanics of registration. There were also clear instructions on the procedures for candidates to go forward for election as poor law guardians and as rural and urban district councillors. Although it was pointed out that 'as yet women are not eligible for membership of Borough and County Councils', there were 'several important offices' for which they could apply. These included 'Sanitary Inspectors, School Attendance Officers, Inspectors of Workhouses ... members of the Governing Committees upon the District Hospitals'.[191] It is likely that Anna Haslam was the author of this work and of *Suggestions for Intending Lady Guardians*, which advised the formation of committees of 'influential men and women of all shades of political opinion and of all religious denominations to promote the election of ... capable and judicious women ... in all the more the important Unions in Ireland'.[192] The *Englishwoman's Review* printed 'Irishwomen and the Local Government Act' by Anna Maria Haslam which contained much the same information as was contained in the two pamphlets and was written in a similar style. These works have been described as 'carefully drafted, clear explanations of new rights and of steps which should be taken to implement them'.[193]

Above all, Anna saw the local government successes as a stage in the battle for the vote rather than an end in itself. In the *Englishwomen's Review* she wrote: 'For my-self personally the Local Government Act is interesting, far more as a political educator than from the specific benefits that may in other directions spring from it.' Heretofore, she argued, many 'women saw no practical good in agitating for reform which never seemed likely to be realised'; instead they involved themselves in charitable works, 'the result of which would be visible in their lifetime'. Now, however, 'sitting side by side with men upon their respective councils will revolutionise their ideas and make them not only desire the Parliamentary vote but willing to take some little trouble to obtain it'.[194] Susan Day, suffragist and poor law guardian, recognized that the election of women to local government bodies was a vital factor in their politicization, and made the case for parliamentary suffrage compelling:

> On County Councils, Boards of Guardians and Committees they have vindicated their public-spiritedness. But her position on administrative boards has only increased woman's demands for the vote. In adminis-tering the law she has learnt how to criticize it, and its weak spots stare up at her in helpless and hopeless and often tragic confusion.[195]

The election of women as public officials empowered them to administer laws that they had no part in formulating, nor had they a vote in the elec-tion of those who did. Women's participation in local government must have created confidence in their competence. Anna Haslam's constant reit-eration of the improvements achieved by women poor law guardians bears witness to this. Their public profile, their canvassing for election, the fact that women could vote in those elections surely lessened fears about women's inability to participate in public life.

An important part of Haslam's campaigning was her agitation for the employment of women as paid public officials. In 1898 she wrote to the Chairman of the Public Health Committee regarding the desirability of appointing lady sanitary inspectors: 'we think it must be self-evident that there are certain departments of the work which most especially require that minute pains-taking investigation in which the vigilant & practical eye of a well trained lady inspector would be peculiarly effective.'[196] In the 1899 report it was noted that the DWSA, apart from its efforts for the parliamen-tary vote, had engaged in valuable work affecting women. Some success was achieved in Dublin where there had been 'several precedents' estab-lished, including the appointment of two women as sanitary officers and four as school attendance officers. There was also a woman inspector appointed for boarded out children and one for the protection of infants.[197] The report of 1900 announced with pride that Dublin now had twenty female inspectors of which five were sanitary officers, thirteen school attend-ance officers, one an inspector of boarded out children and one appointed under the Shops Hours Acts. In Kerry, Lady Castlerosse, a poor law guardian, had been appointed as a member of the County Agriculture and Technical Institute committee; Meath also had a woman on the County Agricultural Committee. However, the Local Government Board had ignored the representations of the DWSA committee regarding the appointment of women as inspectors of boarded out children.[198] The successful endeavours in regard to women's employment notwithstanding, 'women will never be treated equally until they have obtained their legitimate share in the election of the men who have the making of the laws'. Despite setbacks, the writer of the report (almost certainly Thomas Haslam), was sanguine for the future: 'We can entertain no doubt that, long before the year 2000 has dawned upon our successors, every artificial barrier restricting the free political action of our fellow country women will have been removed.'[199] In a 1900 interview, Anna argued for the appointment of women to 'the governing committees of hospitals, asylums, reformatories, gaols and so forth'.[200] This interview featured in the *Queen*, unusual in the reporting of suffrage matters, contained a suggestion of the Irish as 'other', indeed of 'Oirish' whimsy:

> Mrs Haslam's keenness is manifested differently from some of our English pioneers. It is hard to put into words the nature of the difference, one can only suggest it in the very vague statement that she is Irish, and I cannot but think that to be Irish . . . makes the conduct of such business a little more genial, a little more ingratiating, a less point blank.

Mrs Haslam advocated 'women taking their proper part in the administration of local affairs, which after all were the affairs of both sexes', and 'employing women equally with men (and whenever possible for equal pay)'. Readers were informed that 'everybody in Dublin knew Mrs Haslam and I am quite sure everybody likes her whether or not he shares her views'.[201]

As is evident from its labours to involve women all over Ireland in the campaign for the vote, in its efforts to promote the election of women in local government and to encourage the employment of women as public officials, the Dublin Women's Suffrage Association endeavoured to become a countrywide pressure group. Anna had written in 1898 that 'The immediate duty of women's suffrage in Ireland is the establishment of active working Committees' in centres of population 'and to this indispensable work our Dublin Committee are now more especially addressing themselves'.[202] The DWSA did not confine itself to Ireland but also participated in the international women's movement that emerged in the 1880s. The Fisher family's involvement in the anti-slavery and international peace movements would have exposed the young Anna to the common empathy of purpose which could unite peoples of different countries in reforming movements. The international women's movement originated in the United States and had connections with the anti-slavery movement. Indeed, the exclusion of the American female delegates from the first international anti-slavery conference held in London in 1840 was the catalyst for the formation of the American women's rights movement.[203] The International Council of Women (ICW) was founded by the American suffrage pioneers Susan B.

Anthony and Elizabeth Cady Stanton, who visited Great Britain in 1883 in an attempt to persuade 'old friends from anti-slavery times and many younger ones that an international suffrage association be formed'. On their return to the United States the women were persuaded not to form an international group solely dedicated to suffrage. Instead the ICW set out to unite all women's organizations, 'from which would follow the attainment of all reform goals, suffrage included'.[204]

The first international convention was held in Washington DC in 1888. The DWSA decided not to send delegates to Washington as the committee did not know the objects of the convention.[205] There were, in fact, only eight European delegates and sixty Americans in attendance. The published report of this meeting, however, contained a message, signed by Anna Haslam, which expressed 'deep regret' for the inability of Irishwomen to attend, and hoped for the 'rapid hastening of those further measures of justice for which women everywhere are longing'. The message pointed out that although 'Irishwomen still suffer grievously from numerous political and other disabilities', there had been advances, 'chiefly in the direction of educational justice in the last decade'.[206] The copy of the published report of the Washington meeting held in the National Library of Ireland, bears on the flyleaf an inscription dedicated to 'Mrs Anna Maria Haslam with the compliments of the I.C.W. committee of arrangements', signed by Susan B. Anthony.

The founders of the ICW believed that 'women of all nations' could achieve 'the best good of humanity' by a 'greater unity of thought, sympathy and purpose'.[207] The Council met in London in 1899, under the presidency of Lady Aberdeen, lately Vicereine of Ireland. Anna Haslam and Margaret Dockrell represented Ireland at this conference, the delegates of which were 'accorded a reception' by Queen Victoria. The 'old and frail' queen passed 'slowly in her carriage between the long ranks of women of all ages, races, and nations', and afterwards invited them to tea in Windsor Castle where they were served 'in great state, with the famous gold plate set out'.[208] The proceedings of the conference were published in seven volumes, one of which, *Women in Politics*, included contributions from Anna and Thomas Haslam and from Margaret Dockrell. The speeches of Anna and Margaret Dockrell were designed to bring the conditions peculiar to Ireland to the attention of an international audience, while Thomas addressed the universality of the women's question. Dockrell's address, called 'Irish Women in Local Government', explained that

> Ireland is in a transition state. The governing power on local affairs has passed from the Unionists to the Nationalists, from the educated, cultured and leisured classes to the traders, small farmers, and, in many cases even to the labourers; but the women . . . elected nearly all belong to the highly-educated class, and some of them are Unionists and Protestants.

While this presented some difficulty to women entering public life, her 'own individual experience' as a unionist and Protestant was encouraging. She served on a council which was two-third nationalist and Catholic, but was 'unanimously elected to be deputy vice-chairman', and placed on several committees 'including being made chairman of the Dwellings for the Very Poor'. She added disarmingly that she was quite old-fashioned in some respects: 'I still believe in husbands and babies and frocks.' She saw herself as 'a connecting link between the old type of woman who thought men must be always right and the new type who think they are always wrong'. Margaret Dockrell, although unionist, did not see the accession of power by nationalists as a necessarily bad thing but felt that upon women devolved 'the task of reconciling the opposing forces, softening asperities and cementing all classes'.[209] It could be argued that such sentiments conformed to the stereotype of woman as peacemaker and conciliator, rather than radical innovator. There was also a submission from a 'Miss Hasland' of Dublin, which from the context and the evidence of her having been present, almost certainly refers to Mrs Haslam.[210] She cited the statistics of the elections of poor law guardians since the passing of the 'Irish Local Government Act in 1885' (sic). She was very happy that a large number of lady guardians were Roman Catholic. She had 'waited upon the Roman Catholic Bishop of Ireland [sic] to learn his idea on the subject' of women guardians, 'and he had stated that he had no objection . . . provided that they did not turn out a good Roman Catholic man'.[211] No comment was offered on the sexist and denominational implications contained in the bishop's statement. The sensitivity to the views of the hierarchy was most certainly pragmatic; presumably potential Roman Catholic women candidates were anxious not to alienate church leaders, and Haslam sought to reassure them by seeking hierarchical approval. Alternatively she may have sought to deflect church criticism by ensuring approval prior to seeking Roman Catholic candidates to stand for election. It is noteworthy that both Margaret Dockrell and Anna addressed questions in an international arena that were not commented upon in the annual reports or minutes of their organization at home. Anna also attended the women's suffrage meeting at the Queen's Hall, organized in conjunction with the conference.[212] Delegates 'from the United States and nine other countries' were welcomed to this 'enthusiastic gathering'.[213] Thomas was resolutely optimistic in his address. He cited the eighty-five 'ladies in Ireland' who were poor law guardians, the thirty rural district councillors and four urban district councillors, as examples of the 'revolution in Ireland' pertaining to the 'political position of women'. This 'stride in the path of progress', notwithstanding, 'he was forced to the belief that they would never be successful in their agitation until the day universal suffrage dawned'.[214]

The International Congress in Berlin in 1904 was noted in the annual report and in the minutes of the Irish Women's Suffrage and Local Government Association (IWSLGA) as the DWSA was now called, but no mention was made of Irish delegates. However, by this time an International Woman Suffrage Alliance (IWSA) had been formed and was acknowledged as a separate entity, which fact the IWSLGA minute book noted with approval.[215] Mrs Haslam and Margaret (now Lady Dockrell), attended the

1909 IWSA conference in London. The Stockholm conference of 1911 and the 1913 conference in Budapest were also attended by Margaret Dockrell as the IWSLGA delegate.[216] The ICW and IWSA succeeded in providing a forum for women for the exchange of ideas and the sharing of experience. The IWSA was a 'central bureau for the collection, exchange and dissemination of information concerning the methods of suffrage work and the general status of women in the various countries'.[217] It is difficult to ascertain the overall impact of the ICW and the IWSA. Commenting on the 1899 London congress, *The Times* expressed 'difficulty in apprehending what the objects of this formidable organisation are or how it expects to promote them'. Beatrice Webb judged it 'not a failure but hardly a success'.[218] Lady Aberdeen's summing up of the ICW in 1925 suggests that it had not yet achieved its aims. She felt that its success was dependent on rousing 'the rank and file of women all over the world to realise their power', an admission that she considered that it had not succeeded in doing so in the decades since its foundation. She also conceded that the work was hampered 'ever since its inception' by 'lack of funds'.[219] Nonetheless, as the reports of congresses show, the ICW and its offshoot the IWSA prove that at the very least, 'women could successfully organise a large-scale forum for the public discussion of a wide range of current, often controversial, topics'.[220] The ICW strove to achieve consensus and to provide a forum for the exchange of ideas and for shared experiences. The members believed that 'the universe must be a moral one'.[221] The IWSA fulfilled the need of political activists to have an organization of their own and provided a forum for the 'collection, exchange and dissemination of information concerning the methods of suffrage work and the general status of women in the various countries'.[222] The participation of Anna Haslam in international meetings where women read papers, exchanged ideas and dedicated themselves to the causes for which she worked all of her life, must have been heartening and made ultimate victory seem inevitable. Both organizations left a lasting idea of a global 'sisterhood' which ultimately influenced the League of Nations, 'not only on matters pertaining to women's rights but on the vital issue of peace'.[223]

Anna Haslam was also a prominent member of the National Union of Women Workers of Great Britain and Ireland (NUWW), which was not, as its name suggests, a trade union, but rather an association of voluntary women workers who were interested in furthering the interests of women generally. The organization dated from the mid-1870s and was essentially a 'Friendly Society with Trade Union overtones'.[224] It saw itself as a body for disseminating information to women and for fostering sympathy and co-operation among them. It also strove 'to promote the social and religious welfare of women in general'.[225] Its founders were involved with suffrage, and also with the campaign against the Contagious Diseases Acts. Josephine Butler was a subscriber and Millicent Fawcett was a trustee. The NUWW fostered a spirit of class co-operation; it campaigned on working conditions of women and on the provisions of the Factory Act. The association lobbied against 'protective' (called by then 'restrictive'), legislation for working women; such legislation, in effect, served to take jobs away from women and ensured that they received lower wages than men. Membership was open to housewives, indicating perhaps a recognition of them as 'workers'; it is more than likely that such women were also engaged in voluntary effort. The association was 'marked by a strange mixture of feminism, trade unionism and middle-class attitudes'.[226]

In 1899 the NUWW Occasional Paper included an article entitled 'What Irish Women are Doing'. This mentioned Mrs Haslam's 'valuable leaflet' on the Irish Local Government Act of 1898 and also featured her paper 'The Public Duties of Irishwomen' given in the judge's room of Dungannon Courthouse in February 1899. Her address 'was exceedingly interesting and was listened to with great attention'. She had expressed gratitude to the Ulster members, T.W. Russell and William Johnston for their 'zeal' in ensuring the passage of the Local Government Act. The speech, which was reported at length, detailed the progress of the women's movement mainly in education and local government.[227] Anna regularly travelled to England to NUWW meetings. These meetings were models of careful organization: The NUWW handbook for its 1896 Manchester meeting included names and addresses of hosts on whom delegates were billeted. Mrs Haslam stayed with the Reverend S. A. Steinthal of 81 Nelson Street.[228] From 1897 she was a member of the general committee of NUWW.[229] The 1900 DWSA report described the NUWW as a non-sectarian organization that 'embodies within its membership a large proportion of the most zealous philanthropic workers of the United Kingdom'. It commented on its Brighton meeting in October where many practical topics, including 'women as government officials', were discussed.[230] The IWSLGA report of 1907 stated that Mrs Haslam had been appointed as vice-president of the NUWW, and had attended the Manchester meeting.[231] Women's Franchise noted that there was a demonstration in favour of women's suffrage in the Manchester Free Trade Hall at the conclusion of the NUWW conference. The 'distinguished platform audience' was named and included such luminaries as Mrs Fawcett, Mrs Pethick Lawrence, Mrs Bertrand Russell, Mrs Wolstenholme Elmy and Mrs Haslam.[232] The report of 1915 rejoiced that the IWSLGA had affiliated to the NUWW and that 'Mrs Haslam, once again elected Vice-President has long desired to form a branch in Dublin', and this was now effected.[233] The introduction of the NUWW to Ireland was, however, criticized in the pages of the Irish Citizen because it was British and not likely 'to unite women of every shade of opinion', as its officers and committee were 'women of precisely the same shade of opinion'.[234]

In 1901 Anna was part of a delegation to the Chief Secretary at Dublin Castle which impressed on him 'the need for several urgent reforms' in the poor law system. She stressed the need for the appointment of lady inspectors. Mr Wyndham, it was noted, was most encouraging, and 'has always been an advocate of women's suffrage'. While he was 'highly complimentary' and in favour of the delegation's suggestions, he made no positive promise.[235] Sir Horace Plunkett's contribution as an influential friend of the cause of women's advancement was acknowledged in the 1901 report.[236] As vice-president of the newly formed Department of Agriculture and Technical Instruction, he recognized 'the claims of qualified women to an equitable share in the remunerative appointments at their [the department's] disposal in the most exemplary manner'. Technical schools were now in all industrial centres, where 'Lady instructors will lecture upon such subjects as Laundry Work, Dressmaking, Cookery, Domestic Economy and Hygiene, Poultry Rearing'.[237] Plunkett was praised again in the 1902 report for his appointment of a (presumably female) director of needlework and inspectors.[238]

Suggestions that women be co-opted rather than elected as poor law guardians in order that they might be saved 'the worry and turmoil of a popular election' were rejected with vehemence as an 'unwarrantable usurpation of the prerogatives of ratepayers who have the right to elect women or not'. Women who were co-opted, it was argued, 'would be no more than subordinate nominees' of those who appointed them. Furthermore, women thus appointed would lack the necessary clout to discharge their 'onerous duties', as they would not receive 'official deference'.[239] Anna's high profile, and her efforts to improve the services available to the poor were recognized when she gave evidence to the Vice-Regal Commission on Irish Poor Law Reform. She said that she had been interested in reform of the poor law for thirty years. She recounted the superior conditions in English workhouses visited by her. She suggested that male guardians would be educated by women to look after things a little better, a remark that was greeted with laughter. She recommended that children be boarded out in cottage homes and that 'a number of women inspectors should be appointed for Work-houses and wherever a second doctor was appointed it ought to be a woman.'[240] The recommendations of Mrs Haslam and of women guardians who gave evidence, seem enlightened and humane. They suggested the conversion of workhouses into district hospitals, the abolition of the pauper ward, extension of outdoor relief, removal of children from the workhouse, provision of separate rooms or cottages for aged married couples, and the provision of cottage hospitals and a district nursing service.[241]

Thomas Haslam's participation in suffrage agitation was ongoing if low-key. As we have seen, he was to the fore in the 1870s when he published his feminist *Women's Advocate* and was a founding member of the DWSA. He would appear to have been subdued in suffrage terms between the early 1880s and 1904. Although he attended committee meetings, and proposed and seconded resolutions at public meetings arranged by the committee, the magisterial voice is strangely silent. A detailed search for published works written by him in the 1880s drew a blank. There is evidence that he regularly participated in the Saturday night sessions in the Contemporary Club, a well-known debating society. He was a frequent speaker at the weekly meetings of the Dublin Friends' Institute 'where he read well-prepared lectures on innumerable subjects and was always a welcomed and useful speaker'.[242] He travelled to Cork in 1881 to deliver a lecture on 'the prevention of pauperism' to the Cork Mutual Improvement Association; his solution was to advocate a variety of social insurance'.[243] His major enterprise of this era, a book of literary criticism, *Good English for Beginners*, was published in 1892. This was a primer intended to improve the written English of the reader by providing a critical analysis of selected passages from eminent writers. The book would appear to have been very successful and was widely reviewed. It reveals Haslam as familiar with an impressive array of literature and also as a competent, if idiosyncratic, critic.[244] The *Irish Times*, in one of the many favourable reviews, said it was 'delightful reading'. The *Speaker* called it 'an excellent book . . . admirable in arrangement, lucid in exposition, comprehensive in scope, and everywhere bearing marks of judgement, taste and common sense'.[245] A notice at the end of the book calls the book 'a labour of pure love on the part of the author, and the product of ten years' careful preparation'.[246] The labour involved in researching and writing *Good English for Beginners* may well have been the reason for Thomas Haslam's reduced effort on behalf of suffrage in this period.

By the end of the nineteenth century, the Haslams had been engaged in the cause of suffrage for over thirty years. The suffrage organization they had founded was in its twenty-fifth year. Much had been achieved in legislation: the extension of the provisions of the Married Women's Property Act, the repeal of the CDAs, the participation of women in local government, the increased availability of education to women, the increase of employment opportunities. The criticism levelled against the nineteenth-century suffrage movement, with the Haslams at its head, was that they were conformist, ineffective and middle class. But by their patient and decorous methods they had achieved reforms central to the basic cause of equality. Millicent Fawcett understood the importance of the gradual reforms:

> Women's suffrage will not come, when it does come, as an isolated phenomenon, it will come as a necessary corollary of the other changes which have been gradually and steadily modifying during this century the social history of our country. It will be . . . based upon social, educational and economic changes which have already taken place . . . The revolution has been quietly taking place.[247]

The Haslams worked within the existing power structures but in reality they were challenging the very fundamental tenet that political life was the prerogative of a male government. From her surviving speeches it is clear that Anna Haslam was not a passionate or inspiring speaker. She appealed to the reason of her listeners. She was a respected figure who in her person made nonsense of the gibes of 'howling viragos', or 'shrieking sisterhood', which were levelled at the women who wanted the vote. While she rationally argued women's right to the vote, helped by the writings of her feminist theorist husband, she was also determined to demonstrate that by their responsible actions and devotion to duty, they deserved it.

In the early twentieth century, Thomas re-emerged as pamphleteer and public speaker on behalf of votes for women. In 1904, and the years following, Thomas addressed public meetings in Dublin, Belfast, London,

Cork and other places, on the topic of women's suffrage. These addresses were published in two 'widely disseminated' pamphlets.[248] His *Women's Suffrage from a Masculine Standpoint* (1904) opens disarmingly: 'A lady, whom I hold in very high regard [presumably Anna], has asked me to give you an address from a *masculine* point of view, upon women's suffrage.' He declares himself a 'woman-suffragist' for over half a century and credits Herbert Spencer with settling the question for him 'for once and for ever when [in 1851] he enunciated the memorable principle: "Equity knows no difference of sex. The law of equal freedom manifestly applies of the whole race, – female as well as male."' In the fifty years of support for this principle he had 'never met with one conclusive argument in contravention of the equal political rights of the two sexes'.[249] He now robustly rebutted the 'separate sphere' argument, about which it has been argued above, he was deliberately ambivalent in the *Women's Advocate*:

> There are many reputed admirers of the 'fair sex' – that is their favourite manner of speaking, – who affect to believe that dropping their voting paper . . . into the Parliamentary ballot-box . . . would unsex the poor innocents . . . Women, being physically much weaker than men, . . . being taught from their cradles to consider themselves less important than men have . . . . been treated as inferior beings; have been converted most frequently into household drudges . . . not infrequently into drawing-room playthings, – as has best suited *our* convenience.[250]

Men, he argued, do not want their wives 'to inter-meddle in public affairs . . . Let them remain at home, look after their housekeeping and their children, and leave politics to those who can understand them . . . [Men] still look upon their wives and daughters as inferior beings, whose duty and pleasure it should be to keep their proper place.' Haslam was full of hope for future 'political and social revolutions' in the twentieth century, the most important of which would be 'the instalment of women in their rightful position in our social and political organisations'. In the chronicle of suffrage achievements, he proudly cited the Mill petition signed by 1,499 'presumptuous ladies of whom my wife was one'. Although he spoke harshly of his own sex he conceded that every 'single step in the process of women's enfranchisement' had 'been *instrumentally* due to the action of chivalrous men'. The actions of such men were due to 'a growing consciousness of what is right'.[251] His appeal was addressed to two sections of society to 'come forward and actively co-operate in our movement'. These were 'generous-hearted men, . . . conscious of the injustices under which women have laboured in past generations . . . [and] women . . . of the refined and cultured classes'. He regarded the lack of involvement of such women, with noble exceptions, as a major impediment to the cause. If Mrs Gladstone and Queen Victoria 'had been cordial supporters of our movement – the Franchise might have been included in Mr Gladstone's Representation of the People Act of 1884'. Wives and 'lady friends' of legislators were in a position to influence their votes.[252] Thomas Haslam was, like Anna, an opponent of Home Rule; he simultaneously acknowledged 'seven centuries of misgovernment' and the efforts of parliament 'in the wearisome task of removing the grievances' of the Irish 'since the Legislative Union of the islands was accomplished'.[253]

In *The Rightful Claims of Women* (1906) Haslam's plea is for amelioration of inequality in all spheres that affect the lives of women. Despite recent advances, he argued, women were still not 'recognised as capable, reasonable beings, entitled to the same rights and privileges as their husbands and brothers', nor did they enjoy equality of educational opportunity. As workers 'they are seldom remunerated as equitably as their male competitors; as *wives and mothers* ... they are legally subjected to dishonouring disabilities'.[254] Haslam wrote indignantly: 'To my mind there is something dastardly in first denying women their rightful measures in the *kind* of education which would render them more capable in all the relations of life, and then casting their inequality in their teeth.'[255] Those few women who received university education, despite 'most distinguished careers as students' were never appointed as 'Professors and Tutors and Fellows, and Senators'. Women were judged suitable 'for the servile drudgery of the nurse and the *sage-femme*', but until recently were debarred from becoming doctors. Although now allowed a legal education and degree, women were 'still denied admission to all remunerative practice'.[256] Women who did not marry were frequently untrained to make a decent living. If qualified they were paid less than men and 'accused of taking the bread out of the mouths of the men whose places they may appear to occupy'. Although they rarely wasted money on drink or tobacco, 'nearly twice as many destitute women as destitute men have to fall back upon Pauper-relief in their declining years'.[257]

The most fundamental claim of women was for

> their rightful share in the moral government of the world ... the *predominant* share in whatever especially concerns themselves and their children. For thousands of years ... we, men have excluded women from any recognised participation in the enactment, and administration of the laws, no matter how *vital*, or no matter how *fatal*, those laws may have been to themselves and those dearest to them.[258]

When women all over the world obtained 'their rightful political recognition' wars would 'gradually, but inevitably, come to an end'. If women were granted the vote they would use it to support social and political reform.[259] The superior wisdom of men was a delusion; Haslam was convinced that women were 'more conscientious ... more alive to the sense of duty ... more self-sacrificing', and they would 'not much longer consent to so degrading a subserviency'. Many conscientious men shared his conviction and were 'resolved that the present inequitable system must come to an end'.[260]

Haslam returned to the topic of immorality which he had first written about thirty years earlier. Here, probably because the pamphlet was the text of an address delivered in public, his language is guarded and euphemistic and he does not use the word prostitution but refers to it as the 'deadliest scourge'. Haslam judged that the problem of prostitution could best be solved by 'the superior morality of our women'. While women were allowed to control the education of their daughters, 'the *sons* have been virtually taken out of their hands from the earliest age'.[261] Haslam's conviction of the moral superiority of women is present in all of his writings. If this conviction were predicated on the Victorian stereotype of the asexual lady whose very asexuality granted her moral superiority, then Thomas cleverly exploited this stereotype in order to testify to the incontrovertible right of women to full legal and political equality. Very clearly, however, he did not subscribe to the corollary of the stereotype – that women were to be protected from entry to the public sphere – as is shown by his enthusiastic support of his wife's public campaigning.

The twentieth century, in Haslam's opinion, was 'destined to be immortalised by the elevation of women somewhat nearer to their rightful place, as co-workers with men, upon the footing of equality for the moral elevation of mankind'. When women say these things they are called the 'shrieking sisterhood'. Thus men must speak out on their behalf, a point he had made thirty years previously in the *Women's Advocate*. Haslam ends his pamphlet in apocalyptic tones with a utopian vision of a future in which women have achieved the removal of their 'disabling shackles':

> And great achievements will issue from them, both in the intellectual and moral spheres, such as the world has never heretofore seen. And the two sexes no longer paralysed by enfeebling mutual jealousies will go onward, hand in hand, enacting laws and establishing institutions, which will have for their paramount object, – not the mere temporary satisfaction of our lower impulses, – but the moral and physical regeneration of the world.[262]

Thomas accompanied his wife on her frequent visits to England where he was fêted as a suffrage pioneer. On their visit to North Hackney, London in 1905 a letter from the secretary of the local suffrage society called him 'one of the earliest champions of the cause of Woman's Suffrage ... [whose] chivalrous efforts have not ceased for 53 years'. The writer urged attendance at a meeting at which the Haslams were to speak: 'It is an exceptional honour to receive pioneers with such a magnificent record of unselfish work behind them, and the younger women among us will cherish the remembrance of that honour, long after the recognition of the principles for which they have stood have been granted.'[263] A local newspaper gave considerable coverage to the visit:

> The meeting was exceptionally favoured in the presence and speeches of two of the pioneers of women's suffrage ... Mr Haslam, in an admirably lucid and forceful speech, stated that he had been a convinced claimant for the enfranchisement of women for 54 years, his conversion being due to Herbert Spencer's ethical axiom ... Mrs

Haslam followed with a charming bright speech which made it almost impossible to believe that she has been working for the public weal since 1845.[264]

In 1906 Mr and Mrs Haslam addressed four drawing-room meetings in London, and in the following year they spoke at suffrage gatherings in Llandudno. The headline in the *Llandudno Advertiser* announced, 'Irish Suffragists at Llandudno'.[265] These visits, and the adulation they received, must have been very gratifying to the couple. Thomas appears to have been judged as equally important in suffrage terms as his wife, a perception one does not get in Ireland. Thomas was eighty-two and Anna seventy-eight in 1907. In the light of the precarious state of Thomas's health over forty years previously, the speech-making and travelling of his advanced years seem almost miraculous. Nonetheless, Thomas and Anna were to remain actively involved in the suffrage campaign for more than another decade.

The split in the movement, the turbulent years of the militant campaign, the involvement of a new generation of impatient young women, character-ized the twentieth-century suffrage campaign that was to culminate in the granting of the vote.

6

'Clear brains and able hands';[1]
Moderation in the age of militancy

The first years of the twentieth century were marked by intensive suffrage activity and a significant increase in membership of the IWSLGA. Subscriptions received increased from £34 18s 6d in 1898 to £63 10s 0d in 1908.[2] The failure in 1907 to include Ireland in the legislation for the participation of women in County Council and Borough elections was a major cause of disappointment. In September the IWSLGA had noted that Irish MPs had been requested to see that the 'Women's Co. Council Bill' be extended to Ireland.[3] The exclusion was referred to as 'iniquity' in the account of IWSLGA events in *Women's Franchise*.[4] The association had not waited until after the event to campaign for inclusion in the legislation. In April 1907 a letter was sent to Campbell-Bannerman, the Prime Minister, pointing out that the proposed Local Authorities (Qualification of Women) Bill must be extended to the women of Ireland as 'it would be deplorable if through a fresh enfranchising Act for England, they should again be placed in a position of inferiority by the arbitrary denial of a right to which they are morally entitled upon all constitutional grounds'.[5] A circular was also sent to IWSLGA members asking them to write to all members of parliament in their town or county to exert influence in 'the present crisis'. A handwritten addendum asked them to write *especially* to the Chief Secretary.[6] Again in July a letter was sent to 'all Irish members' informing them that it was 'the confident trust' of the IWSLGA that the recipients would do all in their power to ensure that the Bill, which had passed its third reading in the House of Lords, would be 'extended to the women of Ireland'.[7] Frank Sheehy Skeffington, writing on the exclusion of Irishwomen from the legislation, asserted that

> There were curious rumours at the time which have never been denied, as to the precise agency by which this exclusion was effected . . . Sir Henry Campbell Bannerman declared in the House that he was willing to include Irishwomen if there was any demand; and it was said that some of those who ought to have been foremost in pressing the claims of Irishwomen acted in a contrary direction.[8]

Presumably Sheehy Skeffington meant Irish Members of Parliament, rather than the IWSLGA in his reference to those who should have pressed the claims of Irishwomen. His summed up: 'The general moral was plain. Englishwomen had secured the privilege because they had an active militant Suffrage agitation; Irishwomen had been denied it because they had not.'[9] His use of the words 'contrary direction' suggest that there were those who worked against the extension of the legislation to Ireland. In the Commons, however, no Irish members spoke against it, but very few spoke in favour. Indeed there was scarcely any participation by Irish members in the debates on the Qualification of Women Bill. In the Commons debate, Hugh Law, the Irish Party member for Donegal, asked whether steps would be taken 'to extend the Qualification of Women (County and Borough Councils) Bill to Ireland... if not whether it is the intention of the Government to introduce legislation of a similar character in the case of Ireland'. Mr Campbell-Bannerman replied that if there was 'any general desire by members for Ireland for the extension of this bill to that country an opportunity will no doubt occur to this effect while the bill is passing through the House'. He stated categorically that there was 'no intention of introducing a separate bill for Ireland'.[10] Walter Long, the Conservative member for Dublin South was 'rather surprised that the Bill did not extend to Ireland'. He pointed out that local authorities in Ireland were the same as in the United Kingdom. He expressed the hope that 'amendments might be proposed to extend whatever privileges the House decided to grant to women whether they were members of English, Irish, or Welsh local bodies'.[11] Walter Long was an unlikely champion; he was featured in a series entitled 'Prominent Anti-Suffragists', on the front page of the *Anti-Suffragist Review* of June 1911.[12] No one mentioned the exclusion of Ireland at the committee stage, nor in the debate in the House of Lords. If there were those who were active agents in the exclusion of Ireland, it was done behind the scenes. It seems, from the reading of the debates, to have been a sin of omission which Campbell-Bannerman was willing to put right if pressed. Why did not the Irish supporters of suffrage speak out? The evidence of their having been lobbied has been cited above. Was Sheehy Skeffington correct in his assertion that the reason lay in the lack of a militant suffrage movement in Ireland? This seems unlikely given that the introduction of militancy to Ireland resulted, not in increased parliamentary support for women's suffrage from Irish MPs, but in the defeat of the 1912 Conciliation Bill, 'due in part to the withdrawal of Irish Nationalist support'. Twenty-six Liberal and Conservative members who had pledged support also voted against it in this instance. The constitutional suffragists blamed militancy for this.[13] Is there an argument that in 1907 it was not in any party's interest to have woman candidates in city and county council elections? Or were Irish members merely apathetic on the topic despite being assiduously lobbied?

When the first suffrage bill passed its second reading in 1870 by a majority of thirty-three, the pioneer suffragists were full of 'happy anticipation of easy achievement' which proved 'delusive'.[14] Forty-eight years were to pass before women were granted the vote. Why? One practical reason was the difficulty of introducing a private members' bill, a procedure subject to numerous hazards. Such bills could easily be stymied and needed the government's tacit support or, at the very least, the absence of government hostility. Private bills had time allocated to them by ballot at the beginning of each parliamentary session. In the event of success in the ballot, it was still possible, and indeed all too easy, for the previous business on the agenda to be prolonged so that no time remained for the private bill. If the bill were reached on the order of business, the debate could be prolonged until the limited private member's time expired and the bill was 'talked out'. In 1905, for example, 'a second reading victory was . . . averted by Mr. Labouchere, who in order to ward off a possible suffrage success, distinguished himself by speaking for some hours about the lighting of vehicles.'[15] Even if the bill successfully passed the first stage, it was notoriously difficult to find time for the later stages, as it had to join the queue of other private members' bills. One way of frustrating a bill was to commit it to a committee of the whole house, rather than a standing committee; this meant that time had to be found on the floor of the house for the committee stage, an event easy to frustrate. However, despite the frequent frustration of unsuccessful private members' bills, the suffragist leaders encouraged and supported them, for they considered that they were the only course open to them, and that they always engendered publicity for the cause.[16]

Constitutional suffragists' campaigns were also frustrated by the vicissitudes of party politics. A fundamental difficulty was that the major parties neither officially supported nor opposed women's suffrage but allowed members a 'free vote'. The Conservative Party's leaders seemed supportive, but the rank and file were largely antagonistic; Liberal leadership was on the whole hostile, while its parliamentary members were favourable. Harold Smith, in his 1998 history of suffrage, summarizes the party political position thus:

> The majority of the MPs supporting women's suffrage were Liberals but their party loyalty was greater than their commitment to women's suffrage. Liberal Party leaders opposed reform, in part because they believed the majority of women enfranchised would vote Conservative. While Conservative Party conferences repeatedly endorsed women's suffrage, and Conservative leaders expressed their support for it, they made no attempt to introduce legislation when in office, perhaps because the vast majority of Conservative MPs opposed it. This stalemate might have been overcome if public opinion had been aroused in support of reform but . . . [suffrage] leaders preferred secret negotiations with parliamentary cliques.[17]

By the end of the nineteenth century the futility of the strategy of introducing private members' bill was causing frustration within the more radical sections of the suffrage movement, which resulted eventually in the militant suffrage campaign. The roots of the British radical, and eventually militant suffrage society, the Women's Social and Political Union (WSPU), were in the 'campaigns among the textile workers promoted by Esther Roper and the Manchester Society', and also in the radical Women's Franchise League (WFL) which, in the 1890s, 'developed new sources of suffrage support among organised working women'. The WFL also provided Emmeline

Pankhurst, the militant leader of the WSPU, with her 'apprenticeship' as a suffrage leader.[18]

In her recent work Sandra Holton stresses that we should think of the continuities between the nineteenth-century campaign and the militancy of the twentieth century; militancy evolved from the earlier campaign. David Rubenstein, too, argues that there was continuity between the nineteenth century and the militant movements. He cites evidence of increased support for women's suffrage in the 1890s, demonstrated especially in the 'Appeal from Women of all Parties and all Classes' – a petition which succeeded in collecting nearly a quarter of a million signatures in 1894. Among those who signed were working-class women, 'many women eminent in the professions and arts, and most of the leading women educationalists of the day'.[19] Mrs Haslam ran a countrywide campaign to obtain signatures, including letters to twenty newspapers. From Ireland 5,753 names had been sent, the IWSLGA having mounted a campaign to obtain signatures.[20] The widening of the social base of the movement to include working-class women, the growth of disillusionment with their parliamentary 'friends', the increased self-confidence of some women resulting from educational opportunity and a quarter of a century of campaigning in the public sphere, all combined in the evolution of the militant movement in Britain. The founders of the WSPU were also involved in the Independent Labour Party (ILP), indeed the WSPU was originally conceived as a ginger group within it. Women within the ILP were disappointed to discover that party 'support for women's franchise was not by any means universal'.[21] Recent research has also shown that the militant movement did not supersede the constitutional, non-militant movement, nor was that movement moribund. In fact, by 1910, the constitutional National Union of Women's Suffrage Societies (NUWSS), of which Anna Haslam was a vice-president, 'was a much stronger organization ... than it had been in 1900'.[22] The non-militants and militants both believed in the equality of women but the militant women deliberately sought to 'undermine gender boundaries'. They insisted that they did not want the vote 'to be given to women; they would be empowered only if they forced the government to concede it'.[23] They objected to what they perceived as the 'lady-like behaviour' of the older suffrage association. They railed against women 'tamely' accepting their position, and 'denounced the false dignity earned by submission and extolled the true dignity accorded by revolt'.[24]

The WSPU was founded in Manchester in 1903 by Emmeline Pankhurst, and had the motto 'Deeds, not words'. Though not originally a militant organisation "deeds" soon came to mean militant methods.'[25] In 1905, Mrs Pankhurst listened from behind the grille in the Ladies' Cage, as Henry Labouchere's verbosity ensured the sudden death of yet another suffrage bill's chances. She left the House and immediately organized an impromptu meeting which included members of the neophyte WSPU. She dated the onset of militancy from this protest. Shortly afterwards her daughter Christabel and a companion were ejected from a meeting when they challenged Sir Edward Grey on votes for women. Outside, Christabel committed a 'technical assault on a policeman', which resulted in the arrest and eventual imprisonment of the two women, when they refused to pay the fine incurred.[26] She correctly anticipated that this ploy would bring press attention and 'attract new members to the WSPU'.[27] The association had a powerful appeal for young women; it encouraged them to throw off restrictions imposed upon them by stereotyped gender roles. Margaret Haig, a suffragette, vividly conveys this appeal:

> [F]or me, and for many young women like me, militant suffrage was the very salt of life. The knowledge of it had come like a draught of fresh air into our padded, stifled lives. It gave us release of energy . . . hope of freedom and power and opportunity. It gave us scope at last, and it gave us what normal healthy youth craves – adventure and excitement.[28]

The young women attracted to the WSPU satisfied the criteria which typified 'the new woman'. The term, invented by the novelist Sarah Grand, was a journalistic and literary construct beloved of newspaper editors who used it to great effect in caricatures.[29] The 'new woman', however, had a basis in reality. She was a product of the increased educational and employment opportunities created by the first wave feminist movement, and availed of by the generation who came after them. The term was not a synonym for feminist but the 'new woman' was likely to hold feminist views. Lucy Bland defines her as

> a middle-class or upper middle-class young woman, concerned to reject many of the conventions of femininity and to live and work on free and equal terms with the opposite sex. She was given to reading 'advanced' literature, smoking cigarettes and travelling unchaperoned, often on a bicycle. Her hallmark was *personal* freedom.[30]

Militants were known as suffragettes, a word coined by the *Daily Mail* journalist, Charles E. Hands in January 1906, 'to identify the supporters of the recently formed . . . WSPU and their more aggressive form of campaigning. It was subsequently taken up by the militants to distinguish themselves from the suffragists.'[31] 'Suffragist' was in common currency for some years before the start of the women's suffrage campaign. *The Oxford English Dictionary* defines it as 'an advocate of the extension of the political franchise', often used with a prefixed word such as 'woman's' or 'universal' or 'complete'. It dated its use in relation to women from 1885.

The obstructive tactics of Parnell in parliament would appear to have impressed the founders of the WSPU. Emmeline Pankhurst believed that Parnell's policy was absolutely right:

> With his small party he could never hope to win home rule from a hostile majority, but by constant obstruction he could in time wear out the government, and force its surrender. That was a valuable object lesson, one that years later I was destined to put into practice.[32]

Teresa Billington-Grieg[33] also emphasized the influence of Parnell on the thinking of suffragette leadership:

> Parnell believed in angering and shocking the enemy; so does Miss Pankhurst . . . It is said that Parnell was unscrupulous in his methods, that he looked only at the end, caring little how he got there. This is an outstanding characteristic of the present militant movement.[34]

Initially the suffragettes developed the technique of being a nuisance; they undertook sit-ins on the steps of No. 10 Downing Street, they heckled from the Ladies' Cage in the Commons, they held vociferous protests in public.[35] The WSPU attracted increasing public attention from 1906 onwards and, in Ireland, younger suffragists sought to emulate it. Hanna Sheehy Skeffington wrote that the militant movement 'stirred a responsive chord in some Irish feminist breasts . . . stimulated by English revolt, a group of us got together and planned an Irish 'Suff' group'.[36]

Hanna Sheehy Skeffington (1877–1946), opened her autobiographical 'Reminiscences of an Irish Suffragette' with an acknowledgement of Anna Haslam's leadership of the Irish suffrage movement:

> Anna Maria Haslam, a Quaker rebel, one of the most consistent and ardent feminists I have known, of the old school, the New Woman one, led the movement for Women's suffrage, ably assisted by her husband Thomas, a libertarian in many fields . . . I first became aware of Mrs. Haslam, (or, rather, she of me) through Esther Roper (Eva Gore Booth's lifelong friend) when the latter was organising women graduates in Manchester by means of a gigantic Petition to the House.[37]

Her inclusion of Anna in the ranks of 'new women' is surprising. It would seem that Hanna herself was a more suitable candidate for that appellation according to the definition of the term discussed above. While Anna Haslam undoubtedly lived and worked 'on free and equal terms with the opposite sex', it is doubtful that she smoked or travelled by bicycle. Hanna would appear to have used the term to mean simply 'nineteenth-century feminist', which, coupled with her use of 'rebel', suggests that despite her ultimate disillusionment with the staid methodology of Haslam, she recognized the radical nature of her original campaign. The consigning of the older woman to the 'old school' suggests that her day was done.

Anna Haslam was almost fifty years older than Hanna Sheehy Skeffington and the women came from different backgrounds.[38] Anna was a Quaker with unionist loyalties, while Hanna was a Roman Catholic born into a prominent nationalist family; her father, a nationalist MP, was a supporter of Fenianism and had been imprisoned for his part in the Land War in the 1880s. Hanna had attended the Royal University in Dublin where she 'achieved the distinction of an MA with first class honours and a special prize of £25'.[39] She was a member of the new self-confident Catholic bourgeoisie. Her biographer, Margaret Ward, suggests that Hanna's mother saw herself as 'presiding over the birth of a new ruling class – those who would run the country when Home Rule was won'.[40] The two women, however, had much in common. Obviously both were feminist and worked tirelessly for the cause of suffrage. Their husbands were feminist theorists who edited suffrage journals. Each woman, untypically for the eras in which they lived, supported herself and her husband. Both Anna and Hanna founded and led suffrage organizations. Their acquaintance, through the Roper petition, introduced Hanna to suffrage activism and ultimately resulted in the formation of the first militant suffrage society in Ireland. Thus Anna Haslam was responsible for the recruitment of young educated Irishwomen who had already benefited from her endeavours. The letter from Anna requesting Hanna to become involved in the suffrage movement survives:

> It is exceedingly important that we should have as many educated women as possible amongst our published list of supporters. Your name has been forwarded to me by Miss Roper BA, Manchester as one of those who signed the Women Graduates' Petition in March.[41]

Esther Roper, graduate of Manchester University, was secretary of the Lancashire and Cheshire Women's Suffrage Society. She sought 'to win the support of working-class women through local socialist and Labour movement organisations, most especially the Women's Cooperative Guild and branches of the textile workers' union'.[42] There are references to the Lancashire Textile Workers' Union with which she was associated in the IWSLGA archive, and it was noted in the 1902 report that 38,000 signatures in favour of women's suffrage had been obtained from those employed in textiles.[43] Together with Eva Gore-Booth, Roper is credited with obtaining 67,000 signatures in all from workers in the textile trades.[44] The IWSLGA was envious of the widening of the movement's appeal in England; its 1903 report speaks rather wistfully of the huge working-class support for the cause of women's suffrage there and concludes that support from such a source was 'unimaginable' in Ireland 'except perhaps in Belfast'.[45] Thomas Haslam, in a newspaper interview, stated that the movement was no longer an upper- and middle-class one, but that in England 'artisans and working classes have taken the matter in hand and urged it forward with all the power at their command'.[46]

Roper obviously used the names of graduate women obtained in the petition as a recruitment source, with Irish leads efficiently followed up by Anna Haslam who, in fact, wrote to fifty-four Irish graduates in 1902.[47] The higher education of women was, of course, a cause dear to Haslam, as evidenced by her committee work in the cause of education. She was a founder member of the awkwardly named Central Association of Irish Schoolmistresses and Others Ladies Interested in Education (CAISM). This association was formed in 1882 with the objectives of furthering the cause of higher education for women and of keeping a watching brief on 'the interests of girls especially with regard to Intermediate Education and the Royal University'.[48] The 1922 annual report of the CAISM stated that the association was founded at Anna's initiative, and, at the very first meeting, she had read a paper describing her aims as the promotion of the higher education and the protection of girl's interests in the Intermediate Certificate, aims which were adopted as the central tenets of the association. 'Since that time until her death, Mrs Haslam was a member of the Executive Committee and in spite of many public activities she was always keenly interested in the work of the Association and rarely failed to attend the Committee meetings.'[49] The minute book for 1889 confirms that Anna was, indeed, a regular attender at meetings and had much to contribute, but was not a leader of the movement.[50] The committee was particularly active in pursuing the objective of entry of women to degree courses in Trinity College. Members also campaigned vigorously for equality within the Intermediate system.

Anna Haslam was particularly interested in standards of teaching, and repeatedly broached the question of statutory registration of teachers in Ireland. She wished inspectors to have had teaching experience and also suggested the appointment of women inspectors.[51] Although the CAISM was 'limited to the Protestant section of the community' of necessity, as 'ladies who conduct the education of Roman Catholic girls' were 'debarred from taking part in public action by their religious profession', the minute book reveals correspondence and cooperation between the committee and nuns of teaching orders.[52] The CAISM argued that women, whether they chose the 'social, philanthropic, political, professional or industrial life; or whether they exercise the narrower but closer influence of home life', needed 'thorough mental training and high moral and intellectual culture'.[53] Anna and Thomas Haslam were deeply committed to the cause of education, a commitment that was recognized and acknowledged:

It is impossible to name an educational movement in Dublin that the Haslams did not help forward. The founding of Alexandra College in 1866; the opening of medical degrees to women in the Irish College of Physicians and Surgeons; the inclusion of girls' schools in the benefits of the Intermediary System; the granting of University degrees to girls in the Royal University of Ireland; the complete opening both of teaching and of degrees to them in Trinity College, much useful work in the Association of Irish Schoolmistresses, were sections of the educational vineyard in which they bore the burden and heat of the day. They stimulated the demand for education and helped to supply it.[54]

Anna was very anxious to attract women graduates to the cause of suffrage. Keen to exploit the publicity value of recruits, who represented the crème de la crème of female intellectual life, she was punctilious always to include details of members' degrees in suffrage committee and subscription lists. The presence of Hanna Sheehy Skeffington at a meeting of the IWSLGA committee was first noted in the minutes of the 24 September 1903. She was present again on 22 October of the same year and soon she was a regular attender at meetings.[55] In February 1905 Anna and Hanna combined to address the Nursing Association, a meeting which was attended by ninety people, five of whom joined the suffrage association.[56] Although, by no means the first woman graduate to join the IWSLGA, Hanna's recruitment to the cause signals the start of Irish women graduates' activism. Increased educational opportunities for young women led inevitably to articulate voices demanding reform. The Irish Association of Women Graduates (IAWG) was founded in March 1902. Alice Oldham and Mary Hayden, president and vice-president respectively, were both members of the IWSLGA. The 1903 report credited the association of Women Poor Law Guardians as the catalyst for the increase in members and subscriptions but the increased availability of higher education for women and the formation of the IAWG must surely have been a factor. Hanna Sheehy Skeffington's membership of the association is contemporaneous with a noticeable increase in subscribers whose names are followed by the distinguishing letters of their educational qualifications. Despite the poor response to a graduate recruiting drive in 1902, when it was noted that only five of the fifty-four Irish women graduates written to had joined the association, a few months later, Mrs Haslam proudly recorded that among their subscribers were twenty-one university graduates and eleven medical practitioners.[57]

Hanna's husband Francis, a committed feminist, addressed a Mansion House meeting of the association on the 14 January 1904 at which the principal speaker was Thomas Haslam, who delivered his *Women's Suffrage from a Masculine Standpoint* address.[58] There were marked similarities between the two men. Both, obviously, were feminists. Thomas, the senior by nearly fifty years, was influenced by John Stuart Mill; Sheehy Skeffington's first feminist paper was, 'The Progress of Women', which introduced Hanna to the feminist writings of Mill.[59] Both men were initially employed as teachers, Thomas in Ackworth and Francis in St Kieran's College, Kilkenny. Thomas left teaching for the business world from which he retired for reasons of ill-health. Francis became registrar of University College Dublin from which he resigned on being censured for challenging college policy on equality of treatment for women.[60] Thereafter Francis made a precarious living from journalism and eventually was editor of the *Irish Citizen*. Hanna's earnings from teaching were the Sheehy Skeffington's main source of income, just as the Haslams had been dependent on Anna's stationery business. Both men were members of the Contemporary Club, a notable debating society, where Thomas 'often took a vigorous part in the Saturday Night Talks'.[61] Frank, having reached 'an intellectual decision', became 'a vehemently committed atheist'. His son called his parents 'convinced rationalists and humanists'.[62] There is evidence to suggest that Haslam too had abjured religion. While the murder of Francis by British forces in 1916 altered the course of Hanna Sheehy Skeffington's life, her married life bears striking similarities to that of Anna Haslam.

Having joined the IWSLGA, Hanna was also successful in recruiting family members as subscribers. Ward writes:

> Mrs Sheehy Skeffington, a member of the committee, was busily engaged in recruiting as many of her family as could be prevailed

upon to join. Her three sisters paid their shilling subscriptions that year [1903] and would do so for the next three years. [Her brother] Dick Sheehy's name appeared on the subscription list for two years and, for 1904, the 'Rev. E. Sheehy[63] of County Limerick' contributed a generous five shilling subscription.[64]

From the correspondence surviving, Anna appears to have made many demands on the busy younger woman. She always addressed her as Mrs Skeffington, rather than use the Sheehy Skeffington adopted by both Hanna and her husband Francis on their marriage in 1903 as a symbol of their equality. Years later, in a letter to Marie Stopes, who retained her maiden name on marriage, Anna wrote: 'I always wished to have my husband's name and was proud of it.' Although the Haslams' marriage was not a 'traditional' one in many ways (their commitment to equality, their involvement in reform causes, their marriage ceremony in a registry office, Thomas's financial dependence on Anna all bear testimony to this), in this respect she was deeply conventional. Anna knew Marie Stopes's mother and was therefore aware that Stopes was not using her husband's name. She wrote to Stopes of her ideal of marriage, with heavy emphasis: 'The *complete union* of the husband & wife *in everything* was always our aim, there was no *mine & thine* it was always *ours*. We had no separate purse.'[65]

Among the correspondence between Anna Haslam and Hanna Sheehy Skeffington, there is a request for Hanna to 'kindly say a few words for us' at a proposed meeting 'as you did so nicely on Saturday'.[66] Again, Anna asked her to help to get copies of Thomas Haslam's address onto the tables of Rathmines newspaper rooms, 'and also distributed in St Mary's College or where you teach'. One wonders if Hanna resented the rather peremptory tone used by the writer who always signed herself A. M. Haslam: 'I will give you as many as you can manage to put out usefully.' Obviously Hanna was expected to collect the pamphlets: 'I expect to be home this evening or Friday and Saturday till 8p.m.'[67] A postscript to a note asks baldly: 'Have you seen the Sanitary Inspectors?' In December 1904, another note with underlined emphasis is dispatched: 'You said today, some were thinking of joining us. Could you get them to do so *next week or week after Xmas* . . . Could you see Miss Quigley BA Blackrock.'[68] On the sad occasion of the death of 'Miss Alice Oldham BA', Hanna was offered transport to the funeral: 'Mr. Oldham is sending a carriage in the morning. If you and Mr. Skeffington would care to be here *sharp at 8.30* we shall be glad to have you.' Disarmingly the postscript adds, 'A's untimely death is an exceeding grief to us'. As though the underlined admonition to be on time were not enough, 'TJH' added tersely, 'Could you say on postcard if we may expect you. The one word yes would suffice.'[69] The fussy instructions perhaps are indicative of the advanced age of the Haslams, usually belied by their active lives. Perhaps the gesture also reveals the regard Anna felt for the younger woman; one would be careful, after all, of one's choice of companions at the funeral of a friend who has died without warning. This regard is also demonstrated in some short notes from Anna in which Hanna is invited to call and see the Haslams: 'It is a long time since we saw you – suppose you are too busy – we expect to be at home on Friday and Saturday evening. Any hope of seeing you then.'[70] And: 'We were sorry to hear you were ill – trust earnestly you are improving each day. I had hoped to have called up to see you but was prevented.'[71] An instance of the warmth of the relationship between the women is given in Hanna's suffrage memoir. When prisoners in Mountjoy, the suffragettes were allowed daily visits. Many supporters came to see Hanna including Countess Markievicz and Fr Eugene Sheehy.

> Mrs Haslam came with a difference. 'Don't think I approve – but here's a pot of verbena I brought you. I am not here in my official capacity, of course – the Irish Women's Suffrage and Local Government Association strongly disapprove of violence as pulling back the cause. But here's some loganberry jam – I made it myself.' This well summed up the attitude of many of our visitors. I appreciated and understood.[72]

Writers on suffrage in Ireland all record the formation of the Irish Women's Franchise League (IWFL) in 1908 as an event of real significance, which of course it was. This association, was 'avowedly militant', but was dedicated, as was the IWSLGA, to the granting of the parliamentary franchise to women on the same basis as to men.[73] Its founders, Hanna Sheehy Skeffington and Margaret (Gretta) Cousins, influenced by the Women's Social and Political Union in England and 'impatient with the IWSLGA', resolved to 'follow the lead of the WSPU by using militancy as a weapon if it should prove necessary'. The IWFL, however, would not be simply an 'Irish branch of that organisation', but would be independent as 'they were perfectly competent to lead themselves'.[74] Gretta Cousins, medium, theosophist, committed vegetarian, graduate, has left an account of her life in an autobiography jointly written with her husband, James Cousins.[75] She, too, had been an active member of the IWSLGA and held a drawing-room meeting in her house in Sandymount in January 1907, 'presided over by Lady Dockrell, with Anna and Thomas Haslam as speakers'.[76] Her husband, James Cousins, was also a committed feminist who wrote poems with a feminist theme published in *Votes for Women*, the organ of WSPU. His visit to a committee meeting in 1907 is noted in the IWSLGA minutes.[77] We are indebted to Gretta for a pen picture of Thomas and Anna in 1906:

> Mr. and Mrs. Haslam, a remarkable old pair, devoted to one another and dedicated to the case of the advancement and enfranchisement of women. They were nearly seventy [in fact Thomas was eighty-one and Anna seventy-six] when I met them; always in the best of health; she a dynamo of energy, small and sturdy; he intellectual, tall rather like a university don, a good speaker, very refined and kindly.[78]

In November 1908, the Cousinses and Sheehy Skeffingtons decided that they were ready to formally launch the IWFL, a 'militant suffrage society on

Irish lines'.[79] A small group went to inform Anna Haslam of this decision; the 'dear old leader of the constitutional suffragists' (then aged 79), although deploring the duplication of effort, gave the group her blessing and they 'parted as friends agreeing to differ on means though united in aims and ideals'. Gretta described Anna as 'congenitally, a person of peace, non-violent, law-abiding to the finger-tips', who nonetheless 'sensed the Time Spirit' of their endeavour. This I am sure was Gretta's perception rather than Anna's assertion; 'Time Spirit' seems rather an unlikely phrase for the intensely practical Anna to have uttered.[80] Frank Sheehy Skeffington was damning of the IWSLGA, which he accused of having failed 'entirely to awaken popular enthusiasm or sympathy, and the masses of the population had never heard of it'.[81] It is true that by the 1900s the tactics of the constitutional IWSLGA had become somewhat stale and seemingly ineffectual. Twenty-five years previously 'it was considered daring for women to speak in public', but now 'the public had become accustomed to the campaign and were inclined to ignore it'.[82] Hanna Sheehy Skeffington was impatient with the constitutional methods of the IWSLGA. In an obvious reference to English militants, she is recorded as regretting Irishwomen's 'apathy as compared to Englishwomen'.[83] However, she resigned from the committee in January 1906, over two years before the formation of the IWFL, in a dispute regarding the wording of the annual report for the previous year. Hanna, seconded by Jenny Wyse Power,[84] 'supported' by 'Mary Hayden MA' and Mrs Hogg, suggested amendments to the language of the report, e.g. it was proposed that 'British' be substituted for 'our own' in the phrase 'our own enterprising colonies'. The amendment was defeated and Hanna Sheehy Skeffington and Jenny Wyse Power resigned.[85] The dissidents obviously had much support; Mrs Haslam reported in March that she had received letters 'impugning the action of the Committee in adopting the report'. However, in a gesture that seems typical of the IWSLGA's tendency to avoid controversy, it was ruled out of order to reopen the discussion.[86] The topic was the subject of a letter to Hanna, where the stance taken by Anna and Thomas was justified:

> Mr. Haslam desires me to add that he is fully prepared to justify everything that he had done with regard to the proposed amendments, but he does not see any use in continuing the controversy. We have no doubt that the course adopted by the majority of the committee on Thursday represents the sentiments of nine-tenths of our subscribing members.[87]

Obviously the incident and the loss of two talented members was of major significance, an impression not gained from the terse entries in the minute book, although one tiny concession was made to the dissenters in the report: 'the' was substituted for 'our' in the phrase 'our colonies'. The episode would appear to suggest that the catalyst for Hanna's resignation from the committee of the IWSLGA was an aversion to the language of loyalism inherent in the report. While the IWSLGA was non-party and had within its ranks many of nationalist leanings, its ethos of loyalty to the Crown was obviously anathema to some of the younger members. One should not, however, dismiss the IWSLGA as merely a unionist organization. In the letter quoted above, Anna conceded that ten per cent of the wider membership of the association would have sympathized with Hanna Sheehy Skeffington. In the nature of things, Anna would have estimated the lowest possible credible figure as supporting the opposite point of view to her own.

While the sympathies of Anna and Thomas were undoubtedly unionist, the association they founded was much more heterogeneous than is usually acknowledged. Among its supporters in the early days were many committed to Home Rule to which, as we have seen Anna was vehemently opposed. David Sherlock, one of the association's influential early members was a Catholic, a Liberal member of parliament, and an enthusiastic supporter of Home Rule. Maurice Brookes, Liberal member for Dublin, and faithful supporter of the DWSA, was pro-Home Rule, as was Justin McCarthy. Willie Redmond, nationalist member for Wexford, and later East Clare, was lavishly praised for his speech in the House of Commons in favour of Sir Charles McLaren's resolution 'that the disabilities of women in respect of the Parliamentary Franchise ought to be removed by legislation'. The 1904 report declared that Redmond had delivered 'one of the most effective speeches in favour of the resolution', and quoted at length from his speech. Redmond was again said to have been especially 'remarkable' in the 'very effective debate' on the 1907 Suffrage Bill.[88] While the Haslams were devoted and loyal to the union with Britain, their organization welcomed support from all who proffered it, irrespective of political allegiances. The IWFL claimed also to be non-political, but, as the founders of the IWSLGA were unambivalently unionist in sympathy, so were its leaders nationalist: 'We were as keen as men on the freedom of Ireland, but . . . we women were convinced that anything which improved the status of women would improve, not hinder, the coming of real national self government.'[89] Thus, it could be said that the IWSLGA and the fledgling IWFL, in many ways miles apart, each dedicated itself to the procurement of the vote, and welcomed members irrespective of political conviction.

The presence of those of nationalist sympathies on the IWSLGA committee did not prevent a message of sympathy being sent to Queen Alexandra on the death of King Edward VII.[90] A letter of acknowledgement 'of our message of sympathy from the King and Queen Mother' was read at a subsequent meeting.[91] Irish nationalism was remarkably heterodox in the early twentieth century. Home Rulers were not separatists, nor were they republicans. Many Irish Parliamentary Party supporters were loyal to the king, and their vision of Home Rule included the monarch. Many nationalists were pro-Imperial.[92] Sean O'Faolain has written that he had 'two loyalties, to the Empire and to Ireland'.[93] On the outbreak of war in 1914, 'nationalist Irishmen enlisted in the war-effort in approximately the same proportions as unionists did'.[94] The phenomenon of nationalists who had previously enrolled in the overwhelmingly Catholic Irish Volunteers, supporting the war effort in such numbers, demonstrates that many Irish nationalists were still pro-British in 1914. In 1903, when King Edward visited Ireland, he had enjoyed the hospitality of the Irish hierarchy at Maynooth where the walls of his room were 'draped in His Majesty's racing colours and carried two admirable engravings of royal horses'.[95] The extending of sympathy to the widowed Queen Alexandra, therefore, would not necessarily have been taken amiss by members of the IWSLGA, even by those of a nationalist persuasion. Had Hanna Sheehy Skeffington still been a committee member at this time, it is safe to assume that the sending of such a message would at least have been put to the vote.

Initially the tactics of the IWFL did not altogether differ from those of the IWSLGA. Meetings and letters to Irish MPs were the order of the day. Hanna wrote:

> We were strongly Irish-minded, most of us, realizing that, though the House of Commons was still the arbiter of Irishwomen's as well as Irishmen's destinies we should have to . . . begin at once on our own MPs pressing to have a clause embodying Votes for Women in our measure of Home Rule.[96]

Although Anna Haslam, as the voice of the IWSLGA, wanted Westminster to continue to rule Ireland, she too targeted the Irish MPs. I imagine by 'our own' Hanna meant Irish Party members, while Anna wrote to all Irish members irrespective of allegiances. The IWFL was not aligned to any political party, but because of members' nationalist aspirations, they were constantly bedevilled by ideological sniping from women, who though suffragist, felt strongly that all endeavour should be expended on national freedom. Initially Inghinidhe na hÉireann, and subsequently Cumann na mBan, engaged in debate with the women of the IWFL. This debate has been well documented by historians of Irish women's movements in the early years of the century.[97] Briefly, the argument was a question of priorities; suffragists argued that without the vote, 'the national question would be resolved without women being consulted'.[98] The women of the separatist movement, on the other hand, used the counter argument that, although they too wanted the vote, to accept it from Westminster was to acknowledge British domination. To them the national question was the more important; once that was resolved women's rights would be granted in recognition of the effort made by them in the struggle. Both points of view were argued vehemently, but before 1916 at least, neither succeeded in changing the other's convictions. The IWSLGA, however, never became embroiled in this ideological quagmire.

Anna Haslam's reaction to the emergence of the militant movements in England and in Ireland was complex. In 1907, in a report printed in *Women's Franchise,* the IWSLGA

> recognised the impetus which their [the militants'] behaviour has given to the cause and refused to condemn the women who had been goaded into it by the flagrant injustice, and in some cases, brutal personal violence to which they had been subjected.[99]

The IWSLGA report of 1908 stated that, although many 'sincere suffragists' had 'sincerely censured' the actions of militants, and, although the Dublin committee thought that such tactics were 'not suited to the condition of things in Ireland', it deplored 'the easy and not very chivalrous denunciation of the women, who under the severest provocation, and in some cases, subjecting themselves to brutal outrages', had adopted the militant line of action.[100] Thomas, too, justified differences of opinion within the suffrage ranks, which he described 'as independence of thought'.[101] The 1908 report stoutly defended the women who were in prison in England for militant activities:

> The continued denial of those rights by Government after Government for nearly half a century has become an intolerable grievance; and the women who have gone to prison, in their efforts to remove it, are entitled to our warmest gratitude and none the less because we . . . have not felt called upon to follow in their example.[102]

These sentiments were warmly endorsed by the *Women's Franchise* journal, which called the report admirable, and could not 'refrain from quoting . . . *in extremis*' the paragraph relating to militancy, reproduced above.[103] The entry of the IWFL on the suffrage scene was generously welcomed by the IWSLGA, even though many members had defected to the new association. 'The IWFL is another proof of the freshly awakened interest . . . intended to stretch our movement in directions which our resources have not enabled us to reach.' The committee wished the IWFL every success in their efforts.[104] In October 1909, there was a 'warm debate' at a committee meeting regarding the vexed question of whether or not to condemn the 'militant sisters' in England. A proposal to write to the papers condemning their actions was defeated.[105]

A letter from Anna to Miss Strachey, written in 1909, acknowledged the 'honour' of being asked to be a vice-president of the London Women's Suffrage Society.[106] Anna wrote that the IWSLGA was losing members 'owing to the action of the Militants', which she felt was very unfair as '*we* [the IWSLGA] have *no connection* with these militant societies'. She went on to say that neither she nor her organization had ever subscribed to militant societies 'tho' some of our *members* sympathise with them'. She described the 'two new W.S. Societies' started in Ireland, giving in the description her perception of the IWFL: 'Some young enthusiasts – members of our association feeling that we were too slow etc. have formed a more militant – Nationalist – R.C. association.' She also mentioned the Conservatives and Unionists Women Suffrage Association, which established a branch in Ireland in 1909.[107] Haslam told Strachey unambivalently where the IWSLGA stood: '*We* are the *old* central body – in touch with both, feeling that there is work for them in a way we independents – non party could never undertake. We cannot do *election* work – can only help to educate.' She called her letter long and discursive, and asked, as vice-president, to be called Mrs. A. M. Haslam.[108] The *Englishwomen's Review* described the IWSLGA as at the 'centre with a left, or Nationalist wing, and a right or Unionist'.[109] Thomas Haslam's attitude to Westminster and Home Rule parliaments would seem to have been 'a plague on both their houses', at least where women's rights were concerned:

> I do not believe that our women will ever receive equitable treatment from either an Imperial or a Home Rule Parliament until they have a fair proportion of seats, in either case, in both the House of Commons and the Cabinet.[110]

Undeniably, the emergence of the militant movement meant that the cause of suffrage won considerable publicity, a fact acknowledged by Anna Haslam. The WSPU, in particular had very early on displayed great flair and ingenuity in capturing public attention:

> The processions, demonstrations, bazaars and badges and regalia, parlour games and illustrated post cards, have all been copied by subsequent political agitations and exemplify the ingenuity with which public notice was directed to the demand for votes for women.[111]

In January 1909, three suffragettes chained themselves to the grille of the Lady's Gallery. In February they ballooned over London 'showering leaflets on those below'.[112]

Ray Strachey notes the increased interest in the women's suffrage caused by the militants' actions:

> Day after day, as the militants provided fresh headlines for the newspapers ... the comments flowed out from the domestic hearth to railway trains, smoking rooms, clubs, and public-houses ... The wide notoriety of the movement had a marked and not unnatural effect upon women.[113]

While some were shocked by the perceived scandalous behaviour of the suffragettes, others, particularly those who had been passive supporters, were forced by the debate resulting from the 'sterling advocacy and flaming challenge' of the suffragettes to defend their belief in women's suffrage. Many of the erstwhile 'passive' supporters, those who would have willingly signed petitions, now joined non-militant suffrage societies. The records of the IWSLGA show a steady increase of members and subscribers. Subscription had almost doubled between 1900 and 1911.[114] In 1912 the IWSLGA was credited with a membership of between 700 and 800.[115] Ray Strachey, initially a suffragette, afterwards a supporter of Mrs Fawcett's constitutional suffrage society, in her first-hand account of the period, conveys the realization of such women, not hitherto actively involved in the cause of suffrage, of the real importance to them of the vote:

They saw that this thing in which they had passively believed [votes for women] was after all the key to the whole position. Driven by their own arguments, they realised that philanthropy without political power was but a patching up of old abuses; that education without enfranchisement was but selfishness. They began to look at themselves and their mission in the world in a new light, and poured into the suffrage societies ... These women, the backbone of the new Suffrage movement, did not see the struggle as the militants did ... What they saw in it and what they wanted from it, was an extended power to do good in the world.[116]

In Ireland, the new association's intent to bring the message of suffrage all over the country, fulfilled a need long recognized by the IWSLGA: 'Outside Dublin, Belfast, Cork and one or two other towns, Ireland is still an untilled field as far as women's suffrage is concerned.' Despite efforts over the years to bring the message to the provinces, paucity of resources meant that efforts were more or less confined to Dublin and its suburbs. Discreet as ever, the report continued: 'For reasons which lie upon the surface, our fellow countrywomen generally remain far more interested in other questions which we need not specify.' The report regretted that so few women had become 'trained public speakers; and the day for their addressing huge public gatherings has hardly yet arrived'.[117] However, IWFL members were not shy of addressing public, or even open-air meetings; they brought its message all over Ireland. Margaret Cousins described her participation in suffrage speaking tours in her autobiography: 'Usually we set off two by two on tours. There were difficulties in securing places for meetings ... in securing hotel accommodation or a press which would urgently print notices of our meetings.'[118] The IWFL conducted an 'Open Air Campaign' in the West of Ireland in 1912 which was reported in the *Irish Citizen.* They travelled as far west as Dunquin, Co. Kerry, preaching the message of suffrage. The accommodation problem was solved by camping.[119]

The IWSLGA eventually became vocal in their disapproval of the ever increasing militancy of the IWFL. Militancy was

> a significant factor in the Irish suffrage movement between 1912 and 1914. This is equally true with regards to those suffragettes who were non- or anti-militant. A large proportion of their time was now spent in disassociating themselves from the militants and condemning their actions.[120]

But the IWSLGA also conceded that militant tactics brought results. The 1910 annual report announced that, whatever about the methods of the IWFL, 'they had succeeded in coercing Mr. Birrell to receive a deputation from their Body'.[121] Augustine Birrell, Chief Secretary of Ireland, was pro-suffrage but was unwilling to receive a deputation of women from the combined suffrage societies. The minute book of 3 November 1910 reports with some chagrin: 'Some members of the IWFL having heckled Mr Birrell at the Law Society meeting and also at Greystones, he consented to receive a deputation from them.' Frank Sheehy Skeffington 'wrote proudly of that victory, proof that the militant path was the right one'.[122]

While the IWSLGA conceded that it had lost some members of militant tendency, and despite the seeming success of militant methods, it was determined to stick to its constitutional methods:

> Ever since the establishment of our association in 1876, our action has been consistently non-party and constitutional . . . at the eleventh hour when we are on the brink of victory, we can see no reason for changing our methods of procedure.[123]

The Irish situation, where the principal suffrage players were the long established, constitutional, law-abiding IWSLGA and the neophyte, young, militant IWFL, was essentially a mirror image of the English situation where Mrs Fawcett's National Union of Women's Suffrage Societies and the Pankhursts' Women's Social and Political Union were, respectively, the non-militant and militant societies. The WSPU differed from the IWFL, however, in that its roots were in the textile unions of the north of England and in the Independent Labour Party. While the IWFL's roots were firmly fixed in the groves of academe, it shared premises in Great Brunswick Street 'with the newly inaugurated Independent Labour Party of Ireland'. Francis Sheehy Skeffington was 'in the thick of that too, so there was a constant flow of radicals in and out of the building'.[124] The IWFL membership was of course mainly nationalist – a dimension which did not have a parallel in the English movement.[125] As already mentioned, the IWFL was urged by separatists to wait 'until freedom for men was won . . . to ask for inclusion in the British measure of Home Rule was to acknowledge Britain'.[126]

Cliona Murphy has written that the IWFL was not just a group looking for the vote but

> were very much part of the Fin de Siècle era and the Irish Renaissance with an opinion about everything and visions for an ideal society . . . The individuals involved in the IWFL, Frank Sheehy Skeffington, Hanna Sheehy and her sisters and their husbands . . . the Cousinses . . . the Palmers, the Oldhams and Mary Hayden were all part of the intellectual life that was going on in Dublin at the beginning of the twentieth century . . . a number of them were vegetarians, anti-inoculation, anti-vivisection . . . others declared themselves to be atheists.[127]

The members of the IWFL, it would appear, inhabited a different Ireland to that of the IWSLGA. The heady mix of the language revival, bicycling women, the Abbey Theatre, the flourishing nationalist movement and militant feminism must have made for an exciting ambience especially compared with the staid world of the drawing-room meeting and the petition. But the two worlds were not mutually exclusive. Mary Hayden, mentioned above as an IWFL member, remained involved with the

IWSLGA for many years after the formation of the IWFL. She agreed to hold 'education meetings' under the umbrella of the IWSLGA in 1910. She addressed an evening meeting on 'Why university and professional women want the vote' in December 1911. She delivered a 'warm vote of thanks' to Miss C. Corbett MA for a speech delivered at the IWSLGA committee meeting in November 1911.[128] She was a member of the subcommittee appointed to choose a successor to Mrs Haslam in 1913.[129] Margaret Ward credits her with speaking at an IWFL meeting in February 1909 which was held in the Abbey theatre, while *Women's Franchise* describes her as 'the only lady in the Senate of the new National University', and mentions her as presiding at a drawing-room meeting at the home of Mrs Keatinge under the auspices of the IWSLGA.[130] The Oldhams, too, are interesting in that they would appear to have straddled both organizations. Margaret Ward names Kathë Oldham, wife of the Trinity professor Charles Oldham, as first president of the IWFL, appointed in November 1908. She speculates that this appointment was because 'presumably she was the most "respectable" name they could muster'.[131] Kathë was the sister-in-law of the late Alice Oldham who had been a member of the IWSLGA and CAISM. Despite Kathë's presidency of the IWFL, she cooperated with Mary Hayden 'to hold education meetings in the evenings' under the auspices of the IWSLGA.[132] Her husband Charles, although a generous friend of the Sheehy Skeffingtons, continued his connection with the IWSLGA and was a member of a subcommittee appointed to discuss a proposed joint suffrage meeting.[133]

The vegetarian, anti-vivisection, etc. profile was not unique to the IWFL circle. The Haslams had moved in such a milieu as far back as the 1870s. Francis Newman, correspondent of Thomas Haslam, was vegetarian and anti-vivisection – in fact, he called himself 'anti-everything'. Mrs Hogg, a 'devoted member' of the IWSLGA committee, was the inappropriately named vice-president of the Irish vegetarian society. Thomas Haslam's own writings reveal him, at the very least, to have had doubts about the existence of God. His correspondence with leading humanists makes it likely that he, too, was interested in humanism. While there is no evidence to suggest that the Haslams were actively involved in the cultural renaissance, it is likely that, Thomas at least kept abreast of literary trends. He was said to be 'keenly alive to literature, classical and modern, and every new movement'.[134] Nonetheless there were social, generational and ideological differences between the IWFL and IWSLGA leaderships. The IWFL was part of the new Ireland of strong, self-confident, Catholic nationalism. The era was one of great optimism for nationalists who 'could reasonably feel that their country was on an upward spiral'. In 1909 John Dillon was quoted as saying that Ireland had 'made more progress in the last ten years than during the previous two hundred years . . . [T]he whole face of the country is changing and the spirit of the people with it.'[135] Home Rule was now merely a matter of time. Did Anna Haslam share in the jubilation expressed in a *Freeman's Journal* editorial of 1907 at the perceptible 'chorus of confidence' in Ireland which brought not only 'cheerfulness but strength . . . a brightness and hope too often lacking in the past'?[136]

The IWFL participated in the 'census resistance' campaign in 1911, a campaign spearheaded in Great Britain, which consisted mainly of evading registration rather than resisting it.[137] Ward claims that the census campaign succeeded in uniting 'all the suffrage groups in a determination to resist. Militant and non-militant were in agreement that until the state recognised them as citizens they would refuse to cooperate with the state.'[138] An IWSLGA meeting of March 1911 suggests that not all suffrage women were united in resistance. This meeting decided that the IWSLGA would 'not give any support to the movement for refusing to fill up the census papers as such action would vitiate the returns for the next ten years'.[139] The decision not to participate in the campaign further demonstrates the extreme caution of the IWSLGA, a caution that forbade their involvement in any resistance, however peaceful, and also their respect for the census as an important social document. The campaign was reported in the suffrage press as a notable success, but its practical effect at sabotaging the accuracy of the census was impossible to quantify, as many enterprising enumerators inserted the names of the missing women.[140] Nonetheless, 'the evasion of the census, was not just an exercise in undermining the machinery of the state but was also of profound psychological and symbolic importance to the women involved'.[141]

The perception, gained from the anti-census campaign, that the IWSLGA was condemned to the sidelines of the suffrage movement by its own inherent law-abiding caution, is somewhat altered by the scale of activities detailed in the 1911 report. In June, a huge suffrage march took place in London when '40,000 resolute women of every social grade, marching in a continuous, magnificently ordered procession', included 'our own' Irish contingent of approximately sixty, headed by Mr and Mrs Haslam.[142] The fact that Thomas, now aged eighty-nine, and Anna eighty-two, were still sufficiently resilient to undertake the sea and train journeys to London, and to participate in what was probably an exhausting procession, is in itself remarkable. The IWSLGA also invited Margaret Ashton, member of Manchester City Council, founder of the Manchester Women's Guardian Association, chairman of Manchester Suffrage Society, to address meetings in Cork, Mallow, Limerick, Waterford and Dublin. Miss Ashton 'generously refused to take her travelling expenses'; her meetings were very successful and 'a large number of new members joined as a consequence'.[143] Mrs Haslam also attended the conference of NUWW in Glasgow and participated in a Health Congress in Dublin under the auspices of Lady Aberdeen.[144] The Local Authorities (Ireland) Act, for which the association had worked so hard, passed all stages in 1911, thus enabling women both to vote in, and contest, county council and borough elections. Almost immediately, in January 1912, two women were elected: Sarah Harrison to Dublin Corporation and Dr Mary Strangman to Waterford.

There were many suffrage societies in Ireland by 1911, established to 'cater for particular regional, religious or political groups'.[145] Louie Bennett and Helen Chenevix founded the non-party, non-militant Irish Women's Suffrage Federation (IWSF), 'to link together the scattered suffrage societies in Ireland in the effort to obtain the Vote as it is, or may be granted to men'.[146] Despite repeated requests, discussed at committee meetings, the IWSLGA did not join the federation. Opinions were canvassed 'from Branches and absent members' as a result of which 'it was unanimously decided that . . . such a union would be absolutely impracticable and that our association can work much more efficiently by acting independently'.[147] News of a 'Women's Suffrage League in Munster on the same lines as our Cork Branch' was greeted in a more hostile manner. The committee objected that 'as the parent body of women's suffrage in Ireland', it was 'impossible to ignore our Branch in Cork and to unite with any other society working in the same district. We deplore very much that there should be any schism among women acting with apparently identical aims.'[148]

The 1912 report of the IWSLGA rejoiced that 'the general apathy which so long prevailed has now entirely passed away . . . the movement has become truly national'. The fact that this increased profile was most likely due to the activities of the militants was not acknowledged. Ray Strachey called the years 1906–1912, 'the great years of the women's movement . . . it was the flowering time . . . the long years of preparation and slow growth were forgotten and the Cause seemed to be springing new born from the enthusiasm of the time'.[149] This perception of the movement as 'new born' perhaps also helps to explain how historians of the movement have under-valued the Trojan efforts of Anna Haslam in the thirty years preceding the 'flowering time'. The flowering in Ireland was manifested in the mushroom-like growth of suffrage societies. By 1913, nine local societies from Ulster were affiliated to the IWSF. The Munster Women's Franchise League (MWFL) had branches in Cork, Skibbereen, Queenstown, Waterford, Bandon and Limerick. Connaught women had an association in Galway, and Nenagh and Birr also had local associations.[150] In 1912 it was calculated that there were 'well over three thousand' suffragists in Ireland.[151] This may have been an optimistic figure, but all the evidence points to a healthy increase in involvement in militant and non-militant suffrage at this time. Increased membership, also a feature of the English movement and the general upsurge in interest in the question, was, according to Strachey, a 'natural and inevitable' development: 'it was the consequence of what had gone before; and the startling advocacy and flaming challenge of the militants did not create it; but they did undoubtedly, hasten and quicken what was already coming to birth.'[152]

The suffrage paper, the *Irish Citizen,* launched in 1912, was a valuable addition to the cause. It was founded by Frank, husband of Hanna Sheehy Skeffington, and James, husband of Margaret Cousins. This suggests another interesting parallel with Thomas Haslam, founder of the *Women's Advocate.* James Cousins credits Frank with first articulating the need for a paper 'to keep the British and Irish suffrage movements distinct and carry on propaganda along our own lines'. Ironically, James wrote to the Pethick-Lawrences of the British WSPU requesting money to start the paper.[153] Haslam's *Women's Advocate* was acknowledged as 'the first suffrage paper in Ireland – all honour to our valiant predecessor!'[154] Although it was managed by the IWFL (both men were associate members married to its founders), the

Irish Citizen was still very much 'the paper of the movement', and Louise Ryan refers to it as 'a forum for debate among the various scattered suffrage societies in Ireland'.[155] While the paper's alliance with the IWFL could be said to give the militant point of view an unfair advantage, it consistently chronicled the activities of the non-militants, including the IWSLGA, and printed letters from readers condemning militancy. In reply to a 'correspondent – a lady prominent in one of the Irish Women's Suffrage Societies', who feared that the paper would become the 'organ of militancy', it was stated simply: 'But it is already the organ of militancy – and also of nonmilitancy . . . It is the organ of both in that its pages are open to the fullest and fairest possible record of the woman's suffrage movement of Ireland.'[156] Over the years it paid generous tributes to Anna and Thomas Haslam, and in 1915 published in full Thomas's paper, *Some Last Words on Women's Suffrage*, which was read at an IWFL meeting in November 1915.[157]

The period in which the suffrage movement expanded was one of constantly frustrated expectation. The usual private members' bills were introduced and continued to meet their inevitable failure. The Labour Party alone consistently supported general adult suffrage regardless of property qualification. After the election of 1910, a cross-party 'conciliation committee' was formed to draft a women's suffrage bill acceptable to all parties. This committee introduced a number of Conciliation Bills, all of which were unsuccessful due to party political machinations. A letter from Augustine Birrell, Chief Secretary for Ireland, to the Irish Parliamentary Party MP, John Dillon, reveals the difficulties of achieving the successful passage of legislation acceptable to all, particularly when there was no consensus at cabinet level: 'Both the Conciliation Bill and the wider amendment [married and single female suffrage] will be lost, the one because it doesn't go far enough and the other because it goes too far. This might be plainly called trickery.'[158] The IWSLGA report of 1912 was damning of the behaviour of Irish MPs in the matter of the Conciliation Bill. The defeat of the Bill (which had a large majority of 167 in 1911), by fourteen votes in 1912 was described as catastrophic and was due, in part

> to the tergiversation of a large proportion of our representatives who feared . . . that the Bill might delay passage of Government of Ireland [Home Rule] Bill . . . and also it is alleged, in no small measure, to the disgust produced in the minds of a large number of our parliamentary friends by the fresh outburst of militancy. [159]

The further defeat of an amendment to the Home Rule Bill which sought to include a clause granting women's suffrage 'to all women who possess the Local Government vote – a very modest proposal', was also noted in the report. Despite a campaign in which many IWSLGA subscribers wrote to all Irish MPs, of the 103 Irish members only eleven voted for the amendment and seventy-one against it. It was defeated by 173 votes.[160] The IWSLGA censure of the militants, the accusation of antagonizing MPs who were previously pro-suffrage, was not unique to the Irish association. Constance Rover has attributed the defeat of the Conciliation Bill to 'loss of support through reaction against suffragette disturbance', as well as to the 'defection of Irish Nationalists'.[161] This, of course, was a reference to agitation in England, where the militant campaign had escalated and many women were in prison. Hugh Law, a supporter of suffrage who had successfully sponsored the Local Authorities (Ireland) (Qualification of Women) Bill, thus allowing women to sit on County Councils and County Boroughs, said in the House that militancy 'has been exceedingly inneffective except in exciting hostility for woman suffrage'.[162]

The part played by the Irish Parliamentary Party in the defeat of the Conciliation Bill and of the franchise amendment to the Home Rule Bill in 1912 has been well described in works on suffrage in Ireland.[163] Rosemary Owens summed up:

> The Home Rule struggle ... was to dog the path of the Woman Suffrage in Ireland, and hindered its progress at many stages. Many Irish MPs were in favour of Votes for Women but when the Home Rule manoeuvrings became really critical, they stepped into line under ... John Redmond ... [who] was anxious to avoid any issue which might adversely affect the granting of Home Rule. Thus the voting of Irish Members was responsible for the defeat of ... 'The Conciliation Bill' – and for the similar defeat of Women's Suffrage amendment to the Home Rule Bill.[164]

Hanna Sheehy Skeffington wrote that the frustration caused by the exclusion of 'Irishwomen from the Vote in the Home Rule Bill' was the catalyst that caused the first stone to be flung 'as a protest'.[165] Hitherto, the members of the IWFL had confined themselves to poster protests and the heckling of MPs. On 13 June 1912, the organized breaking of windows by members of the IWFL, in the GPO, the Custom House and Dublin Castle, was the real start of militant action in Ireland, and resulted in the imprisonment of the perpetrators.[166] Now the IWSLGA's patience with, and seeming tolerance of, the militants was truly at an end: 'Owing to the actions of the extreme branch of the militants we have refrained from prosecuting our cause in public as the majority of people were made so antagonistic to it by these violent and unwise methods.'[167] The *Irish Citizen* printed a letter from Mrs Anna M. Haslam, who wrote 'from London':

> Owing to my absence in London, I am unable to summon our committee, but I know that I am embodying their sentiments when I express my strong disapproval of the breaking of windows as a means of advancing our cause. It is my conviction that the adoption of such action by a section of our supporters here was one of the chief contributory causes of the defeat of the Conciliation Bill, and I do not believe that it will promote the passing of a woman's suffrage amendment to our Home Rule Bill if carried. Our association which has been in existence since 1876, has always consistently disapproved of what are called militant methods in the advancement of our cause.[168]

This letter had reverberations at the IWSLGA meeting of September 1912 when three members, including Mrs Oldham, resigned 'in consequence of the letter sent by the honorary secretary to the newspapers in June'. The majority of the committee sided with Mrs Haslam, however, as the following resolution was passed: 'This committee desire to express their approval of Mrs. Haslam's letter to the papers in June re the breaking of windows in Dublin.' It was also noted that branch secretaries in Cork, Limerick and Mallow had written supporting Mrs Haslam's letter.[169]

The criticism was not all one way. A public meeting of the IWSLGA was reported in the *Irish Citizen*. While the main speakers, Councillor Rathbone of Liverpool and Councillor Strangman of Waterford (both women), were praised, the paper deplored that

The harmony of the evening was somewhat marred by the ill-judged attacks on militant suffragists made from the platform . . . It was also noted . . . that *The Irish Citizen* was not procurable within the hall, though at least one suffragist organ of English origin was on sale . . . It is also regrettable . . . that no question or discussion was invited as is usual in suffragist meetings.[170]

Thomas Haslam advanced what he called his 'very moderate' opinion regarding the damage done to the cause by the militant movement in a letter printed by the *Irish Citizen*. He cited such authorities as Lloyd George, a sincere 'friend of Women's Suffrage', and Keir Hardie who had observed that 'the Women's Social and Political Union had done more to damage Women's Suffrage than all other causes put together'.[171]

Anna Haslam tendered her resignation as honorary secretary in 1913. The minutes do not give any explicit information, other than the resolution passed in January: 'It is hereby resolved that in consequence of the resignation of the hon. sec. and for various other reasons we shall consider dissolution of this association.'[172] Without any further detail, we can only speculate as to why this course was considered. While for many, Mrs Haslam obviously *was* the association, in reality there were many other prominent members of the committee. Mary Hayden was a high-profile figure, Professor of History and member of the senate of the Royal University. She was a seasoned chairperson at suffrage meetings and a practised public speaker. Margaret, Lady Dockrell, another long serving committee member was a member of Blackrock Urban District Council, had attended many international suffrage meetings on behalf of the IWSLGA and was, too, a seasoned speaker. Why then did they want to throw in the towel 'in consequence of the resignation' of Anna Haslam? What were the 'various other reasons?' Was it disillusionment with the prevarication of the House of Commons or a desire to bow out gracefully as the militants continued the campaign of civil disobedience? Perhaps they felt the injustice of alienated public opinion which did not discriminate between suffragists and suffragettes. By 13 February, however, it was decided that a subcommittee, which included Miss Hayden and Lady

Dockrell, would consider a successor to Mrs Haslam, who in the meantime consented to stay on until June.[173]

Anna Haslam had been the virtual ruler of the IWSLGA for almost forty years. From notes inscribed on the minute book in her own hand, we know that she had attended all of the 213 committee meetings. Rose McDowell was joint secretary for many years, but nowhere is it suggested that she was of equal stature to Anna, nor was she replaced after her death. The description of Rose as 'a kindly co-worker in the struggle' suggests a figure in the background. The *Irish Citizen* wrote of the IWSLGA that, 'in the eyes of the public Mrs. Haslam was the society and the society Mrs. Haslam'.[174] This may have been an implicit criticism of the association as well as praise of Mrs Haslam. However, the association survived her resignation for many years, as will be discussed later in the chapter. While there is little explicit evidence to suggest that the IWSLGA was ever anything but a democratic organization, there is nonetheless an impression that Mrs Haslam frequently got her own way. An intriguing entry in the minute book for 1900 states that, 'Miss McKerlie's letter and Mrs. Haslam's replies having been considered', members of the committee 'are unanimously of the opinion, that Mrs Haslam did not make any mistake regarding Miss McKerlie's subscription'. Obviously a claim had been made by Miss McKerlie and contested by Mrs Haslam, that the former had paid her subscription. Anna had served as treasurer and secretary simultaneously. The committee went on to 'regret very much that any friction should have arisen and deprecate the annoyance and worry which have thereby been occasioned to Mrs. Haslam'. At the next meeting Miss McKerlie's resignation was accepted.[175] Miss McKerlie was not a new recruit; she had accompanied Anna on an official visit to Birmingham in 1895. Without the correspondence between Mrs Haslam and Miss McKerlie, and not knowing anything of the latter, it is impossible to know what really went on. From the brief account in the minute book, however, the impression is given that Mrs Haslam was uncompromising when convinced that right was on her side. Her letter to the papers in 1912, in which, without consultation, she claimed that she was 'embodying' the sentiments of the committee in condemning the Irish militants, is another case in point.[176] The subsequent resignations from the committee demonstrate that her views did *not* embody the sentiments of all committee members, but she felt empowered to speak out on such a sensitive measure without prior consultation. The letter quoted above (p. 161), sent to Hanna Sheehy Skeffington regarding the proposed amendment to the minutes, while quoting Thomas, smacks a little of Anna Haslam laying down the law. Thus surviving evidence suggests the possibility that Anna had controlled and been the prime mover of the committee, which would explain why the immediate response to her signalled resignation was a motion to disband.

In the final days of Mrs Haslam's stewardship, the committee appears to have become demoralized. The negativity emanating from the minutes is striking. Perhaps the caution exhibited is understandable, caused by the distress felt by the non-militants at the suffragettes' actions. In April 1913, for example, it was decided 'not to join in the proposed deputation to John

Redmond during the Whitsun holidays'.[177] Again: 'It was decided after considerable discussion, not to unite with the proposed appeals to Bonar Law and Lloyd George to receive deputations from women's suffrage as it might prove too compromising.'[178] The committee decided not to join the women's suffrage week in December as it would also be 'too compromising'.[179]

Despite the reluctance to take part in any suffrage activity for fear of becoming tarred with the suffragette brush, the minutes reveal that the committee was still prepared to justify the motivation of the militants:

> The Committee of the IWSLGA, while deeply deploring the fresh outburst of outrages on the part of a small number of misguided suffragists which is following the rejection of Mr. Dickinson's Bill, regret that they cannot exonerate our Irish representatives who voted against the proposed measure of justice to women from a large share of the responsibility for the recurrences of these outrages.[180]

Anna Haslam's resignation from the secretaryship, which for most of her thirty-seven-year reign had meant virtual leadership of the movement in Ireland, thus came at a time when the Irish Party in Westminster were stymieing suffrage amendments to successive Home Rule Bills, and the militant wing of the movement had declared war on the government. The 1913 annual report included an account of Anna's resignation, and her appointment to the newly created post of president of the association. One might have expected a more fulsome tribute than the following:

> Our honorary secretary, Mrs. Haslam, who has acted in that capacity since the formation of the association in 1876 has now reached the advanced age of nearly eighty-five years, having requested to be released from an office whose duties she does not any longer consider herself able to discharge efficiently, we decided . . . to accept her resignation.[181]

Perhaps this low-key report of Mrs Haslam's leaving was due to her own innate modesty; as secretary presumably she took the minutes. Thomas compiled the annual reports from 1896 to 1913 and perhaps, as her husband, did not think it fitting to laud her.[182] Included, however, was a generous tribute from the Cork Branch who noted 'with deep regret . . . Mrs. Haslam's proposed resignation', which came after a 'life of strenuous and conscientious work . . . in women's best interest'.[183] The *Irish Citizen* carried a report of Mrs Haslam's retirement which acknowledged the importance of her influence on the Irish suffrage scene:

> All the new societies which have sprung into existence in Ireland within the last five years have built upon the foundations laid by Mrs. Haslam, and every worker in the movement looks up to her as one of the pioneers whose work will endure for ever, because knitted into the very fabric of society.[184]

Mrs Haslam was the 'embodiment of the women's cause in Ireland; and the work which she accomplished . . . should never be forgotten by the generations to come'.[185]

The association's reports subsequent to the resignation of Anna as secretary never fail to mention her. In 1913, the year of her resignation, accompanied by Mr Haslam, she took part in a 'memorable pilgrimage' to London culminating on 26 July in a magnificent demonstration in Hyde Park. Five or six thousand women who were the 'most intelligent, level-headed and law-abiding in England', travelled 'in fair weather and foul' to London where the demonstration was a 'triumphant success'. Hospitality and support was received from mayors, councillors and clergymen.[186] This brief account refers to the National Union of Women's Suffrage Societies, who in 1913

> planned and executed a great pilgrimage . . . [W]omen set out on foot from the far corners of the kingdom, and, marching with banners and bands along eight main routes, they converged upon London. As they went along they were joined by others living on the routes, and the processions grew daily.[187]

This event seems more characteristic of the militants, but it was planned and executed by the law-abiding NUWSS. It demonstrates how the onset of militancy had changed, in England at least, the methodology of the constitutional suffragists. One must assume that Mr and Mrs Haslam had not walked to London with the procession but merely joined in the London demonstration. The Haslams and many other members of the IWSLGA took part in many of the large suffrage processions in London. Such processions did not feature in the Irish suffrage campaign, although the IWFL organized outdoor meetings. The 1908 report explained that in Ireland, 'owing to the very great differences in our social and political conditions we have had nothing analogous to these immense gatherings'.[188] The significant cultural taboos that had to be overcome by women who participated in those first public parades should not be underestimated:

> three thousand women [marched] . . . long skirts trailing on the ground and hearts in which enthusiasm struggled successfully with propriety. In that year [1907] the vast majority of women still felt that there was something very dreadful in walking in procession through the streets . . . and many of the demonstrators felt that they were risking their employments and endangering their reputations, besides facing a dreadful ordeal of ridicule and public shame.[189]

The 1907 annual report had hinted at the difficulties for women of participating in public demonstrations. The 'Great Suffrage Demonstration' in London in February 1907 was attended by '[d]istinguished women [who] felt themselves bound in conscience to descend to the streets in public demand of an act of elementary justice'.[190] Mrs Haslam, while disapproving of militant demonstration, does not appear to have had any problem with appearing in public. She had, after all, first appeared on a public platform sixty years previously when she stood with Elihu Burritt in the cause of international peace. Anna wrote proudly of the 'grand procession from the Embankment to Albert Hall' in 1908, when '[n]early one hundred of our fellow countrywomen headed by nine members of our Dublin committee', including Thomas and herself 'followed two Irish banners . . . There is not one of us who does not feel honoured by the privilege of taking part in so magnificent a demonstration.'[191]

The occasion of Mrs and Mr Haslam's sixtieth wedding anniversary was marked by celebrations which demonstrated the regard and affection felt for them. The *Irish Citizen* published an essay by Frank Sheehy Skeffington which described Thomas and Anna as 'The Pioneers of Feminism in Ireland', and outlined the life of Anna, and to a lesser degree that of Thomas, in glowing terms. There is, however, an elegiac air about the piece as though the 'venerable couple' were already dead. Their achievements, according to Sheehy Skeffington, were all too often forgotten by those who 'have entered into the harvest of their labours'. The impression of the baton having been passed on by Mrs Haslam is tempered somewhat by the essay's conclusion: 'She has, indeed, been a fighter all her life, and still is a fighter, to get things done; and all who value progress and the bettering of human conditions will pay their homage to her and her devoted husband and co-worker.' The anniversary was the occasion of a large party at which the couple were presented with an illuminated address and a purse of sovereigns.[192]

The outbreak of war was described, in Ireland, as threatening the cause of women's suffrage 'with a temporary burial'.[193] In Britain 'the suffrage societies at once suspended their political activities, and the Government . . . issued an amnesty to all the suffragette prisoners'. The WSPU ceased its militancy, closed its offices and applied itself to war work. The non-militant NUWSS 'decided that their strength and their machinery should be . . . used to the utmost for the relief of distress caused by the war'.[194] In Ireland the response by suffrage societies to the outbreak of war varied. The IWSLGA applied itself, immediately and enthusiastically, to relief works. In Cork the Munster Women's Franchise League presented an ambulance to the military authorities.[195] The militant IWFL opposed the involvement of suffrage societies in war work:

Our movement was founded with the definite aims of securing the political freedom of women. To this work, we have pledged ourselves, and to no other . . . What possible affinity between women struggling for freedom and the forces responsible for precipitating the present horrible catastrophe? Let those who have plunged the nation in war be made to shoulder the full responsibility for their deed.[196]

The *Irish Citizen*'s editorial policy was strongly pacifist although the paper also provided a forum for those suffragists who were involved in war relief work. It also disagreed with the suspension of suffrage activities for the course of the war. It printed a letter from Mrs J. Spring Rice at the outset of war in which she expressed the hope that suffragists who 'feel strongly inclined to give up active propaganda work' in order to devote themselves to relief work, would 'undertake such works as suffragists and, as much as possible, through suffrage societies'. The writer felt that this line of action would help the cause. The editor, Frank Sheehy Skeffington, added a foot-note to this letter: 'We trust that the strong inclination to give up active propaganda will be strenuously resisted. Now is the time for increasing activity of propaganda.'[197] In Ireland the situation was further complicated by the growing separatist movement, and specifically by the formation of Cumann na mBan and the ensuing debate between its members and the women of the IWFL. Neither Anna Haslam nor her organization became embroiled in this ideological battle.

The IWSLGA report for 1914, while still noting suffrage news, applied itself to matters pertaining to the outbreak of war. Despite Mrs Haslam's res-ignation as secretary the previous year owing to her stated inability to carry out duties due to increasing age, the report is almost exclusively devoted to her activities. We are told that Mrs Haslam, 'our president', inaugurated a joint committee consisting of representatives from societies in Dublin inter-ested in social work. Fourteen associations were involved in the committee, including, intriguingly, the 'National League for opposing Women's Franchise'. It was proposed that this joint committee should assist in the work for the election of poor law guardians. In 1914 there were 124 female poor law guardians and nine town and urban councillors.[198] Miss Harrison T.C. proposed, and Mrs Haslam seconded the resolution to set up a com-mittee urging the government to appoint an Irish advisory committee of women in connection with relief work schemes. The Lord Lieutenant 'intensely approved', and the committee, after an interview with the Chief Secretary, was in place.[199] Mrs Haslam, it was noted, had resigned from the vice-presidency of the NUWW, a fact which perhaps demonstrates that she was making an effort to cut down on some of her activities. She was reported as having collected £15 1s 0d towards the provision of a bed in Dublin Castle for wounded soldiers.[200] Mrs Haslam had worked in the cause of peace in her youth, when she was a member of an Olive Leaf Circle. Her endeavours on behalf of wounded soldiers does not necessarily mean that she had abandoned her pacifist principles. The IWSLGA does not appear to have engaged in bellicose language – the war is 'terrible', not glo-rious, Germans are not vilified. Many pacifists went to France as ambulance drivers; engaging in work for the relief of suffering did not necessarily mean that one did not have pacifist ideals.

Thomas Haslam's succinct, lucid prose was no longer a feature of the annual report.[201] In 1915 'suffrage work, as such, was in abeyance' during the 'terrible war'. Mrs Haslam's bed for wounded soldiers, known as the IWSLGA bed, was now in use in the Red Cross Hospital in Dublin Castle. In a wonderfully ambiguous phrase, it is mentioned that 'members of the com-mittee make a point of interesting themselves, alas, in the successive inmates of the bed'.[202] Presumably this was a comment on the numbers of injured soldiers repatriated for hospitalization.

Shortly after the outbreak of war, Anna proposed that because of 'these abnormal times we should agitate for the employment of trained women as police women on patrols'. She had collected a mass of information on the topic which she had presented to the committee.[203] None of this has survived and it is difficult to discover precise information regarding the aims and methods of the Dublin patrols. Reports of their activities tend to presume knowledge of the patrols on the part of their readers. The *Irish Citizen* was initially cynical at the suggestion of voluntary policewomen: 'Fancy, anyone asking a policeman whether he would be paid or act as a volunteer! There is plenty of money available to pay for women police.'[204] Despite these misgivings, it printed a brief correspondence between the Under Secretary for Ireland and the Chairman of the Joint Committee which confirmed the Lord Lieutenant's approval of women patrols. Each patrol member's identity card was to be signed by the Chairman and countersigned by the Chief Commissioner of the Dublin Metropolitan Police. Volunteers were asked to apply to Mrs Haslam for further information.[205] By January 1915, the *Irish Citizen* judged that the introduction of women's patrols 'is principally desirable because, under the present purely male administration of the law, women require further protection'. Usefully, this is a prescriptive piece which gives some clues to the activities of the patrols. They should not confine themselves to keeping 'the numerous young girls', whose presence was a 'danger to themselves and others', off the streets, but should also ensure 'that innocent women are not made the victims of unscrupulous, and sometimes brutal policemen and that guilty women are brought to the police station in a civilised way'.[206] There are clear echoes here of the CDA debates of the nineteenth century, fuelled perhaps by the threat of the reintroduction of the Acts.[207] There is also the suggestion that the patrols were engaged in safeguarding young women at risk of seduction, as well as working with prostitutes in a preventative capacity. While the system of patrols did not 'altogether satisfy' the *Irish Citizen* writer, it was clear 'from Mrs Haslam's statement' that it did 'not satisfy the promoters either, and that they regard it as merely a preliminary step to greater things'.[208] An account of the 'Experiences of a Woman Patrol' in the *Irish Citizen* described how 'the whole locality of Sackville Street' at night 'appears to be like one great low saloon where young girls, soldiers and civilians loiter about. It goes to one's heart to see how very young most of the girls are; also how drunk many of them are.' The writer complains of the sexual double standard; 'no other vocation in life' was open to these girls: 'once they have taken to the streets; they have not the same chance as men of living an immoral life and being received by respectable people, and having excuses made for them if they are found out.'[209] A further account suggests that the patrols were engaged also in dealing with disturbances. It described a street scene of infernal proportions:

> Everything very filthy with street doors wide open ... four women drinking out of bottles ... I knew it was useless our trying to do anything if there was any row or unseemly behaviour; what use would

two women be, with no powers, and not even a whistle to call for help
. . . We did our best to disperse the crowd . . . we went to find a policeman.[210]

The piece included an appeal for better housing conditions for the urban
poor.

The foundation of the women's patrols in Ireland was obviously influenced by the English situation. In the first weeks of the war, the NUWW in
England 'inaugurated a scheme of voluntary patrols for specific welfare
work in areas in which military camps and centres were being established'.
The work of patrols 'was regarded solely as a war-time measure . . . voluntary patrols are neither police, nor rescue workers, but true friends of the
girls'.[211] However, there was contemporaneously, in England at least, a volunteer women's police force, many of whom were 'prominent workers for
Women's Suffrage'. This small group quickly became the Women Police
Service which operated with the aid of voluntary contributions until 1916
when it received a government grant.[212] Modern scholarship on the phenomenon of women's patrols forges a link between the social purity
movement and 'the wider feminisit ambition catalyzed initially by the
struggle over the Contagious Diseases Acts'.[213] The women's patrols were
'organised primarily, with a view to the care of girls and women, who are
not prostitutes and would not ordinarily come under notice of police, and
. . . their object is mainly preventative'.[214] From the evidence of the activities
of the Dublin Women's Patrols, their work, too was preventative. Anna
Haslam succeeded in having policewomen appointed:

> Miss [sic] Haslam and her colleagues had been agitating for some time
> for the appointment of women police officers to look after female and
> child offenders in the courts. Her war-time volunteers . . . gained a
> hard core of knowledge of the shadowy under side of the world of
> bright lights when Government resistance broke down so far as to
> agree to setting up a force of women police limited in number and
> scope.[215]

Six women were appointed in Dublin by the British authorities but, after
independence, 'the Dublin Women's Police Force, far from expanding in
proportion to the increasing awareness of the social necessity for it, dwin-
dled as member after member reached retirement age'. The last member of
'Dublin's small and singularly restricted women's police force', Miss
Elizabeth Watters, retired in 1956.[216] The foundation of patrols was regarded
as a significant achievement of Anna's. An obituary by M. T. H. (probably
Mary T. Hayden) stated:

> She founded in 1915 the Irish Women's Patrols and, until a few months
> ago, regularly attended the meetings of the Executive. She even . . .
> went on patrol. The Chief Commissioner of the Dublin Metropolitan
> Police, Colonel Johnston, had the highest opinion of Mrs. Haslam's

judgement, and relied much on her opinion in the selection of police-women and in kindred matters.[217]

Thus women's patrols obviously outlived the war. If the writer is indeed Mary Hayden, she is well qualified to speak with authority on women's patrols. In the 1916 report Miss Hayden MA was named as joint president of the patrol committee.[218]

Amazingly Mrs Haslam was back as vice-president of the National Union of Women Workers in 1915, and rejoiced that there was now an affiliated Irish branch. She had 'long desired to form a branch in Dublin'.[219] Anna's reappointment as vice-president of the NUWW and the affiliation of the Dublin branch was obviously connected with the founding of women's patrols.

In 1915 Anna Haslam addressed a meeting of the Women's National Health Association, chaired by Lady Aberdeen, on the subject of women's patrols, 'which had lately been instituted in Dublin'. There were now twenty women's patrols concentrated in the central streets of the city. 'It was very important that more Catholic ladies should volunteer for the work.' Clubs, both Catholic and Protestant were needed to which the patrols could direct girls.[220] It is not stated why more Catholic women were needed for the work. One can only deduce that because of the moral questions involved, it was desirable that coreligionists of the girls who were perceived to be at risk were involved in patrolling the streets. In March 1916, Mrs Haslam reported that 'their appeal for more Catholic ladies as patrols had been successful and now more Protestant ladies were wanted'.[221]

Women's patrols were judged a complete success by the IWSLGA: 'the presence of those devoted women in our streets, quietly watchful, tactfully alert to every opportunity to assist or advise must be of enormous moral effort.'[222] In 1916 it was noted that Mrs Haslam 'kept in touch with Colonel Johnston, Chief Commissioner of the Police who has already taken two of our patrols for regular police work and intends taking others as they are trained and he has openings for them'. There was also a recreation room for girls in Middle Abbey Street, regarded as an 'important factor in the advancement' of the work of the patrols. Later in the report 'our respected president' was congratulated 'on her untiring philanthropic work, viz. her success in being able to appoint two policewomen for duty in Dublin'.[223] The *Irish Citizen* was not uncritical of the patrols; it named the women appointed as 'Mrs. Farquharson and Miss McLoughlin', and hoped that 'an adequate salary is paid to these ladies and that the Government are not adding to their list of sweated labour'.[224]

The *Irish Citizen* reported the findings of a committee of women who attended court cases in order to 'ensure that while offences against women and children are being heard, some authoritative women should be present in court to collect information and give publicity to points, often unreported, in regard to such cases'.[225] Mrs Sanderson, an IWSLGA member, wrote a blistering account of the first court case she witnessed as one of the committee of 'Women Watching the Courts', in which she recounted her horror, as a suffragist, at the legal inequity of the case, which was one of seduction. She emphasized the need for women as jurors, as counsel and as judges.[226] The trials on which members of the 'Women Watching the Court Committee' reported in the *Irish Citizen* usually dealt with seduction and sexual assault, and the accounts included the, usually caustic, comments of the 'watcher'. The lawyers in a civil case of seduction in which the man pleaded guilty, were said to have:

> laughed and talked about 'human nature'. The girl's agony and ruined life were estimated at the munificent sum of £120, and she and her baby dismissed with a wave of the hand . . . There was no hint of marriage; the word was never mentioned.[227]

Obviously the writer felt that some effort should be made to have the seducer marry the 'ruined' girl. Thomas Haslam had suggested the same solution forty years previously.[228] The *Irish Citizen*'s editorial and features coverage of sexual matters suggests that there was no difference of approach to these questions between the militant and non-militant suffrage societies, and also agreed broadly with the theories expressed by Thomas Haslam in his nineteenth-century works. Dana Hearne, in an analysis of the paper, concluded that between August 1912 and December 1913, there were at least thirty-five articles, fourteen of which were editorials, on 'white slavery' or 'commercialized prostitution'.[229] Some *Irish Citizen* pieces bordered on the hysterical and seem far-fetched to today's reader. An account of an attempted attack on three young girls which had been foiled by the intervention of a 'plucky' young solicitor ended: 'What strikes the mere woman about the tale is the fact that such a foul outrage could be committed . . . and that no attempt to lynch the would be assassin of maidenhood is recorded.'[230] Another report detailed the attempted abduction of young girls in 'a well-known [but unnamed] Dublin suburb', by giving them sweets which were 'proved to contain morphia'.[231] However, many thoughtful analytical pieces on prostitution were also published. James Cousins, one-time editor of the *Irish Citizen*, delivered a speech to the Liverpool WSPU which was reported at length in the paper. In it he blamed 'the low and selfish character' of men for the existence of prostitution, because 'in matters of sex, man is the natural aggressor'. The solution was 'the attainment of power by women to mould effectively the legislation that is on all sides encroaching on the affairs of women as well as men'.[232] Cousins's words are an echo of the ideas put forward by Thomas Haslam in his pamphlet published over forty years previously. Haslam had named '*men's* unchastity and *men's* injustice' as the causes of prostitution. He too linked the solution of the problem of prostitution with the granting of female suffrage, which would allow women 'their rightful voice in the passing of those laws upon which the well-being of both sexes is equally dependent'.[233]

The English militant leader, Christabel Pankhurst, wrote, in a pamphlet praised by the *Irish Citizen,* that the cure for venereal disease was 'Votes for Women and Chastity for men'. She thought that state regulation of prostitution was futile; the 'observance of the same moral standard' for men and women was 'indispensable' to the ending of the 'Great Scourge'.[234] The writings on prostitution of Christabel Pankhurst and of the Irish militant opinion shapers were very similar to, if not influenced by, those of Thomas Haslam. Some feminists in the early twentieth century strove to construct a positive female sexuality which asserted that 'sexual feeling and emotion were natural and beneficial, and that repression was harmful socially, emotionally and psychologically'.[235] A short-lived feminist journal called the *Freewoman* published in England from November 1911 to May 1912, put forward an alternative point of view on male and female sexuality. Contributors included Rebecca West, Havelock Ellis and H. G. Wells, whose writings challenged contemporary opinions on marriage, sexuality, sexual enjoyment and contraception. Such taboo topics as lesbianism and menstruation were discussed, but far from winning converts to the idea of a broader forum for sexual debate, the journal provoked 'much displeasure among the leaders of the suffrage campaign'.[236]

Suffragists attacked the double standard of sexuality which justified the existence of prostitution. They did not recommend sexual freedom for women, however, but sought rather to end the acceptance of male sexual licence. Women in parliament and as voters would be empowered to strive for moral reform. Lady Chance of the constitutional National Union of Women Suffrage Societies argued that as long as women were denied the vote 'the double standard of morality for men and women' would continue. She wrote that suffragists wished to convince public opinion that 'it is equally wrong for both sexes to transgress the moral law ... the Women's Movement is in fact a great Moral Movement'.[237] In England as in Ireland, suffrage writings and utterances on sexuality were predicated on a belief in the moral superiority of female sexual behaviour. Dana Hearne has written that the key function of the discourse on sexuality in the *Irish Citizen* 'was to show that women's voices and power were needed in the public realm in order to transform a world ... in this new world, male sexuality would be controlled, and the female standard of chastity would become the norm'.[238] Women's patrols, although engaged in a 'definitionally masculine and authoritarian occupation', were essentially feminist, devoted to protecting women from immorality – a dominant motif of the women's movement of the period.[239]

Possibly because of the extent of its wartime activities, Anna Haslam felt obliged to reiterate the IWSLGA's commitment to suffrage in 1915, when she proposed a resolution that the committee 're-affirms its adherence to its chief aims' of the parliamentary vote for women on the same terms as men. Women must be included 'in any scheme formulated for the future of Ireland'. All Irish MPs were circulated with a copy of the resolution.[240]

The 1915 IWSLGA report congratulated Mr Haslam on his ninetieth birthday. 'We rejoice that Mr. and Mrs. Haslam are still with us with clear brains and able hands ever working to further our interests ... [with] unflinching devotion to the women's cause, the advancement of which is the *one and only* foundation for sound reform.' On 8 November 1915,

Thomas Haslam 'veteran champion of the cause', read his paper *Some Last Words on Women's Suffrage* to an IWSLGA audience. The following week he addressed the militant Irish Women's Franchise League on the same topic and his speech was printed in full in the *Irish Citizen*. [241] The IWFL notes in the 'Irish Suffrage Activities' column was also devoted to the Haslam speech. He was compared to Mr Gladstone, 'who also grew more progressive as years went on'. Mrs Sheehy Skeffington in proposing the vote of thanks to Thomas said that the Haslams' lives were 'an inspiration to us all'. Obviously no legacy of bitterness or personal animosity resulted from the differences between the Haslams and IWFL. The report hoped that Mrs Haslam would 'give [the IWFL] . . . a special evening and tell us more of her wonderfully interesting life experiences'.[242]

Thomas's paper, published in 1916, could be said to be an apologia for his life's work. It is a stylish, convincing, closely argued polemic that conclusively demonstrates the unimpaired mental capabilities of this ninety-year-old man. Haslam uses 'we' throughout, referring perhaps to the partnership of Anna and himself, or perhaps he is including the audience of suffragist supporters.[243] The experience of working for fifty years for women's suffrage has been 'upon the whole' satisfactory. Despite the failure to attain 'the main object of our exertions' much had been achieved. He predicted correctly that some form of enfranchisement would be granted at the end of the war. He demanded nothing less than full adult suffrage: 'We should abandon . . . paltry exclusions, . . . adopt the frankly democratic principle . . . for all capable women . . . in other words, *all our adult women.*'[244] He argues that, without representation, no group is ever treated equitably, citing as an example 'the repressive treatment which our Trade Unionists received until Mr. Disraeli and Mr. Gladstone carried their respective democratic extensions of the Franchise in 1867 and 1884'. Furthermore he urged that women must 'obtain an adequate representation . . . in the House of Commons and possibly in the House of Lords . . . likewise in the *Cabinet*'. The property qualification had no 'ethical validity'. It is precisely those without property who most urgently needed the vote. The rich had protection; 'the Law Courts, the Police Force, and, in the last resort the Soldiery are always more or less at their service'.[245]

He wrote of the militant movement more in sorrow than in anger. 'Suffrage has been so long withheld that a few of our more impulsive women, grown weary of the protracted struggle, as a practical protest, have allowed themselves to be goaded into regrettable acts of violence.'[246] The cause of women's suffrage had gained general acceptance. Trades union congresses evidenced no opposition to full adult suffrage; even the attitudes of conservative classes indicated a remarkable change in the general feeling.[247] He quoted from the 1914 debate in the House of Commons, an extract from a speech of Mr Clough which, he says, summed up the entire case for women's suffrage in a nutshell:

> I want Honourable Members . . . to admit that . . . their mothers, their sisters, their daughters and their wives, are as fully entitled to the

Parliamentary Franchise, *on absolutely equal terms,* as their fathers, their brothers, their sons and themselves; and if this be established in regard to the female relatives of Honourable Members of this House, it logically follows that it consistently and justly applies in every house throughout the length and breadth of the United Kingdom.[248]

Haslam forecast correctly that 'if all our adult women were enfranchised, they would add not a revolutionary, but a reasonably conservative element to our electorate'. He did not propose resumption of agitation until war had concluded. In the event of Home Rule, he was sure that 'whatever course is adopted by the Parliament at Westminster will be followed at College Green'.[249] He ended by stressing that the extent of the franchise measure that would certainly 'follow the termination of war on both sides of the Channel', would depend on the 'attitude and earnestness displayed by our women themselves'.[250]

This speech, delivered by a very old man, is as its title suggests, a valedictory statement; it is also a personal credo. It is required reading for anyone who dismisses Haslam as typically conservative and middle-class. While it could be argued that the language is paternalistic – 'our women' – the ideas expressed are radical and inclusive. The civil rights of the poor are privileged over those of the rich. It is not enough to give all adult women the vote, they must also win seats in parliament. He recognized that women must achieve cabinet positions, in order that they might influence legislation pertaining to their lives. Other points raised by him include the injustice of laws of inheritance, 'which so often confer the bulk of the bequeathed property upon the *sons,* to the exclusion of the *daughters'*. Reference to the war, couched in careful language, is far from bellicose and demonstrates at the very least an ambivalence on his part. He talks about the self-sacrificing spirit 'in which our mothers, in obedience to what they have believed to be the call of duty, have sent hundreds of thousands of their dearly loved sons to die'.[251] The united strength of men and women was needed to solve the problem of

> our ruinous system of *Aggressive Wars,* which is wasting the energies of all our leading nations; it is we, men, who uphold it for the gratification of our selfish ambitions; our women are its helpless victims; and, until they obtain their legitimate influence in the Councils of the world, I can see no prospect of its termination.[252]

Women's participation was also needed to solve the temperance problem, the problem of pauperism, and 'what is euphemistically called the *Social Evil'*. The latter problem would never be solved by men alone because 'it is we, men, who are mainly responsible for its existence'.[253]

These were indeed Thomas's last words on suffrage. He died in January 1917 in his ninety-second year, of influenza. The IWSLGA report for 1916 had not yet gone to press and when published included the shocked announcement: 'A calamity has befallen the suffrage cause in Ireland. We have lost a champion by the death of Mr. T. J. Haslam.' The obituary, on a page edged with a deep black border, stated that Thomas had 'beautiful faith in woman's ability to use for the good of the world those advantages he worked so hard to obtain for them'. A meeting on 22 February passed a resolution proposed by Lady Dockrell which recorded the 'sense of irreparable loss' suffered by the committee, conveyed 'heartfelt sympathy' to Anna, and noted their 'deep feeling of appreciation for his long and unwearied efforts on behalf of women's suffrage and his unselfish devotion to the service of humanity'.[254] Recognized in the obituary was Thomas's conviction that the empowerment gained by women by the granting of the franchise, would result in the improvement of mankind, a point argued compellingly in his final pamphlet. The conviction that woman was not merely equal, but in many cases superior, to the male of the species is a recurring theme in his work. His final pamphlet was a bold assertion of his radical beliefs, so different from the relatively modest suggestions of his early works on suffrage. Perhaps it is possible to trace an evolution in his feminism from his suffrage pamphlets; it is, however, more likely, as has been argued here, that he always held the convictions expressed in his last pamphlet. He was careful in his earlier works not to antagonize potential supporters by advancing ideas which would be judged too radical. As the prolonged suffrage campaign gradually educated public opinion, his arguments became bolder. Sadly, his death was less than two years before his wife first cast her vote. The *Irish Citizen* summed up 'his outstanding qualities . . . Truth, Simplicity, Activity and Love of Peace'.[255]

The 1917 IWSLGA report contained the terse phrase: 'our cause is won'.[256] This referred to the decision of the government to compile a new register of voters based on war service in order to overcome the difficulties of including fighting men in the event of an election being called. The NUWSS wrote to the prime minister pointing out that women were carrying out war work and, although they had no wish for controversy while war continued, they could not allow a change in conditions for the male voter without pressing the claims of women.[257] Suffrage work resumed, albeit of the most restrained and subdued variety. MPs were lobbied. Public opinion was with the women. The *Observer* and many other newspapers once opposed to the cause were now in favour: 'In the past we have opposed the claim . . . We were wrong.'[258] The deliberations of the government ultimately resulted in a women's suffrage clause being inserted in the Representation of the People Bill, which was passed without a division. The *Irish Citizen* announced: 'A great triumph has been achieved', but regretted that 'so deeply are women pre-occupied with other affairs . . . it would seem the power of the vote were being put into an inert hand'. The victory was attributed to 'the sacrifices and labour of other days'.[259] In February 1918, the 'Royal Assent' was given to the Representation of People Act, which enfranchised women over thirty who were householders or the wives of householders, occupiers of property with a £5 'annual value', graduates of a British university, or those who had fulfilled the qualification for graduation but were not being allowed to graduate (as in Cambridge University).[260]

Mrs Haslam was not prepared to rest on her laurels. She regarded the victory as 'limited' and attempted to foster cooperation between the different societies in Ireland to work together for 'certain reforms'. In March 1918, she organized meetings 'of delegates from most of the Irish Suffrage Societies'. Three meetings took place, but 'the delegates unanimously decided not to form, for the present, any amalgamation . . . The feeling of the conference being that political differences are at present so strong in Ireland that a closer union in a society or federation would be out of the question.' Despite Mrs Haslam's failure to unite suffragist women of different political persuasions, her achievement in convening the meetings was acknowledged:

This further work of Mrs. Haslam for the cause of feminism in Ireland is much appreciated, and it is significant of the esteem in which she is held by Irish suffragists of all political creeds that they are uniting in the presentation of an address of congratulation to her upon the realisation of her life's work.[261]

The election of December 1918, the first general election in which women (or at least some of them) could vote and stand for election, was marked by a touching tribute to Mrs Haslam:

On Election Day the League was represented with its banners and colours at joint demonstrations organised by the various suffrage and women's organisations for Mrs. Haslam the veteran Irish suffrage leader. She recorded her vote in the midst of an admiring feminine throng to cheer her, was presented with a bouquet in suffrage colours for the occasion . . . It speaks well for the broadmindedness of the new women voters that women of all parties – Unionist, Irish Party and Sinn Féin – joined heartily to honour Mrs. Haslam and suffrage.[262]

The *Freeman's Journal* stated simply that 'Mrs. Haslam voted at William Street Courthouse. She is 90 years old, and made a speech in this election in support of Sir Maurice Dockrell. She . . . looked charmingly venerable.'[263] The writer of this account did not think it necessary to explain to readers who Mrs Haslam was, which suggests that her status would be instantly recognizable to readers. Anna's only regret was that Thomas 'was not present to share her joy'.[264] The *Irish Citizen* also regretted that 'her devoted husband . . . a life long friend of the cause did not live to see its victory'.[265] An analysis of voting preferences in the Rathmines constituency showed that suffragists did not vote en bloc: 'Mrs. Kettle and Professor Mary Hayden back one candidate, the Irish Party nominee, while Mrs. Haslam swears allegiance to the Conservative, Sir Maurice Dockrell, and Mrs. Sheehy Skeffington supports Sinn Féin.'[266] It was pointed out that all of the candidates supported by these women were themselves suffragists.

Countess Markievicz was elected as a Sinn Féin member for South Dublin, the only woman to be elected in Great Britain and Ireland. Seventeen other women candidates were defeated including prominent campaigners such as Christabel Pankhurst, Charlotte Despard, Emmeline Pethick-Lawrence and Ray Strachey. The election of Constance Markievicz, of great significance in the history of suffrage, was inextricably linked to her participation in the Rising of 1916 and the Sinn Féin landslide in 1918.

The work of the IWSLGA was not over. 'In view of the partial victory obtained under the Representation of the People Act', the committee resolved to devote its energies to the promotion of the extension of the vote 'to women on the same terms as men'. It would henceforth promote the election of suitable women as MPs and work to ensure the registration of qualified women voters.[267] In 1918 the IWSLGA was rechristened the Irishwomen Citizens' and Local Government Association (IWCLGA). The substitution of the word 'citizens' for 'suffrage' in the title celebrated the attainment of citizenship; citizen was a significant word in the dictionary of feminism. James Cousins had earlier defined it, 'not merely as an academic idea' but as a social reconstruction 'in which the feminine and masculine sides of humanity should share equally the work of life, and enjoy equally the products of their work'.[268] The members of the IWCLGA saw citizenship not merely as a right to be enjoyed, but as a state which brought with it duties and responsibilities.

Although Anna Haslam was ninety in 1919, she travelled to London for the reading of the Emancipation Bill.[269] She described her activities while in London as going 'to the House of Commons to interview MPs on the Bill, attending to a meeting on proportional representation in the Carlton Hall, visiting various friends and relations and going to a *medium*'.[270] Obviously, neither the attainment of the vote nor her great age prevented her from continuing to take an active interest in reform. Anna also described a meeting in Dublin, held under the auspices of 'our Association' to advocate proportional representation:

> I was one of the names proposed at test election. Unfortunately the Sinn Féiners were in the majority in the Hall + the Countess Markievicz got 6 more votes than I did tho' she did not get a single vote no. 1 + I got 20 – it was a very interesting experiment.[271]

Anna Haslam was active up to the last few weeks of her life. On her ninety-third birthday in April 1922, there was a 'touching little function' at which she was 'the recipient of a presentation' from members of the IWCLGA and other friends. 'The accompanying address spoke of the stimulus and inspiration' of her life to others. Mrs Haslam was grateful for the 'generous gift and kind words'. The writer concluded, 'it is for us to thank her'.[272] A few days before her death she was visited at home by the first female Clerk of the Petty Sessions, Miss Frost. Anna had lobbied for the appointment of a woman to the post and 'started a subscription to meet the legal expenses involved'.[273]

The IWCLGA was prominent in feminist campaigns in post-independent Ireland. The 1925 Civil Service Regulation (Amendment) Bill proposed to exclude women from the higher grades in the civil service. The 1927 Juries

Act sought to deny women the right to sit on juries, a basic duty of citizenship, on the grounds that the vast majority of women citizens would be grateful to be relieved of jury duty.[274] The IWCLGA protested that employment in the civil service should be based, not on the gender of the candidates, but on their competence for the job. One can hear the voice of Anna Haslam in the IWCLGA's protest against the proposed Juries Act: 'Women had no right to evade any duties and responsibilities involved in citizenship.'[275] The Civil Service Act was defeated in the Seanad. The Juries Act became law, however, but an amendment was added which allowed women to sit on juries, but only if they specifically applied. Despite its efforts to unite 'Irish women of all politics and all creeds for the study and practice of good citizenship', the association remained a small Dublin-based group.[276] Members included Senator Jenny Wyse Power and Mary Hayden. The association merged in 1947 with a 'new and vigorous group', the Irish Housewives' Association.[277]

The *Irish Citizen's* claim in 1918, that Irishwomen had achieved the vote 'Thanks mainly to the efforts of the Irish Women's Franchise League', must be challenged.[278] The victory in Ireland was an inextricable part of the wider British victory. The relative importance of the constitutional and militant societies in the winning of the vote continues to be a matter of debate. While it is undeniable that the entry of the militants into the fray generated an enormous upsurge of interest in the suffrage movement in Ireland as in England, in reality 'the constitutional societies absorbed many new members who were roused by the militant drum but could not march to it'.[279] The tactics of militants undoubtedly alienated parliamentary support and may actually have impeded legislative progress. Women of the IWFL, however, had an input into the eventual inclusion of full adult suffrage in the Irish Free State Constitution of 1922, which gave the vote to all women over twenty-one.[280]

The constitutional IWSLGA may have seemed staid and cautious when compared with the flamboyant behaviour of the IWFL but it was not replaced by it. The analysis in this chapter of the twentieth-century campaign of the IWSLGA challenges the impression created by historians of the Irish suffrage campaign, that the IWFL effectively superseded the outmoded older organization. Admittedly the IWSLGA was at a disadvantage in that its leadership was part of the dying fall of southern unionism, while the IWFL was lifted by the buoyant vibrancy of self-confident nationalism. The IWSLGA, despite the unionism of the leadership, kept true to its non-party credo, while the IWFL was repeatedly drawn into a debate with those of feminist leanings within the separatist movement. Despite their differences, the minute book and reports of the IWSLGA and the pages of the *Irish Citizen* reveal the mutual respect and regard the leadership of each organization felt for the other. Comparisons between the writings on suffrage and sexuality in the *Irish Citizen* and in the works of Thomas Haslam reveal that the two organizations shared an ideology, and were divided only by their methodologies.

Anna and Thomas Haslam devoted almost fifty years of their lives to the fight for suffrage. Their methods were constitutional, peaceful, law-abiding and inclusive. They repeatedly stressed that their claim was 'reasonable and moderate' – that 'women should have the votes upon the same terms as men'.[281] Their perseverance, despite repeated disappointments, demonstrates their unshakeable conviction of the justice of the cause.

Conclusion

Anna Haslam's death on 28 November 1922 was almost synonchronic with the birth of the Irish Free State. While the constitution of the new state granted universal adult suffrage, 'votes for women' did not herald the emergence of an enlightened social policy as prophesied by Thomas and Anna Haslam. The era of the socially radical politicized woman was at an end, helped by the abstensionist policies of the Civil War that ensured that five of the six women elected in 1922 did not take their seats in the Dáil. Their connections with dead heroes became the criterion for the selection of women as political candidates by the major parties and, when elected, they toed the party line. Anna Haslam's death would appear to have signalled the end, rather than the beginning of a Brave New World for women. Two days after her death, however, the *Irish Times* printed an article, 'The Great Unpaid: Another Demand for Reform', calling for an end to 'so many inequalities of rights' between husbands and wives. The writer demanded that, within marriage, 'woman must receive reward' for her work within the home, not as 'favours flung by a generous hand' but as a 'just and legitimate right'.[1] The inclusion of such a piece in the very issue of the conservative *Irish Times* that announced the death of 'A Woman Pioneer' seems apt and may not have been coincidence.

The lives of Thomas and Anna Haslam were dedicated to the attainment of equality for women. They were feminists before the word was coined. In an era when respectable women were not supposed to know of the existence of prostitutes, Anna became empowered to do the unthinkable – not only to speak in public, but to discuss openly matters sexual, and to attack the double standard of sexuality that was enshrined in the official treatment of prostitutes. The life-long commitment of the Haslams to the cause of women's suffrage never faltered, despite the repeated discouragement of the fate of bills defeated in the House of Commons.

Anna Haslam's life was a textbook example of the evolution of a feminist. Her Quaker upbringing, her practical espousal of the anti-slavery cause in early childhood, her education and brief career as a teacher, and her administrative skills were characteristic of the feminist profile. Her marriage, like those of Millicent Fawcett, Margaret Cousins and Hanna Sheehy Skeffington, was to an active suffragist. The involvement of men in a movement essentially led and operated by women in a world in which men had hegemony is remarkable. The story of women's struggle for equality incorporates men who were forging a new construct of 'masculinity'. Thomas

Haslam would appear to have been comfortable with his acknowledged role as his wife's helper. One could argue that his auxiliary capacity was not unrelated to his financial dependence on his wife. This is unlikely to be the case; his formulation of a feminist theory appears to have been predicated as much upon the necessity of rethinking the nature of man as upon the rights of women. He recognized the injustice of the prevailing double standard of morality and demanded of men the same standards of behaviour as society had previously demanded of women. 'Chastity for men' was the message. 'Manliness' was henceforth to be characterized by sexual self-control. The connections he forged between male chastity and feminist principles were exemplified in his own life. It must be stated that his message of 'chastity for men' would not appear to have involved any change of lifestyle for himself. His theories of heredity presented him with the heady prospect of his works impinging beneficially on the lives of future generations.

The Haslams' seemingly celibate marriage, ironically for a couple interested in birth control, was the inevitable outcome of their decision not to have children. Perhaps it was equally an inevitable result of the marriage of feminist ideas with a belief in the Victorian stereotype of the asexual woman. Thomas was undoubtedly the feminist theorist of the couple. Anna was a 'ceaseless reader' of material that 'fortified her ambitions', who applied feminist ideas to various campaigns for reform. Although their endeavours took place in Ireland they saw themselves as part of a wider movement for the transformation of society. It is a matter of regret that Anna did not commit her ideas to paper as she was 'forceful and adroit in her argument' and adept at exploitation of events to hammer home her message.[2]

The Haslams represented an Ireland that did not survive them. While they were dedicated to the union with Westminster, they worked happily with those who applied themselves to its destruction. Although in many ways they exemplified the virtues of their Quaker backgrounds, they did not subscribe to any organized religion. Despite living in straitened circumstances, they were part of an urban intellectual elite and participated in the social and cultural life of Dublin for over fifty years.

It is tempting to speculate how the Haslams would have fared in post-independence Ireland; Hanna Sheehy Skeffington, who had impeccable nationalist credentials, was effectively marginalized. It is likely that they would have protested against discriminatory legislation in their usual law-abiding manner but, in a country that quickly developed an overwhelmingly Roman Catholic ethos, would they have had a voice or a constituency? Ironically, Thomas's teaching on chastity would have found favour with the Roman Catholic hierarchy; his message was disseminated in a simpler and more pious form in numerous Catholic Truth Society pamphlets. The Protestant minority never sought to subvert the institutions of the state, was careful not to criticize, and kept its collective head down. Dáil Éireann was not bombarded with petitions for the restoration of divorce facilities or the unbanning of birth control. Those who sought such amenities obtained them quietly 'in another jurisdiction'. Fifty years were to pass before the condom-wielding 'comely maidens' erupted on to the front pages of the Sunday papers. They were, one imagines, the spiritual descendants of the militant rather than the constitutional suffrage movement.

When Mary Robinson was elected to the presidency of Ireland in 1991 she referred to her election as a victory for 'Mná na hÉireann', 'the women of Ireland'. she sent the principle of rights for women, however, as something which still needed advocacy eighty years after the death of Anna and Thomas Haslam.

> Once and for all we need to commit ourselves to the concept that women's rights are not factional or sectional privileges, bestowed on the few at the whim of the many. They are human rights. In a society in which the rights and potential of women are constrained no man can be truly free.[3]

Notes

Introduction

[1] Mary Cullen, 'Anna Maria Haslam (1829–1922)' in Mary Cullen and Maria Luddy (eds.), *Women, Power and Consciousness in Nineteenth Century Ireland* (Dublin: Attic Press, 1995), pp. 161–96.

[2] Mary Colum, *Life and the Dream* (New York, 1947), p. 153.

[3] James Cousins and Margaret Cousins, *We Two Together* (Madras: Ganesh, 1950), p. 129.

[4] In 1876 the Haslams founded the Dublin Women's Suffrage Association (DWSA) which later became the IWSLGA.

[5] Obituary for Thomas Haslam stated that his papers had been deposited in the National Library of Ireland (NLI). See C. H. Oldham, 'Thomas Joseph Haslam: 1825–1917 – Man and Social Reformer', *Freeman's Journal*, 3 Feb. 1917. The staff of the NLI are satisfied that the papers were never deposited there. It is interesting to note that published suffrage material in the NLI (journals and conference reports, etc.) all bear Anna Haslam's name. In correspondence with Marie Stopes, Anna, commenting on correspondence on birth control, does not mention any material on deposit in the NLI. Stopes, however, wrote on her copy of *The Marriage Problem*: 'Thomas Joseph Haslam ... Diaries, letters, Mss etc. in the National Library of Ireland.' A letter received from Dublin Friends' Historical Library states that 'the legal papers belonging to the Haslam Estate appear to have been destroyed many years ago when there was a big 'paper drive'. This information came from a solicitor now decd.' DFHL, 19 Sept. 1996.

Chapter 1

[1] 'Letter from our Country Women's Meeting in Lancashire to be Dispersed abroad among the Women's meetings everywhere.' It was sent between 1675 and 1680 'to women on both sides of the Atlantic'. Cited in Elisabeth Potts Brown and Susan Mosher Stuard (eds.), *Witnesses for Change: Quaker Women over Three Centuries* (New Brunswick: Rutgers U. P., 1989), p. 27.

[2] There are many works on the religious beliefs of the Society of Friends. Especially helpful are Elisabeth Potts Brown and Susan Mosher Stuard (eds.), *Witnesses for Change*; Richard S. Harrison, 'Spiritual Perception and the Evolution of the Irish Quakers', in Kevin Herlihy (ed.), *The Religion of*

Irish Dissent (Dublin: Four Courts Press, 1996), and Isabel Grubb, *Quakerism in Ireland* (London, 1927).

3   For an account of the history of Quakers in Ireland see Maurice Wigham, *The Irish Quakers: A Short History of the Religious Society of Friends in Ireland* (Dublin: Historical Committee of the Religious Society of Friends in Ireland, 1992); Richard S. Harrison, *A Biographical Dictionary of Irish Quakers* (Dublin: Four Courts Press, 1997), and Thomas P. O'Neill. 'The Society of Friends and the Great Famine', *Studies*, June 1950, pp. 203–13.

4   Cyril Gerard Brannigan, 'Quaker Education in Eighteenth- and Nineteenth-Century Ireland', *Irish Educational Studies*, vol. 4, no. 1, 1984, pp. 59–60.

5   Susan Mosher Stuard, 'Women's Witnessing: A New Departure', in Brown and Stuard, *Witnesses for Change*, p. 15.

6   Letter written sometime between 1675 and 1680 and sent from the Lancashire Meeting of Women Friends to other women's meetings on both sides of the Atlantic. Ascribed to Sarah Fell, daughter of Margaret Fell whose second husband was the founder of the Quakers. Cited in Brown and Stuard (eds.), *Witnesses for Change*, pp. 27–8.

7   Susan Mosher Stuard, 'Women's Witnessing', pp. 15–16.

8   Wigham, *Irish Quakers*, p. 36.

9   Susan Mosher Stuard, 'Women's Witnessing', p. 16.

10 Ibid., p. 17.

11 Ibid., p. 16.

12 This is evident from documents such as 'The Diary of Elizabeth Clibborn of Anner Mills, Clonmel, Co. Tipperary, 1807–1813', Dublin Friends' Historical Library (DFHL). In 1810 she 'Left home in company with James Abell, Benjamin White etc., parted my dear husband and sweet children under strong emotions' to attend a meeting in Dublin, 'a uniting instructive time'. Despite having 'gone through much conflict respecting the propriety of leaving my dearest husband' she then travelled to Holyhead and from thence 'travelled 163 miles in 2 days' to Birmingham where she attended two meetings. She drove to London to the Yearly Meeting, which 'continued to that day week in much harmony'. She also visited an asylum near Bristol, a home for the blind in Bristol 'and some other affecting institutions'. On the way home 'the wind was contrary' and the voyage to Waterford took thirty hours.

13 Stuard, 'Women's Witnessing', p. 4.

14 Elders and overseers, appointed by the monthly meeting, were originally older Friends respected for their wisdom. Overseers were appointed to help the membership practically at different stages of life. See Harrison, *Biographical Dictionary*, p. 17.

15 Typescript of speech delivered by Anna Haslam, n.d. Irish Housewives Association (IHA) archive. Cited in Mary Cullen, 'Anna Maria Haslam (1829–1922)', in Mary Cullen and Maria Luddy (eds.), *Women, Power and Consciousness in Nineteenth Century Ireland* (Dublin: Attic Press, 1995), p. 165.

16 'The Pioneers of Feminism in Ireland', *Irish Citizen*, 21 Mar. 1914, p. 347.

[17] Philippa Levine, *Feminist Lives in Victorian England: Private Lives and Public Commitment* (Oxford: Blackwell, 1990), pp. 32, 17.

[18] The duty of the 'clerk' to a Meeting was to ascertain 'the sense of the meeting' and record decisions in the form of an agreed minute. See Harrison, *Biographical Dictionary*, p. 17.

[19] Fisher family biographical notes, DFHL.

[20] Joseph Fisher of Youghal to Lord Liverpool, 11 Oct. 1816. BL Add. MS 38263.

[21] Harrison, Richard S. '*Dublin Quakers in Business*' (unpublished thesis, M. Litt., Trinity College Dublin, 1988), p. 316.

[22] *Slater's Directory* (Manchester: Slater, 1846), p. 411.

[23] The main source of information on the life of Jane Fisher is her lengthy obituary in the *Annual Monitor, or, Obituaries of the Members of the Society of Friends for the year 1877* (London, 1879), pp. 79–81.

[24] Anna Haslam to Marie Stopes, 20 Aug. 1818. Hull University Library, DX/66/2b.

[25] Elizabeth Clibborn, a Quaker woman from Clonmel, who was active in ministry and was married with children, wrote that she 'hesitated about the propriety of leaving my little flock . . . but the prospect brightens'. See 'The Diary of Elizabeth Clibborn', DFHL.

[26] 'Mrs. Anna Maria Haslam – The "At Home" to celebrate her Eightieth Birthday', unidentified newspaper article, 5 Mar. 1909, in DFHL scrap-book, p. 20.

[27] In her obituary (see note 5 above) it was stated that Jane left her younger children in the care of her older children.

[28] Mary White Fisher, born in 1822, was actually the sister next to Anna in age but as her birth date is the only information available on her life, I strongly suspect she did not survive infancy.

[29] John Reader, *Of Schools and Schoolmasters: Some Thoughts on Quaker Education as Seen in their Schools in England* (London: Quaker Home Service, 1979), p. 27.

[30] Ibid. See also Brannigan, *Quaker Education*, and W. A. Campbell Stuart, *Quakers and Education as Seen in their Schools in England* (London: Epworth Press, 1953).

[31] Maurice Wigham, *Newtown School Centenary 1898* (Waterford: Newenham Harvey & Co., 1898) pp. 35, 25, 23, 33.

[32] For an account of educational opportunities at the Mount see Reader, *Of Schools and Schoolmasters*, p. 34, and Campbell Steward, *Quakers and Education*, p. 66.

[33] Ibid., p. 97.

[34] Joseph Spence Hodgson, *Superintendents, Teachers and Principal Officers of Ackworth School from 1779–1894: A list compiled from official documents with historical notes and short biographies* (Ackworth: Ackworth Old Scholars' Association, 1895), pp. 62–3.

[35] Papers of Famine Relief Commission, NAI, RLFC. 3/2/6/133 and 2/441/39.

36 Richard S. Harrison, *Cork City Quakers 1655–1939* (privately published, 1991), p. 59.

37 *Annual Monitor*, 1900, p. 69.

38 'The Pioneers of Feminism in Ireland', *Irish Citizen*, 14 Mar. 1914, p. 347.

39 Ibid., 28 Mar. 1914, p. 355.

40 Autobiographical sketch of Anna Haslam, IHA MS.

41 Anna Haslam to Frank Sheehy Skeffington, 16 Mar. 1914. Sheehy Skeffington Papers, NLI, 21,625.

42 Extract from letter received from Youghal dated 8 March 1852. Jonathan Pim, Secretary, Society of Friends Relief of Distress Papers, NAI, 2/506/42.

43 'Mrs. Anna Maria Haslam: The "At Home" to celebrate her Eightieth Birthday.'

44 Alex Tyrrell, 'Making the Millennium: the mid Nineteenth-Century Peace Movement', *Historical Journal*, no. 20, pt. 1, 1978, p. 86.

45 Jill Liddington, *The Road to Greenham Common: Feminism and Anti-Militarism in Britain since 1820* (Syracuse: Syracuse U. P., 1991), p. 15.

46 Alex Tyrrell, 'Women's Mission and Pressure Group Politics in Britain (1825–1860)', *Bulletin of the John Rylands University Library of Manchester*, vol. 63, no. 1, 1980, p. 218.

47 Peter Moor Fisher (1809–99), eldest brother of Anna Haslam. At the Paris conference, Richard Webb, also a Quaker, and Fisher were the only delegates from Ireland. Fisher was an intrepid traveller. He visited Egypt, Malta and Palestine and travelled to North America to buy corn and wheat. See *Annual Monitor*, 1900, pp. 70–71.

48 Tyrrell, 'Making the Millennium', p. 75.

49 Tyrrell, 'Women's Mission', p. 218.

50 *The Olive Leaf: or, Peace Magazine for the Young*, vol. 33, no. 4, 1847, p. 33.

51 Wigham, *Irish Quakers*, p. 58.

52 Letter to author from Robert Haslam, Calgary, Alberta, Canada, 16.07.1998.

53 Registers of Births, Marriages and Deaths of the Society of Friends, DFHL.

54 Minute of the Mountmellick Monthly Meeting held in Mountrath on the 10th day of the 11th month, 1840, DFHL (Quakers did not use what they considered the pagan names of days and months).

55 See Wigham, *Irish Quakers*, p. 81. 'The most extreme case was of two girls who removed their clothing and walked through the town of Longford clothed only in chestnut leaves.'

56 Letter from Mary Haslam, Rosenallis 17th day of the 5th month, 1841, in Mountmellick Monthly Meeting Book, DFHL.

57 Harrison, *Biographical Dictionary*, p. 65. See also Wigham, *Irish Quakers*, pp. 80–82, and Isabel Grubb, *Quakerism in Ireland* (London, 1927), p. 127.

58 Wigham, *Irish Quakers*, p. 82.

59 *One Hundred Years of Mountmellick School* (Dublin: Webb, 1886), pp. 85–6.

60 Ibid., p. 59.

61 Ibid., pp. 29, 30, 31–2.

62 *Annual Monitor*, 1918, p. 75–7.

[63] Campbell Steward, *Quakers and Education*, p. 88.

[64] *Annual Monitor*, 1918, pp. 75–7.

[65] Hodgson, *Superintendents*, pp. 27–8.

[66] Ackworth School Wages Book, pp. 218, 239. Registry of Deeds, Wakefield. Ref. C678/2/8/2.

[67] Fisher family biographical notes, DFHL.

[68] Anna Haslam to Marie Stopes, 20 Aug. 1918. Hull University Library, DX/66/2b.

[69] James Westwood (ed.), *Forty-second Report of the Ackworth Old Scholars' Association*, 1923–24, p. 85.

[70] Minute of Mountmellick Meeting, 19th day of the 2nd month, 1851; Testimony of Disownment, p. 92, DFHL.

[71] Wigham, *Irish Quakers*, p. 60.

[72] Ibid.

[73] Marriage certificate of Anna and Thomas Haslam, DFHL. Reuben Fisher may have been Anna's older brother who was born in 1812 and who died in 1871 in Florida. However, his wife was called Eliza. Reuben was a common Fisher name and this witness may have been a cousin. Julia was not a Quaker name. Perhaps this Reuben had also 'married out' and thus agreed to be Anna's witness. John Haslam, Thomas's brother would surely have been witness had he been at the wedding. He called his second son, born in 1858, Thomas Joseph, so presumably was not estranged from his brother.

[74] Testimony of Disownment, p. 423, DFHL.

[75] Wigham, *Irish Quakers*, p. 96.

[76] *Annual Monitor*, 1918, 1923, pp. 75–77, 81.

[77] *Annual Monitor*, 1918, p. 77.

[78] Anna Haslam to Marie Stopes, 12 Aug. 1918. Hull University Library, DX/66/2a.

[79] Anna Haslam to Marie Stopes, 20 Aug. 1918. Hull University, DX/66/2b.

[80] Marie O'Neill, 'The Dublin Women's Suffrage Association and its Successors', *Dublin Historical Record*, vol. 38, no. 4, Sept. 1985, p. 129.

[81] History of Mountmellick, p. 37.

[82] *Freeman's Journal*, 3 Feb. 1917.

[83] 'Mrs. Anna Maria Haslam: The "At Home" to Celebrate her Eightieth Birthday', p. 20.

[84] Westwood (ed.), *Forty-second Annual Report*, pp. 85–6.

[85] O'Neill, 'The Dublin Women's Suffrage Association', p. 129.

[86] See *Slater's Trade Directory* and Dublin trade directories.

[87] Francis Newman to T. J. Haslam, April 1868; John Stuart Mill to T. J. Haslam, Feb. 1868. Hull University Library, DX/66/1.

[88] 'Thomas J. Haslam Our Veteran Suffragist', *Irish Citizen*, 20 Nov. 1915.

[89] C. S. Bremner, 'Thomas Haslam', in *The Herald*, DFHL scrapbook.

[90] 'Suffragists Diamond Wedding, March 20, 1914', *Irish Citizen*, 21 Mar. 1914.

[91] C. H. Oldham, 'Thomas Joseph Haslam: 1825–1917 – Man and Social Reformer', *Freeman's Journal*, 3 Feb. 1917.

[92] Anna Haslam to Marie Stopes, 12 Aug. 1918. Hull University Library, DX/66/2a.

[93] *Irish Citizen*, 4 Apr. 1914, p. 366.

[94] Œdipus [Thomas J. Haslam], *The Marriage Problem* (Dublin: Webb, 1868).

[95] See letters of Anna Haslam to Marie Stopes. Hull University Library, DX/66/2.

[96] Anna Haslam to Marie Stopes, 20 Aug. 1918. Hull University Library, DX/66/2b.

[97] Anna Haslam to Marie Stopes, 28 Nov. 1918. Contemporary Medical Archive Centre, Wellcome Institute, London (CMAC).

[98] Anna Haslam to Marie Stopes, 20 Aug. 1918. Hull University Library, DX/66/2b.

[99] Anna Haslam to Marie Stopes, 5 June 1921. BL Add. MS 58689.

[100] Anna Haslam to Marie Stopes, 28 Nov. 1918. CMAC.

[101] Michael Mason, *The Making of Victorian Sexuality* (Oxford: OUP, 1994), p. 265.

[102] See Chapter 3 for a discussion of *Duties of Parents*.

[103] Phyllis Rose, *Parallel Lives: Five Victorian Marriages* (London: Vintage, 1994), pp. 19–20.

[104] Sheila Jeffreys, *The Spinster and Her Enemies* (London: Pandora, 1985), p. 31.

[105] Rose, *Parallel Lives*, pp. 19–20.

[106] James H. Cousins and Margaret Cousins, *We Two Together* (Madras: Ganesh, 1950), p. 108.

[107] Leah Levenson and Jerry H. Natterstad, *Hanna Sheehy Skeffington: Irish Feminist* (Syracuse: Syracuse U. P., 1986), pp. 16, 22.

[108] Rosamund Jacob diaries, entries for 1 Nov. 1919 and 9 Nov. 1919. NLI.

[109] Rose, *Parallel Lives*, p. 45.

[110] Ibid., pp. 10–11.

[111] Angela V. John and Claire Eustance, 'Shared Histories–Differing Identities: Introducing Masculinities, Male Support and Women's Suffrage', in Angela V. John and Claire Eustance (eds.), *The Men's Share?: Masculinities, Male Support and Women's Suffrage in Britain 1890–1920* (London: Routledge, 1997), p. 7.

[112] C. H. Oldham, 'Thomas Joseph Haslam'.

[113] Westwood (ed.), *Forty-second Annual Report*, pp. 85–86.

[114] See DFHL scrapbook and *Irish Citizen*, 4 Apr. 1914, p. 366.

[115] *Hackney and Stoke Newington Record*, 3 July 1905.

[116] The influence of Spencer's epigram 'Equity knows no difference of sex. The law of equal freedom applies to the whole race – female as well as male' was referred to frequently and was printed under the title of the *Women's Advocate*, no. 1, April 1874.

[117] See especially the first issue of the *Women's Advocate*. This is discussed at length in Chapter 5.

[118] Angela V. John, 'Men, manners and militancy: Literary men and women's suffrage', in Johns and Eustance (eds.), *Men's Share?*, p. 89.

[119] Carolyn Spring, 'The Political Platform and the Language of Support for Women's Suffrage. 1890–1920', in John and Eustance (eds.), *Men's Share?*, pp. 163, 165.

[120] Ibid., p. 165.

[121] John Tosh, 'The Making of Masculinities: The Middle Class in Late Nineteenth-Century Britain', in John and Eustance (eds.), *Men's Share?*, p. 39.

[122] Spring, 'Political Platform', p. 171.

[123] John Holloway, *The Victorian Sage: Studies in Argument* (London: Macmillan, 1953), p. 1.

[124] David Newsome, *The Victorian World Picture: Perceptions and Introspections in an Age of Change* (London: Murray, 1997), p. 259.

[125] John Gross, *The Rise and Fall of the Man of Letters: Aspects of English Literary Life since 1800* (London: Weidenfeld & Nicholson, 1969), p. xiii.

[126] Gertrude Himmelfarb, *Victorian Minds* (London: Weidenfeld and Nicholson, 1968), p. 310.

[127] Newsome, *Victorian World Picture*, p. 199.

[128] Thomas Haslam to Francis Newman, 29 Apr. 1868. Hull University Library, DX/66/1.

[129] Thomas Haslam to Francis Newman, 8 Aug. 1868. Hull University Library, DX/66/1.

[130] Walter Houghton, *The Victorian Frame of Mind* (New Haven: Yale U. P., 1957), pp. 400–01.

[131] M. J. Cullen, *The Statistical Movement in Early Victorian Britain* (Hassocks: Harvester Press, 1975), pp. 135, 136, 137.

[132] Mary E. Daly, *The Spirit of Earnest Inquiry: The Statistical and Social Inquiry Society of Ireland 1847–1997* (Dublin: Statistical and Social Inquiry Society of Ireland, 1997), p. 1.

[133] Ibid., p. 2.

[134] *The Statistical and Social Inquiry Society of Ireland: List of Members of the Society* (Dublin: Webb, 1864).

[135] Daly, *Spirit of Earnest Enquiry*, pp. 74–75.

[136] SSISI list of Members.

[137] Daly, *Spirit of Earnest Enquiry*, pp. 270, 203

[138] [Thomas J. Haslam], *The Real Wants of the Irish People* (Dublin: Webb, 1865), p. 35 and *passim*.

[139] Bessie Rayner Parkes was the organizer of petitions in 1856 'representing the injustice of the law respecting the property and earnings of married women'. She was the co-founder with Barbara Leigh Smith of the feminist periodical *The Englishwomen's Journal*. See Helen Blackburn, *Women's Suffrage: A Record of the Women's Suffrage Movement in the British Isles* (London: Williams & Norgate, 1902), p. 47.

[140] Perhaps the wife of Provost Lloyd of Trinity, an early supporter of suffrage.

[141] Ann Jellicoe (1823–80), was the wife of John Jellicoe, a miller from Mountmellick. She was responsible for the setting up of a lace school in that town. She moved to Dublin and was involved in the foundation of

Alexandra College. She was a member of the Society of Friends and is buried in Rosenallis.

142 Barbara Corlett was a signatory of the John Stuart Mill petition in 1866 and was involved with all early suffrage meetings in Dublin. She was a member of the Society of Friends.

143 'Mrs. Anna Maria Haslam: The "At Home" to Celebrate her Eightieth Birthday', p. 21.

144 Blackburn, *Women's Suffrage*, p. 128; Anne V. O'Connor and Susan M. Parkes, *Gladly Learn and Gladly Teach* (Dublin: Blackwater Press, 1983), p. 7.

145 Anna compiled a list (reproduced here) of societies that she had been connected with; she marked with an 'X' those of which she had been Hon. Sec. or Treasurer:

> Soup Kitchen Youghal; Olive Leaf Youghal X; OP. Post Youghal X ? [I have not identified this association]; Anti slavery Youghal; Queen's Institute Dublin; Women's Suffrage X; Rathmines Night School; CDA X; Social Purity X; Women's Trade Union; St. John's Ambulance; Women Doctors; Rathmines Literary X; Friends Education Society; Schoolmistresses' Association; Women's Liberal Union X; Rathmines Unionist Society X; Central Unionist Committee Grafton St; Women's Patrol and *In a smaller way*: Sanitary Society; Fresh Air Society; Prevention of cruelty; Vigilance Association. Irish Housewives' Association Archive. [This list is held in the archive].

146 Anna Haslam to Marie Stopes, 20 Aug. 1918. Hull University, DX/66/2b.

147 *Irish Times*, 15 Apr. 1895.

148 'Mrs. Anna Maria Haslam – 'The "At Home" to Celebrate her Eightieth Birthday', p. 20.

149 Anna Haslam to Marie Stopes, 26 June 1920. BL Add. MS H14.

150 Ms. account of Anna Haslam's life in her own hand. Irish Housewives' Association Archive.

Chapter 2

1 Thomas Scott to Thomas Haslam, 18 Feb. 1868. Hull University Library, DX/66/1. Scott's comment on the method of birth control advocated by Thomas J. Haslam.

2 Œdipus [Thomas J. Haslam], *The Marriage Problem* (Dublin, 1868). It is perhaps anachronistic to use the term 'birth control' which was not coined until 1914 by the American activist Margaret Sanger. The word 'contraceptive' was coined earlier, in 1886. The terms used in the period under discussion were 'artificial checks', 'artificial limitations', 'preventative checks', 'Malthusian appliances', etc.

3 Ibid., p. 7.

4 Ibid., pp. 15, [2] and note on cover.

5 Ronald Pearsall, *The Worm in the Bud* (London: Pimlico, 1993), p. 214.

6 Thomas Robert Malthus, *An Essay on the Principles of Population* (London: Johnson, 1798).

7   Malthus, *Essay* (1817 edn), vol. iii, p. 393.

8   Malthus, *Essay* (1803 edn), p. 531.

9   Angus McLaren, *Birth Control in Nineteenth-Century England: A Social and Intellectual History* (London: Croom Helm, 1978), p. 65.

10 James Mill, *Supplement to the Encyclopaedia Britannica* (Edinburgh, 1824), III, p. 261.

11 Norman Himes, *Medical History of Contraception* (Baltimore: William & Wilkins, 1936), pp. 212–13.

12 Michael Mason, *The Making of Victorian Sexual Attitudes* (Oxford: U. P., 1994), p. 179.

13 Himes, *Medical History*, p. 213.

14 Facsimile of handbill. Francis Place, *To the Married of Both Sexes of the Working People*. Reproduced in Himes, *Medical History*, p. 214.

15 Haslam, *Marriage Problem*, p. 6.

16 Richard Carlisle, *Everywoman's Book: or What is Love? Containing Important Instructions For the Prudent Regulation of The Principal of Love and The Number of a Family* (London: A. Carlisle, 1838), pp. iv.

17 For example Thomas said of the 'knowledge' contained in his pamphlet: 'Nothing surely can be more simple, natural or important to mankind.' Haslam, *Marriage Problem*, p. 9.

18 Carlisle, *Everywoman's Book*, pp. 31, 8.

19 Ibid., pp. 39–40.

20 Robert Dale Owen, *Moral Physiology, or, A Brief and Plain Treatise on the Population Question*, 3rd edn (London, 1831).

21 Ibid., pp. 66–7.

22 Ibid., p. 61.

23 Ibid., pp. 8, 13.

24 Ibid., p. 68.

25 Ibid., p. 15.

26 Mason, *Victorian Sexual Attitudes*, p. 185.

27 Himes, *Medical History*, p. 224.

28 Warren Sylvester Smith, *The London Heretics 1870–1914* (London: Constable, 1967), p. 46.

29 Charles Knowlton, *Fruits of Philosophy, or, The Private Companion of Young Married People*, 3rd edn (London: Watson, 1841), pp. 33, 34.

30 A Doctor of Medicine [George Drysdale], *The Elements of Social Science or, Physical, Sexual and Natural Religion: An Exposition of the True Cause and Only Cure of the Three Primary Social Evils Poverty, Prostitution and Celibacy*. 11th edn (London: Truelove, 1873), p. 346.

31 Ibid., p. 350.

32 Ibid., p. 338.

33 Ibid., p. 349.

34 Dale Owen, *Moral Physiology*, p. 60.

35 R. T. Trall, *Sexual Physiology: A Scientific and Popular Exposition on the Fundamental Problems in Sociology* (London: J. Burns, 1866). The British Library copy bears Mrs Haslam's name and address. In a letter to Marie Stopes, undated but probably sent in April/May 1921, Anna Haslam

wrote, with reference to *Sexual Physiology*, that she had just 'looked over the passages my darling had marked when he got it in 1866'. Stopes Collection. CMAC, Wellcome Institute for the History of Medicine.

36 M. C. Stopes, *Contraception (Birth Control): Its Theory, History and Practice* (London: Bale, 1923), p. 289.

37 Trall, *Sexual Physiology*, pp. 206–7.

38 Charles J. McFadden, *Medical Ethics* (London: Burn & Oates, 1962), p. 94.

39 Knowlton, *Fruits of Philosophy*, p. 16.

40 McFadden, *Medical Ethics*, pp. 96–8.

41 Trall, *Sexual Physiology*, p. 206.

42 Ibid.

43 Ibid.

44 Himes, *Medical History*, p. 268.

45 Stopes, *Contraception*, p. 289.

46 Trall, *Sexual Physiology*, p. 213.

47 J. Burns to Thomas Haslam, 28 March 1868. Hull University Library, DX/66/1. Burns was the English publisher of Trall's *Sexual Physiology*, which was also published in New York in 1866 by Miller, Wood & Co.

48 Mason, *Victorian Sexual Attitudes*, p. 186.

49 See J. Burns's letter of 28 March 1868, and also letter from J. E. George to Thomas Haslam 6 Aug. 1868. Both Hull University Library, DX/66/1.

50 Haslam, *Marriage Problem*, pp. [3]- 4.

51 Ibid., p. 5.

52 Ibid., p. 6.

53 Trall, *Sexual Physiology*, pp. 212–3.

54 Haslam, *Marriage Problem*, pp. 6–7.

55 Ibid., p. 8–9.

56 Ibid., p. 10–11.

57 Ibid., p. 14–15.

58 Ibid., p. 8.

59 Trall, *Sexual Physiology*, p. 206.

60 J. S. Mill, *Principles of Political Economy* (Toronto: Robson, 1965), p. 372 (1st edn 1848).

61 Trall, *Sexual Physiology*, p. 201.

62 Ibid.

63 Ibid., pp. 201, 204.

64 Haslam, *Marriage Problem*, pp. 11–12.

65 See Margaret Jackson, *The Real Facts of Life: Feminism and the Politics of Sexuality c1850–1940* (London: Taylor & Francis, 1994), pp. 87–8.

66 Lucy Bland, *Banishing the Beast: English Feminism & Sexual Morality 1885–1914* (London: Penguin, 1995), p. 19. The Men and Women's Club was founded by Karl Pearson, later a leading eugenicist, in 1885. The aim of the club was the exchange of ideas between men and women with a consequent breaking down of barriers. Many of the members were committed feminists.

67 Haslam, *Marriage Problem*, p. 12.

68 Bland, *Banishing the Beast*, p. 19.

69 Haslam, *Marriage Problem*, p. 14.

70 Ibid., p. 10.

71 Thomas Haslam to Francis Newman, 29 Apr. 1868. Hull University Library, DX/66/1.

72 Carlisle, *Everywoman's Book*. Cited in McLaren, *Birth Control*, p. 84.

73 John Peel, 'Contraception and the Medical Profession', *Population Studies*, vol. XVIII, no. 2, 1984, p. 134.

74 Michel Foucault, *The History of Sexuality: an Introduction* (London: Penguin, 1994), p. 53.

75 *Lancet*, 2 Nov. 1823. Cited in Peel, *Contraception*, p. 134.

76 *Lancet*, 7 Aug. 1869. Cited in Peel, *Contraception*, p. 215.

77 Ibid.

78 Anna Haslam to Marie Stopes, 20 Aug. 1918. Hull University Library, DX/66/2.

79 Place and Knowlton were especially concerned that women were in control of contraceptive methods.

80 Bland, *Banishing the Beast*, p. 190.

81 Ibid., p. 204.

82 Haslam, *Marriage Problem*, p. 10.

83 The term 'eugenics movement' was first used in 1911 by James A. Field in 'The Progress of Eugenics', *Quarterly Journal of Economics*, no. 26, 1911, p. 3.

84 Pauline M. H. Mazumdar, *Eugenics, Human Genetics and Human Failings: The Eugenics Society, its Sources and its Critics in Britain* (London: Routledge, 1992), p. 2.

85 L. A. Farrall, *The Origin and Growth of the English Eugenics Movement 1865–1925* (New York: Garland, 1985), p. 27.

86 Mazumdar, *Eugenics*, p. 3.

87 Thomas Haslam to Francis Newman, 29 Apr. 1868. Hull University Library, DX/66/1.

88 W. R. Greg, 'On the Failure of Natural Selection in the Case of Man', *Fraser's Magazine*, Sept. 1868. Cited in Farrall, *Origin*, p. 15.

89 Cited in Farrall, *Origin*, p. 15.

90 Gretta Jones, 'Eugenics in Ireland: the Belfast Eugenics Society, 1911–15', *Irish Historical Studies*, xxviii, no. 109, May 1992, pp. 81–95. A meeting was held in Dublin in 1911 with the intention of starting a Eugenics Society. It did not appear to result in the formation of a society, but among those present was Lady Dockrell, a colleague of Anna Haslam's in the suffrage campaign.

91 James Haughton, Some Facts which suggest the idea that the Desire for Alcoholic Stimulants is . . . transmitted by Hereditary Descent . . . and thus strongly tends to deteriorate the Human Race in Mary Daly, *The Spirit of Earnest Inquiry: The Statistical and Social Inquiry Society of Ireland 1847–1997* (Dublin: Statistical Social Inquiry Society of Ireland, 1997), p. 228. Thomas Haslam was, of course, a member of the SSISI.

92 J. A. Banks, *Victorian Values: Secularism and the Size of Families* (London: Routledge and Kegan Paul, 1981), p. 20.

93 Ibid.

94 John Stuart Mill to Thomas Haslam, 19 Feb. 1868. Hull University Library, DX/66/1.

95 Norman E. Himes, 'John Stuart Mill's Attitude to Neo-Malthusianism', *The Economic Journal (Supplement)*, no. 4, Jan. 1929, pp. 481, 482.

96 Francis W. Newman (1805–97). A fellow of Balliol College, he resigned his fellowship in 1830, as he was unable to subscribe to the Thirty-Nine Articles. He was appointed to the Chair of Latin in University College London in 1846.

97 Brian Harrison, *Drink and the Victorians* (London: Faber and Faber, 1971), p. 186.

98 'F. W. Newman on the Population Question', *Barker's Review* 1 (1861), pp. 3–6; 'Marriage Laws', *Frasers Magazine*, 76 (1867), pp 167–89; 'Malthusianism, True and False', *Frasers Magazine*, 3 (1871), pp. 584–98.

99 Marie Stopes, *The Early Days of Birth Control* (London, 1922), p. 14. Michael Mason has written that Stopes 'owned a letter from Newman in which he admitted to an Irish birth control propagandist that his previous "simple revulsion of disgust" against contraception was not appropriate'. Obviously Mason had not seen the original correspondence, as he regretted that 'the date of this letter is not apparent'. Mason, *Making of Victorian Sexual Attitudes*, p. 174.

100 F. W. Newman to Thomas Haslam, 26 Apr. 1868. Hull University Library, DX/66/1, p. 2.

101 Ibid., pp. 2, 3.

102 Ibid., pp. 4, 5.

103 J. G. Sieveking, *Memoir and Letters of F. W. Newman* (London: Kegan Paul, Trench, Trubner & Co., 1909), p. 139.

104 F. W. Newman to Thomas Haslam, 26 Apr. 1868. Hull University Library, DX/66/1, pp. 5, 6.

105 Ibid., pp. 9, 10.

106 Ibid., pp. 11, 12.

107 Thomas Haslam to F. W. Newman, 29 Apr. 1868. MS 'Copy of reply', Hull University Library, DX/66/1, p. 1.

108 F. W. Newman, *Alliance News*, 31 May 1884, p. 342.

109 Thomas Haslam to F. W. Newman, 26 April 1868. Hull University Library, DX/66/1, p. 2.

110 Trall, *Sexual Physiology*, p. 244.

111 Thomas Haslam to F. W. Newman, 29 Apr. 1868. Hull University Library, DX/66/1, p. 3.

112 Ibid.

113 F. W. Newman to Thomas Haslam, 26 April 1868. Hull University Library, DX/66/1, p. 8.

114 Thomas Haslam to F. W. Newman, 29 Apr. 1868. Hull University Library, DX/66/1, p. 3.

115 Trall, *Sexual Physiology*, p. 244.

116 Thomas Haslam to F. W. Newman, 29 Apr. 1868. Hull University Library, DX/66/1, p. 3.

117 Ibid., pp. 3, 4.

[118] Ibid., p. 4.

[119] Ibid., p. 8.

[120] Ibid.

[121] Ibid., pp. 4, 5, 6.

[122] Thomas Haslam to F. W. Newman, 8 May 1868. Hull University Library, DX/66/1.

[123] F. W. Newman to Thomas Haslam, 14 May 1868. Hull University Library, DX/66/1.

[124] A Member of the Statistical and Social Inquiry Society of Ireland [Thomas Haslam], *The Real Wants of the Irish People* (Dublin: Webb, 1865), pp. 38–9.

[125] See Mountmellick Monthly Meeting, 19th day of the 2nd month, 1851. DFHL.

[126] Thomas Haslam to F. W. Newman, 29 Apr. 1868. MS copy in Thomas Haslam's hand, Hull University Library, DX/66/1, pp. 1, 2,

[127] Anna Haslam in her letters to Marie Stopes continually mentions the necessity of educating the poor in birth control methods. In a letter dated 20 March 1921 she wrote to Stopes: 'The middle and upper classes know what to do more or less – but the poor! Oh dear their clergy preach *plenty of children* the *more* the *better*!!!' BL Add. MS 58688, f. 97.

[128] Richard A. Soloway, *Birth Control and the Population Question in England. 1877–1930* (Chapel Hill: University of North Carolina Press, 1982), p. xvii.

[129] Haslam, *Marriage Problem*, p. 12.

[130] Ibid., p. 13.

[131] Thomas Scott (1808–78), was a 'freethought publisher' who began a series of pamphlets in 1868 under the banner of 'Free Inquiry and Free Expression'. There were eventually more than sixty of the Thomas Scott pamphlets, written by Charles Voysey, F. W. Newman, Jeremy Bentham, E. Van-Sittart Neale, John Robertson et al. See Warren Sylvester Smith, *The London Heretics 1870–1914* (London: Constable, 1967).

[132] T. Scott to Thomas Haslam, 18 Feb. 1868. Hull University Library, DX/66/1.

[133] Anna Haslam to M. Stopes, undated. Hull University Library, DX/66/2c.

[134] Letter to author from Dr Huw Walters, National Library of Wales, 11 Sept. 1996, in response to a request for information on George.

[135] A. S. Evans, *Hanes Eglwys Ramoth, Hirwaun* (Blaeanu Ffestinog, 1912), pp. 86–7.

[136] J. E. George to Thomas Haslam, 6 Aug. 1868. Hull University Library, DX/66/1.

[137] J. E. George to Thomas Haslam, 14 Aug. 1868. Hull University Library, DX/66/1.

[138] Letter to author from Dr Huw Walters, National Library of Wales, 11 Sept. 1996. Dr Walters was unable to trace a Welsh translation of Haslam's pamphlet. George's 'short summary' of Haslam's pamphlet would have been of a flimsy and ephemeral nature, material unlikely to have survived. Of course, it may never have been printed.

139 J. Burns to Thomas Haslam, 28 Mar. 1868. Hull University Library, DX/66/1.

140 Haslam, *Marriage Problem*, p. 15.

141 Thomas Haslam to F. W. Newman, 29 Apr. 1868. Hull University Library, DX/66/1, p. 3.

142 Anna Haslam to M. Stopes, 12 Aug. 1918. Hull University Library, DX/66/2a.

143 Anna Haslam to M. Stopes, 20 Aug. 1918. Hull University Library, DX/66/2b.

144 Josephine Butler was the charismatic leader of the campaign against the Contagious Diseases Acts (CDA). See Chapter 4.

145 Anna Haslam to M. Stopes, 20 Aug. 1918. Hull University Library, DX/66/2b.

146 Anna Haslam to M. Stopes, 16 Oct. 1918. CMAC: PP/MCS/A121 [All CMAC items bear the same ref.]

147 This was a small rubber cervical cap 'made on a fine rubber ring which is accurately fixed round the dome-like end of the womb and adhering by suction, remains securely in place, whatever movement the woman makes'. See M. Stopes, *Wise Parenthood* (London: Fifield, 1919), p. 7.

148 Anna Haslam to M. Stopes, 28 Nov. 1918. CMAC.

149 Anna Haslam to M. Stopes, 1 Nov. 1919. BL Add. MS 58685. H 126.

150 Anna Haslam to M. Stopes, 20 Mar. 1921. BL Add. MS 58688 F 97.

151 Ibid.

152 Anna Haslam to M. Stopes, 5 June 1921. BL Add. MS 58689. H122.

153 Soloway, *Birth Control*, p. xvii.

154 Stopes, *Contraception*, pp. 290–3.

155 Ibid., pp. 289–90.

156 Anna Haslam to M. Stopes, 20 Aug. 1918. Hull University Library, DX/66/2b.

157 M. Stopes to Anna Haslam, 30 Apr. 1921. CMAC.

158 Anna Haslam to M. Stopes, 3 May 1921. BL Add. MS. 58689. H6.

159 This pamphlet, although listed on the British Library catalogue, could not be found. The copy listed was part of the Stopes collection and was obviously the one given by Anna Haslam to Stopes.

160 M. Stopes to Anna Haslam, 7 May 1921. CMAC.

161 Anna Haslam to M. Stopes, 13 May 1921. CMAC.

162 Anna Haslam to M. Stopes, BL Add. MS 58689. H122.

163 Leonard Webb to M. Stopes, 12 Dec. 1922. CMAC.

164 M. Stopes to Webb & Webb, 14 Dec. 1922. CMAC.

165 Leonard Webb to M. Stopes, 2 Jan. 1923. CMAC.

166 M. Stopes's secretary to Webb & Webb, 4 Jan. 1923. CMAC.

167 Anna Haslam to M. Stopes, 26 June 1920. BL. Add MS 58687. H14.

168 Anna Haslam to M. Stopes, 13 May 1921. CMAC.

169 Anna Haslam to M. Stopes, undated [May 1921]. Hull University Library, DX/66/2c.

170 M. Stopes to Anna Haslam, 22 Mar. 1921. CMAC.

171 M. Stopes to Anna Haslam, 19 Apr. 1921. CMAC.

[172] George Morant, *Hints to Husbands: A Revelation of Man-Midwife's Mysteries*, 3rd edn (London: Simpkin Marshall, 1857), p. 7.

[173] Ibid., pp. 18, 44–5.

[174] See Stopes, *Contraception*, p. 300; Michael Mason, *The Making of Victorian Sexuality* (Oxford: OUP, 1994), p. 174.

[175] The copy of *The Marriage Problem* in the Hull University Library bears the inscription 'M. C. Stopes From Mrs. Haslam'. For evidence of Himes not having read the pamphlet see p. 52.

[176] F. H. Amphlett Micklewright. 'The Rise and Decline of English Neo-Malthusianism', *Population Studies*, vol. XV, no. 1. July 1961, p. 37.

[177] Maria Luddy, *Women in Ireland 1800–1918: A Documentary History* (Cork University Press, 1995), pp. 32–4.

[178] Himes, *Medical History*, p. 230.

[179] Banks, *Victorian Values*, p. 20.

[180] Himes, 'John Stuart Mill's Attitude to Neo-Malthusianism', p. 464.

Chapter 3

[1] John Holloway, *The Victorian Sage: Studies in Argument* (London: Macmillan, 1953), p. 1.

[2] David Newsome, *The Victorian World Picture: Perceptions and Introspections in an Age of Change* (London: Murray, 1997), p. 259.

[3] Stefan Collini, *Public Moralists: Political Thought and Intellectual Life in Britain 1850–1930* (Oxford: Clarendon, 1991), p. 98.

[4] Lucy Bland, *Banishing the Beast: English Feminism and Sexual Morality 1885–1914* (London: Penguin, 1995), p. 80.

[5] J. D. Y. Peel, *Herbert Spencer: The Evolution of a Socialist* (Aldershot: Gregg Revivals. 1992) p. 188.

[6] Ibid., p. 142.

[7] Collini, *Public Moralists*, p. 94.

[8] Maudsky. Cited in ibid., p. 99.

[9] Haslam, *Duties of Parents*, p. 4.

[10] Ibid., pp. 4, 11–12.

[11] Ibid., pp. 12–13.

[12] Ibid., p. 13.

[13] Herbert Spencer, *The Study of Sociology* (London: Kegan Paul, Trench, Trubner, 1873), pp. 343–4.

[14] Haslam, *Duties of Parents*, pp. 13–14.

[15] 'H.' 'Darwinism and National Life'. *Nature*, 16 Dec. 1869, p. 183.

[16] R. A. Soloway, *Demography and Degeneration: Eugenics and the Declining Birthrate in Twentieth-Century Britain* (Chapel Hill: University of North Carolina, 1990), vii.

[17] Haslam, *Duties of Parents*, p. 17.

[18] F. W. Newman to T. J. Haslam, 15 Nov. 1872. Hull University Library, DX/66/1, p. 4.

[19] The phrase 'eugenics movement' was first used in 1911 by James A. Field in 'The Progress of Economics', *Quarterly Journal of Economics* (26) 1911, p.

3. The word eugenic 'pertaining to the production of fine offspring' was first used in 1883 (OED).

[20] Angus McLaren, *Birth Control in Nineteenth-Century England: A Social Intellectual History* (London: Croom Helm, 1978), p. 144 .

[21] Lindsay Andrew Farrall, 'The Origins and Growth of the English Eugenics Movement' (Ph. D. dissertation Indiana University, 1969). Photocopy (Ann Arbor, Mich.: University Microfilms International, 1991, p. 27.

[22] McLaren. *Birth Control* , p. 144.

[23] Ibid., p. 148–9.

[24] See, for example, Dr. John B. Haycroft, *Darwinism and Race Progress* (1895); Victoria C. W. Martin, *The Rapid Multiplication of the Unfit* (1891); Henry Smith, *A Plea for the Unborn* (1897).

[25] Haslam, *Duties of Parents*, p. 3.

[26] Haslam, *Duties of Parents*, p. 66.

[27] S. F. Finer, *The Life and Times of Sir Edwin Chadwick* (London: Methuen, 1952), p. 218.

[28] Haslam. *Duties of Parents*, p. 72.

[29] F. A. Aalen. 'The Rehousing of Rural Labourers in Ireland under the Labourers (Ireland) Acts 1893–1919', *Journal of Historical Geography*, vol. 12, no. 3, 1986, pp. 287–306.

[30] Haslam, *Duties of Parenst*, p. 73.

[31] Ibid.

[32] Ibid., p. 73–4.

[33] Ibid., p. 132.

[34] Ibid.

[35] Lesley A. Hall, 'The Archives of Birth Control in Britain', *Journal of the Society of Archivists*, vol. 16, no. 2, 1995, pp. 207–8. The Stopes *Married Love* correspondence is held at the Contemporary Medical Archives Centre (CMAC), Wellcome Institute for the History of Medicine, Euston Road, London. It is a rich collection which gives the researcher valuable insight into attitudes to sexuality and birth control in the early twentieth century.

[36] Haslam, *Duties of Parents*, pp. 20, 21.

[37] Michael Mason, *The Making of Victorian Sexuality* (Oxford: OUP, 1994), p. 44.

[38] Haslam, *Duties of Parenta*, p. 22.

[39] Mason, *Making of Victorian Sexuality*, p. 179.

[40] Walter, *My Secret Life*, North Hollywood, Calif.: Brandon House, 1967. v. 1 Book 1, p. 61.

[41] Lesley Hall, 'Forbidden by God, Despised by Man: Masturbation, Medical Warnings, Moral Panic, and Manhood in Great Britain, 1850–1950', in John C. Fout (ed.), *Forbidden History: The State, Society and the Regulation of Sexuality in Modern Europe* (Chicago: University of Chicago Press, 1992), p. 297.

[42] Haslam, *Duties of Parents*, p. 29.

[43] Hall, 'Forbidden by God', p. 295.

[44] Haslam, *Duties of Parents*, pp. 22, 23.

45 Ibid., pp. 23, 24.

46 Ibid., p. 26.

47 Ibid., p. 28.

48 William Acton, *The Functions and Disorders of the Reproductive Organs*, 1st edn (London: 1857). The book was exclusively about male sexuality and combined ideas of medical physiology with moral advice advocating sexual continence and restraint.

49 E. P. Miller, *Vital Force* (New York: Miller & Haynes, 1869). This book was on the list sent by AH to Marie Stopes and was judged by Thomas to be 'an excellent book to place in the hands of young men'.

50 Haslam, *Duties of Parents*, pp. 29, 31, 37.

51 Ibid., pp. 29, 31.

52 Acton, *Functions and Disorders*, pp. 130–1.

53 Ibid.

54 See F. B. Smith. 'Sexuality in Britain, 1800–1900: Some Suggested Revisions', in Martha Vicinus (ed.), *A Widening Sphere: Changing Role of Victorian Women* (London: Methuen, 1980), pp. 182–98; and M. Jeanne Peterson, 'Dr. Acton's Enemy: Medicine, Sex and Society in Victorian England', *Victorian Studies* 29 (1986) pp. 569–90.

55 Hall, 'Forbidden History', pp. 294–5.

56 Bland, *Banishing the Beast*, p. 56.

57 Miller, *Vital Force*. Cited in Haslam, *Duties*, p. 38.

58 Trall, *Sexual Physiology*, p. 245.

59 T. J, Haslam to F. W. Newman, 8 Aug. 1868. Hull University Library, DX/66/1.

60 Haslam, *Duties of Parents*, pp. 36, 37.

61 Ibid., p. 30.

62 Ibid.

63 Ibid.

64 Miller, *Vital Force*. Cited in Haslam, *Duties of Parents*, p. 33.

65 Fleetwood Churchill, *On the Diseases of Women*, 5th edn (Dublin: Fannin, 1864).

66 Haslam, *Duties of Parents*, pp. 34–5.

67 Ibid., p. 33.

68 Miller, *Vital Force*. Cited in Haslam, *Duties of Parents*, p. 33.

69 Haslam, *Duties of Parents*, p. 39.

70 Bland, *Banishing the Beast*, p. 241.

71 Haslam, *Duties of Parents*, pp. 39–40.

72 Margaret Jackson, *The Real Facts of Life: Feminism and the Politics of Sexuality c1850–1940* (London: Taylor & Francis, 1994), p. 142.

73 Bland, *Banishing the Beast*, p. 82.

74 See Bland, *Banishing the Beast*, pp. 79–82; Jackson, *Real Facts*, pp. 6–7; J. A. and Olive Banks. *Feminism and Family Planning in Victorian England* (New York: Schoken, 1964), pp. 107–13.

75 Trall, *Sexual Physiology*, p. 230.

76 James H. and Margaret Cousins, *We Two Together* (Madras: Ganesh, 1950), pp. 108–9.

[77] Herbert Spencer, *The Principles of Sociology*, III, p. 640. Cited in Peel. *Herbert Spencer*, p. 203.

[78] Acton, *Functions and Disorders*. Cited in Haslam, *Duties*, p. 52.

[79] Haslam, *Duties of Parents*, p. 52.

[80] Ibid., p. 45–6.

[81] A. Haslam to M. Stopes, 20 Aug. 1918. Hull University Library, DX/66/2b.

[82] Haslam, *Duties of Parents*, p. 43.

[83] Elizabeth Wolstenholme, suffragist, campaigner against the CDA and for the Married Women's Property Act, also lobbied for the legal recognition of marital rape and for higher education for women. She married Ben Elmy, sometime chairman of National Secular Society, only when 'visibly pregnant' in 1875 and on the insistence of her suffragist colleagues who were worried that her behaviour might damage the cause of women's rights.

[84] It is not clear whether the pseudonym referred to Elizabeth W. Elmy alone or to the joint authorship of husband and wife. Bland ascribes the use to Ben Elmy alone, while Jackson and Sheila Jeffreys (*The Spinster and her Enemies*) state that Elizabeth's pseudonym was Ellis Ethelmer. To Susan Kingsley Kent (*Sex and Suffrage*) the pseudonym represents joint authorship of husband and wife. Sandra Stanley Holton ('Free Love and Victorian Feminism: The Divers Matrimonials of Elizabeth Wolstenholme and Ben Elmy') also thinks that there is good reason to believe that it signified a collaborative effort. I have used the pronoun 'she' in referring to Ellis Ethelmer.

[85] Ellis Ethelmer, *Phases of Love* (Congleton: Women's Emancipation Union, 1897), p. 9.

[86] Ellis Ethelmer, *Women Free* (Congleton, Woman's Emancipation Union, 1893), p. 20.

[87] Ellis Ethelmer. *Phases of Love*, p. 5.

[88] E. C. Wolstenholme to A. and T. J. Haslam. 28 Jan. 1873. Hull University Library. DX/66/1.

[89] Margaret Jackson, *Real Facts of Life*, p. 82.

[90] Frances Swiney, *Women and Natural Law*, 2nd edn (London: League of Isis, 1912) p. 46.

[91] Elizabeth Blackwell, *Pioneer Work on Opening the Medical Profession to Women* (London: Longmans, Green, 1895), pp. 4, 28–30.

[92] William Acton, *The Function and Disorder of the Reproductive Organs* (London: John Churchill, 1875), p. 215.

[93] Ibid. 3rd edn (1862), p. 106.

[94] Ibid. 5th edn (1871), p. 196.

[95] Haslam, *Duties of Parents*, pp. 48–9.

[96] Pat Jalland, *Women, Marriage and Politics 1860–1914* (Oxford: Clarendon, 1986), p. 85.

[97] See E. B. Duffey, *What Women Should Know* (Philadelphia, 1873), pp. 87–9.

[98] Steven Marcus, *The Other Victorians: A Study of Sexuality and Pornography in Mid-Nineteenth Century England* (London: Weidenfeld & Nicolson,

1956); Peter Gay, *The Bourgeois Experience, Victoria to Freud*, vol. 1: *Education of the Senses* (Oxford: OUP, 1984); Michel Foucault, *The History of Sexuality* (London: Penguin, 1981).

99 Roy Porter and Lesley Hall, *The Facts of Life: The Creation of Sexual Knowledge in Britain 1850–1950* (New Haven: Yale U. P., 1995), p. 142.

100 Phyllis Rose, *Parallel Lives: Five Victorian Marriages* (London: Vintage, 1994), pp. 20–21.

101 Jalland, *Women, Marriage and Politics*, p. 171.

102 J. S. Mill, *Principles of Political Economy with some of their applications to social philosophy* (1848), p. 372.

103 Haslam, *Duties of Parents*, p. 135.

104 Rose, *Parallel Lives*, p. 111.

105 Jack Stilleinger (ed.), *The Early Draft of John Stuart Mill's Autobiography* (Urbana: University of Illinois Press, 1961), p. 171.

106 Simon Szreter, *Fertility, Class and Gender in Britain, 1860–1940* (Cambridge: Cambridge University Library, 1996), pp. 456–7.

107 Bland, *Banishing the Beast*, p. 19.

108 Josephine Butler, *Social Purity: An Address Given at Cambridge, 1879*, p. 5.

109 Josephine Butler, 'Introduction', in J. Butler (ed.), *Women's Work and Women's Culture* (London: Macmillan, 1869), p. xxxvii.

110 Thomas Haslam, *A Few Words on Prostitution and the Contagious Diseases Acts* (Dublin: Webb, 1870), p. 3.

111 Anna Haslam to Marie Stopes. 12 Aug. 1918. Hull University Library DX/66/2.

112 Haslam, *Duties of Parents*, p. 39.

113 Ibid., p. 132.

114 Ibid., p. 54.

115 Ibid., p. 98.

116 Ibid., p. 106.

117 Ibid., p. 108.

118 *One Hundred Years of Mountmellick School* (Dublin: Webb, 1836), p. 31.

119 Ibid, pp. 95, 89–90.

120 *36th Annual Report of Ackworth Old Scholars' Association*, p. 61.

121 Haslam, *Duties of Parents*, p. 109.

122 E. C. Wolstenholme to A. and T. J. Haslam, 28 Jan. 1873. Hull University Library, DX/66/1.

123 Maria I. W. Tod to T. J. Haslam, 1 November 1872. Hull University Library, DX/66/1.

124 J. Evans to James Tod, Feb. 1875 (copy in TJH's hand). Hull University Library, DX/66/1.

125 Isabella Tod to A. Haslam, 18 May 1875. Hull University Library, DX/66/1.

126 Anna Varian to A. Haslam, 29 Oct (no year) Hull University Library, DX/66/1.

127 Francis W. Newman to T. J. Haslam. 10 Nov. 1872. Hull University Library, DX/66/1.

128 Ibid., 15 Nov. 1872.

129 Bland, *Banishing the Beast*, pp. 83–4.
130 Ibid., p. 00.
131 Porter & Hall, *Facts of Life*, p. 127–8.

Chapter 4
1 *LNA Annual Report*, 1870, p. 12.
2 Thomas Haslam, *A Few Words on Prostitution and The Contagious Diseases Acts* (Dublin: Webb, 1870).
3 Thomas is listed as a 'Provincial Member' in the 'Vice-Presidents, General Executive and Finance Committees, and Officers Section' of the NARCDA membership list. *Annual Report*, 1881.
4 'Pioneers of Feminism in Ireland', *The Irish Citizen*, 21 March 1914, p. 347.
5 Paul McHugh, *Prostitution and Victorian Social Reform* (London: Croom Helm, 1980), p. 165.
6 Michel Foucault, *The History of Sexuality: An Introduction* (London: Penguin, 1984), p. 33.
7 Ibid.
8 Lynda Nead, *Myths of Sexuality* (Oxford: Blackwell, 1988), p. 97.
9 W. R. Greg, 'Prostitution', *The Westminster Review*, 53, 1850, pp. 456–7.
10 Nead, *Myths of Sexuality*, p. 6.
11 'The Influence of Women', *The Magdalene's Friend*, vol. 5 (1864), p. 174.
12 See W. E. H. Lecky, *History of European Morals from Augustus to Charlemagne* (London, 1897), vol. 2, p. 283. William Acton wrote: 'Some consider that prostitution is the safety valve of society', in *Prostitution Considered in its Moral, Social and Sanitary Aspects in London and other Large Cities and Towns*, 2nd edn (London: Cass, 1972). Facsimile of edn, London: Churchill, 1870, p. 166.
13 Anne Humphreys, 'Biographical Note', in facsimile edn of William Acton, *Prostitution Considered*, p. v.
14 Acton, *Prostitution Considered*, pp. [v], vi.
15 Act for the Prevention of Contagious Diseases at Certain Naval and Military Stations, 27 & 28 Vict. c. 85; Act for the Better Prevention of Contagious Diseases . . . 29 & 30 Vict. c. 96; Act to Amend the CDA, 1866, 32 & 33 Vict. c. 86.
16 The Acts of 1866 and 1869, together with a minor amendment of 1868, were known collectively as the CDAs 1866–1869.
17 Roy Porter and Lesley Hall, *The Facts of Life: The Creation of Sexual Knowledge in Britain 1650–1950* (New Haven: Yale University Press, 1995), p. 138.
18 Philippa Levine, *Feminist Lives in Victorian England* (Oxford: Blackwell, 1990), p. 84.
19 Paul McHugh, *Prostitution and Victorian Social Reform*, p. 18.
20 Brian Harrison, 'Underneath the Victorians', *Victorian Studies*, Mar. 1967, p. 257.
21 Haslam, *Few Words on Prostitution*, p. 7.
22 Harrison, 'Underneath the Victorians', p. 257.

23 Haslam, *Few Words on Prostitution*, pp. 7–8.
24 *Report from the Select Committee on the Contagious Diseases Act 1866; together with the proceedings of the Committee, P. P.,.* 1868–9 (306) VII. Appendix, no. 4, p. 88.
25 Acton, *Prostitution Considered*, pp. 58, 64–5.
26 Ibid., p. 166.
27 Ibid., p. 162.
28 Haslam, *Few Words on Prostitution*, pp. [1]-2.
29 Lecky, *History of European Morals*, p. 283.
30 Acton, *Prostitution Considered*, p. 166.
31 Haslam, *Few Words on Prostitution*, pp. 3, 4.
32 Acton, *Prostitution Considered*, p. 163.
33 William Acton, *The Functions and Disorders of the Reproductive Organs in Childhood, Youth, Adult Age, and in Advanced Life Considered in their Physiological Social and Moral Relations*, 4th edn (London: Churchill, 1865), p. 112. In later editions this became 'happily for society'.
34 W. R. Greg, 'Prostitution', in *Westminster Review*, 53, 1850, pp. 456–7.
35 R. J. Culverwell, *On Single and Married Life: or the Institution of Marriage, its Intent, Obligations, and Physical and Constitutional Disqualifications* (New York: Kline, 1882), p. 47.
36 See Carol Z. Stearns and Peter N. Stearns, 'Victorian Sexuality: Can Historians do it Better?', *Journal of Social History*, Summer 1985, pp. 625–34; Carl N. Degler, 'What Ought to Be and What was: Women's Sexuality in the Nineteenth Century', *American Historical Review*, 79, no. 5 (1974), pp. 1468–91: Peter Gay, *The Bourgeois Experience – Victoria to Freud*, vol. 1, *Education of the Senses* (Oxford: Oxford University Press, 1984).
37 Acton, *Function and Disorders of the Reproductive Organs*, p. 114.
38 Haslam, *Marriage Problem*, p. 12.
39 *Report of Special Assistant Poor Law Commissioners on the Employment of Women and Children in Agriculture* (1843), p. 201. Cited in Keith Thomas, 'Double Standard', *Journal of the History of Ideas*, 20, 1959, p. 206: See also *Lancet*, 10 April 1969, p. 500.
40 Haslam, *Few Words on Prostitution*, pp. 3, 4.
41 Ibid., pp. 4–5.
42 Ibid., p. 5.
43 W. R Greg 'Prostitution', *Westminster Review*, vol. 53, 1850, p. 471.
44 Keith Nield, 'Introduction' *Prostitution in the Victorian Age* (Farnborough: Gregg, 1973), [p. 14].
45 Greg, 'Prostitution', p. 471.
46 Haslam, *Few Words on Prostitution*, p. 3.
47 Judith R. Walkowitz, *Prostitution and Victorian Society: Women, Class and the State* (Cambridge University Press, 1980), pp. 18–19.
48 Ibid., pp. 194, 196.
49 Acton, *Prostitution Considered*, pp. 39–40.
50 Greg, 'Prostitution', p. 458.
51 Haslam, *Few Words on Prostitution*, p. 2.

52 Yves Guyot's account of Butler's address to the Municipal Court of Paris. Cited in Nancy Boyd, *Josephine Butler, Octavia Hill, Florence Nightingale: Three Victorian Women who Changed the World* (London: Macmillan, 1982), p. 49.

53 McHugh, *Prostitution and Victorian Social Reform*, p. 22.

54 Frank Skeehy Skeffington, 'Pioneers of Feminism in Ireland', *Irish Citizen*, 21 March 1914, p. 347.

55 Kathleen Barry, *The Prostitution of Sexuality* (New York: New York University Press, 1995), p. 93.

56 Boyd, *Josephine Butler*, pp. 38–9.

57 Keith Thomas, 'The Double Standard', *Journal of the History of Ideas*, 20, 1959, p. 199.

58 Philippa Levine, 'Women and Prostitution: Metaphor, Reality, History', *Canadian Journal of History*, XXVIII, Dec. 1993, p. 486.

59 *Daily News*, 31 Jan. 1869, reproduced in Patricia Hollis, *Women in Public 1860–1900: Documents of the Victorian Women's Movements* (London: Allen & Unwin, 1979), pp. 208–9.

60 F. B. Smith, 'The Contagious Diseases Acts Reconsidered', *Social History of Medicine*, 3 (1990), p. 204.

61 Josephine Butler, *An Autobiographical Memoir* (Bristol: Arrowsmith, 1909), p. 90.

62 Haslam, *Few Words on Prostitution*, pp. 9–10.

63 See *Shield*, 7 Mar. 1870, p. 8.

64 Haslam, *Few Words on Prostitution*, p. 10.

65 Cited in Porter and Hall, *Facts of Life*, p. 134.

66 Haslam, *Few Words on Prostitution*, p. 10.

67 Ibid., pp. 10, 11.

68 Smith, 'Contagious Diseases Acts Reconsidered', p. 198.

69 Porter and Hall, *Facts of Life*, p. 137.

70 Ray Strachey, *The Cause: A Short History of the Women's Movement in Great Britain* (London: Virago, 1978), reprint of 1928 edn, p. 194.

71 Smith, 'Contagious Diseases Acts Reconsidered', p. 201.

72 *Report of the Royal Commission upon the Administration and Operation of the Contagious Diseases Acts 1866–1869* (1871), P. P., 1871 (c.408. 1), XIX. Question 18476, p. 666.

73 Smith, 'Contagious Diseases Acts Reconsidered', p. 201.

74 Ibid.

75 Deborah Dunsford, 'Principle versus Expediency: A Rejoinder to F. B. Smith', *Social History of Medicine* (1992), p. 508.

76 Smith, 'Contagious Diseases Acts Reconsidered', p. 208.

77 McHugh, *Prostitution and Victorian Social Reform*, p. 149.

78 *Report of the Royal Commission*, 1871. Qs. 15657, 15660, p. 554.

79 Smith, 'Contagious Diseases Acts Reconsidered', p. 215.

80 Walkowitz, *Prostitution and Victorian Society*, p. 83.

81 McHugh, *Prostitution and Victorian Social Reform*, p. 64.

82 Walkowitz, *Prostitution and Victorian Society*, p. 93.

83 Maria Luddy, 'Isabella M. S. Tod', in Mary Cullen and Maria Luddy

(eds.), *Women, Power and Consciousness in Nineteenth-Century Ireland* (Dublin: Attic Press, 1995), pp. 212–15.

84 The Contagious Diseases Act (1866) Schedule defined the Irish 'subjected districts' as, the Curragh: 'The limits of the ... parishes of Kilcullen, Kildare, Ballysar, Great Conwell, Morristown-beller'; Cork: The limits of the borough of Cork for municipal purposes', and Queenstown: 'The limits of the town of Queenstown for the purposes of town improvement.' *Report on the Committee appointed to enquire into the Pathology and Treatment of the Venereal Diseases with a view to diminish the injurious effects on the men of the Army and Navy. 1868* (4031), P. P. 1868. XXXVII, p. lxxiii.

85 *Cork Examiner*, 10 Feb., 1860.

86 *Report from the Select Committee on Contagious Diseases Acts; with the Proceedings of the Committee, Minutes of Evidence, Appendix and Index*, 1882, P. P., 1882 (c. 340), IX. Qs. 11192, 11194, p. 472.

87 *Shield*, 15 Apr., 1871, p. 461.

88 *Report of the Select Committee*, 1882. Q. 11340, p. 481.

89 *Royal Commission on the Contagious Diseases Acts*, 1871. Qs. 18. 471–3, p. 666.

90 *Leinster Express*, 27 Oct., 1855. Cited in C. Costelloe, *A Most Delightful Station* (Cork: Collins Press, 1996), pp 148–9, 151.

91 James Greenwood, *The Wren of the Curragh* (London: Tinley Bros, 1867), pp. vii, 14, 16–17.

92 *Pall Mall Gazette*, 23 Oct. 1867. Cited in Maria Luddy, 'An Outcast Community: The Wrens of the Curragh', *Women's History Review*, vol. 1, pt. 3, p. 351.

93 Ibid., p. 346.

94 *Report of the Royal Commission*, 1871. Qs. 15816–7, p. 560.

95 Greenwood, *Wren*, pp. 27–8.

96 *Report of the Select Committee*, 1882. Qs. 11256–7, p. 476.

97 Ibid. Q. 11278, p. 477.

98 Ibid. Qs. 11299–11301, p. 478.

99 Ibid. Q. 5481, p. 242.

100 Ibid. Q. 5482, p. 242.

101 *Special Report from the Select Committee on the Contagious Diseases Bill*, 200 with the proceedings of the committee, 1866. Q5971, 577.

102 Brian Griffin, 'The Irish Police: Love, Sex and Marriage in the Nineteenth and Early Twentieth Centuries', in Margaret Kelleher and James H. Murphy (eds.), *Gender Perspectives in Nineteenth-Century Ireland: Public and Private Spheres* (Dublin: Irish Academic Press, 1997), p. 169.

103 Ibid., p. 171.

104 Ibid., p. 172.

105 *Report from the Select Committee*, 1882. Q. 2504, p. 101.

106 Ibid. Qs. 2534, 2536, p. 102.

107 *Report from Royal Commission*, 1871. Q. 3435–7, p. 106.

108 *Shield*, 7 Mar., 1870, p. 8.

109 *Report of Select Committee*, 1882. Appendix no. 27, p. 612.

[110] *Report from the Select Committee on the Contagious Diseases Acts*, 1881. P. P., 1881 (351). VII. Q. 6440, p. 291.

[111] Ibid.

[112] Ibid. Qs. 6438–9 p. 291.

[113] Ibid. Appendix no 16, p. 475.

[114] Ibid. Appendix no. 15, p. 474.

[115] *Report from the Select Committee on the Contagious Diseases Acts*, 1880. P. P., 1880 (114), VIII. Appendix no. 2, p. 51.

[116] Ibid.

[117] Walkowitz, *Prostitution and Victorian Society*, p. 111.

[118] *Shield*, 30 May 1870, p. 99.

[119] *Shield*, 10 Nov. 1875, p. 294.

[120] Walkowitz, *Prostitution and Victorian Society*, p. 159.

[121] *Shield*, 30 May 1870, p. 102.

[122] *Shield*, 10 Nov. 1875, p. 294.

[123] *Cork Examiner*, 27 June 1876.

[124] Sheehy Skeffington, 'Pioneers of Feminism in Ireland', p. 347.

[125] Susan Kingley Kent, *Sex and Suffrage in Britain, 1860–1914* (London: Routledge, 1987), p. 9.

[126] *Shield*, 7 Mar. 1870, pp. 1, 7.

[127] Ibid., 28 Mar. 1870.

[128] Ibid., 23 May 1870, pp. 92–3.

[129] Ibid., 23 May 1870, p. 96.

[130] Ibid., 16 May 1870, p. 86.

[131] *LNA Annual Report*, 1870, p. 12.

[132] Ibid.

[133] Ibid., pp. 27, 33.

[134] Ibid., pp. 8, 16.

[135] Ibid., pp. 19–20.

[136] Maria Luddy, *Women and Philanthropy in Nineteenth-Century Ireland* (Cambridge: Cambridge University Press, 1995), p. 139.

[137] *Report of the Commission on the Contagious Diseases Acts*, 1871. Qs. 18,798, 18, 830–1, p. 677.

[138] Ibid. Qs. 18,799, 18,801, p. 677.

[139] *Shield*, 30 May 1870, p. 99.

[140] Ibid., 23 May 1870, p. 92.

[141] Ibid., 23 May 1870, p. 93.

[142] Ibid., 4 Mar. 1871, p. 407.

[143] Ibid., 29 Apr. 1871, p. 478.

[144] *LNA Annual Report*, 1871, pp. 10–11.

[145] Ibid., pp. 17–18.

[146] Ibid., 1873, p. 15.

[147] *Report of the Fifth Annual Meeting of the LNA held at Victoria Rooms Bristol October 14, 1874* (Bristol: Arrowsmith, 1874), pp. 7, 8.

[148] *LNA Annual Report*, 1875. List of executive committee members.

[149] Ibid., p. 13.

[150] Ibid.

[151] Ibid., pp. 13–14.
[152] *LNA Annual Report*. 1876, p. 16.
[153] Walkowitz, *Prostitution and Victorian Society*, p. 103.
[154] *LNA Annual Report*, 1876, p. 15.
[155] Ibid.
[156] Ibid., 1877, p. 23.
[157] Ibid., 1878, p. 9. (Sir Harcourt Johnstone's bill for the repeal of the Acts, was debated in the House but went no further.)
[158] Ibid., pp. 9–10.
[159] Ibid., p. 10.
[160] Speech delivered by J. Butler at Croydon in 1871. Reproduced in Barbara Denis and David Skilton (eds.), *Reform and Intellectual Debate in Victorian England* (London: Croom Helm, 1987), pp. 162–3.
[161] Anna Haslam to Marie Stopes, 20 Nov. 1918. CMAC. PP/MCS/A121.
[162] Extracts from a letter of an Irish 'Friend' describing an interview with Josephine E. Butler. MS 24. 121(99), Mary Estlin Collection, Dr Williams's Library, London.
[163] *LNA Annual Report*, 1878, pp. 51–2.
[164] Ibid., p. 21. (I am indebted to Richard Harrison, author of *A Dictionary of Quaker Biography*, for this information on membership of the Society of Friends.)
[165] Ibid., p. 23.
[166] Ibid.
[167] *Shield*, 25 Nov. 1874, p. 247.
[168] *LNA Annual Report*, 1878, pp. 28, 29.
[169] *Shield*, 16 Nov. 1878, p. 274.
[170] Ibid.
[171] *LNA Annual Report*, 1878, p. 34.
[172] *Shield*, 16 Nov. 1878, p. 276.
[173] *Freeman's Journal*, 2 Nov. 1878.
[174] *LNA Annual Report*, 1878, p. 35.
[175] *The Times*, 4 Nov. 1878.
[176] *LNA Annual Report*, 1878, p. 35.
[177] Sheehy Skeffington, 'The Pioneers of Feminism in Ireland', p. 347.
[178] *LNA Annual Report*, 1878, p. 35.
[179] Ibid., p. 37.
[180] Ibid., p. 38.
[181] *Shield*, 16 Nov. 1878, p. 279.
[182] Ibid., p. 280.
[183] Ibid., p. 279.
[184] *Freeman's Journal*, 2 Nov. 1878.
[185] *LNA Annual Report*, 1878, p. 40.
[186] *Irish Times*, 4 Nov. 1878.
[187] *Freeman's Journal*, 2 Nov. 1878.
[188] *The Times*, 4 Nov. 1878.
[189] *Freeman's Journal*, 2 Nov. 1878.
[190] *Irish Times*, 4 Nov. 1878.

191 *Report of the Royal Commission on the Contagious Diseases Acts*, 1871. Q. 18,798, p. 677.

192 McHugh, *Prostitution and Victorian Reform*, p. 131.

193 *LNA Annual Report*, 1875, pp. 13–14.

194 Ibid., p. 13; 1878, p. 9.

195 *LNA Annual Report*, 1878, pp. 36–7.

196 Ibid., p. 40.

197 Walkowitz, *Prostitution and Victorian Reform*, pp. 132, 133.

198 *LNA Annual Report*, 1880, p. 43.

199 Ibid., 1881, p. 27.

200 *Immoral Legislation* (Dublin: LNA, 1880).

201 *LNA Annual Report*, 1880, p. 13.

202 Ibid., 1881, pp. 26–7.

203 Ibid., 1882, pp. 23–4.

204 *Hansard*, 3rd series (20 Apr. 1883), p. 278, col. 749ff.

205 *LNA Annual Report*, 1884, pp. 16–7.

206 Ibid., 1886, p. 19.

207 Ibid., p. 19.

208 Ibid., 1887, p. 19.

209 Walkowitz, *Prostitution and Victorian Society*, p. 134.

210 Levine, *Feminist Lives*, p. 92.

211 Frank Mort, *Dangerous Sexualities: Medico-moral Politics in England since 1830* (London: Routledge & Kegan Paul, 1987), p. 94.

212 *LNA Annual Report*, 1885, pp. 24–5.

213 Edward J. Bristow, *Vice and Vigilance* (Dublin: Gill and Macmillan, 1977), p. 94.

214 Judith R. Walkowitz, 'Male Vice and Female Virtue: Feminism and the Politics of Prostitution in Nineteenth-Century Britain', *History Workshop: A Journal of Socialist and Feminist Historians*, 13, Spring 1982, p. 86.

215 Bristow, *Vice and Vigilance*, p. 104.

216 *LNA Annual Report*, 1885, p. 25.

217 Anna Haslam to M. Stopes, 16 Oct. 1918. CMAC.

218 Walkowitz, 'Male Vice and Female Virtue', p. 86.

219 Typescript. IHA Archive.

220 Walkowitz, *Prostitution and Victorian Society*, p. 252.

221 Bristow, *Vice and Vigilance*, p. 104.

222 Walkowitz, *Prostitution and Victorian Society*, p. 247.

223 Bristow, *Vice and Vigilance*, p. 114.

224 Sheehy Skeffington, 'Pioneers of Feminism in Ireland', p. 347.

225 *LNA Annual Report*, 1886, p. 25.

226 McHugh, *Prostitution and Victorian Reform*, p. 266.

227 Millicent Fawcett, *Josephine Butler: Her Work and Principles and their Meaning in the Twentieth Century* (London, Association for Moral & Social Hygiene, 1927), p. 105.

228 Strachey, *Cause*, p. 204.

229 Luddy, *Women and Philanthropy*, p. 143.

230 Philippa Levine, *Victorian Feminism 1850–1950* (London: Hutchinson, 1987), p. 148.

231 Mort, *Dangerous Sexualities,* p. 91.

232 *The Suffragette,* 11 July 1913, p. 660.

Chapter 5

1 Helen Blackburn, *Women's Suffrage: A Record of the Women's Suffrage Movement in the British Isles with Biographical Sketches of Miss Becker* (London: Williams & Norgate, 1902). Blackburn's description of Anna Haslam: 'In Mrs Haslam the Women's Suffrage cause had . . . found a worker full of perseverance and buoyant energy', p. 129.

2 The Dublin Women's Suffrage Association was founded in 1876. Anna and Thomas Haslam were founder members.

3 Rosemary Cullen Owens, *Smashing Times: A History of the Irish Women's Suffrage Movement 1889–1922* (Dublin: Attic Press, 1984), pp. 23, 27.

4 Louise Ryan, *Irish Feminism and the Vote* (Dublin: Folens, 1996), p. 7.

5 Margaret Ward, *Hanna Sheehy Skeffington: A Life* (Cork: Attic Press, 1997), p. 15.

6 Cliona Murphy, *The Women's Suffrage Movement and Irish Society in the Early Twentieth Century* (New York: Harvester Wheatsheaf, 1989), p. 303.

7 Hanna Sheehy Skeffington, 'Reminiscences of an Irish Suffragette', Andrée Sheehy Skeffington and Rosemary Owens (eds), *Votes for Women: Irish Women's Struggle for the Vote* (Dublin: Sheehy Skeffington & Owens, 1975), p. 12

8 Here 'first wave' is used to define the nineteenth-century movement, and 'second wave' the twentieth-century militant movement.

9 David Rubenstein, *Before the Suffragettes: Women's Emancipation in the 1890s* (Brighton: Harvester, 1986), pp. x, xv.

10 Ibid., p. xv.

11 Fenner Brockway, 'Foreword', in Constance Rover, *Women's Suffrage and Party Politics in Britain 1866–1914* (London: Routledge & Kegan Paul, 1967), p. v.

12 Ray Strachey, *The Cause: A Short History of the Women's Movement in Great Britain* (London: Virago, 1978), p. 103.

13 Petition, *To the Honourable the Commons of the United Kingdom of Great Britain and Ireland in parliament assembled,* presented by John Stuart Mill on 7 June 1866.

14 Strachey, *Cause,* p. 105.

15 Michael St. John Packe, *The Life of John Stuart Mill* (London: Secker & Warburg, 1954), p. 492.

16 Mill to the editor of the *Anti-Slavery Standard,* 4 July 1867. Cited in Packe *Life of John Stuart Mill,* p. 492

17 Blackburn, *Women's Suffrage,* pp. 58–9. Helen Blackburn (1842–1903) was a native of Valentia Island, Co. Kerry, secretary to the Central Committee of the National Society for Women's Suffrage from 1880–95 and editor of

the *Englishwomen's Review* from 1881–9. Her *Women's Suffrage* is a valuable source for the history of the first wave of suffrage activism. Perhaps because of her Kerry origins, the work includes much information on Ireland and on the Haslams.

18 Ibid., p. 63.

19 J. S. Mill to Thomas Haslam, 17 Aug. 1867. DFHL.

20 T. P. Foley, 'Two Letters of John Stuart Mill', in *The Mill Newsletter*, vol. XX, 2 (Summer 1985), p. 13.

21 I am grateful to John Creasey, Librarian, Dr Williams's Library, Gordon Square, London, for bringing this pamphlet to my attention. The copy held by Mr Creasey bears the inscription, 'Professor Francis W. Newman with the author's kind regards. Thomas J. Haslam'.

22 J. S. Mill to T. J. Haslam, 17 Aug. 1867. Hull University Library, DX/66/1.

23 J. E. Cairnes (1823–75), son of a Drogheda brewer was educated at Trinity College Dublin, and was called to the Irish Bar. He was appointed Whately professor of political economy in 1856. He developed and restated J. S. Mill's doctrines.

24 J. S. Mill, *The Later Letters of John Stuart Mill* (Toronto: University of Toronto Press, 1972), p. 1315.

25 Alfred Webb (1834–1908), was a Quaker printer who espoused many philanthropic causes. In 1870 he became involved in the Home Rule movement and became MP for Waterford in 1890. Members of the Webb family were subsequently involved in the DWSA and the LNA.

26 Mill, *Later Letters*, p. 1315.

27 Ibid.

28 J. S. Mill to T. J. Haslam, 19 Feb. 1868. Hull University Library, DX/66/1.

29 *Englishwoman's Review*, vol. 1 (new series), p. 13.

30 *Freeman's Journal*, 10 Apr. 1870.

31 List of signatories of Mill petition in IHA Archive.

32 'The Pioneers of Feminism in Ireland', in *Irish Citizen*, 21 Mar. 1914, p. 347.

33 Joy Melville, *Mother of Oscar: The Life of Jane Francesca Wilde* (London: Murray, 1994), p. 69.

34 *Freeman's Journal*, 10 Apr. 1870.

35 Ibid. Jacob Bright, MP had attempted to advance the cause of suffrage in parliament after J. S. Mill lost his seat in 1868.

36 A pamphlet issued by the National Association for Women's Suffrage in 1869, referred to Miss Robertson, Blackrock, Dublin as one of the Association's honorary secretaries.

37 *Freeman's Journal*, 10 Apr. 1870.

38 *Irish Citizen*, 21 March 1914, p. 347.

39 Blackburn, *Women's Suffrage*, pp. 86, 105.

40 Ibid., pp. 97, 98. 99.

41 Ibid., pp. 116–7.

42 NSWS Central Committee, *Annual Report of the Executive Committee*, 28 May 1875 (London: Dunlop, 1875), pp. 8, 14

43 *Englishwoman's Review*, no. 2, Apr. 1870, p. 107.

44 MS note on IWSLGA minute book, IHA Archive.

45 Blackburn, *Women's Suffrage,* p. 129.

46 Ibid., p. 119.

47 A note in *Englishwoman's Review,* no. 13, Jan. 1873, states: 'The London National Society, of which John Stuart Mill is president, has just ordered for circulation in England, one thousand copies of the essay, "Women's Need of Representation", written lately by Miss Anne I. Robertson, President of the Irish Society.'

48 A. I. Robertson, *Women's Need of Representation: A Lecture upon the Necessity of Giving Women the Parliamentary Franchise* (Dublin: Webb, 1873), p. 15.

49 Maria Luddy, 'Isabella M. S. Tod', in Mary Cullen and Maria Luddy (eds), *Women, Power and Consciousness in Nineteenth-Century Ireland* (Dublin: Attic Press, 1995) pp. 215–16.

50 *The Journal of Charles Ryan* (Wed. 13 May 1874), TCD MS 10349. f 39.

51 Blackburn, *Women's Suffrage,* pp. 127–9.

52 Ibid.

53 NSWS Central Committee, *Annual Report,* 28 May 1875, p. 7.

54 *Englishwoman's Review,* no. 5, Jan. 1871, p. 57.

55 Blackburn, *Women's Suffrage,* p. 129.

56 Marie O'Neill, 'The Dublin Women's Suffrage Association and its Successors', *Dublin Historical Record,* vol. 38, no. 4, September 1985, p. 128.

57 Blackburn, *Women's Suffrage: A Record,* p. 129.

58 DWSA minute book, 6 Mar; 4 Apr. 1876.

59 *Women's Advocate,* no. 1, Apr. 1874.

60 Strachey, *Cause,* p. 266.

61 'The Angel in the House' was the title of Coventry Patmore's long poem which idealized the role of the woman within the home. The title has come to epitomize the Victorian preoccupation with the ideal of womanhood eulogized by John Ruskin in *Sesame and Lilies*: 'Her intellect is not for invention, but for sweet ordering, arrangement and decision.'

62 *Freeman's Journal,* 10 Mar. 1874.

63 Ibid.

64 Letter from T. J. Haslam, *Freeman's Journal,* 11 Mar. 1874.

65 *Freeman's Journal,* 19 Mar. 1874.

66 Strachey, *Cause,* p. 270.

67 Letter from T. J. Haslam, *Freeman's Journal,* 25 Mar. 1874.

68 James Thornton Hoskins was a suffragist and author of a pamphlet called *A few words on women's suffrage* (1870).

69 *Freeman's Journal,* 30 Mar. 1874.

70 Strachey, *Cause,* p. 271.

71 Rover, *Women's Suffrage,* p. 25.

72 Rubenstein, *Before the Suffragettes,* p. 143.

73 Thomas Haslam, *Women's Advocate,* no. 1, April 1874.

74 Thomas Haslam, *Women's Suffrage from a Masculine Standpoint* (Dublin: IWSLGA, 1906), p. 4.

75 *Women's Advocate,* no. 2, May 1874.

76 Lydia Becker (1827–90), was a worker for the cause of suffrage from 1866. She was secretary to the Manchester Suffrage Society from 1867. She was 'a woman of unusual political insight' who was intellectually convinced of the rightness of the suffrage cause. See Strachey, *Cause*, p. 106; and Blackburn, *Women's Suffrage*, pp. 23–43.

77 *Irish Citizen*, 21 Mar. 1914, p. 347.

78 *Women's Advocate*, no. 3, July 1874.

79 Charles Eason (1823–99), was the founder of the bookselling and stationery firm Eason & Son.

80 DWSA minute book, 21 Feb. 1876.

81 Ibid., 6 Mar. 1876.

82 O'Neill, 'The Dublin Women's Suffrage Association', p. 127.

83 The 'lovely' Miss Ashworth was reputedly popular as a speaker in that, according to Strachey, she successfully belied the stereotype of the 'rather hirsute female with spectacles and large feet who figured so freely in the comic Press', Strachey, *Cause*, p. 120.

84 *Freeman's Journal*, 21 Jan. 1876, p. 6.

85 Thomas Wallace Russell, Liberal MP for North Tyrone from 1886–1910, and for South Tyrone from 1911–18. He was created a Baronet in 1917.

86 Maurice Brookes, Liberal MP, pro-Home Rule, was member for Dublin between 1874 and 1885.

87 Colonel Thomas Edward Taylor was a Conservative MP. He was Chancellor of the Duchy of Lancaster in the period during which he was involved with the DWSA. Colonel Taylor initially voted against Mill's amendment to the Representation of the People Bill on 20 May 1867, but he afterwards voted in favour of women's suffrage. (See Blackburn, *Women's Suffrage*, p. 255.) He died on 3 February 1883.

88 William Johnston was a Conservative MP for Belfast from 1868 until 1902. He was educated at TCD.

89 David Sherlock QC was a member for King's County, 1868–80. He was at various times Chairman of the Board of Excise and Sergeant-at-Arms. He was a Liberal, pro-Home Ruler who died in 1884. He was a Roman Catholic.

90 *Reports of the Irish Women's Suffrage and Local Government Association from 1896 to 1918* (Dublin: Ormond, 1918), pp. 7–8.

91 Cliona Murphy, 'The Religious Context of the Women's Suffrage Campaign in Ireland', *Women's History Review*. vol. 6, no. 4, 1997, p. 550.

92 Cited in Murphy, *Women's Suffrage Movement and Irish Society*, p. 17.

93 Richard Harrison, *A Biographical Dictionary of Irish Quakers* (Dublin: Four Courts Press, 1997), p. 102.

94 Ibid., p. 25.

95 Blackburn, *Women's Suffrage*, p. 128. See also *Annual Reports of the Queen's Institute (Female Professional Schools)* Anne V. O'Connor and Susan M. Parkes, *Gladly Learn and Gladly Teach* (Tallaght: Blackwater Press, 1983), p. 7.

96 Blackburn, *Women's Suffrage*, pp. 223–4

97 'Mrs Anna Haslam: 'At Home' to celebrate her eightieth birthday.'

Newspaper cutting (unidentified) 5 Mar. 1909 in scrapbook. pp 20–1. DFHL.

98   See L. M. Cullen, *Eason & Son; A History* (Dublin: Eason, 1989), p. 147.
99   DWSA minute book, 15 January, 1879.
100 See death notices in newspapers for 17 April 1905.
101 Helena Moloney, 'James Connolly and Women', *Dublin Labour Year Book*, 1930. Cited in Murphy, *Women's Suffrage Movement and Irish Society*, p. 21
102 IWSLGA *Annual Report*, 1903, p. 10. Delegates to a convention in Holborn reported the 'newly awakened zeal throughout England' including considerable working-class support. Such support 'unimaginable in Ireland, except, perhaps, in Belfast'.
103 Jessie Craigen trained as a child actress and subsequently used her 'magnificent voice' in the service of various reform movements. She was a radical suffragist who sought working-class support and was employed by Lydia Becker as a speaker on suffrage. See Sandra Holton, *Suffrage Days* (London: Routledge, 1996), pp. 50–1.
104 *Reports of the Irish Women's Suffrage and Local Government Association*, p. 5.
105 DWSA minute book, 11 July 1877.
106 Ibid., 10 July 1878.
107 Ibid., 20 Sept. 1876.
108 Ibid., 7 Mar. 1877.
109 Ibid., 29 Apr. 1879.
110 Ibid., 15 Jan. 1879.
111 Ibid., 20 Sept. 1876.
112 Ibid., 22 Jan. 1877
113 Ibid. List entitled 'Suffrage journals sent to the following.' Although undated, it would appear from its position in the volume, to refer to 1879.
114 Ibid., 13 Feb. 1878.
115 Ibid., 29 Apr. 1879.
116 Ibid., 8 Sept. 1880.
117 Blackburn, *Women's Suffrage*, p. 126.
118 DWSA minute book, 4 Nov. 1880.
119 *Englishwoman's Review*, no. 110, 13 Oct. 1880, p. 469.
120 Preface, *Reports of the Irish Women's Suffrage and Local Government Association*, p. 5.
121 Jessie Craigen, 'A Visit to Bodyke', in Brian Ó Dálaigh (ed.), *The Stranger's Gaze: Travels in County Clare 1534–1950* (Ennis: Clasp Press, 1998), pp. 291–4.
122 Cullen Owens, *Smashing Times*, pp. 23, 27.
123 Ryan, *Irish Feminism and the Vote*, p. 7.
124 DWSA minute book, 11 July 1877.
125 Ibid.
126 Ibid., 5 Nov. 1877.
127 Ibid., 15 Jan. 1879.
128 Ibid., 29 Apr. 1879.
129 Ibid., 1 Feb. 1882.

130 Ibid., 4 Aug. 1881.
131 Ibid., 18 Feb. 1880.
132 Ibid.
133 Niamh O'Sullivan, 'The Iron Cage of Femininity: Visual Representation of Women in the 1880s Land Agitation', in Tadgh Foley and Seán Ryder (eds.), *Ideology and Ireland in the Nineteenth Century* (Dublin: Four Courts Press, 1998), p. 181.
134 Blackburn, *Women's Suffrage*, p. 154.
135 Circular with letter head of DWSA in Haslam, scrapbook in IHA Archive.
136 Ibid.
137 Ibid.
138 Letter from Anna Haslam in *Daily Express*, 17 Mar. 1884 (from scrapbook).
139 DWSA minute book, 26 June 1884.
140 DWSA minute book, 27 Oct. 1884.
141 *The Woman's Leader*, 8 Dec. 1922, p. 358.
142 Strachey, *Cause*, p. 277.
143 Letter from the Chief Secretary's Office to Anna Haslam, 15 Jan. 1884, in Haslam scrapbook, DFHL.
144 Blackburn, *Women's Suffrage*, p. 257.
145 Draft MS letter from Anna Haslam, Secretary of DWSA to Rt. Hon, G. O. Trevelyan. Scrapbook, DFHL.
146 Letter from Ladies to Members of Parliament, May 1884. Cited in Blackburn, *Women's Suffrage*, pp. 264–6.
147 Strachey, *Cause*, pp. 277–8
148 Blackburn, *Women's Suffrage*, pp. 161–2
149 Letter from Mr W. Gladstone to Mr W. Woodall MP (the proposer of the clause to include women). Cited in Blackburn, *Women's Suffrage*, p. 163.
150 *Women's Suffrage Journal*, July 1884. Cited in Blackburn, *Women's Suffrage*, pp. 164–5.
151 Strachey, *Cause*, p. 278.
152 Ibid., p. 280.
153 Blackburn, *Women's Suffrage*, p. 175.
154 DWSA minute book, 28 Dec. 1888.
155 Ibid., 4 Jan. 1889.
156 Ibid., 26 Feb. 1890.
157 Strachey, *Cause*, p. 281.
158 DWSA minute book, 18 Sept. 1900.
159 For an account of the Ladies' Land League see Ward, *Unmanageable Revolutionaries* (London: Pluto Press, 1987).
160 MS in Anna Haslam's hand in IHA archive. Speech delivered on 22 June 1888 to 'Mrs Russell and ladies'. Mrs Russell was the wife of T. W. Russell, MP, suffrage supporter and speaker at CDA repeal meetings.
161 Blackburn, *Women's Suffrage*, p. 172. The Women's Liberal Unionist Association was a group of Liberal supporters who were anti-Home Rule.
162 *Irish Times*, 25 Apr. 1895.
163 MS of speech in IHA archive.

164 Hanna Sheehy Skeffington, 'Sinn Féin and Irish Women', in *Bean na hÉireann*, Nov. 1909. Cited in Margaret Ward, *Unmanageable Revolutionaries: Women and Irish Nationalism* (London: Pluto, 1983), pp. 71–3.

165 A Member of the Statistical and Social Inquiry Society of Ireland (Thomas J. Haslam), *The Real Wants of the Irish People* (Dublin: Webb, 1865), p. 50.

166 Blackburn, *Women's Suffrage*, p. 169.

167 Strachey, *Cause*, p. 284.

168 *DWSA Annual Report*, 1896, p. 3

169 DWSA minute book, 5 March 1896.

170 *DWSA Annual Report*, 1896, p. 4.

171 DWSA minute book, 15 Sept. 1896

172 Ibid.

173 Ibid., 11 Nov. 1896.

174 Address by Anna Haslam at an election meeting in Dublin in support of Mrs Lawrenson's candidacy as poor law guardian, 10 Feb. 1897. Scrapbook in IHA archive.

175 The DWSA briefly became the Dublin Women's Suffrage (and Poor Law Guardian) Association. Next known as the Dublin Women's Suffrage and Local Government Association, its name was changed in 1901 to Irish Women's Suffrage and Local Government Association (IWSLGA), which name lasted until 1918. To avoid confusion I have used only two versions, viz. DWSA and IWSLGA.

176 *DWSA Annual Report*, 1897, p. 4.

177 Ibid., p. 5.

178 Ibid., p. 7.

179 *DWSA Annual Report*, 1898, p. [3].

180 Virginia Crossman, *Local Government in Nineteenth-century Ireland* (Belfast: The Institute of Irish Studies, 1994), p. 94.

181 *DWSA Annual Report*, 1898, pp. [3]–4.

182 Anna Haslam to Arthur Balfour, 20 July 1898, and reply of 22 July 1898. IHA Archive.

183 Crossman, *Local Government*, pp. 94–5.

184 *DWSA Annual Report*, 1899, p. [3].

185 Ibid., p. 7.

186 Ibid.

187 'Women and Local Government in Ireland: A Chat with Mrs Haslam', *Sunday Times*, 8 July 1900.

188 Anna Haslam, 'Irishwomen and the Local Government Act', reprinted from *Englishwoman's Review*, 15, Oct. 1898. Copy in Haslam scrapbook, IHA Archive.

189 DWSA, *Suggestions for Intending Lady Guardians* (leaflet). Scrapbook IHA Archive.

190 Anna Haslam to the editor of the *King's County Chronicle*, 9 Nov. 1900.

191 DWSA, *Suggestions for Intending Women Workers under the Local Government Acts*, rev. edn (Dublin: DWSA, n.d.), pp. 1–8.

[192] DWSA, *Suggestions for Intending Lady Guardians* (Dublin: DWSA, n.d.).

[193] O'Neill, 'The Dublin Women's Suffrage Association and its Successors', p. 150.

[194] Anna Haslam, *Irishwomen and Local Government Act*, reprinted from the *Englishwoman's Review*, 15 Oct. 1898. Haslam scrapbook, IHA Archive.

[195] Susan Day, *Women in a New Ireland* (Cork: MWFL, 1912), p. 3.

[196] Letter from Anna Haslam to the Chairman of the Public Health Committee, City Hall Dublin, 5 Nov. 1898.

[197] DWSA, *Annual Report*, 1899, p. 8.

[198] Ibid., 1900, pp. 8–9.

[199] Ibid., pp. 11, 13.

[200] Women and Local Government in Ireland': A chat with Mrs Haslam, *Sunday Times*, 8 July 1900.

[201] M. B., 'Notes on Women's Work in Dublin', *Queen: The Ladies' Newsletter*, 26 May 1900. Cutting in Haslam scrapbook, IHA Archive.

[202] Anna Haslam, *Irishwomen and the Local Government Act* (Dublin: IWSLGA, n.d.).

[203] See Jane Rendall, *The Origins of Modern Feminism* (London: Macmillan, 1985), p. 300, and Alex Tyrrell '"Woman's Mission" and Pressure Group Politics in Britain (1825–1860)' in *The John Rylands University Library Journal*, vol. 63, no. 1, autumn 1980, p. 194.

[204] Edith F. Hurwitz, 'The International Sisterhood', in Renate Bridenthal and Claudia Koonz (eds), *Becoming Visible: Women in European History* (Boston: Houghton Mifflin, 1977), p. 329.

[205] DWSA minute book, 9 Dec. 1887.

[206] *Report of the International Council of Women assembled by the National Woman Suffrage Association* . . . 1888 (Washington, DC: National Women's Suffrage Association, 1888), p. 42.

[207] Earl and Countess of Aberdeen, *'We Twa': Reminiscences of Lord and Lady Aberdeen*, vol. 2 (London: Collins, 1925), p. 296.

[208] Ibid., pp. 299–300.

[209] Mrs Maurice Dockrell, 'Irish Women in Local Government' in Countess of Aberdeen (ed.), *The International Congress of Women 1899*, vol. 5: *Women in Politics* (London: International Congress of Women, 1900), pp. 88–9.

[210] Anna Haslam was at the conference as a delegate (see minute book 14 Sept. 1899; IWSLGA Annual Report, 1899, p. 4). There is no other mention of a Miss Hasland and the concerns expressed by this speaker are similar to the frequent references made by Mrs Haslam to the election of women poor law guardians. This misprint is followed by another error in the dating of the Local Government Act. A 'Mr Hasland' (almost certainly Thomas) also addressed the convention.

[211] Aberdeen, *International Congress of Women*, 1899, vol. 3, p. 94.

[212] DWSA minute book, 14 Sept. 1899.

[213] Blackburn, *Women's Suffrage*, pp. 214–5.

[214] Aberdeen, *International Congress of Women*, 1899, vol. 3, p. 61.

[215] IWSLGA, Minute Book, 26 July 1904.

[216] Ibid., 18 Sept. 1913.

[217] Hurwitz, 'International Sisterhood', p. 334.

[218] _The Times_, 29 June 1899; _The Diary of Beatrice Webb_ (Virago: London, 1983), p. 162. Both items cited in Rubenstein, _Before the Suffragettes_, p. 162, n. 65.

[219] Aberdeen, _'We Twa'_, vol. 2, p. 307. The cost of travel to far-flung conferences would have been considerable, which suggests that perhaps Lady Dockrell, the wife of a wealthy businessman, financed her own visits to Stockholm and Budapest.

[220] Rubenstein, _Before the Suffragettes_, p. 152.

[221] Hurwitz, 'International Sisterhood', p. 330

[222] Ibid., p. 334.

[223] Ibid., p. 328.

[224] Sandra Stanley Holton, _Suffrage Days: Stories from the Women's Suffrage Movement_ (London: Routledge, 1996), p. 35.

[225] _NUWW: An Occasional Paper_, Oct. 1896.

[226] Holton, _Suffrage Days_, p. 36.

[227] _NUWW: An Occasional Paper_, no. 13, Feb. 1899, p. 21

[228] _Official Handbook for the Annual Conference of NUWW to be held in the Central Hall, Oldham St._, Oct. 27–30, 1896, p. 22.

[229] _Official Handbook for the Annual Conference of NUWW to be held in Croydon ... 1897_, p. 5.

[230] _DWSA Annual Report_, 1900, p. 5.

[231] _IWSLGA Annual Report_, 1907, p. 11. Much of Mrs Haslam's indefatigable work for the employment of women was consistent with NUWW policy.

[232] _Women's Franchise_, no. 19, 7 Nov. 1907, p. 210.

[233] _IWSLGA Annual Report_, 1915, pp. 7–8

[234] _Irish Citizen_, 20 Nov. 1915, p. 65

[235] _IWSLGA Annual Report_, 1901, pp. 8–9.

[236] Horace Plunkett (1854–1932), the pioneer of the co-operative movement in Ireland, recruited Irish politicians of all parties into the Recess Committee in 1895, the recommendations of which were realized in the creation of the Department of Agriculture and Technical Instruction in 1899, and in the extension of technical education.

[237] _IWSLGA Annual Report_, 1901, p. 13.

[238] Ibid., 1902, p. 8.

[239] Ibid., 1903, p. 8.

[240] _Freeman's Journal_, 27 June 1903.

[241] _IWSLGA Annual Report_, 1903, p. 6.

[242] C. H. Oldham, 'Thomas J. Haslam: 1825–1917 – Man and Social Reformer', _Freeman's Journal_, 3 Feb. 1917.

[243] Richard Harrison, 'Cork Mutual Improvement Association (1859–1884) and its Antecedents', _The Journal of the Friends' Historical Society_, vol. 56, no. 4, 1993, p. 281.

[244] Thomas J. Haslam, _Good English for Beginners_ (Dublin: Eason, 1892). A passage from George Eliot was cited as an example of how not to write!

245 Examples from the twenty-seven reviews from Irish and British publications included at the end of *Good English for Beginners*.

246 T. Haslam, *Good English*, [n.p.].

247 Millicent Fawcett, *Nineteenth Century*, May 1886. Cited in Rover, *Women's Suffrage*, p. 2.

248 Thomas J. Haslam, *Women's Suffrage from a Masculine Standpoint* (Dublin: Ormond, 1906), and *The Rightful Claims of Women* (Dublin: Ormond, 1906). There were earlier editions also, as the *IWSLGA Annual Report*, 1905 states that Haslam's *Women's Suffrage from a Masculine Standpoint* had been 'widely disseminated'. Seven thousand copies in all were distributed thanks to 'the generosity of a subscriber who desires to withhold her name from publication', p. 14. Three thousand copies of *The Rightful Claims of Women* were printed. This address had been delivered at 'several meetings in London'. *IWSLGA Annual Report* 1906, p. 13.

249 Haslam, *Women's Suffrage*, p. 3.

250 Ibid., pp. 8, 12.

251 Ibid., pp. 14–15.

252 Ibid., pp. 22–3.

253 Ibid., p. 16.

254 Haslam, *Rightful Claims*, p. 4.

255 Ibid., p. 7.

256 Ibid., p. 11–12.

257 Ibid., p. 13.

258 Ibid., pp 15–16.

259 Ibid., pp. 17, 18.

260 Ibid., p. 20.

261 Ibid., p. 21.

262 Ibid., p. 21–2.

263 Letter in Haslam scrapbook from Annie Craig, sec. of the North Hackney division of the Central Society for Women's Suffrage, undated, referring to a meeting on 22 June 1905 which the Haslams addressed.

264 *Hackney and Stoke Newington Gazette*, 3 July 1905. Cutting Haslam scrapbook, IHA Archive.

265 IWSLGA minute book, 13 Sept. 1906; 6 Sept. 1907; *Llandudno Advertiser*, 15 July 1907.

Chapter 6

1 *IWSLGA Annual Report*, 1914, p. 12: 'We rejoice that Mr and Mrs Haslam are still with us with clear brains and able hands ever working to further our interests. '

2 Ibid., 1898, 1910. The minimum subscription was one shilling but some subscribers gave larger amounts.

3 IWSLGA minute book, 6 Sept. 1907.

4 *Women's Franchise*, no. 7, 12 Sept. 1907, pp. 116–17.

5 Anna Haslam to Campbell-Bannerman MP, Prime Minister, April 1907. IHA Archive.

6 Anna Haslam to members of IWSLGA, 6 March 1907. IHA Archive.

7 IWSLGA 'to all Irish Members', 27 July 1907. IHA Archive.

8 F. Sheehy Skeffington, *Votes for Women*, 11 Nov. 1910, p. 83. Cited in Cliona Murphy, *Women's Suffrage Movement and Irish Society in the Early Twentieth Century* (New York: Harvester Wheatsheaf, 1989).

9 Ibid.

10 *Hansard Parliamentary Debates*, 4th series, vol. 189, 1 Jul. 1907, cols. 343–4.

11 Ibid., 12 Aug. 190, col. 929.

12 Cited in Constance Rover, *Women's Suffrage and Party Politics in Britain 1866–1914* (London: Routledge & Kegan Paul, 1967), p. 176.

13 Harold Smith, *The British Women's Suffrage Campaign, 1866–1928* (London: Longman, 1998), p. 45.

14 Helen Blackburn, *Women's Suffrage: A Record of the Women's Suffrage in the British Isles with Biographical Sketches of Miss Becker* (London: Williams & Norgate, 1902), p. 67.

15 Strachey, *The Cause: A Short History of the Women's Movement in Great Britain* (London: Virago, 1978; reprint of 1st ed. London: G. Bell, 1928), p. 291.

16 Rover, *Women's Suffrage and Party Politics*, p. 190.

17 Smith, *British Women's Suffrage Campaign*, p. 10.

18 Sandra Stanley Holton, *Suffrage Days: Stories from the Women's Suffrage Movement* (London: Routledge, 1996), pp. 106–7. The WFL was founded in 1899 by Elizabeth Wolstenholme Elmy, correspondent of the Haslams, and 'became the voice' of radical suffrage. The WFL tried to link with working-class women and with the Labour movement. They argued that women's labour, whether paid or unpaid, entitled them to full citizenship (See Smith, *British Women's Suffrage Campaign*, pp. 12–13).

19 David Rubenstein, *Before the Suffragettes: Women's Emancipation in the 1890s* (Brighton: Harvester, 1986), p. 147.

20 IWSLGA minute book, 24 Oct. 1893; 1 May 1894; 10 Oct. 1894.

21 Holton, *Suffrage Days*, p. 108.

22 Smith, *British Women's Suffrage Campaign*, p. 15. See also Rubenstein *Before the Suffragettes*, and Holton, *Suffrage Days*.

23 Ibid., p. 29.

24 Emmeline Pethick-Lawrence, *My Part in a Changing World* (1938). Cited in Smith, *British Women's Suffrage Campaign*, p. 92.

25 Smith, *British Women's Suffrage Campaign*, p. 29.

26 Holton, *Suffrage Days*, p. 110.

27 Smith, *British Women's Suffrage Campaign*, p. 29.

28 Margaret Haig, *This was my World* (1933). Cited in Smith, *British Women's Suffrage Campaign*, p. 91.

29 Sarah Grand first used the term in her novel *The Heavenly Twins* (1893); however, she 'claimed to have invented the term in an article she wrote for *The North American Review* in 1894'. (Lucy Bland, *Banishing the Beast: English Feminism and Sexual Morality 1885–1914* (London: Penguin, 1995), p. 340.

30 Bland, *Banishing the Beast*, p. 144.

31 Holton, *Suffrage Days*, p. 253, n. 3. See also entries for *suffragette* and *suffragist* in *OED*.

32 Emmeline Pankhurst, *My Own Story* (London: Eveleigh Nash, 1914), p. 18.

33 Teresa Billington-Grieg (1877–1964), was one of the first WPSU organizers and author of suffrage works including a history of the militant movement cited below.

34 Teresa Billington-Grieg, *The Militant Suffrage Movement* (London: Palmer, 1911), p. 200.

35 See Strachey, *The Cause*, pp. 310–11; Rover, *Women's Suffrage and Party Politics*, pp. 80–81.

36 Hanna Sheehy Skeffington, 'Reminiscences of an Irish Suffragette', in Andrée Sheehy Skeffington and Rosemary Owens (eds) *Votes for Women Irish Women's Struggle for the Vote* (Dublin: Sheehy Skeffington & Owens, [1975]), p. 12.

37 Ibid.

38 Although coincidentally, prior to his becoming an MP, David Sheehy, like Anna's father, Abraham Fisher, was a miller.

39 Ward, *Hanna Sheehy Skeffington: A Life* (Cork: Attic Press, 1997), p. 15.

40 Ibid., p. 7.

41 Ibid., p. 23.

42 Holton, *Suffrage Days*, p. 99.

43 *IWSLGA Annual Report*, 1902, p. 4.

44 Roger Fulford, *Votes for Women: The Story of a Struggle* (London: Faber, 1957), p. 104.

45 *IWSLGA Annual Report*, 1903, p. 10.

46 *Irish Independent*, 7 April 1906, p. 7.

47 IWSLGA minute book, 25 Sept. 1902.

48 *First Report of the Association of Irish Schoolmistresses and Other Ladies Interested in Education* (Dublin: Webb, 1883).

49 Typescript of AISM 1922 report. TCD 9722/1–47.

50 Minute book of the Committee of AISM commenced 19 Feb. 1889. TCD 9722/1–47. Annual reports date from 1882.

51 Ibid., 3 Jan. 1999; 9 May 1906; 18 Dec. 1908.

52 Alice Oldham, *A Sketch of the Work of the Association of Irish Schoolmistresses and other Ladies interested in Education from its Foundation in 1882 to the year 1890* (read at the annual meeting, 25 Nov. 1890, and included in the 1890 report of the association), pp. 22–3. For examples of communication between nuns and the committee, see AISM, minute book, 27 Jan. 1906: Letter from Revd Mother Mary Patrick received via Mrs Byers, 'calling attention to the necessity of at once taking steps to lay the claims of the University teaching of women before the Government in view of the possible approaching legislation in Irish University education'. On 22 Apr. 1901 a letter was received from Loreto Abbey regarding students who had passed First Arts taking teachers' diplomas.

53 Oldham, *Sketch of the work of AISM*, pp. 23–24.

54 C. S. Bremner, *Thomas J. Haslam*. Scrapbook in DFHL.
55 See IWSLGA minute book for 24 Sept. and 22 Oct. 1903 and thereafter.
56 Ibid., 24 Feb. 1905.
57 Ibid., 25 Sept. 1902; 22 Jan. 1903.
58 *IWSLGA Annual Report*, 1903. Margaret Ward incorrectly states that this meeting took place in January 1903 in her biography of H. Sheehy Skeffington. It was included in the 1903 report, which probably accounts for the error. The meeting is also referred to in the minute book for 4 Jan. and 5 Feb. 1904.
59 Ward, *Hanna Sheehy Skeffington*, p. 20–21. See also Sheehy Skeffington, 'Reminiscences', p. 12.
60 Ward, Hanna Sheehy Skeffington, pp. 21, 33.
61 Ibid., p. 37; *Freeman's Journal*, 3 Feb. 1917.
62 Ward, *Hanna Sheehy Skeffington*, p. 40.
63 Father Eugene Sheehy, Hanna's uncle, was a major influence on her. He was prominent in the Land League and was imprisoned in Kilmainham during the first phase of the Land War.
64 Ward, *Hanna Sheehy Skeffington*, pp. 23–4. See also IWSLGA *Annual Reports*, 1903–1906.
65 Anna Haslam to Marie Stopes, 18 Oct. 1918. CMAC. A MS note on the death certificate of Thomas states that their current and deposit accounts were 'in joint names of Thomas and Anna Maria Haslam'. DFHL.
66 Anna Haslam to H. Sheehy Skeffington, 29 Feb. 1904. Sheehy Skeffington Papers, NLI, MS 33603 (22).
67 Anna Haslam to H. Sheehy Skeffington, 2 Dec. 1904. Ibid.
68 Anna Haslam to H. Sheehy Skeffington, 17 Jan. 1904. Ibid.
69 Anna Haslam to H. Sheehy Skeffington, n.d. [1907]. Ibid.
70 Ibid.
71 Ibid.
72 Sheehy Skeffington, 'Reminiscences', pp. 20–21.
73 Rosemary Cullen Owens, *Smashing Times* (Dublin: Attic Press, 1984), p. 42.
74 Ward, *Hanna Sheehy Skeffington*, p. 47
75 James and Margaret Cousins, *We Two Together* (Madras: Ganesh, 1950).
76 Ward, *Hanna Sheehy Skeffington*, p. 46.
77 IWSLGA minute book, 21 Mar. 1907.
78 Cousins, *We Two*, p. 129.
79 Ward, *Hanna Sheehy Skeffington*, p. 46.
80 Cousins, *We Two*, p. 164.
81 Cited in Murphy, *Women's Suffrage Movement and Irish Society*, p. 29.
82 Rover, *Women's Suffrage and Party Politics*, p. 69.
83 This was at a meeting at which Thomas Haslam delivered a paper. See *Women's Franchise*, no. 43, 23 (Apr. 1908), p. 501.
84 Jenny Wyse Power (1858–1941), was a member of Ladies' Land League, Inghinidhe na hÉireann, Cumann na mBan. She became a senator from 1923.
85 IWSLGA minute book, 11 Jan. 1906.

86 IWSLGA minute book, 22 Mar. 1906.
87 Letter from Anna Haslam to H. Sheehy Skeffington, 13 Jan. 1906. Sheehy Skeffington Papers, NLI, MS 33603 (22).
88 *IWSLGA Annual Report*, 1904, p. 5; 1907, p. 7.
89 Cousins, *We Two*, p. 185.
90 IWSLGA minute book, 19 May 1910.
91 IWSLGA minute book, 7 July 1910.
92 See Tom Garvin. *The Evolution of Irish Nationalist Politics* (Dublin: Gill and Macmillan, 1981), p. 91 and *passim*. See also R. F. Foster, *Modern Ireland 1600–1972* (London: Allen Lane, 1988), p. 431 and *passim*.
93 Sean O'Faolain, *Vive Moi!* (London: Rupert Hart Davis, 1965), p. 30.
94 Conor Cruise O'Brien, *Ancestral Voices: Religion and Nationalism in Ireland* (Dublin: Poolbeg, 1994), p. 94.
95 Ibid., p. 75.
96 Sheehy Skeffington, 'Reminiscences', p. 12.
97 See, for example, Ward, *Unmanageable Revolutionaries* (cited below); Murphy, *Women's Suffrage Movement and Irish Society*; Owens, *Smashing Times*.
98 Margaret Ward, *Unmanageable Revolutionaries: Women and Irish Nationalism* (London: Pluto Press, 1987), p. 73.
99 *Women's Franchise*, no. 33, 13 Feb. 1908, p. 373.
100 IWSLGA *Annual Report*, 1908, p. 14.
101 *Women's Franchise*, no. 14, 3 Oct. 1907, p. 151. [Thomas Haslam to editor]
102 IWSLGA *Annual Report*, 1908, p. 14.
103 *Women's Franchise*, no. 31, 28 Jan. 1909, p 365.
104 IWSLGA *Annual Report*, 1908, p. 8.
105 IWSLGA minute book, 21 Oct. 1909.
106 The London Society for Women's Suffrage had existed from the beginning of the campaign. John Stuart Mill was a founding member. By 1909 when Anna Haslam was asked to become vice-president it was dominated by conservative suffragists and was an important constituent member of the National Union of Women's Suffrage Societies (NUWSS).
107 See Owens, *Smashing Times*, p. 42.
108 Anna Haslam to Miss Strachey, 21 Nov. 1909. Autograph collection, Fawcett Library.
109 *Englishwomen's Review*, April 15 1909, p. 102.
110 *Irish Citizen*, 15 Feb. 1913, p. 309.
111 Rover, *Women's Suffrage and Party Politics*, p. 84.
112 Ibid., p. 85.
113 Strachey, *The Cause*, p. 304.
114 See IWSLGA *Annual Reports*, 1900 and 1911 (£40 19s 6d and £77 17s 6d respectively).
115 *Irish Citizen*, 25 May 1912, p. 7.
116 Strachey, *The Cause*, pp. 304–5.
117 IWSLGA, *Annual Report* 1906, pp. 12–13.
118 Cousins, *We Two*, p. 167.

119 *Irish Citizen*, 6 Jul. 1912, p. 55 .
120 Murphy, *Women's Suffrage Movement and Irish Society*, p. 90.
121 *IWSLGA Annual Report*, 1910, p. 13.
122 Ward, *Hanna Sheehy Skeffington*, p. 69.
123 *IWSLGA Annual Report*, 1910, p. 14.
124 Ward, *Hanna Sheehy Skeffington*, p. 60.
125 Sheehy Skeffington, 'Reminiscences', p. 12.
126 Sheehy Skeffington, 'Reminiscences', p. 13.
127 Murphy, *Women's Suffrage Movement and Irish Society*, p. 28.
128 IWSLGA minute book, 9 Nov. 1911.
129 Ibid., 13 Mar. 1913.
130 Ward, *Sheehy Skeffington*, p. 49; *Women's Franchise*, vol. 2, no. 36 (4 Mar. 1909), p. 431.
131 Ward, *Hanna Sheehy Skeffington*, p. 47.
132 IWSLGA minute book, 6 Jan. 1910.
133 Ibid., 11 Apr. 1912.
134 *Irish Citizen*, 20 Nov. 1915, p. 170.
135 Tony Farmar, *Ordinary Lives: The Private Worlds of Three Generations of Ireland's Professional Classes* (Dublin: Farmar, 1995), p. 18.
136 *Freeman's Journal*, 17 Mar. 1907.
137 Ward, *Hanna Sheehy Skeffington*, p. 73.
138 Ibid., p. 74.
139 IWSLGA minute book, 9 Mar. 1911.
140 See *Votes for Women*, 24 and 31 Mar. 1911.
141 Murphy, *Women's Suffrage Movement and Irish Society*, p. 36.
142 *IWSLGA Annual Report*, 1911, pp. 10–11.
143 IWSLGA minute book, 11 May 1911.
144 Lady Aberdeen, wife of the Lord Lieutenant, was a campaigner against disease, particularly tuberculosis, in Ireland. As seen in Chapter 5, she was a prominent member of the international women's movement. She was an enthusiastic promoter of Irish handicrafts. A staunch ally of Haslam, she was continually heckled by members of the IWFL who made her life and that of her husband 'a misery'. (See Ward, *Hanna Sheehy Skeffington*, p. 112).
145 Owens, *Smashing Times*, p. 42.
146 Rosemary Owens, 'How We Won the Vote', in Sheehy Skeffington and Owens (eds) *Votes for Women*, p. 7.
147 IWSLGA minute book, 14 Sept. 1911.
148 Ibid., 9 March 1911. The 'League' was presumably the Munster Women's Franchise League in which Edith Somerville and Violet Martin (Somerville and Ross) were officers.
149 Strachey, *The Cause*, p. 305.
150 *Irish Citizen*, 17 May 1913, p. 417.
151 Owens, *Smashing Times*, p. 47.
152 Strachey, *The Cause*, p. 305.
153 Cousins, *We Two Together*, pp. 203–4. James Cousins wrote of a mysterious woman whose 'personal deportment was noticeably . . . above her

common dress' who arrived at his door a few days after the request for cash. She handed over a 'sheaf of bank-notes'. There was no covering letter, no sender's name or address, but the amount handed over was almost identical to the amount requested, and so the paper was started. Cousins did not have any theories as to the reason for the cloak-and-dagger tactics.

154 *Irish Citizen*, 20 Nov. 1915, p. 169.
155 Louise Ryan, *Irish Feminism and the Vote* (Dublin: Folens, 1996), p. 10.
156 *Irish Citizen*, 29 June 1912, p. 44.
157 *Irish Citizen*, 20 Nov. 1915, pp. 166–167.
158 Augustine Birrell to John Dillon 15 Jan. 1912. Cited in Owens, *Smashing Times*, p. 47.
159 *IWSLGA Annual Report*, 1912, p. [4].
160 Ibid., p. 5.
161 Rover, *Women's Suffrage and Party Politics*, p. 222.
162 *Hansard Parliamentary Debates*, 5th series, vol. 43, 5 Nov. 1912, col. 114.
163 See especially Murphy, *Women's Suffrage Movement and Irish Society*, pp. 164–95.
164 Owens, 'How we won the vote', p. 292.
165 Sheehy Skeffington, 'Reminiscences', p. 18.
166 Ibid., pp. 18–20.
167 *IWSLGA Annual Report*, 1912, p. 20.
168 *Irish Citizen*, 22 June 1912, p. 39.
169 IWSLGA *Minute Book*, 12 Sept. 1912.
170 *Irish Citizen*, 23 Nov. 1912, p. 215.
171 Ibid., 28 Dec. 1912, p. 254.
172 IWSLGA minute book, 9 Jan. 1913.
173 Ibid., 13 Mar. 1913.
174 *Irish Citizen*, 10 Jan, 1914, p. 265.
175 IWSLGA minute book, 13 Dec. 1900 and 17 Jan. 1901.
176 *Irish Citizen*, 22 June 1912, p. 39.
177 IWSLGA minute book, 10 Apr. 1913.
178 Ibid., 16 Oct. 1913.
179 Ibid., 13 Nov. 1913.
180 Ibid., 8 May 1913.
181 *IWSLGA Annual Report*, 1913, p. 16.
182 *Irish Citizen*, 20 Nov. 1915, p. 170.
183 *IWSLGA Annual Report*, 1913, p. 17.
184 *Irish Citizen*, 10 Jan. 1914, p. 265.
185 Ibid.
186 *IWSLGA Annual Report*, 1913, pp. 5–6.
187 Strachey, *The Cause*, p. 334.
188 *IWSLGA Annual Report*, 1908, p. 6.
189 Strachey, *The Cause*, pp. 305–6.
190 *IWSLGA Annual Report*, 1907, p. 5.
191 A copy of 'letter to the editor', 16 June 1906, from Anna Haslam. Scrapbook DFHL. Unidentified newspaper.

192 *Irish Citizen*, 21 Mar. 1914, p. 347; *Irish Citizen*, 4 Apr. 1914, p. 366; Scrapbook DFHL.

193 Ibid., 15 Aug. 1914, p. 98.

194 Strachey, *The Cause*, pp. 337–8.

195 Owens, *Smashing Times*, p. 97.

196 *Irish Citizen*, 19 Sept. 1914, p. 139.

197 Ibid., 15 Aug. 1914, p. 98.

198 *IWSLGA Annual Report*, 1914, pp. 4–5.

199 Ibid., p. 8.

200 Ibid., pp. 10, 27.

201 *Irish Citizen*, 20 Nov. 1915, p. 170: 'He wrote from 1896 to 1913 the annual report of the society which is a valuable record and summary of suffrage work in Ireland year by year.'

202 *IWSLGA Annual Report*, 1915, p. 5.

203 Ibid., p. 7.

204 *Irish Citizen*, 14 Nov. 1914, p. 201.

205 Ibid., 9 Jan. 1915, p. 268.

206 Ibid., 2 Jan. 1915, p. 253.

207 Ibid., 9 Jan. 1915, p. 258.

208 Ibid.

209 Ibid., 9 Oct. 1915.

210 Ibid., 4 Dec. 1915, p. 182.

211 Commandant Mary S. Allen, *The Pioneer Policeman* (London: Chatto & Windus, 1925), pp. 11–12.

212 Ibid., pp. 12, 13, 21.

213 Phillipa Levine, '"Walking the Streets in a Way no Decent Woman Should": Women Police in World War 1', *Journal of Modern History*, vol. 66, no. 1 (Mar. 1994), p. 40.

214 Form letter, Home Office to Chief Constables, 20 Nov. 1911. Cited in Levine, 'Walking the Streets', p. 44.

215 *Irish Independent*, 9 Mar. 1957.

216 Ibid.

217 *The Women's Leader*, 8 Dec. 1922, p. 358.

218 *IWSLGA Annual Report*, 1917, p. 6.

219 Ibid., 1915, pp. 6–9.

220 *Irish Times*, 15 Apr. 1915.

221 *Irish Citizen*, May 1916, p. 217.

222 *IWSLGA Annual Report*, 1915, p. 6.

223 Ibid., 1916, pp. 6, 8.

224 *Irish Citizen*, Apr. 1917, p. 253.

225 *IWSLGA Annual Report*, 1915, p. 6.

226 Mrs E. Sanderson, 'Watching the Courts', *Irish Citizen*, 19 June 1915, p. 34.

227 *Irish Citizen*, 20 Nov. 1915, p. 171.

228 Haslam, *A Few Words on Prostitution*, p. 5.

229 Dana Hearne, 'The Development of Irish Feminist Thought: a Critical

Analysis of The Irish Citizen, 1912–1920' (unpublished Ph.D, York University, 1992), Ottawa: National Library of Canada, 1993), p. 144.

230 *Irish Citizen*, 3 May 1913, p. 393.

231 Ibid., August 1917, p. 39.

232 James Cousins, 'White Slavery: Its The Cause and Cure', *Irish Citizen*, 12 July 1913, p. 60.

233 Thomas J. Haslam, *A Few Words on Prostitution and the Contagious Diseases Act* (Dublin: Webb, 1890), pp. 3, 5.

234 Christabel Pankhurst, *The Great Scourge and How to End It*. Cited in Smith, *British Women's Suffrage*, p. 96. An *Irish Citizen* editorial of 18 Oct. 1913 urged readers to buy the pamphlet, p. 76.

235 Susan Kingsley Kent, *Sex and Suffrage in Britain 1860–1914* (London: Routledge, 1995), p. 215.

236 Ibid., p. 217.

237 Lady Chance, *Women's Suffrage and Morality: An Address to Married Women* (London: NUWSS, 1912), pp. 6, 9.

238 Hearne, 'Development of Irish Feminist Thought', p. 161.

239 See Levine, 'Walking the Streets'; Lucy Bland, 'In the Name of Protection: The Policing of Women in the First World War', in Julia Brophy and Carol Smart (eds.), *Women-in-Law: Family and Sexuality* (London: 1985), p. 41.

240 *Irish Citizen*, Nov. 1916, p. 236.

241 *IWSLGA Annual Report*, 1915, p. 8; *Irish Citizen*, 20 Nov. 1915, pp. 166–7.

242 *Irish Citizen*, 20 Nov. 1915, p. 171.

243 Thomas J. Haslam, *Some Last Words on Women's Suffrage* (Dublin: Ormond, 1916).

244 Ibid., pp. 3–5.

245 Ibid., pp. 6–8.

246 Ibid., p. 11.

247 Ibid., p. 13.

248 Ibid., pp. 14–15.

249 Ibid., p. 17.

250 Ibid., p. 18.

251 Ibid., p. 10.

252 Ibid., p. 12.

253 Ibid.

254 *IWSLGA Annual Report*, 1916, p. 11.

255 *Irish Citizen*, Feb. 1917, p. 245.

256 *IWSLGA Annual Report*, 1917, p. 4.

257 Strachey, *The Cause*, p. 352.

258 *Observer*, 13 Aug. 1916. Cited in Strachey *The Cause*, p. 354 .

259 *Irish Citizen*, July 1917, p. 367

260 Rover, *Women's Suffrage*, p. 223.

261 *Irish Citizen*, Apr. 1918, p. 605.

262 *Irish Citizen*, Jan. 1919, p. 643.

263 *Freeman's Journal*, 16 Dec. 1918, p. 5.

264 *The Woman's Leader*, 8 Dec. 1922, p. 358.

265 *Irish Citizen*, Jan. 1919, p. 643.

266 *Irish Citizen*, Dec. 1918, p. 633.

267 Dora Mellone, Preface to *Reports of the IWSLGA* from 1896 to 1918 (Dublin: Ormond, 1919), pp. 8–9.

268 *Irish Citizen*, 17 May 1913, p. 411.

269 This was a Labour Party private member's bill designed 'to remove at one sweep all the remaining disabilities of women'. The Bill was eventually quashed by the Lords. See Strachey, *The Cause*, p. 375.

270 Anna Haslam to Marie Stopes, 7 Feb. 1919. BL. Add MS 58685, postcard.

271 Anna Haslam to Marie Stopes, 1 Nov. 1919. BL Add MS 58685, H126.

272 *Woman's Leader*, 17 Apr. 1922, p. 82.

273 Ibid., 8 Dec. 1922, p. 318.

274 Catriona Beaumont 'Women and the Politics of Equality: The Irish Women's Movement 1930–1943', in Maryann Gialanella Valiulis and Mary O'Dowd (eds.), *Women in Irish History* (Dublin: Wolfhound, 1997), p. 175.

275 Ibid.

276 Ibid., p. 176

277 Hilda Tweedy, *A Link in the Chain: The Story of the Irish Housewives' Association 1942–1992* (Dublin: Attic Press, 1992), p. 22.

278 *Irish Citizen*, Dec. 1918, p. 633.

279 Roger Fulford, *Votes for Women: The Story of a Struggle* (London: Faber, 1957), p. 299.

280 See Owens, *Smashing Times*, p 130; Ward, *Hanna Sheehy Skeffington*, pp. 249–51.

281 *DWSA Annual Report*, 1899, p. 7.

Conclusion

1 *Irish Times*, 30 Nov. 1922.

2 *Freeman's Journal*, 1 Dec. 1922.

3 President Mary Robinson, 'Striking a Balance. The Allen Lane Foundation Lecture', delivered 25 Feb. 1992, from press release.

Bibliography

Archival Sources

Cambridge

Girton College
The Helen Blackburn Collection

Dublin

Friends' Historical Library, Swanbrook, Dublin 4 (DFHL)
Diary of Elizabeth Clibborn of Anner Mills Clonmel, Co. Tipperary
Death certificates of Anna and Thomas Haslam
Fisher family biographical notes
Marriage certificate of Anna and Thomas Haslam
Minute of Clonmel Monthly Meeting
Minute of Cork Monthly Meeting
Minute of Mountmellick Monthly Meeting
Minute of Youghal Preparative Meeting
Registers of Births, Marriages and Deaths of the Society of Friends
Testimonies of Disownment of the Society of Friends

Irish Housewives' Association
Irishwomen's Suffrage and Local Government Association Minute Book
Scrapbook containing IWSLGA newspaper cuttings and letters
Folder containing miscellaneous letters and manuscripts pertaining to Anna
Haslam

National Archives of Ireland
Papers of the Central Relief Committee
Society of Friends Relief of Distress papers
Last will and testament of Anna Haslam

National Library of Ireland.
Diaries of Mary Hayden, MS 16641 (A).
Diaries of Rosamund Jacob
Sheehy Skeffington Papers, MSS 21,625–6.

Trinity College Dublin
Letter from Ruskin College to Mrs A. M. Haslam, 6 Apr. 1904, PA/777/3
Memorial to the Board of Trinity College from 'Ten Thousand Irishwomen of the Upper and Middle Classes' 1892. MUN P/1/2441
Memorandum from the Board of Trinity College Dublin regarding the admission of women. MUN P/1/2526/3
The Journal of Charles Ryan. MS 10349, f 39

Hull

University of Hull Brynmor Jones Library
Correspondence of Thomas and Anna Haslam. DX/66/1, 2a-c (Presented to the Library by the Marie Stopes Memorial Foundation)

London

British Library
Letter from Joseph Fisher of Youghal to Lord Liverpool, BL Add. MS 38263
Correspondence of Marie Stopes with Anna Haslam, Add. MSS 58685–9

Contemporary Medical Archives Centre. Wellcome Institute for the History of Medicine
Correspondence of Anna Haslam with Marie Stopes, Marie Stopes Papers PP/MCS.A.121

Dr Williams's Library
Extracts from a letter of an Irish 'Friend' describing an interview with Josephine E. Butler, MS 24.121/99

Fawcett Library
Josephine Butler Collection
Letter from Anna Haslam to Miss Strachey, autograph collection

Library of the Religious Society of Friends in Britiain
Minute of the Westminster Monthly Meeting

Wakefield

West Yorkshire Archive Centre, Registry of Deeds
Ackworth School Wages Book, C678/2/8/2

Annual Reports

Ackworth Old Scholars' Association
Central Association of Irish Schoolmistresses and Other Ladies Interested in Education
Central Committee of the National Society for Women's Suffrage
Irish Women's Suffrage and Local Government Association
Ladies' National Association for the Repeal of the Contagious Diseases Acts
National Association for the Repeal of the Contagious Diseases Acts
National Union of Women Workers
Queen's Institute (of Female Professional Schools) for Improving the Education of Women
Women Poor Law Guardians

Public Documents

Hansard's Parliamentary Debates
Report of the Royal Commission upon the Administration and Operation of the Contagious Diseases Acts 1866–1869. P. P., 1871 (c.408.1), XIX.
Report from the Select Committee on the Contagious Diseases Acts. 1866; together with the Proceedings of the Committee. P. P., 1868–9 (306), VII.
Report from the Select Committee on the Contagious Diseases Acts.1880. P. P., 1880 (114), VIII.
Report from the Select Committee on the Contagious Diseases Acts. 1881. P. P., 1881 (351), VII.
Report from the Select Committee on the Contagious Diseases Acts; with the Proceedings of the Committee, Minutes of Evidence, Appendix and Index 1882. P. P., 1882 (c. 340), IX.
Report of the Committee appointed to enquire into the Pathology and Treatment of the Venereal Diseases with a View to Diminish the Injurious Effects on the Men of the Army and Navy. (1868) P. P., 1868 (c.4031), XXXVII.
Special Report from the Select Committee on the Contagious Disease Bill with the proceedings of the committee 1866, pp. 1866 (c.200) XI.

Contemporary Journals

Annual Monitor
Anti-Suffragist Review
Common Cause
Englishwomen's Review
Fraser's Magazine
Irish Citizen
The Magdalen's Friend
The Olive Leaf, or, Peace Magazine for the Young
Pall Mall Gazette

The Shield
The Suffragette
Votes for Women
The Women's Advocate
The Women's Leader
Women's Franchise
Women's Suffrage Journal

Newspapers

Cork Examiner
Freeman's Journal
Hackney and Stoke Newington Gazette
Irish Independent
Irish Times
King's County Chronicle
Llandudno Advertiser
Leinster Express
Sunday Times
The Times

Works by Thomas J. Haslam

The Real Wants of the Irish People. Dublin: Webb, 1865.
The Marriage Problem. Dublin: Webb, 1868.
A Few Words on Prostitution and the Contagious Diseases Acts. Dublin: Webb, 1870.
Duties of Parents: Reproductive and Educational. London: Burns, 1872.
Good English for Beginners. Dublin: Eason, 1892.
The Rightful Claims of Women. Dublin: Ormond, 1906.
Some Last Words on Women's Suffrage. Dublin: Ormond, 1916.
Woman's Suffrage from a Masculine Viewpoint. Dublin: Ormond, 1906.

Contemporary Printed Sources

Aberdeen, Countess of (ed.) *The International Congress of Women 1899*. Vol. 5: *Women in Politics*. London: International Congress of Women, 1900.

Aberdeen, Earl and Countess of. *'We Twa': Reminiscences of Lord and Lady Aberdeen*. Vol. 2. London: Collins, 1925.

Acton, William. *Prostitution Considered in its Moral, Social and Sanitary Aspects in London and other Large Cities and Towns*. 2nd edn, London: Cass, 1972. Facsimile of edn, London: Churchill, 1870.

——. *The Functions and Disorders of the Reproductive Organs*. London: John Churchill, 1875.

Allen, Commandant Mary S. *The Pioneer Policeman*. London: Chatto & Windus, 1925.

Billington-Grieg, Teresa. *The Militant Suffrage Movement*. London: Palmer, 1911.

Blackburn, Helen. *Comments on the Opposition to Women's Suffrage*. London: NSWS, 1878.

——. *Because*. Bristol: Arrowsmith, 1888.

——. *Women's Suffrage: A Record of the Women's Suffrage Movement in the British Isles with Biographical Sketches of Miss Becker*. London: Williams & Norgate, 1902.

Blackwell, Elizabeth. *Pioneer Work on Opening the Medical Profession to Women*. London: Longmans, Green, 1895.

Brooke. W. R. *Statement of the Movement for the Admission of Women to Trinity College Dublin and Correspondence in Reference Thereof*. Dublin: University Press, 1895.

Butler, Josephine. *Women's Work and Women's Culture*. London: Macmillan, 1869.

——. *Social Purity: An Address Given at Cambridge*. 1879.

——. *An Autobiographical Memoir*. Bristol: Arrowsmith, 1909.

Carlisle, Richard. *Everywoman's Book: or What is Love? Containing Important Instructions For the Prudent Regulation of The Principal of Love and The Number of a Family* (London: A. Carlisle, 1838).

Chance, Lady. *Women's Suffrage and Morality: An Address to Married Women*. London: NUWSS, 1912.

Churchill, Fleetwood. *On the Diseases of Women*. 5th edn. Dublin: Fannin, 1864.

Culverwell, R. J. *On Single and Married Life: or the Institution of Marriage, its Intent, Obligations, and Physical and Constitutional Disqualifications*. New York: Charles J. C. Kline, 1862.

'Darwinism and National Life', *Nature*. 16 Dec. 1869.

Day, Susan. *Women in a New Ireland*. Cork: Munster Women's Franchise League, 1912.

——. *The Amazing Philanthropist*. London: Sidgewick & Jackson, 1912.

Dockrell, Margaret (Mrs. Maurice). 'Irish Women in Local Government' in Countess of Aberdeen. (ed.), *The International Congress of Women 1899*. Vol. 5: *Women in Politics*. London: International Congress of Women, 1900, pp. 87–9.

Donegan, C. O'Kane. *Law Students' Debating Society of Ireland: Women's Suffrage an Address Delivered in the Dining Hall, King's Inns, Dublin . . . on 20th October 1892 by the Auditor.* Dublin: Dublin University Press, 1892.

Drysdale, George. *The Elements of Social Science or, Physical, Sexual and Natural Religion: An Exposition of the True Cause and Only Cure of the Three Primary Social Evils, Poverty, Prostitution and Celibacy.* 11th edn, London: Truelove, 1873.

Duffey, E. B. *What Women Should Know.* Philadelphia, 1873.

Ethelmer, Ellis. *Women Free.* Congleton: Woman's Emancipation Union, 1893.

——. *Phases of Love.* Congleton: Women's Emancipation Union, 1897.

Evans, A. S. *Hanes Eglwys Ramoth Hirwaun.* Blaenau Ffestiniog, 1912.

Fawcett, Millicent. *Women's Suffrage: A Short History of a Great Movement.* London: Jack, 1912.

——. *Josephine Butler: Her Work and Principles and Their Meaning in the Twentieth Century.* London: Association for Moral & Social Hygiene, 1927.

Greenwood, James. *The Wren of the Curragh.* London: Tinley Bros., 1867.

Greg, W. R. 'Prostitution', *The Westminster Review,* 53, 1850, pp. 448–506.

Haycraft, John B. *Darwinism and Race Progress.* London: S. Sonnenschein, Scribner, 1895.

Hodgson, Joseph Spence. *Superintendents, Teachers and Principal Officers of Ackworth School from 1779–1894: A list compiled from official documents with historical notes and short biographies.* Ackworth: Ackworth Old Scholars' Association, 1895.

Knowlton, Charles. *Fruits of Philosophy, or, The Private Companion of Young Married People.* 3rd edn. London: Watson, 1841.

Lecky, William E. H. *History of European Morals from Augustus to Charlemagne.* Vol. 2, 3rd rev. edn, New York: Appleton, 1897.

Malthus, Thomas Robert. *An Essay on the Principles of Population.* London: Johnson, 1798, and 1817 edns.

Martin, Victoria C. W. *The Rapid Multiplication of the Unfit.* 1891.

McCarthy, Justin, M. P. *The Political Enfranchisement of Women: Speech delivered at Corn Exchange Bedford, 26th February, 1890.* Thornton Heath, 1890.

Mill, James. *Supplement to the Encyclopaedia Britannica.* Edinburgh, 1824.

Mill, John Stuart. *Principles of Political Economy.* Totonto: Robson, 1965; 1st edn. 1848.

Mill, John Stuart. *The Later Letters of John Stuart Mill.* Toronto: University of Toronto Press, 1972.

Miller, E. P. *Vital Force.* New York: Miller & Haynes, 1869.

Morant, George. *Hints to Husbands: A Revelation of Man-midwife's Mysteries.* 3rd edn, London: Simpkin Marshall, 1857.

Newman, F.W. *A Lecture on Women's Suffrage delivered in the Guildhall Bath on January 28th 1870.* Bristol: Arrowsmith, 1870.

Newtown School Centenary 1898: History of the School, Papers Read at Centenary Meeting, Record of Proceedings, List of Old and New Scholars. Waterford: Newenham Harvey & Co., 1898.

Opinions of Women on Women's Suffrage. London Committee of NSWS, 1879.

Owen, Robert Dale. *Moral Physiology, or, A Brief and Plain Treatise on the Population Question*. 3rd edn. London, 1831.

Pankhurst, Emmeline. *My Own Story*. London: Eveleigh Nash, 1914.

Report of International Council of Women: Assembled by the National Women's Suffrage Association, Washington, D.C., March 25 to April 1, 1888. Washington: National Women's Suffrage Association, 1888.

Roberstson, A. I. *Women's Need of Representation: A Lecture upon the Necessity of Giving Women the Parliamentary Franchise*. Dublin: Webb, 1873.

Sheehy Skeffington, Hanna. 'Reminiscences of an Irish Suffragette', in AndréeSheehy Skeffington and Rosemary Owens (eds) *Votes for Women: Irishwomen's Struggle for the Vote*, Dublin: Sheehy Skeffington & Owens, [1975].

Sieveking, J. G. *Memoir and Letters of F. W. Newman*. London: Kegan Paul, Trench, Trubner & Co., 1909.

Smith Henry. *A Plea for the Unborn: An Argument that . . . Man may Become Perfect by Means of Selection and Stripculture*. London: Watts, 1897.

Some Account of the Life and Religious Labours of Sarah Grubb. Dublin: Jackson, 1792.

Southwell, Rose M. *The Youghal Lace Industry*. Dublin: Browne & Nolan, n.d.; reprinted from *The Irish Rosary*, June 1898.

Spencer, Herbert. *The Study of Sociology*. London: Kegan Paul, Trench, Trubner, 1873.

Stopes, Marie C. *Early Days of Birth Control*. London: Putnam, 1922.

——. *Contraception (Birth Control), Theory, History and Practice: A Manual for the Medical and Legal Profession*. London: Bale & Danielson, 1923.

Strachey, Ray. *The Cause: A Short History of the Women's Movement in Great Britain*. London: Virago, 1978. (Reprint).

Swiney, Frances. *Women and Natural Law*. 2nd edn, London: League of Isis, 1912.

The Statistical and Social Inquiry Society of Ireland: List of Members of the Society. Dublin: Webb, 1864.

Townsend, Mary A. *One Hundred Years of Mountmellick School: History of the School with Proceedings of the 1886 Centenary and A Complete List of Scholars*. Dublin: Webb, 1886.

Trall, R. T. *Sexual Physiology: A Scientific and Popular Exposition on the Fundamental Problems in Sociology*. London: J. Burns, 1866.

Women's Peace Association. Dublin: Chapman, 1883.

Secondary Sources

Aalen, F. A. 'The Rehousing of Rural Labourers in Ireland under the Labourers (Ireland) Acts 1893–1919', *Journal of Historical Geography*, vol. 12, no. 3, 1986, pp. 287–306.

Ahern, Michael. 'The Quaker Schools in Clonmel', *Tipperary Historical Journal*, 1990, pp. 128–32.

Banks, J. A. and Olive. *Feminism and Family Planning in Victorian England*. New York: Schoken, 1964.

——. *Victorian Values: Secularism and the Size of Families*. London: Routledge and Kegan Paul, 1981.

Barry, Kathleen. *The Prostitution of Sexuality*. New York: New York University Press, 1995.

Beaumont, Catriona. 'Women and the Politics of Equality: The Irish Women's Movement 1930–1943', in Maryann Gialanella Valiulis and Mary O'Dowd (eds.), *Women in Irish History*. Dublin: Wolfhound, 1997, pp. 173–88.

Benn, J. Miriam. *The Predicaments of Love*. London: Pluto Press, 1992.

Bland, Lucy. 'The Domain of the Sexual: A Response', *Screen Education*, 39, Summer 1981. pp. 56–67.

——. *Banishing the Beast: English Feminism & Sexual Morality 1885–1914*. London: Penguin, 1995.

——. 'In the Name of Protection: The Policing of Women in the First World War', in Julia Brophy and Carol Smart (eds.), *Women-in-Law: Family and Sexuality*. London: Routledge & Kegan Paul, 1985, pp. 23–49.

Boyd, Nancy. *Josephine Butler, Octavia Hill, Florence Nightingale: Three Victorian Women who Changed the World*. London: Macmillan, 1982.

Brannigan, Cyril Gerard . 'Quaker Education in 18th and 19th Century Ireland.' *Irish Educational Studies*. vol. 4, no. 1, 1984. pp. 54–72.

Breathnach, Eibhlín. 'Women and Higher Education in Ireland (1879–1914)', *Crane Bag*, vol. 4, no.1, 1980, pp. 560–7.

——. 'Charting New Waters: Women's Experience in Higher Education, 1879–1908', in Mary Cullen (ed.), *Girls Don't Do Honours: Irish Women in Education in the 19th and 20th Centuries*. Dublin: WEB, 1987, pp. 55–78.

Bristow, Edward J. *Vice and Vigilance*. Dublin: Gill and Macmillan, 1977.

Brown, Elisabeth Potts and Jean R. Soderlund. 'Sources on Quaker Women', in Elisabeth Potts Brown and Susan Mosher Stuard (eds.), *Witnesses for Change: Quaker Women over Three Centuries*. New Brunswick: Rutgers University Press, 1989, pp. 157–75.

Butler, Tony. 'The White Quakers', *South Tipperary Today*, 10 July 1995.

Collini, Stefan. *Public Moralists: Political Thought and Intellectual Life in Britain 1850–1930*. Oxford: Clarendon, 1991.

Colum, Mary. *Life and the Dream*. New York, 1947.

Costello, Con. *A Most Delightful Station: The British Army on the Curragh of Kildare, 1855–1922*. Cork: Collins Press, 1996.

Craigen, Jessie. 'A Visit to Bodyke', in Brian Ó Dálaigh (ed.), *The Strangers' Gaze: Travels in County Clare 1534–1950*. Ennis: Clasp Press, 1998, pp. 291–4.

Crossman, Virginia. *Local Government in Nineteenth-century Ireland*. Belfast: The Institute of Irish Studies, The Queen's University of Belfast, 1994.

Cullen, L. M. 'Eighteenth-Century Flour Milling in Ireland', *Irish Economic and Social History*, 4, 1977, pp. 5–25.

——. *Eason & Son; A History*. Dublin: Eason, 1989.

Cullen, M. J. *The Statistical Movement in Early Victorian Britain*. Hassocks: Harvester Press, 1975.

Cullen, Mary. 'Anna Maria Haslam (1829–1922)', in Mary Cullen and Maria Luddy (eds.), *Women, Power and Consciousness in Nineteenth-Century Ireland*. Dublin: Attic Press, 1995, pp. 161–96.

D'Arcy, F. 'The Malthusian League and the Resistance to Birth Control Propaganda in Late Victorian Britain', *Population Studies*, vol. 31, 1977, pp. 429–48.

Daly, Mary E. *The Spirit of Earnest Inquiry: The Statistical and Social Inquiry Society of Ireland 1847–1997*. Dublin: Statistical and Social Inquiry Society of Ireland, 1997.

Degler, Carl N. 'What Ought to Be and What Was: Women's Sexuality in the Nineteenth Century', *American Historical Review*, 79, no. 5 (1974), pp. 1468–91.

Denis, Barbara and David Skilton (eds.). *Reform and Intellectual Debate in Victorian England*. London: Croom Helm, 1987.

Dockrell, John H. 'Blackrock – Town Hall and Baths: Some Reflections', *Proceedings of the Blackrock Society*, vol. 2, 1994.

Dunsford, Deborah. 'Principle versus Expediency: A Rejoinder to F.B. Smith', *Social History of Medicine*, vol. 5, 1992, pp. 505–13.

Eaton, George. 'The Quaker Tradition in Neath: A Study in Religious, Social and Commercial Attitudes', *Neath Antiquarian Society Transactions* (1978), pp. 14–34.

Eversley, D. E. C. 'Demography of Irish Quakers 1650–1850' in J. M. Goldstrom and L. A. Clarkson (eds), *Irish Population, Economy, and Society*. Oxford: Clarendon Press, 1981, pp. 57–88.

Farmar, Tony. *Ordinary Lives: The Private Worlds of Three Generations of Ireland's Professional Classes*. Dublin: Farmar, 1995.

Finegan, John. *The Story of Monto*. Cork: Mercier, 1978.

Finer, S. F. *The Life and Times of Sir Edwin Chadwick*. London: Methuen, 1952.

Foley, T. P. 'Two Letters of John Stuart Mill', *The Mill Newsletter*, vol. XX, 2, Summer 1985.

Foster, R. F. *Modern Ireland 1600–1972*. London: Allen Lane, 1988.

Foucault, Michel. *The History of Sexuality: an Introduction*. London: Penguin, 1994.

Fryer, Peter. *The Birth Controllers*. London: Secker & Warburg, 1965.

Fulford, Roger. *Votes for Women: The Story of a Struggle*. London: Faber, 1957.

Garvin, Tom. *The Evolution of Irish Nationalist Politics*. Dublin: Gill and Macmillan, 1981.

Gay, Peter. *The Bourgeois Experience – Victoria to Freud*. Vol. 1, *Education of the Senses*. Oxford: Oxford University Press, 1984.

——. *The Bourgeois Experience – Victoria to Freud*. Vol. 4, *The Naked Heart*. London: Fontana, 1997.

Gross, John. *The Rise and Fall of the Man of Letters: Aspects of English Literary Life since 1800*. London: Weidenfeld & Nicholson, 1969.

Grubb, Isabel, *Quakerism in Ireland*. London, 1927.

Haight, Gordon S. 'Male Chastity in the Nineteenth Century', *Contemporary Review*, 219, 1971, pp. 252–62.

Hall, Lesley A. 'Forbidden by God, Despised by Man: Masturbation, Medical Warnings, Moral Panic, and Manhood in Great Britain, 1850–1950' in John C. Fout (ed.) *Forbidden History: The State, Society and the Regulation of Sexuality in Modern Europe*. Chicago: University of Chicago Press, 1992.

Hall, Lesley A. *Hidden Anxieties: Male Sexuality, 1900–1950*. Cambridge: Polity Press, 1991.

——. 'The Archives of Birth Control in Britain', *Journal of the Society of Archivists*, vol. 16, no. 2, 1995, pp. 207–18.

——. '"I Have Never Met the Normal Woman": Stella Browne and the Politics of Womanhood', *Women's History Review*, vol. 6, no. 2, 1997, pp. 157–82.

——. 'Suffrage, Sex and Science', in Joannou Maroula and June Purvis (eds), *The Women's Suffrage Movement: New Feminist Perspectives*. Manchester: Manchester University Press, 1998, pp. 186–200.

Hall, Ruth. *Marie Stopes: A Biography*. London: Quality Book Club, 1977.

Harrison, Brian. 'Underneath the Victorians', *Victorian Studies*, March, 1967.

——. *Drink and the Victorians*. London: Faber and Faber, 1971.

——. *Separate Spheres*. London: Croom Helm, 1978.

——. 'A Different World for Women', *Twentieth-Century British History*, vol. 3, no.1, 1992, pp. 76–83.

Harrison, Richard S. 'Irish Quaker Perspectives on the Anti-Slavery Movement', *Journal of the Friends' Historical Society*, vol. 56, no. 2, 1991, pp. 106–25.

——. '*Cork City Quakers: A Brief History 1655–1939*. Published privately, 1991.

——. *Irish Insurance: Historical Perspectives 1650–1950*. Published privately, 1992.

——. *Richard Davis Webb: Dublin Quaker Printer*. Published privately, 1993.

——. 'Cork Mutual Improvement Association (1859–1884) and its Antecedents' *Journal of the Friends' Historical Society*, vol. 56, no. 4, 1993. pp. 272–86.

——. 'Spiritual Perception and the Evolution of the Irish Quakers.' Kevin Herlihy (ed.), *The Religion of Irish Dissent*. Dublin: Four Courts Press, 1996, pp. 68–82.

——. *A Biographical Dictionary of Irish Quakers*. Dublin: Four Courts Press, 1997.

Hazelkorn, Ellen. 'The Social and Political Views of Louie Bennett, 1870–1956', *Saothar: Journal of the Irish Labour History Society*, 13, 1988, pp. 32–44.

Himes, Norman E. 'John Stuart Mill's Attitude to Neo-Malthusianism', *The Economic Journal (Supplement)*, no. 4, Jan. 1929, pp. 457–84.

——. *Medical History of Contraception*. Baltimore: William & Wilkins, 1936.

Himmelfarb, Gertrude. *Victorian Minds*. London: Weidenfeld and Nicolson, 1968.

——. 'Mayhew's Poor: A Problem of Identity', *Victorian Studies*, vol. 14, no. 3, 1972, pp. 307–20.

Hollis, Patricia. *Women in Public, 1850–1900: Documents of the Victorian Women's Movement*. London: Allen & Unwin, 1979.

Holloway, John. *The Victorian Sage: Studies in Argument*. London: Macmillan, 1953.

Holton, Sandra. 'The Suffragist and the Average Woman', *Women's History Review*, vol. 1, no.1, 1992, pp. 9–23.

Holton, Sandra Stanley. 'Free Love and Victorian Feminism: The Divers Matrimonials of Elizabeth Wolstenholme and Ben Elmy', *Victorian Studies*, vol. 37, no. 2, 1994, pp. 199–222.

——. *Suffrage Days: Stories from the Women's Suffrage Movement*. London: Routledge, 1996.

Houghton, Walter. *The Victorian Frame of Mind*. New Haven: Yale University Press, 1957.

Hudson, Derek. *Man of Two Worlds: The Life and Diaries of Arthur J. Munby 1828–1910*. London: Abacus, 1974.

Hurwitz, Edith F. 'The International Sisterhood', in Renate Bridenthal and Claudia Koonz (eds.), *Becoming Visible: Women in European History*. Boston: Houghton Mifflin, 1977, pp. 325–45.

Ingram, Angela J. C and Daphne Patai (eds). *Rediscovering Forgotten Radicals: British Women Writers, 1889–1939*. Chapel Hill: University of North Carolina Press, 1993.

Jackson, Margaret. *The Real Facts of Life: Feminism and the Politics of Sexuality c.1850–1940*. London: Taylor & Francis, 1994.

Jalland, Pat. *Women, Marriage and Politics 1860–1914*. Oxford: Clarendon, 1986.

—— and John Hooper (eds). *Women from Birth to Death: The Female Life Cycle in Britain 1830–1914*. Brighton: Harvester, 1986.

Jeffreys, Sheila. *The Spinster and her Enemies: Feminism and Sexuality 1880–1930*. London: Pandora Press, 1985.

John, Angela V. and Claire Eustance. 'Shared Histories–Differing Identities: Introducing Masculinities, Male Support and Women's Suffrage', in Angela V. John and Claire Eustance (eds), *The Men's Share?: Masculinities, Male Support and Women's Suffrage in Britain 1890–1920*. London: Routledge, 1997, pp. 1–37.

Jones, Gretta. 'Eugenics in Ireland: the Belfast Eugenics Society, 1911–15', *Irish Historical Studies*, xxviii, no. 109, May 1992, pp. 81–95.

Kamm, Josephine. *Rapiers and Battleaxes: The Women's Movement and its Aftermath*. London: Allen & Unwin, 1966.

Kent, Susan Kingsley. *Sex and Suffrage in Britain 1860–1914*. London: Routledge, 1995.

Levenson, Leah and Jerry H. Natterstad. *Hanna Sheehy-Skeffington: Irish Feminist.* Syracuse: Syracuse University Press, 1986.

Levine, Philippa. *Victorian Feminism 1850–1950.* London: Hutchinson, 1987.

——. *Feminist Lives in Victorian England: Private Lives and Public Commitment.* Oxford: Blackwell, 1990.

——. 'Women and Prostitution: Metaphor, Reality, History', *Canadian Journal of History,* 28 Dec. 1993, pp. 480–94.

——. 'Walking the Streets in a Way no Decent Woman Should: Women Police in World War I', *Journal of Modern History,* vol. 66, no. 1, Mar. 1994, pp. 34–78.

Lewis, Jane. *Women and Social Action in Victorian and Edwardian England.* London: Edward Elgar, 1991.

Liddington, Jill. *The Road to Greenham Common: Feminism and Anti-Militarianism in Britain Since 1820.* Syracuse: Syracuse University Press, 1991.

Luddy, Maria. 'An Outcast Community: The "Wrens" of the Curragh', *Women's History Review,* vol. 1, no. 3, 1992, pp. 341–55.

——. 'Women and the Contagious Diseases Acts 1864–1886', *History Ireland,* Spring 1993, pp. 32–4.

——. 'Isabella M. S. Tod' in Mary Cullen and Maria Luddy (eds), *Women, Power and Consciousness in Nineteenth-Century Ireland.* Dublin: Attic Press, 1995, pp. 197–230.

——. *Women in Ireland 1800–1918: A Documentary History.* Cork: Cork University Press, 1995.

——. *Women and Philanthropy in Nineteenth-Century Ireland.* Cambridge: Cambridge University Press, 1995.

——. 'Abandoned Women and Bad Characters: Prostitution in Nineteenth-Century Ireland', *Women's History Review,* vol. 6, no. 4, 1997, pp. 485–503.

—— and Cliona Murphy. *Women Surviving: Studies in Women's History in the 19th and 20th Centuries.* Dublin: Poolbeg, 1990.

Marcus, Steven. *The Other Victorians. A Study of Sexuality and Pornography in Mid-Nineteenth-Century England.* London: Weidenfeld & Nicholson, 1956.

Mason, Michael. *The Making of Victorian Sexual Attitudes.* Oxford: Oxford University Press, 1994.

Mazumdar, Pauline M. H. *Eugenics, Human Genetics and Human Failings: The Eugenics Society, its Sources and its Critics in Britain.* London: Routledge, 1992.

McFadden, Charles J. *Medical Ethics.* London: Burns & Oates, 1962.

McHugh, Paul. *Prostitution and Victorian Social Reform.* London: Croom Helm, 1980.

McKillen, Beth. 'Irish Feminism and Nationalist Separatism, 1914–23', *Éire–Ireland,* vol. 18, pt. 3, 1982, and vol. 18, pt. 4, 1982, pp. 72–90.

McLaren, Angus. *Birth Control in Nineteenth-Century England: A Social and Intellectual History.* London: Croom Helm, 1978.

Melville, Joy. *Mother of Oscar: The Life of Jane Francesca Wilde.* London: Murray, 1994.

Mennell, James E. 'The Politics of Frustration: "The Maiden Tribute of Modern Babylon" and the Morality Movement of 1885', *North Dakota Quarterly*, 49, 1, 1981, pp. 68–80.

Micklewright, F. H. Amphlett. 'The Rise and Decline of English Neo-Malthusianism', *Population Studies*, vol. 15, no. 1. July 1961, pp. 32–51.

Mitchel, Geraldine. *Deeds not Words: The Life of Muriel Gahan*. Dublin: Town House, 1997.

Mort, Frank. *Dangerous Sexualities: Medico-moral Politics in England since 1830*. London: Routledge & Kegan Paul, 1987.

Murphy, Cliona. *The Women's Suffrage Movement and Irish Society in the Early Twentieth Century*. New York: Harvester Wheatsheaf, 1989.

——. 'The Religious Context of the Women's Suffrage Campaign in Ireland', *Women's History Review*, vol. 6, no. 4, 1997, pp. 549–62.

Nead, Lynda. *Myths of Sexuality*. Oxford: Blackwell, 1988.

Newsome, David. *The Victorian World Picture: Perceptions and Introspections in an Age of Change*. London: Murray, 1997.

O'Brien, Conor Cruise. *Ancestral Voices: Religion and Nationalism in Ireland*. Dublin: Poolbeg, 1994.

O'Connor, Anne V. 'The Revolution in Girls' Secondary Education in Ireland, 1860–1910', in Mary Cullen (ed.), *Girls Don't Do Honours: Irish Women in Education in the 19th and 20th Centuries*. Dublin: WEB, 1987, pp. 31–54.

—— and Susan M. Parkes. *Gladly Learn and Gladly Teach: A History of Alexandra College and School. 1866–1966*. Dublin: Blackwater, 1983.

O'Faolain, Sean. *Vive Moi!* London: Rupert Hart Davis, 1965.

O'Flynn, Gráinne. 'Aspects of Concern in the Religious Society of Friends with Education in Ireland, 1627–1812', *The Capuchin Annual*, 1975, pp. 320–36.

O'Keeffe, Regina. *The Quakers of Mountmellick: A Short History of the Religious Society of Friends in the Town of Mountmellick 1650–1950* . Mountmellick: Mountmellick Development Association, 1996.

O'Neill, Marie. 'The Dublin Women's Suffrage Association and its Successors', *Dublin Historical Record*, vol. 38, no. 4, Sept. 1985, pp. 126–40.

——. *From Parnell to De Valera: A Biography of Jennie Wyse Power, 1858–1941*. Dublin: Blackwater, 1991.

O'Neill, Thomas P. 'The Society of Friends and the Great Famine', *Studies*, June 1950, pp. 203–13.

O'Sullivan, Niamh. 'The Iron Cage of Femininity: Visual Representation of Women in the 1880s Land Agitation', in Tadgh Foley and Seán Ryder (eds), *Ideology and Ireland in the Nineteenth Century*. Dublin: Four Courts Press, 1998, pp. 181–96.

Owens, Rosemary. 'How We Won the Vote' in Andrée Sheehy Skeffington and Rosemary Owens (eds), *Votes for Women: Irish Women's Struggle for the Vote*. Dublin: Sheehy Skeffington & Owens, 1975, pp. 4–11.

Owens, Rosemary Cullen, 'Votes for Ladies, Votes for Women': Organised Labour and the Suffrage Movement', *Saothar: Journal of the Labour Society*, 9, 1983, pp. 32–45.

——. *Smashing Times: A History of the Irish Women's Suffrage Movement 1889–1922*. Dublin: Attic Press, 1984.

Packe, Michael St. John. *The Life of John Stuart Mill*. London: Secker & Warburg, 1954.

Parnell, Anna. *The Tale of a Great Sham*. ed. with an introduction by Dana Hearne. Dublin: Arlen House, 1986.

Pearsall, Ronald. *The Worm in the Bud*. London: Pimlico, 1993.

Peel, J. D. Y. *Herbert Spencer: The Evolution of a Socialist*. Aldershot: Gregg Revivals, 1992.

Peel, John. 'The Manufacture and Retailing of Contraceptives in England', *Population Studies*, vol. 17, 1964, pp. 22–35.

——. 'Contraception and the Medical Profession', *Population Studies*, vol. XVIII, no. 2, 1984, pp. 113–25.

Peel, Robert A. *Marie Stopes: Eugenics and The English Birth Control Movement*. London: Galton Inst., 1997.

Peterson, M. Jeanne. 'Dr. Acton's Enemy: Medicine, Sex and Society in Victorian England', *Victorian Studies*, 29, 1986, pp. 569–90.

Porter, Roy and Lesley Hall. *The Facts of Life: The Creation of Sexual Knowledge in Britain, 1850–1950*. New Haven: Yale University Press, 1995.

Preston, Margaret H. 'Lay Women and Philanthropy in Dublin, 1860–1880', *Éire–Ireland*, 38, 4, 1993, pp. 74–81.

Prostitution in the Victorian Age: Debates on the Issue from 19th Century Critical Journals. Farnborough: Gregg, 1973.

Quane, Michael. 'The Friends' Provincial School, Mountmellick', *Journal of the Royal Society of Antiquaries of Ireland*, vol. LXXXIX, pt. 1, pp. 59–89.

Reader, John. *Of Schools and Schoolmasters: Some Thoughts on Quaker Education*. London: Quaker Home Service, 1979.

Rendall, Jane. *The Origins of Modern Feminism*. London: Macmillan, 1985.

Robertson, William H. *An Illustrated History of Contraception*. London: Parthenon, 1990.

Robson, John M. *Marriage or Celibacy: The Daily Telegraph on a Victorian Dilemma*. Toronto: University of Toronto Press, 1995.

Rose, June. *Marie Stopes and the Sexual Revolution*. London: Faber & Faber, 1992.

Rose, Phyllis. *Parallel Lives: Five Victorian Marriages*. London: Vintage, 1994.

Rover, Constance. *Women's Suffrage and Party Politics in Britain 1866–1914*. London: Routledge & Kegan Paul, 1967.

Rubenstein, David. *Before the Suffragettes: Women's Emancipation in the 1890s*. Brighton: Harvester, 1986.

——. *A Different World for Women: The Life of Millicent Garrett Fawcett*. Brighton: Harvester Wheatsheaf, 1991.

Ryan, Louise. 'Women Without Votes: The Political Strategies of the Irish Suffrage Movement', *Irish Political Studies*, 9, 1994, pp. 119–39.

——. *Irish Feminism and the Vote*. Dublin: Folens, 1996.

Smith, F. B. 'Sexuality in Britain, 1800–1900: Some Suggested Revisions', in Martha Vicinus (ed.), *A Widening Sphere: Changing Role of Victorian Women*. London: Methuen, 1980, pp. 182–98.

———. 'The Contagious Diseases Acts Reconsidered', *Social History of Medicine,* vol. 3, 1990, pp. 197–213.

Smith, Harold. *The British Women's Suffrage Campaign, 1866–1928.* London: Longman, 1998.

Smith, Warren Sylvester. *The London Heretics 1870–1914.* London: Constable, 1967.

Soloway, Richard A. *Birth Control and the Population Question in England, 1877–1930.* Chapel Hill: University of North Carolina Press, 1982.

———. *Demography and Degeneration: Eugenics and the Declining Birthrate in Twentieth-Century Britain.* Chapel Hill: University of North Carolina, 1990.

Somerville Large, Peter. *Irish Eccentrics.* London: Hamilton, 1975.

Spring, Carolyn. 'The Political Platform and the Language of Support for Women's Suffrage. 1890–1920', in Angela V. John and Claire Eustance (eds), *The Men's Share? : Masculinities, Male Support and Women's Suffrage in Britain 1890–1920.* London: Routledge, 1997, pp. 158–81.

Stearns, Carol Z. and Peter N. Stearns. 'Victorian Sexuality: Can Historians do it Better?', *Journal of Social History,* Summer 1985, pp. 625–34.

Steward, W. A. Campbell. *Quakers and Education as Seen in their Schools in England.* London: Epworth Press, 1953.

Stilleinger, Jack (ed.). *The Early Draft of John Stuart Mill's Autobiography.* Urbana: University of Illinois Press, 1961.

Stuard, Susan Mosher. 'Women's Witnessing: A New Departure', in Elisabeth Potts Brown and Susan Mosher Stuard (eds.), *Witnesses for Change: Quaker Women over Three Centuries.* New Brunswick: Rutgers University Press, 1989, pp. 3–24.

Szreter, Simon. *Fertility, Class and Gender in Britain, 1860–1940.* Cambridge: Cambridge University Library, 1996.

Thomas, Keith. 'The Double Standard', *Journal of the History of Ideas,* 20, 1959, pp. 195–216.

Tone, Andrea. 'Contraceptive Consumers: Gender and the Political Economy of Birth Control in the 1930s', *Journal of Social History,* Spring 1996, pp. 485–506.

Tosh, John. 'The Making of Masculinities: The Middle Class in Late Nineteenth-Century Britain', in Angela V. John and Claire Eustance (eds), *Men's Share?: Masculinities, Male Support and Women's Suffrage in Britain 1890–1920.* London: Routledge, 1997, pp. 38–59.

Tweedy, Hilda. *A Link in the Chain: The Story of the Irish Housewives' Association 1942–1992.* Dublin: Attic Press, 1992.

Tyrell, Alex. 'Making the Millennium: the mid-Nineteenth Century Peace Movement', *Historical Journal,* no. 20, pt.1, 1978, pp. 75–95.

———. 'Women's Mission and Pressure Group Politics in Britain (1825–1860)', *Bulletin of the John Rylands University Library of Manchester,* vol. 63, 1, 1980, pp. 194–230.

Walkowitz, Judith R. 'Male Vice and Female Virtue: Feminism and the Politics of Prostitution in Nineteenth-Century Britain', *History Workshop: A Journal of Socialist and Feminist Historians,* 13, Spring 1982, pp. 79–92.

Walkowitz, Judith R. *Prostitution and Victorian Society: Women, Class and the State.* Cambridge: Cambridge University Press, 1980.

Ward, Margaret. 'Suffrage first above all else!: An Account of the Irish Suffrage Movement', *Irish Feminist Studies,* 10, 1982, pp. 22–36.

——. *Unmanageable Revolutionaries: Women and Irish Nationalism.* London: Pluto Press, 1987.

——. *In Their Own Voice.* Dublin: Attic Press, 1995.

——. *Hanna Sheehy Skeffington: A Life.* Cork: Attic Press, 1997.

——. 'The Ladies' Land League' in Ida Blom, Karen Hagemann, Catherine Hall (eds.), *Gendered Nations: Nationalisms and Gender Order in the Long Nineteenth Century.* Oxford: Berg, 2000.

Warren, Sylvester Smith. *The London Heretics 1870–1914.* London: Constable, 1967.

Wigham, Maurice. *The Irish Quakers: A Short History of the Religious Society of Friends in Ireland.* Dublin: Historical Committee of the Religious Society of Friends in Ireland, 1992.

——. *Newtown School Waterford 1798–1998: A History.* Waterford: Newtown School, 1998.

Williamson, Arthur. 'Enterprise, Industrial Development and Social Planning: Quakers and the Emergence of the Textile Industry in Ireland', *Planning Perspectives,* 7, 1992, pp. 303–28.

Unpublished Theses

Ahern, Michael. 'The Grubbs of Clonmel'. MA, NUI, University College, Cork, 1998.

Harrison, Richard S. 'Dublin Quakers in Business'. M. Litt., Trinity College Dublin, 1988.

Hearne, Dana. 'The Development of Irish Feminist Thought: A Critical Historical Analysis of The Irish Citizen, 1912–1920'. Ottawa: National Library of Canada, 1993, Ph.D. dissertation, York University, 1992; reproduced on microfiche.

Index